The Occult Sciences in the Renaissance

The Occult Sciences
in the Renaissance

A Study in Intellectual Patterns

WAYNE SHUMAKER

University of California Press, Berkeley, Los Angeles, London

University of California Press
Berkeley and Los Angeles, California
University of California Press, Ltd.
London, England

Second Printing, 1973

Library of Congress Catalog Card Number: 70-153552
International Standard Book Number 0-520-02021-9
Designed by James Mennick
Printed in the United States of America

VERITATI

quae super rupes altas

aspera inter saxa non facilis accessu est

neque quidem comperta

semper affectibus desiderioque obsequitur

quae autem est hominibus

boni atque felicitatis

fundamentum inexpugnabile

Contents

⌒ List of Illustrations

The figures are all reproduced from books of the Rare Book Collection at the University of California or books at the Henry E. Huntington Library, San Marino, California. More come from the latter than from the former. To both libraries I am grateful for generous co-operation and many courtesies. With one exception, full bibliographical details are given under the reproductions but not in this list.

⟍⟋ Preface

Since astrology, witchcraft, white magic, alchemy, and Hermetic theology can be examined by many methods and in many tones, it is only fair that I should explain to the prospective reader what awaits him in the chapters which follow.

First of all, the study is not written by a believer. I do not offer a key to esoteric knowledge which will unlock mysteries and confer power. Unlike the Rev. Montague Summers, who wrote credulous books about witchcraft, and A. E. Waite, who contrived in his publications on alchemy to imply that he was an initiate, I do not believe that former ages possessed bodies of esoteric wisdom which far exceeded ours. The reason is not, of course, that I assume a steady progress within which later things are automatically better than earlier. Anybody in possession of his senses knows that society is now in crisis, that ancient and Renaissance art and literature—indeed, even Victorian—were in some legitimate sense of the word greater than our own, and that even in the mechanical arts good products are often replaced by worse. No simplistic generalization can define the relation of old to new. In ethics, for example, we have made tremendous advances in sympathy for the unfortunate but have forgotten the important cardinal virtues of prudence, justice, temperance, and fortitude. I am so far from being an undiscriminating admirer of modernity that by temperamental inclination, as well as by professional responsibility, my reading is mostly in old books. In one area, however, that of the physical sciences, progress has been real, whatever one may think of the applications made of the discoveries. Anyone who now believes that the elements are "really" earth, water, air, and fire, that a fig tree has the power of taming a wild bull tied to it, or that planets become "unfriendly" to each other when separated by ninety degrees must do so not because his knowledge is especially advanced but because he is the victim of some special psychological need. The reader who continues beyond this Preface will discover that in the first chapter I argue explicitly against the view that there is "something in" astrology, and from point to point the explanations given of Renaissance beliefs refer not to the actual behavior of matter but to tendencies in mind. I urge, therefore, that modern occultists who carry on through what is to follow do so with a clear realization that they will often be irked and sometimes, perhaps, enraged.

Nonetheless, the intention has been to present the occult systems honestly and rather fully. Reading simultaneously with two parts of the mind is not difficult, and my aim has not been predominantly to judge but to understand. Understanding inevitably awakens some sympathy, and I can perceive rather alluring values in the very delusions which I reject. For one thing, on the magical hypothesis the universe is permeated not only by soul and will but also by meanings, so that the magician who failed to produce his effects at least may have felt a heartening significance in the most trivial details of consciousness. If he has wasted time, property, and energy without attaining his object, at least he has evaded boredom; and I myself rate interest so high that I would choose fear over apathy. A considerable part of the present unrest derives from the disappearance of cosmic meanings which the magician took for granted. My immediate point, however, is that disbelief has not (I hope) got in the way of comprehension. I trust that the comprehension has been made accessible to readers, so that, conceivably, a skeptical book might enrich the bag of tricks manipulated by an occultist whose convictions and activities I deplore.

Why, then, have I expended so much energy in the study of notions I think mistaken? The most basic single explanation is that, through a series of accidents, I found an unexpectedly rich strain of esoteric thought in the literary period in which I specialize and wanted to learn more about it. The book is intended primarily as history of ideas, as research into mental patterns of a distant period from which we have inherited much that is precious but which also was retrospective, backward–looking, and uncritically syncretic in ways, or to a degree, not widely appreciated. What most shocked me was the discovery of a learned, and evidently very serious, Latin literature on *occulta* which could not be interpreted as playful. By writing in Latin, the authors addressed an educated European audience; and their knowledge of ancient literature, if not consistently accurate, was often astonishingly wide. Moreover, they refer constantly to a Neo-Latin literature whose central importance to the intellectual life of the period is seldom realized. It was not by accident that of nearly six thousand books in the Bodleian Library in 1605 only thirty-six were in English. One remembers, with new understanding, Milton's reluctant abandonment of Latin as a medium for poetry and the prohibition of English at Cambridge except for conversation in chambers. In a word, my sense of the intellectual climate of the Renaissance has been lastingly affected by the findings, and I should imagine that some, at least, of my readers will be affected in a similar way. The Renaissance was different from what I had thought, and its literature often had meanings of which I had been unaware. My own attitude toward the *occulta* was irrelevant to the fact of their currency.

As I read, however—often in Latin and sometimes in the continental vernaculars, but in English if that was the language of the original or if a trustworthy English translation could be found—I perceived a relevance to our own times in what the authors were saying. Although I believe that the movement has begun to recede, no university teacher can be ignorant that many contemporary young people have revolted strongly against reason. One of my best graduate students once said to me, during a discussion of magic, "I *believe* in it." In the production of the musical *Hair* which I saw, the numerical square attributed by Cornelius Agrippa to Saturn was painted on the floor, and a thematic song was entitled "The Age of Aquarius." As I walked from my home to the University I sometimes passed a house which had over the door large wooden letters that said "Witchcraft," and occasionally, intended for what possibly obscene use I do not know, a caged rabbit or other small animal could be seen beside the entrance. Local newspapers frequently carried stories about a witchcraft church in San Francisco, and a popular moving picture, "Rosemary's Baby," had to do with the begetting of a Devil's child. The examples could be multiplied indefinitely. A graduate student I am presently coaching in Renaissance Latin is a practising astrologist. A ten-minute comment at the end of a lecture on Hermetic mysticism brought a rush of students to the podium. Possibly, I told myself, I will be able somewhat to discourage such faddishness by bringing the shaky foundations of traditional occultism into the light. This is the reason for the common-sense refutation of astrology offered in the first chapter and for certain other shorter passages which the historian of science may find intrusive. A decade ago I would not have written them, and in another decade I hope they will again become unnecessary. At the moment, I could not in conscience omit them.

The decision to undertake such a refutation—not page by page, but from point to point—implies no criticism of "irrelevant" scholarship. The traditional specialist was satisfied to let his readers make their own applications of his discoveries for several reasons: because he knew the limitations of his expertness; because he respected his audience's intellectual freedom while deploring its factual and theoretical misapprehensions; and because he assumed some instrumental as well as intrinsic value in all knowledge. For me, at least, the assumption was correct. Quite without professorial exhortation, the study of Anglo-Saxon transformed my preconceptions about the direction of social change. Readings in anthropology caused a revolution in my notions of native human endowments. Research into early epic disclosed an unexpected dominance of "primitive" thought by religion. With every such revelation my total orientation to myself and the world altered. Nevertheless I am not sorry for the opportunity to attempt some explication of meanings. If some readers are irritated by what might be unfairly described as a "see-the-quaint-errors-to-which-Progress-has-made-us-immune" tone, the factual information which is included may enable them to do so somewhat more knowledgeably.

A second special quality of the book may be mentioned. Much academic discourse is highly specific, and much is general, but generality and high specificity seem rarely to be combined. A philosophical essay or book may be almost totally devoid of particulars, whereas antiquarian research is often content merely to put facts in order. German scholarship is sometimes accused of ponderous emptiness, and British scholarship is often exclusively antiquarian. Perhaps because I underwent an initial intellectual awakening at an old-fashioned liberal arts college, but more probably because of a native bent, my own tendency is to push toward the definition of meanings; but I cannot do so comfortably without amassing quantities of details to satisfy myself that the generalizations are responsive to large bodies of data and are not spun out of sheer mind. It is well that the reader of this book should be advised that he is likely to find stretches of it either pettifogging or misty, as he may yearn for analytical thought or raw data. Since no man is a reliable judge of his own competencies, I cannot promise that either aspect of what appears to me to be a single task is done well. I do urge, however, that the two halves of the discussion are complementary.

The resistance to what has seemed to me to be adequate specificity may provoke an objection that the book is too long. It will appear so, certainly, to readers whose interest flags; and it may appear so also to academic minds which disapprove on principle of protracted summaries of documents. To readers of the former class the remedy is at hand: they can skip as much as they wish. The divisions of the long chapters into sections are intended not only to help coherence but also to suggest points at which fresh starts can be made. It is easier for the half-interested to disregard what is on the page than for the absorbed to imagine what might be there but is not. To readers of the second class a different response must be made. That convenient eighteenth-century abstraction, the Candid Reader, will acknowledge that a first-hand acquaintance with the documents is unusual. Besides Lynn Thorndike's monumental *History of Magic and Experimental Science* and Kurt Seligmann's *The Mirror of Magic* (New York: 1948), few really scholarly books treat more than a fraction of my subject matter. Even the specialist typically knows a good deal about astrology, or witchcraft, or magic, or alchemy, or Hermes but not about all these. And there is a further reason for explicitness, the fact that direct access to the documents is made difficult, and for many persons impossible, by inaccessibility and by linguistic barriers. Instead of inviting attention constantly to my own analysis (as, for instance, by subordinating citations of documents to my inferences from them), in some sections I have preferred to put primary emphasis on the Renaissance writings, believing that a special value of the study might lie in the opportunity it offered to watch the minds of intelligent Renaissance men at work on problems they thought important.

It remains to comment briefly on the successive chapters. In the first chapter, on astrology, it seemed necessary to begin with an explanation of astrological principles. Although I am acquainted with many people who to some degree believe in astrology, few appear to understand in detail how it works, and fewer still to grasp its fundamental assumptions. Next, in order to weaken, at the earliest possible moment, an anticipated tendency in some readers to salute all the oddities which lie in wait for them as profundities, I offer the commonsense refutation already mentioned. (This may of course be skipped.) The remainder of the chapter follows a Renaissance controversy about astrology generated by Giovanni Pico's celebrated attack. The second chapter, on witchcraft, is organized differently. Instead of separating Renaissance treatises on the subject into *pro* and *contra* and discussing them more or less in chronological order, I leap back and forth among a relatively large number of documents, making citations wherever they seem useful. The third chapter, which has to do with white or natural magic, differs from the former two in being based on only three documents. Here, if anywhere, the documentation may seem thin. Since many of the treatises cited in the second chapter also have sections on magic, the horizontal reference could easily have been widened; but in fact Della Porta, Ficino, and Cornelius Agrippa not only cover the ground adequately but also supplement one another very neatly. Indeed, the whole chapter might have been focused on Agrippa, whose work is a *summa* without rival in its area. Ficino, however, did too much to encourage a spiritualizing philosophy not to receive special notice somewhere, and natural magic is described with exceptional fullness by Della Porta. It may also be appropriate to remark that because the beliefs here are not (I think) likely to be seductive, summary is less interrupted than elsewhere by commentary. The fourth chapter, on alchemy, reverts to the method of the second and draws upon many documents without fully describing any. In the fifth and last of the substantive chapters, an attempt is made to interpret the Hermetic philosophy in isolation from the other esoteric systems fathered upon Hermes Trismegistus and to say something about its influence. Everywhere I have worked chiefly from primary sources, and in very large part I have done so in the original languages. Where this has been impossible, or where I have availed myself of help offered by a modern translation in Italian, French, German, or English, acknowledgment is made in a note.

The avowing of indebtedness is an anxious business because—as I am not the first to remark—those persons tend to be forgotten whose thought has been so pervasively influential that it has become a form of the writer's awareness. Thus the name of Ernst Cassirer, by whose *Philosophie der symbolischen Formen* I was first drawn to an interest in extralogical patterns, appears nowhere in the following pages. Similarly I have benefited more from the studies of Frances Yates, D. P. Walker, and other historians of thought and of science than could be guessed from my references to them. I have also drawn ideas from conversations with many people, some of them not academics, on topics both related and unrelated to the subject of this study. A chance remark sometimes modified my understanding of common pre-assumptions, so that I altered my expository strategy slightly, or, less frequently, it opened up a fresh line of thought.

More specific instances of indebtedness are comparatively few. I am grateful to Francis Maddison and J. D. North, Curator and Associate Curator of the Museum of the History of Science at Oxford, for help in the understanding of astrolabes, and to the latter for sympathetic reading of the introductory section of the chapter on astrology. The chapter on witchcraft was read and commented on most helpfully by Rossell Hope Robbins, of the State University of New York at Albany. My brother, Dr. Paul R. Shumaker, checked the chapter on alchemy for errors in chemistry, and Jacob J. Finkelstein, of Yale, sharpened the accuracy of a passage about Assyro-Babylonian backgrounds of astrology. I acknowledge with gratitude the assistance of J. B. Trapp, Librarian of the Warburg and Courtauld Institute of the University of London, for instructing me in the use of that admirable library's resources and for putting me on the track to an understanding of the puzzling term *gimetria*. Nicolas J. Perella, of my own university, kindly read a much shorter version of Chapter V, paying attention mainly to Italian backgrounds. I owe thanks to two graduate students at the University of California, Maurice Hunt, who by a seminar paper first drew my serious attention to Hermes Trismegistus, and Anne Janet Braude, whose interest in the subject has sustained me and whose knowledge of it in some areas exceeds mine. For illustrations, which I had not at first expected to provide, I am indebted chiefly to the resources of the University of California library at Berkeley and to the Henry E. Huntington Library at San Marino, California. My thanks are due especially to Leslie S. Clark, of our own Rare Books Collection, for aid in finding books and procuring photographs, and to Robert O. Dougan, Librarian of the Huntington Library, for permission to reproduce illustrations from books not available here.

My wife, Grace Smith Shumaker, who offered constantly the sort of encouragement without which difficulties would sometimes have appeared overwhelming, also helped by searching out illustrations during our brief but enjoyable period at the Huntington. Finally, I am especially indebted to the University of California at Berkeley for the grant of a Humanities Research Fellowship which made it possible for me to stretch a one-quarter sabbatical into a full year. It is hardly necessary to add that the responsibilities for whatever faults remain—and no doubt there are many that I do not suspect—are mine alone.

Wayne Shumaker
Berkeley, California
March 29, 1971

CHAPTER ONE

Astrology

I. Introduction

Like alchemy, judicial or divinatory astrology is a subject too complicated to be
thoroughly mastered in less than a lifetime. Its methods are involved, its history long,
and the disputes among and within its schools numerous. The languages in which its
capital documents are written include not only Latin and Greek but also Arabic,
Egyptian, and "Chaldaean" or Assyro-Babylonian; and modern scholarship, which
is vast enough to intimidate, is also in a number of languages and often highly
specialized. In the discussion to be offered here attention will be focused chiefly on
intellectual patterns as these are revealed by Renaissance documents. And yet for a
variety of reasons it will be necessary first to consider at some length how astrology
works and whether it can make a valid claim to "truth." Its methods and assumptions
are not widely understood, and implication in the Renaissance controversies otherwise than as a musing observer will most effectively be avoided if we maintain the
psychic distance attainable through prior realization that, in the long pull, one set of
arguments was inevitably to triumph over the other. Readers for whom such preparation is unnecessary may skip at once to page 16.

Although predictive astrology often has to do with "elections," or the regulation
of behavior in terms of actions to be initiated or avoided, a description of its methods
can most conveniently be centered on birth horoscopes. The procedures are always

similar and the basic assumptions constant. An effort will be made to keep the discussion mainly general, but it will not on that account be simple. As Bouché-Leclercq remarked, "Whoever goes to an astrologer must arm himself with patience." [1]

The casting of a horoscope begins, once the exact day, hour, and minute of the birth have been learned—if this is possible—by a series of calculations necessary to determine the positions of the planets (which include the sun and moon). In remote periods the astrologer began with a set of "tables," the use of which required long training. By the Renaissance, these were being replaced by the Ephemeris, to which our attention may be confined. This gives planetary positions day by day in terms of degrees within zodiacal signs: for example, Saturn, 18° 23′ of Aries; Mars, 7° 48′ of Taurus; Mercury, 26° 44′ of Capricorn. These data require, however, two kinds of adjustment. The first is for place: the Ephemeris will have been computed for a large city, not, usually, for the exact spot of the birth, so that the planets will have moved beyond the indicated positions or will not yet have reached them. The second is for time: the birth is not likely to have occurred exactly at noon, the moment for which the positions are given. To illustrate simply, if the time of birth was 1:00 p. m. instead of noon the earth will have revolved 1/24 of 360°, or 15° beyond the positions shown in the tables.[2] Once these adjustments have been made—and making them is often a very complex operation—the astrologer is ready to enter the positions on a diagram in which a small earth is surrounded by a band containing symbols which represent the zodiacal signs.

The next step, which is even more complicated, is the drawing of lines to indicate the divisions of the twelve "houses." These are twelve segments of the celestial equator so drawn that the part of the sky in the zodiacal band—which includes, or is presumed to include, the planets—is cut into pie-shaped pieces with their points toward the earth. The process is very complex and may be carried out in various ways. A modern handbook describes briefly eight methods, attributed to Ptolemy, Porphyry, Alcabitius, Campanus, Regiomontanus, Morin, Placidus, and Zariel.[3] The source of the difficulty is that account must be taken not only of the observer's longitude but also of his latitude. If this were not done, all persons born at the same moment on a single line of longitude would have identical horoscopes. The result is that although the circle is ultimately cut by six diameters passing through the earth the houses do not contain equal numbers of degrees. In an example from the seventeenth-century French astrologer Morin the divisions contain, respectively, 32, 29, 37, 19, 45, 18, 32, 29, 37, 19, 45, and 18 degrees.[4] Once this has been done and a double line has been drawn to mark the visual horizon which divides the twelfth house (above the eastern horizon) from the first (just below it), the horoscope takes some such form as that shown below.[5] For the reader's ease I have interpreted the zodiacal and planetary symbols and marked the numbers of the houses, adding by each number the conventional one-word Latin explanation of the department of life to which it relates.

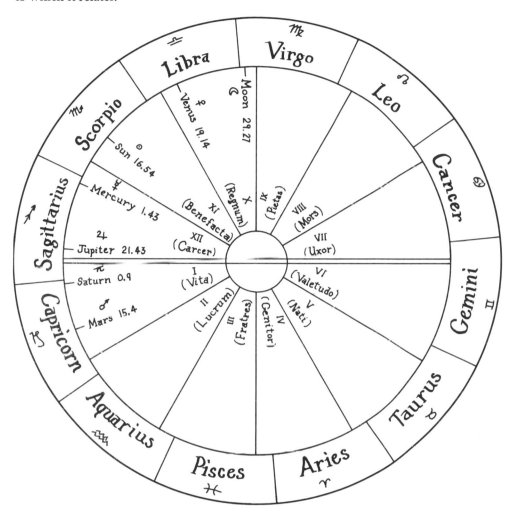

It should be added that until modern times the traditional diagram was drawn differently, the houses being shown thus:

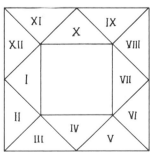

The difference is, however, merely visual: the larger diagram shows the actual divisions more clearly, the other, when filled in, their results.

On the basis of this diagram, or a somewhat more complex one which includes certain refinements—for example, the moon's nodes and, in recent centuries, the positions of additional planets—the astrologer is prepared to begin his reading. It should be understood that he has not, probably, gone up to his rooftop bearing instruments to measure celestial longitudes and latitudes (or "right ascension" and "declination") but has remained within his study. He has not, in fact, looked at the stars at all, nor did he need do so in the Middle Ages or Renaissance. The clerk in Chaucer's *Franklin's Tale,* when contriving the astrological magic which was to make the coastal rocks disappear for a time, consulted his "tables Tolletanes" or Toledo tables, making proper adjustments which included allowance for the position of Dorigen's village.

Before interpreting the sample horoscope, that of King Edward VII,[6] we must pause to notice what kinds of data will be significant.

A general principle is that the planets exert basic forces on character, the zodiacal signs modify these, and the houses "show the earthly sectors, or departments, of everyday life in which the modified forces operate."[7] Position is important, the critical factors being Right Ascendant or position above the eastern horizon and planetary positions relative to the zodiacal signs and to each other. The last are measured by angles, which need not, however, be exact, each planet being considered to "project the rays of its virtue about itself in every direction." According to a typical view, the "sphere of virtue" of Saturn covered 9° of the celestial equator, that of Mars 8°, that of Jupiter 9°, that of the sun 15°, that of Venus 7°, that of Mercury 7°, and that of the moon 12°.[8] If, within these limits, two planets are roughly aligned for an earthly observer they are said to be "in conjunction." For example, since Jupiter projects its virtue for 4° 30′ in every direction and the sun for 7° 30′, Jupiter and the sun can be 12° apart and yet in conjunction. When they are roughly 180° apart—on opposite sides of the earth—they are "in opposition"; when roughly 120° apart "in trine"; when roughly 90° apart "in quartile"; and when roughly 60° apart "in sextile." And so with the other planets within the varying numbers of degrees determined by their respective spheres of virtue. Of these relationships, the trigonal is "good," the sextile also "good" but in somewhat lesser degree, the tetragonal or quartile "bad," and opposition worst of all. Conjunction is good or bad as the planetary characteristics may determine: bad, for example, when Saturn and Mars come together, good when Jupiter and the sun, mixed when Saturn and Jupiter.

The significance of the houses is also very great. These are numbered from one to twelve, proceeding downward and to the right from the one immediately beneath the eastern horizon. Degrees within them, as within the signs, are computed counter-clockwise, each being divided into three "faces" of 10° each. They "rule" or "govern" the departments of life as follows: I (*Vita*), personality, appearance, and childhood; II (*Lucrum*), possessions and money; III (*Fratres*), family, relatives, communication, and speech; IV (*Genitor*), parents, childhood home, and seclusion; V (*Nati*), children, sexual activities, and creativity; VI (*Valetudo*), subordinates, work, and health; VII (*Uxor*), marriage, partnership, and close friends; VIII (*Mors*), death, accidents, and mysticism; IX (*Pietas*), study, mental exploration, and travel; X (*Regnum*), career, ambitions, and attainments; XI (*Benefacta*), ideals, worthy causes, and societies; and XII (*Carcer*), restrictions, sorrow, and illness. This system is subject to some variation but is reasonably steady in its essentials.

Next, each of the planets possesses a complex of inherent "virtues" or "powers," some of which will be alluded to as the discussion proceeds. Something will be implied by adjectives derived from the planetary names: "saturnine," "jovial," "mercurial," "martial." "Lunatic" suggests the connection of the moon with madness as well as with chastity, purity, childbirth, and much else. Mars is associated not only with war but also with anger, ferocity, and an overbearing temperament, much of this being inferred from its redness and the fact that it is "hot." Because Saturn is cold, moves slowly, and rules the heaviest of the metals, lead, it produces a melancholy temperament but is also associated with gravity (a metaphorical extension of "weight"), profundity, and wit. Burton's *Anatomy of Melancholy* was addressed to scholars, who were thought regularly to be saturnine but sometimes, happily, had some admixture of mercurial qualities. The most powerful good influence was believed to be the sun's; but it required some tempering by the milder Jupiter or Venus. Ficino's *De vita coelitus comparanda* is full of directions about how these softer influences may be attracted. Jupiter's influence, because it resembled the sun's but lacked the threat of excessiveness, was perhaps the most favorable of all. Venus, in consequence of a softness produced by her moisture, combined her influence favorably with that of the dry, and therefore desiccating, sun but alone tended to produce sensuality. Mercury was lord, among other things, of learning and eloquence. In all this legends about the Roman gods, or their Greek equivalents, played an important role. When the planet once called Phosphoros or Light-Bringer became identified with the goddess of love, it was inevitably thought to have qualities sharply different from those of the Mars to whom Venus had been united in an uncongenial marriage.

The "qualities" of heat, cold, dryness, and moisture were distributed to all seven planets in pairs. The sun was hot and dry, the moon cold and moist, Venus hot and moist. Othello's observation, in a fit of jealousy, that Desdemona's hand was hot and moist associated her immediately with Venus and lechery. The zodiacal signs were "fiery" (hot and dry), "airy" (hot and moist), "watery" (cold and moist), or "earthy" (cold and dry). These attributes were distributed around the zodiac in a schematic order, with the result that expectations are sometimes violated. For example, Aquarius, the Water-Carrier or Water-Pourer, was not watery but airy, and Scorpio, a land creature, was watery. The signs as well as the planets also had gender, these again alternating regularly around the zodiac. Further, each zodiacal sign ruled a separate part of the body. Aries had responsibility for the head, Taurus the neck, Gemini the arms, Cancer the breast, Leo the sides and back, Virgo the loins, Libra the buttocks, Scorpio the genitals, Sagittarius the thighs, Capricorn the knees, Aquarius the legs, and Pisces the feet. This system once more followed the order of the signs, beginning with the sign thought to be in the ascendant when the universe was freshly created. *Orderliness* appears to have been a source of both mental satisfaction and emotional reassurance. If a rigid schematism sometimes produced awkwardness, as in giving the Archer, Sagittarius, control over the thighs instead of the arms, it also sometimes produced a happy fitness, as in the assignment of the genitalia to Scorpio, which bore a sting in its tail.

Predictions having to do with health of course relied heavily on these associations. For instance, the presence of a malevolent planet in Cancer might suggest weakness in the heart or lungs, and if both Cancer and the planet happened to be in the eighth house, *Mors,* the prognostication might be especially gloomy. The location of any planet in a sign which it "ruled"—that is, in its "domicile"—strengthened its influence. The sun ruled Leo, and if it happened to be in that sign at the time of birth might be more powerful than the ascendant sign. The moon's sign was Cancer. The remaining five planets had both day and night houses, the day house being regularly given first in the following list: Saturn, Capricorn and Aquarius; Jupiter, Sagittarius and Pisces; Mars, Scorpio and Aries; Venus, Libra and Taurus; and Mercury, Virgo and Gemini.

Finally, it must be added that each of the planets ruled one of the seven ages of man. The moon ruled infancy, Mercury ruled childhood, Venus ruled adolescence, the sun ruled early maturity, Mars ruled late maturity, Jupiter ruled vigorous age, and Saturn ruled extreme age or senility, the sequence following the order of the planets from the nearest to the farthest. A prediction from the nativity horoscope of the whole course of life would of course take note of these associations.

From this summary, which is more fragmentary and approximate, by far, than the novice may suppose, we may proceed to a brief reading of Edward VII's horoscope. I borrow the interpretation from Christopher McIntosh's *The Astrologers and Their Creed,*[9] which is also the source of the horoscope.

> . . . the sign of Sagittarius is, for several reasons, remarkably strong: first, because it is in the ascendant; secondly, because its own ruler, Jupiter, is present in the sign; thirdly, because Mercury is also in the sign. Here is a clear case of the ascendant being stronger than the Sun-sign which, in this instance, is Scorpio. The Sagittarian qualities

were unusually pronounced in Edward. He was generous, exuberant and jovial. And, as might be expected, his joviality tended at times to vulgarity. The Sun in Scorpio made him sensitive beneath his boisterous exterior, strong-willed, emotional, aggressive, and passionate in love. His amorous side was strengthened by the fact that Venus is in her own sign, Libra.

Another remarkable thing about the chart is that the planet nearest to the ascendant, Saturn, is in its own sign of Capricorn, giving a strong Saturnian flavour to the nativity. The combination of Saturn and Capricorn in the first house suggests a hard and difficult childhood. Edward was indeed subjected to a rigidly disciplined upbringing.

Both of the two strongest planets, Saturn and Jupiter, are square in aspect (i.e. at ninety degrees) to the moon. The square aspect indicates difficulty and conflict, and the Moon often represents the person of the mother. In this case there is a strong indication that the native had a thoroughly inharmonious relationship with his mother —which, in the case of Edward, was true.

On the whole it is a strong chart, and one suitable for a king.

Although these details might be expanded indefinitely, the illustration will be adequate for our purpose.

The reaction of some persons to the foregoing description of astrology may be lively interest. Even from the little that has been said it is evident that the system has not only considerable richness but also a certain neatness. One can play with it enjoyably, and ingenious minds, if they are willing to take pains, can readily invent further predictions about Edward. Moreover, the effort required to carry out a number of rather exacting calculations before the horoscope can be drawn may evoke a comfortable sense of precision. What involves considerable trouble and, when checked and rechecked, is found to be "correct" is unlikely (we feel) to be altogether pointless. Nevertheless we must confront as briefly as possible the question whether there is "something in" astrology, whether, as it may please even some academic readers in the present intellectual climate to believe, prescientific thought is more profound than scientific. The historical scholar must try his best to maintain an intellectual balance which will allow him the advantage of perspective. Living in one age, he can sometimes look back on another from a moment beyond that at which issues were resolved and hence see bygone disputes in a pattern. In what follows, only enough will be said to suggest that, however pardonable belief in astrology may have been in the Renaissance, in modern times faith in it is likely to tell us more about psychic needs than about the actual workings of the cosmos.

First of all, the Renaissance defense of astrology rested very heavily on the alleged power of "rays" (*radii*) to exert influence by means of light and heat.[10] The rays of the sun operated on us sensibly, and those of the moon, which was known to produce the tides, could be concentrated sufficiently by a concave mirror to produce warmth. Is it credible that cosmic rays from the planets and zodiacal stars can affect us?

So far as the sun is concerned, the answer is unhesitatingly "Yes." Some influence may also be admitted in the moon, which may shine very conspicuously—enough, sometimes, to disturb sleep—and since Newton's time is recognized to have a strong gravitational pull on the earth. For the rest of the seven planets the answer is clearly "No." They have no intrinsic luminosity, and the small quantities of light reflected by them, coming as they must first from the sun, from which they are millions of miles distant, and then across another area of space so vast that the planets themselves appear to an earthly observer as mere points, are very unlikely indeed to determine character and destiny. The sum total of light and heat reaching us from all the planets together is minuscule compared to that of a single electric light bulb, which in a street lamp can make the planets invisible. Neither is there any non-mythological reason to believe that the planets exude energy of a kind not detectable by the most sensitive instruments yet devised. If the existence of occult powers in them is claimed, the support must lie in something other than modern astronomy or physics.

Even if the theoretical possibility of influence from the planets were admitted (or, perhaps, not denied on the plea that much must go on in the universe of which we are unaware), no adequate justification of the specific powers ascribed to them can be offered. The powers are largely inferred from ancient stories about the gods whose names the planets bear and are described differently in countries where Greek and Roman religion had little currency: for example, India and China. Even in Egypt the redness of Mars was not associated with fire and blood; Venus was thought to be male, the "Phoenix-star of Osiris"; and Mercury was considered malevolent.[11]

Let us turn next to the alleged importance of aspects. These depend mainly on a numerological mysticism derived, in the West, from Pythagoras and already important in Plato's *Timaeus*. The trigonal angle is good because special powers were ascribed to the number three, and the sextile also is good, although less decisively so, because six is the product of three and the first even number, two, also regarded as having mystical potency. To the mind sensitive to analogies, "opposition" implied face-to-face confrontation, as in war or vigorous dispute. Other inferences have been drawn from the supposed properties of regular polygons, by which ancient geometricians were fascinated and which seemed to them to play a role in the cosmic harmony. For the rest, the notion that the planets saw each other best (*ad-spectare*) at certain angles appears to derive from the idea of a cosmic dance in which a planet a fourth or a third of the way round the circle was more easily visible than an adjacent one. Unlike human beings, however, the planets do not have eyes only in the fronts of their heads, so that unless some obstacle intervened only distance and the direction of the illumination from the sun would have mattered to them. In any event, no really plausible reason can be given why an angle of 90° is unfriendly and angles of 60° and 120° friendly. Like other *amicitiae* and *inimicitiae,* and like the exaltations and dejections of planets in domiciles, the doctrine of aspects results from a humanizing of impersonal forces, ultimately traceable to an animism which imagined a daemon in every luminary. As for the limits of the spheres of virtue, these are not measured but guessed at on the basis of the planets' brilliance, size, and supposed dignity. Exact angles could not be demanded, for none would be found in the typical horoscope. There exist only eight possibilities out of 360 that any two planets will be at precisely 0°, 60°, 90°, 120°, or 180° to an earthly observer.[12] But to say — for instance—that the sun and moon are at a right angle when at the limits of their spheres they may be separated by any number of degrees between 76° 30′ and 103° 30′ is to work by arbitrary convention, and to imagine the influences of the angles unimpeded by the interposition of the earth's thickness is to carry credulity to an extreme.

The doctrine of the twelve houses is no more soundly based. Since Mercury moves through the zodiac at a mean daily rate of 4.1° and Venus at a mean daily rate of 1.6°, it may occasionally happen that one or the other will have crossed a cusp, or that Mercury, especially, will have altered its aspect with another planet by the time it has moved halfway or further round the earth. But in any event the horoscopal readings are of situations within the houses at a given moment, not predictions based on the certainty that—for example—the sixth house, together with whatever planets may be in it, will appear over the eastern horizon some twelve hours after the birth. If this is so, it must be assumed that the influence of the planets, operating, as we have seen, by means of rays, is not weakened by having to pass through up to 8,000 miles of earth. Yet the reason usually given for basing the horoscope on the moment of birth rather than that of conception or the introduction of the soul into the foetus is that only upon issuing from the womb is the child exposed to radiation.

The necessity that astrologers should ignore this difficulty is perfectly clear. If King Edward VII had been born some 6 hours earlier, all the planets would have been beneath the horizon, and there would have been no horoscope. It strains belief too far, however, to suppose that reflected light from a planet can penetrate the earth's diameter when we know that even direct sunlight can be shut off by a thin partition. And there remains the additional problem of explaining how it comes about that the situations in the twelve houses have exactly the asserted relationships to the departments of life and character: how, for instance, the planet or zodiacal sign in the seventh house, *Uxor,* just above the western horizon at the birth, can operate twenty or thirty years later to influence the choice of a wife. If the reply is that the method is unknown but the fact has been demonstrated by experience, we must inquire exactly how this inductive proof has been established. To this question we shall return in a moment.

We consider next the zodiacal stars, which although subsidiary to the planets are not negligible. First, the effects attributed to the signs come, more or less transparently, from the names assigned to them. Thus men born under the Crab (Cancer) are unscrupulous merchants because the crab's pincers imply ruthless seizure. They send out ships overseas because the crab has a marine habitat. They are small and red-faced (crabs turn red when boiled) and "have big joints, broad bones, thick woolly hair, a big, round face, dark skin, round eyes in a broad head." Because crabs, like other marine animals, are sacred to the sea-born Venus, men born under Cancer are prone to love-affairs; but they are emotionally tough because the crab has a hard carapace. They are changeable, partly because the sun appears to change its course in Cancer but also perhaps because the crab's sidewise or backward motion suggests an alteration of intention; and they deal with various kinds of merchandise as hawkers because land crabs are often observed to pick up and carry small stones or bits of wood.[13] Most of the connections are unmistakably analogical. And so with the other signs.

Let us toy for a moment with the other possible explanation, that the influences were discovered first and fantastically appropriate names found afterwards. We must first observe that the attention paid to the zodiac began fairly late, the Babylonians having had no special interest in it and the Egyptians having preferred to give weight to 36 arcs of 10° each which they thought to be governed by an equal number of "decans."[14] There can be no claim of "uncounted ages" of patient induction. That consideration left to one side, however, we may fairly inquire what kind of observation would have permitted the separation of the influence of a few dozen stars in the zodiac from that of trillions of other stars which also presumably radiate influence. The zodiacal stars are distinguished not by extraordinary brilliance or nearness [15] but by lying in the plane of the ecliptic, which coincides roughly with the orbits of the planets. For that reason a planet is always "in" one of the signs. Once it has been granted that effective radiation from any star can reach us, no adequate defense can be urged for the belief that the radiation from all the stars not in this belt is trivial. Those directly overhead, if equally bright, should be more powerful. Since we can see incalculable numbers at once, the influence from any small group or groups would be an infinitesimal part of the total.

We may now confront directly the assertion that the reliability of astrology has been established by immemorial experience. We begin by noting that Chaldaean or Babylonian records cannot have been preserved for several thousands—or hundreds of thousands—of years, as is claimed, not only because the tribes which came to-gether in Babylon about 3000 B.C. had separate histories but also because during nearly the whole of that period the tribes were illiterate. If ancient records went back further, their age must have been doubtful and the system of notation very crude. As it happens, however, we know with some accuracy what the early records were like: if not the earliest, at least old enough to be pre-horoscopal. One large col-lection of tablets now in the British Museum has to do with some general happening or some aspect of the King's behavior or with meteorological phenomena: "If the moon and sun are in opposition on the fourteenth day of the lunar month, the King will have a wide (receptive?) ear"; "If on the fourteenth day of Sivan (May/June) the moon is darkened and the fourth wind (the east wind) blows, enmity will rule; there will be dead people."[16] Interest centers in winds, storms, the catch of fish, famines, the direction from which an enemy will come, palace revolutions, and what-ever may affect the whole land or the King as its symbol and epitome.[17] These tablets were in the library of King Assurbanipal (668–626 B.C.) and point back to a single larger work which Carl Bezold estimates must have dated merely from "well beyond" the seventh century B.C.[18] The earliest individual horoscope, as opposed to the "omen compositions" just described, dates from 410 B.C., a time which A. Sachs, in 1952, found "startlingly early." So it is in comparison—for ex-ample—with that of the earliest known Greek horoscope, that of Antiochus I of Commagene, which is currently dated 62 B.C.[19] Although Sachs does not intend to suggest that "very much more than a relatively crude horoscopic astrology need have emerged from Babylonia," he nevertheless finds it "very tempting," on the evidence of this text, "to set up the working hypothesis that the basic idea of horoscopic astrology was first propounded in Babylonia."[20] All this is very far from encourag-ing faith that the Babylonians, in several thousand years of prehistory, anticipated post-Baconian research methods by meticulously, and detail by detail, comparing celestial phenomena with individual fortunes: a process which, moreover, could hardly have predated the emergence of twelve equal zodiacal signs after 500 B.C.

Beyond this, it must be remembered that whatever astrological theories were "proved" by Babylonian induction have not survived unchanged into modern times. Babylonian presumptions were altered when astrology spread into Egypt, and these were again changed by the Greeks, to whom Western practices have been chiefly indebted. There has never, perhaps, been a time when conflicting opinions were not held and practices were not being modified. If at first glance such tinkering might be thought to imply constant experimental rectification, no one who has read much astrological literature is likely to believe this was the cause of the alterations. The appeal is regularly to authorities—Ptolemy, Porphyry, Regiomontanus, Albumasar, Alkindi, and dozens of others—or to abstract reason. I can recall no attempt to "prove" from thirty-six or twenty-nine or fifty-seven actual horoscopes that the influence of, say, Mercury has been misunderstood. As a rigorous methodological discipline, induction emerged only very gradually in the Renaissance. This is to say that the history of any specific astrological precept is usually much shorter than is claimed for the whole system and that the reasons why it prevailed are rarely, if ever, experimental.

In modern times additional claims of inductive proof have been offered, this time on a statistical basis. The most sophisticated work of the kind known to me is that of Paul Choisnard, summarized conveniently in *Les Preuves de l'influence astrale sur l'homme*.[21] Briefly, Choisnard asserts that the examination of large numbers of horoscopes reveals a coincidence of prediction with actuality larger than would have resulted from pure chance. For example, Jupiter is in the zenith in 5.5 per cent of all births but at least in twice that proportion of births of people who have achieved honors or celebrity. The conclusion is that the vertical position of Jupiter "is one of the factors of our inner nature which co-operate to predispose to honors."[22] Other investigations have led to similar results: the trine aspect of the moon and Mercury is two or three times more frequent for philosophers than for other men.[23] And so on.

Undoubtedly, some comfort is accessible here for persons who are determined to believe but have scruples about relying on mere intuition ("The heart stands up and answers, 'I have felt' "). Choisnard's conclusions have been much debated without, apparently, much progress having been made toward agreement. One ground of skepticism is the practice of rectifying the time of birth, which alone might produce the discrepancy or *écart constaté* between random expectations and findings on which the entire argument rests. Instead of pressing this point, however, I wish to draw out briefly the practical meaning of Choisnard's discoveries on the assumption that they are perfectly correct, doing so in connection with a single calculation chosen as persuasive by J. Hieroz, a well-known enthusiast and publisher of astrological texts.

The principle tested here is that "A conjunction of Mars and the sun directly overhead at the moment of birth is a probable sign of early death." The astrological situation occurs frequently enough that of 100,000 people 308 will have been born under it. Tables of mortality show us, further, that of 100,000 people 6,000 die before the age of ten. The equation 308: 100,000 as X: 6,000 yields the results that by pure chance 19 of the 6,000 who die early will have been born under the bad conjunction. If, then, we discover that the actual number was 36 or 40 (again about double the expectation), "Galton's curve allows us to realize that there is only one chance in a hundred thousand, in the first case, and one in a million, in the second, that this excess is the result of chance!"[24] Very well; but let us look at the result from another point of view suggested by Hieroz himself. "Certain readers may be astonished that the death of forty children born under the sign is thought convincing when 5,960 will have died without having been born under it and 268 born under it will have escaped its evil influence."[25] Indeed, yes. If the prediction has been made 308 times and found right only 40 times, it will have been right only 13 per cent of the time, and this only if we accept the figure 40 in preference to 36: not an impressive showing for a divinatory system by which we are expected to guide our actions. And we have consented to accept the assertions about the horoscopes on faith, though on balance it is quite improbable that M. Choisnard has in fact succeeded in ascertaining correctly the birth-moments of all 6,000 children who died young and has resisted heroically the temptation to "rectify" the times in order to avoid horoscopal anomalies.

TRACTATUS PRIMI.
SECTIONIS II.
PORTIO IV.

De animæ vitalis cum intellectuali
Scientia, hoc est, de Gene-
thlialogia.

In qua agitur de Genii cujusque inquirendi ratione.

Robert Fludd, *De supernaturali, naturali, praenaturali, et contranaturali microcosmi historia* (Oppenheim: Hieronymus Gallerus, 1619), p. 71 (after beginning of *Tomus secundus,* which follows p. 277).

An astrologer, on the left, casts a horoscope for a subject seated near him. The customary chart is already being filled in; a globe of the heavens is within reach, and a folio lies open on a reading stand. Outside the room, the moon and stars are visible despite the fact that the sun is still well above the horizon. A row of books above the astrologer's head suggests the complexity of his art and the accessibility of reference materials.

Although statistics rarely played a part in earlier inductive proofs, what was traditionally meant by appeals to experience was that predictions—often reported at second or third or fourth hand, many of them about persons hundreds of years dead —had been successful. The persuasiveness of such case-histories may be considered briefly.

One reason for distrust is the probability that most of the horoscopes are *ex post facto:* what had to be discovered was known from the beginning. Once such knowledge is at hand, ways can easily be found of making the forecasts accurate. For one thing, the system has considerable vagueness and lability, as do predictions from chiromancy, auspices, and oracles. A person who discovers that he possesses the character traits associated with his own sign may find, if he perseveres, that he also has the traits associated with several other signs, or indeed with all. Hardly anybody is totally devoid of such qualities as impetuosity, amorousness, or timidity. Further, every horoscopal detail has a range of possible meaning. Luca Bellanti of Siena makes the argumentativeness of Socrates a consequence of the presence of Mercury in the house of Mars at his birth.[26] If the same condition had been found in the horoscope of Alexander the Great, the effect might have been the endowing of a general with eloquence. Again, the exact time of the birth was usually unknown, so that the astrologer could test a whole arc of possibility until he found a moment which was suitable. It was common both in the Middle Ages and in the Renaissance to fix the unknown date of a historical event by discovering a celestial configuration which might have produced it, and the assumptions which underlay this practice regularly influenced the casting of horoscopes. A modern handbook, in a chapter entitled "The Time of Birth: Methods of Rectification," suggests two methods, of which the first is "by important events that have occurred during the life,"[27] and older handbooks regularly contained discussions of the same topic. If few facts of the life are known, hints can be obtained from a photograph.[28] Because the astrologer has made an act of faith in accepting the reliability of his art, such juggling arouses no scruple in his conscience.

For the rest, chance correspondences sometimes exist which need no manipulation. Not everything in thousands of predictions can be wrong, especially since the phrasing is general: "will meet with a misfortune," "should be on guard against impulsive decisions," "should avoid travel," and the like. The memory of a person inclined to belief—and if he is not, he is unlikely to have visited the astrologer—retains the correspondences and forgets the discrepancies, as in reports of the truthfulness of dreams. The astrologer, in turn, having met a great many such credulous visitors, is encouraged to believe in his own methods and, when he writes, to select fortunate hits as illustrative of his predictions. In the Renaissance documents we shall consider, however, the evidence is drawn usually from the horoscopes of well-known persons of earlier times whose birth moments are unlikely to have been known.

Last of all, to conclude a discussion which in spite of the omission of much I had hoped to say has become long, I describe with all possible brevity a final curious perversion having to do with the zodiacal signs. Although known to all serious students of astrology it appears not to be generally familiar.

Because of the precession of the equinoxes, a phenomenon too complicated to explain here, the zodiacal band changes its position relative to a given point on the ecliptic by one sign in about 2,000 years. This alteration was known to Hipparchus as early as 130 B.C.; and Ptolemy, who made observations between about 121 and 151 A.D., in order to get rid of the inconvenience invented an arbitrary zodiac bound to the equinoxial points so as never to vary. This purely imaginary zodiac has ever since been used in astrological predictions. Incredible as the assertion may seem, a man said by astrologers to have been born in Aries was actually born in Pisces or Aquarius; for the zodiac has moved round by nearly two full signs since Aries really marked the beginning of spring, as it did about 2000 B.C. and as Ptolemy pretended it did in his day, when there was already a discrepancy of one sign. The degrees given in the Ephemerides for the positions of the planets thus refer to a zodiacal band which is nearly 60° off-phase with the one actually visible. Yet the influence of the imaginary Aries is still supposed to flow from the position already mostly occupied by Aquarius and soon to be wholly occupied by it. And this gross fiction underlies every horoscope cast from Ptolemy's time to our own.

This extraordinary situation, which is altogether certain, has been defended by a number of implausible arguments. The most common appears to be that the section of sky in question was "saturated" so long with Arietal influence that this continues to emanate from the area. No means is suggested by which Aries overcame the influence of Taurus, which was in the same position previously for an equally long period, and yet has remained unaffected by Pisces and then by Aquarius, which in its turn began nearly 2,000 years ago to encroach upon Pisces. Such arguments, however, are not faithful to the mental habits really congenial to astrologers. When they write for each other instead of to convert skeptics their intellectual qualities become evident. For example, in Leo's *Casting the Horoscope* (10th edition, 1969) an unidentified contributor proposes that the arbitrary zodiac is really "the earth's Astral Body" and has nothing to do with the stars in it. Again, another contributor, in a note, decides what exactly is meant by "birth" by quoting the memory of a hypnotized subject who recalled that one of his incarnations began at the instant the umbilical cord was cut.[29] Such mental habits as these, understandable formerly but psychically regressive now, are those appropriate to the "science."

Yet although we reject utterly the astrologer's faith we may find interesting and historically significant the Renaissance disputes to which now, after this long introduction, we turn.

II. The beginning of all-out attack

In the opinion of Gustav Braunsperger, the Renaissance *Blütezeit* of astrology was prepared by a visit to Italy in 1438 of the Byzantine scholar Georgios Gemistos, later to be called Pletho. Although the church council called to explore the possibility of reuniting the Eastern and Roman churches achieved nothing, he was to have lasting influence as an evangel of Platonism. Plato had been known almost exclusively through a Latin translation of the *Timaeus* and was to become a force in Western thought only as a result of Ficino's translation of Greek dialogues hitherto inaccessible and, in any event, unreadable until the linguistic difficulties were overcome. The visit of Pletho, Bessarion, and other Byzantines provided both an opportunity and an impulse for the study of Greek, especially because Pletho propagated vigorously an attractive world-view which included the attributing of souls to the stars and the asserting of a universal harmony within which matter and intelligence were nowhere sharply disjoined. Cosimo de' Medici became interested, and through him his protégé Marsilio Ficino, who attacked successfully a language which had eluded Petrarch. After a delay occasioned by Cosimo's impatience for a Latin rendering of the newly-recovered *Corpus Hermeticum*—discussed in a separate chapter—Ficino turned his whole attention to Plato and, through his Latin translations, initiated a new phase of intellectual history in which Platonic thought, interpreted largely through such later mystics as Plotinus, Porphyry, and Iamblichus, was to combat the dominant Aristotelianism. In the controversies thus generated astrology was to play a surprisingly important role.[30] With Ficino's thought, most explicitly astrological in his *De vita triplici*—also discussed elsewhere—we have nothing to do here. Upon the *Disputationes adversus astrologiam divinatricem* (1495) of his younger friend Giovanni Pico della Mirandola we must, however, pause, for the document provides the best possible reference frame for nearly two centuries of scholarly dispute.

That Pico should have attacked astrology more effectively than any other Renaissance thinker is one of those ironies of which history is full, for in his earlier writings he had combined logical acuity with mysticism. One of the 900 *Conclusiones* which, as a young man, he offered to defend against all comers at Rome was "No science offers greater assurance of Christ's divinity than magic and the cabala" (*Nulla est scientia, quae nos magis certificet de diuinitate Christi, quam Magia & Cabala*).[31] He was one of the earliest Western scholars to study Hebrew, and his *Heptaplus* is a monument to curious Rabbinical learning of the most mystical and credulous

76 TRACT. I. SECT. II. PORT. IV. LIB. I.

hujus Astrologiæ speciei myrothecium ingredi: Nec tamen huic arti fidem certam attribuimus, nisi à Geomantia, quam superiùs animæ scientiam esse explicavimus, confirmaretur: Ubi ergo hæ duæ scientiæ convenerunt, ibi rei veritatem inesse non inefficaciter prædiximus; in loco autem, ubi eas dissentire percepimus, nihil certitudinis, sed potiùs prædictionis inconstantiam esse declaravimus, nec ausi fuimus quicquam asseveranter ore incerto ebuccinare. Quomodo autem duodecim schematis cœlestis domus fortunio aut infortunio nati respondeant ex speculo sequenti poteris ad oculum percipere.

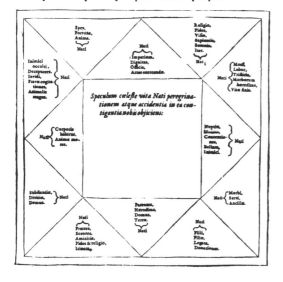

Robert Fludd, *De supernaturali, naturali, praenaturali et contranaturali microcosmi historia* (Oppenheim: Hieronymus Gallerus, 1619), p. 76 (of *Tomus secundus*).

The twelve astrological houses. The writing in the center reads, "Celestial mirror of the native's life, projecting to us his travels and things happening in them." Essentially the diagram expands the usual single-word descriptions of the twelve astrological "houses." The numbering begins at center left and proceeds counterclockwise. I (*Vita*) has to do with what we should call physical and psychological character; II (*Lucrum*) with property, riches, and house; III (*Fratres*) with brothers, sisters, friendship, faith and religion, and journeys; IV (*Genitor*) with parents, inheritance, home, and land; V (*Nati*) with sons, daughters, legacies, and donations; VI (*Valetudo*) with illness and male and female servants; VII (*Uxor*) with marriage, wives, quarrels, war, and enemies; VIII (*Mors*) with death, work, sadness, inherited diseases, and final years; IX (*Pietas*) with religion, faith, vision, wisdom, dreams, and travel; X (*Regnum*) with rule, dignity, duties, and practical arts; XI (*Benefacta*) with hope, fortune, and soul; XII (*Carcer*) with hidden enemies, deceivers, jealous persons, evil thoughts, and large animals. Because of overlappings and other awkwardness, the system is far from neat; but of course it was subject to some fluctuation.

sort. Magic is defined in his *Oratio de hominis dignitate* [32] as consisting of two parts, of which the second, that which does not invite the help of daemons, is "nothing else, when well looked into, but the absolute consummation of natural philosophy." He was fascinated also by numerology, and in general gives the impression of working toward a *summa* of the kind achieved about 1531 by Cornelius Agrippa's three volumes of *Occulta philosophia*. That such a man, gifted though he was with high rank and extraordinary personal graces, should turn at last to hard-headed rationalism is one of the curiosities of intellectual history.

Either or both of two causes may have produced the *volte-face*. Almost two centuries later Antonio Bonatti said that Pico's conversion had resulted from a prediction of his early death by Luca Bellanti of Siena: "Becoming infuriated, he vomited forth many arguments filled with the venom of passion, as if his mind had suddenly lost its control." [33] A similar but expanded story is told earlier by Tycho Brahe, according to whom not one but three Italian astrologers predicted Pico's death in his thirty-third year, the prediction proving true despite the fact that as the time ap-

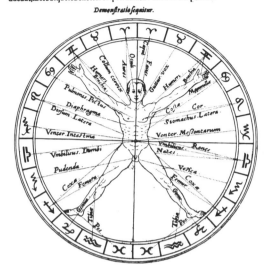

DE MICROCOSMI EXTERNI HARM.   113

nempe. Capricornus, genua, Aquarius, tibiam utramque, & Pisces, pedes exhibet. Qui quidem signorum ad membra respectus tam sanitatem quam corporis concordias naturalibus à Planetis respiciantur, quàm morbos: nam si discordiis & antipathia cum pravis Planetarum dispositionibus concurrant, & per consequens naturæ humanæ dissonent, operationes contra naturæ institutum producunt, morbo; que seu effectus corpori humano infestissimos pariunt.

Demonstratio sequitur.

Est etiam compositio Microcosmi externi cuilibet alii figuræ regulari apta atque conformis, quatenus, pro diversa membrorum protuberantium positione, diverso modo constituitur. Nam in una ejus statione directa, tibiis nullo modo extensis, sed serratis, manibusque cum brachiis ad angulos rectos à corpore expansis, atque in longum ab utroque latere complete porrectis, denotabit verissimam quadrati æquilateralis proportionem. Hujus rei demonstratio inferius sequitur, in qua declaratur, quod hujus etiam quadrati centrum sit pudendorum seu genitalium punctus; quippe cum duæ lineæ rectæ seu diametrales, ductæ ab angulo uno quadrati ad ejus oppositum, faciant intersectio-

P   nem

Robert Fludd, *De supernaturali, naturali, praenaturali et contranaturali microcosmi historia* (Oppenheim: Hieronymus Gallerus, 1619), p. 113.

Diagram of the relationships between parts of the body and the twelve zodiacal signs. The schedule runs as follows: Aries, head, face, eyes, ears; Taurus, throat, voice, neck; Gemini, shoulders, arms, fingers; Cancer, nipples, ribs, lungs, chest; Leo, stomach, sides, diaphragm, back; Virgo, belly, middle and lower intestines; Libra, kidneys, navel, buttocks, loins; Scorpio, testicles, penis; Sagittarius, hips, upper legs; Capricorn, knees; Aquarius, lower legs, feet. Pisces is left without an assignment. Account was taken of these relationships by astrological medicine, which continued to be practised well into the Renaissance.

proached Pico shut himself up in his chamber.[34] (He actually died at thirty-one.) Another and more likely possibility is that the change of attitude was produced by Pico's admiration for Savonarola, who like Luther and Calvin, but unlike Melanchthon, regarded astrology as a superstition unworthy of Christians. At any event, the redirection of interest occurred, and to it we owe a long treatise, in twelve books, which remains not only one of the fullest attacks on astrology but also one of the best informed.

As others were to do after him, Pico began in his *Proœmium* by differentiating astrology from what today we should call astronomy:

When I say astrology I do not mean the mathematical measurement of stellar sizes (*moles*) and motions, which is an exact and noble art . . . but the reading of forecoming events by the stars, which is a cheat of mercenary liars, prohibited by both civil and church law, preserved by human curiosity, mocked by philosophers, cultivated by itinerant hawkers, and suspect to the best and most prudent men; whose practitioners from their nationality (*gentilicio vocabulo*) were called 'Chaldaeans,' or from their practice 'casters of nativities.' " [35]

Such astrology is

the most infectious of all frauds, since, as we shall show, it corrupts all philosophy, falsifies medicine, weakens religion, begets or strengthens superstition, encourages idolatry, destroys prudence, pollutes morality, defames heaven, and makes men unhappy, troubled, and uneasy; instead of free, servile, and quite unsuccessful in nearly all their undertakings." [36]

In the twelve books which follow, these accusations are supported both passionately and astutely. Against Pico it was not easy, although it was nonetheless sometimes done, to bring the charge so often directed against later controversialists, that he was ignorant of his subject.

Since justice could be done to so extended and dense a work only in a separate volume, we can notice here only some of the arguments. In an age when the citation of authorities bore a heavy part in every demonstration, it was appropriate that the first book should undertake to show that Pico himself was not the first skeptic. Laws had been made against astrology by the Caesars (who especially feared predictions of their own deaths); Scriptural prophets condemned it, popes prohibited it, the voices of the most devout men were raised against it, philosophers and mathematicians opposed it.[37] Among the unbelieving philosophers were Pythagoras, Favorinus, Panaetius, Seneca, Cicero, Carneades, Bion, Epicurus, Plato and Aristotle—who nowhere mentioned it—Ocellus, Plotinus, Origines Adamantius, Eudoxus, Averroës, and Avicenna. Most philosophers, indeed, "scorned it rather than confuted it." [38] Further, "This is worthy of note, that the astronomers themselves rejected it." [39] But *Veniamus ad neotericos,* "Let us come to the moderns." Another shorter list follows, including even Ficino, who when advising men about their health (in *De vita triplici*) rather hoped for help from the sky than believed it would come: "I can myself testify faithfully about his state of mind." [40] The imperative in the Renaissance to deny originality was as strong as the desire now to be credited with it. Having demonstrated that he could not justly be suspected of innovation, Pico was ready to proceed with more substantive arguments.

In the first chapter of Book II he undertakes to show that both the art and its foundations are uncertain. Ptolemy himself admitted that "our weakness is too great for us to be equal to so great a work." [41] Arabic and Hebrew philosophers knew that predictions may not come true either because the matter is not suited to receive influence, or free will can intervene, or the Divine purpose may "ordain things otherwise than the usual revolution of the heavens would effect." [42] Anyhow, the portents called "elections" are useless. An astrologer tells us when we should go ahead with our projects, he says in the next chapter, and when we should abstain. But being fortunate consists precisely of being moved by heaven to do things when we should, as Aristotle agreed when he said that council is of no value to a lucky man. At most, such a person could be dissuaded from attempting what he was about to perform happily.[43] Those are much more fortunate "who, having rejected this superstition, use only choice and prudence to lead them," as Francesco Sforza did.[44] If astrology (he continues) advises you to do something which seems wise on other grounds, what has been gained? If it tells you to do something which appears foolish, which are you to trust, the stars or your senses and your reason? [45]

Neither is astrology useful to religion, although Roger Bacon and Pierre d'Ailly argued that by using it we could verify Biblical chronology and show that the events foretold by the prophets coincided with important astrological phenomena. Both, however, were guilty of egregious errors in their calculations, and the Apostle Paul taught us that David's prophecies were inspired.[46] In fact, nothing is more inimical to religion than astrology, which leads to impiety, errors of faith (*malam religionem*), heresies, empty superstitions, desperate morals, and irrevocable evil.[47] Divine miracles are laid to the stars;[48] "Indeed, I have read no one among the principal astrologers who did not subject religion, all laws, and other human affairs to the constellations,"[49] as when Bacon said that Christians ought to abstain from work on Saturn's day, as the Jews did, because it is unpropitious.[50] But this is to demote Moses to an astrologer.[51]

Other arguments follow. The opinions of astrologers differ widely.[52] Ptolemy attacked the Egyptians; and the Indians, Chaldaeans, Egyptians, and Persians are badly at odds.[53] Among the Greeks themselves, what Ptolemy rejects Dorotheus accepts: *alii alii sentiunt et opinantur,* and all claim the support of experience.[54] Modern astrologers suffer from appalling ignorance.[55] If he had not set out to refute the whole art, Pico could point out six hundred errors of which recent practitioners were guilty.[56] The moderns are also lazy, and because they are content to work from an almanach or Ephemeris believe that a planet is at a cardinal point when it is not, or that it is not when it is, and consider only right ascendant without noting the differences made by declination, which are often sufficient to alter the horoscopes materially.[57] In any event, predictions rarely come true—not even of the weather, which Pico had found to be correct for no more than 6 or 7 of 130 days on which he made comparisons.[58] Pino Ordelaffi, Prince of Forlì and Pico's brother-in-law, died in the very year in which a completely secure life was foretold for him.[59] If successes can sometimes be claimed, the explanation is partly that no divinatory art is always wrong, partly that "there is no horoscope in which a complex disposition of stars (*multiplex constellatio*) which has both prosperous and adverse significations is not present," partly that much which is predicted cannot fail to happen, and partly that predictions are ambiguous.[60]

Although so much has been summarized to suggest the energy and scope of Pico's refutation, we must now confine our attention to particulars. As the first of several illustrative passages we look briefly at his comments on the astrological houses, the *loci* or *domus*.

An approach is made through the observation that "Events in the distant future cannot be caused by a present configuration." [61] Astrologers predict the influence on the early part of the life of a planet which lies in the east, and on the late years of a planet which lies in the west; and so on, through many refinements. This, however, is to say that a heavenly force is more powerful when it does not exist than when it does. Forces which are to produce something in the future also produce it more powerfully in the present. To be sure, a baby cannot at once become a king or a philosopher; but astrologers say that the influence ceases during a number of years equal to the number of parts in the signs by which the planet is separated from the ascendant.[62] And this theory Pico finds unacceptable.

The subject is recurred to in Book X, this time specifically in relation to the houses. In space itself Pico will admit no significance beyond that of determining the angle at which rays impinge upon us. Empty areas of the sky possess no inherent "virtue." [63] This is imputed to them, however, by the doctrine of houses, which he proceeds to criticize in detail. Of the five kinds of supporting arguments he undertakes to refute we shall consider only two.

The first defines the houses *ab ordine numerorum,* on the basis that in distinct sequences of numbers the first number of one series corresponds to the first of another, and so on to the end. Thus there are twelve signs and twelve houses; since Gemini is the third sign, the third house must have to do with brothers, and because Jupiter is the second of the planets, after Saturn, and has to do with riches, the second house is the place of wealth (*divitias* for the more usual *lucrum*). The principle leads to absurdities: for example, Saturn is the first of the planets and fire the first of the elements, yet Saturn is cold. And the more equivalents are sought the more contradictions are discovered.[64]

The second justification is based on *parabolica similitudo,* or figurative analogy; and in discussing this Pico comes close to perceiving that all analogical analysis, with which Renaissance thought was permeated, is dangerous. "The father loves his sons, and the fifth house is connected with the ascendant by a trigonal, hence friendly, angle; therefore the fifth house signifies sons." [65] The first house is that of the nativity because *de tenebris prodit in lucem,* from darkness it comes forth into light; and because it travels a short distance in doing so, the same house relates to short journeys, as from one part of a city to another. Similarly, the second house has to do with riches "because, they say, nothing is nearer to a man than riches," and the second house adjoins the first. In fact many things are nearer: the gifts of mind and body, wisdom and health (though these are assigned to the ninth and sixth houses), parents, wife, friends, sons, and glory. The third house is assigned to brothers because the sextile aspect with the nativity is also friendly, but less so than the trine; we love our sons better than our brothers. For a comparable reason the eleventh house, also sextile, is assigned to friends; but the ninth, which like the first is trigonal with the nativity, is not given to sons because it is cadent or falling. The fourth house, in the bad quartile aspect to the first, is given to parents; why is this, if the relation of the native to *his* sons is friendly? We shall not follow the exposition to the end but will move at once to the conclusion: "In this way anything can easily be proved, since nothing exists which it is impossible to imagine by an argument of this kind to have some similarity and dissimilarity with something else." Emphasizing such likenesses resembles the claim that water is like fire because it is as cold as the fire is hot.[66]

The same tough-mindedness about incautious analogy appears elsewhere. Of a neat correspondence suggested by Ptolemy between the four seasons and the moon's quarters Pico remarks, "This is rather very pretty than natural and true."[67] Sometimes he finds correspondences absurd on their own terms, as when he points out that blood, the swiftest of the four bodily humors, is assigned to Jupiter, the next-to-slowest of the planets, and that choler is related to Mars, which has a relatively short cycle, although it is slower than black bile, which is assigned to Saturn.[68] Of course the ratiocinative methods are not consistently modern. Pico accepted the traditional belief that the circle is the perfect figure[69]—a notion which until Kepler's time was to prevent recognition that the planets have elliptical orbits; he denied that the moon causes tides;[70] and he thought that the sun was strongest in eastern parts of the world because gems, perfumes, lions, tigers, and elephants, which were fostered by heat, were found in the Orient.[71] Nevertheless he has moved surprisingly far along the road which was to lead from mythological thought-patterns to scientific, as can be seen from his positive thought about the heavens, and farther still from his own earlier *Conclusiones* and *Heptaplus*.

The principle which underlies most of his denials is that the planets and stars act upon human beings only by light and motion and have no more secret influences (*occultiores afflatus*) at all. Special properties do not have an astrological origin but originate in "the peculiar nature of things themselves and in proximate and related causes."[72] Further, the light, together with the heat which it contains and the heavenly motions to which he elsewhere ascribes effects we would now assign to gravity, acts universally and cannot be held responsible for individual differences in human beings.[73] Lions, he says sensibly, are born from lions under any zodiacal sign, and whenever children are born they are sons and daughters of their parents.[74] Finally, "aside from the sun and the moon the other heavenly bodies act upon us not at all or, at most, very slightly."[75] For the time, these insights were exceptional.

Because the establishment of this positive view required a detailed negation of

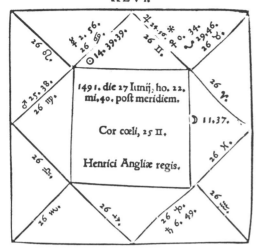

HI. R. CARDANI LIB.
XLVI.

1491. die 27 Iunij, ho. 22.
mi.40. post meridiem.

Cor cœli, 25 II.

Henrici Angliæ regis.

H Ac genitura, ubi bona nulla melior, ubi mala nulla deteri-
or: nam quòd Venus in 9 loco cum Aldebaran posita cū
cauda, & in sextili Mercurij est, mutationem legis ostendit, nec
reuertetur, fixa enim adiacet. Luna etiam in septimo loco in Solis quadrato, Saturno Venerem sic positam respiciente, & Ioue
Marte dominum septimi, diuortium, & multa circa uxores in-
conuenientia declarant, ut etiam illarum unam capite mulcta-
uerit. Saturnus in Mercurij opposito, quoniam Mercurius in
supremo

Hieronymus Cardanus (Jerome Cardan), *Libelli quinque, quorum duo priores, iam denuo sunt emendati, duo sequentes iam primum in lucem editi, & quintus magna parte aucta est* (Nuremburg: apud Iohan. Petreium, 1547), sig. 148r.

Horoscope of King Henry VIII of England. The twelve houses (*loci*) are to be numbered from the triangle at left center in a counter-clockwise direction, so that the twelfth house has a common boundary with the first, the "horoscope" proper. The time of Henry's birth is given as 22:40 p.m. on June 27, 1491—i.e., 10:40 a.m. on June 28, the actual day of the birth. The astrologer's "day" began at noon.

The part of the reading shown here can be translated as follows: "This horoscope, in which there could be no greater good or any greater evil—because Venus is in the ninth house with Aldebaran and the Tail and in sextile with Mercury—shows a change in the laws which will not be revoked but will remain settled. Also the moon, in the seventh house and in quartile with the sun, while Saturn is in trine aspect with Venus, placed as has been described, and Mars is in trine with the lord of the seventh house, Jupiter, announces divorce and much trouble with wives, to the point that one will be capitally punished. Saturn is in opposition with Mercury, since Mercury . . ."

beliefs commonly held, most of Pico's space is given over to refutation. For example, radiation is strongest when it comes from directly overhead, weakest at the horizons, and non-existent when the source is outside the line of sight. Even astrologers admit the weakness of bodies in the twelfth house (just above the eastern horizon), calling them *torpides et cessatrices et imbecillas;* but they assert inconsistently that from directly beneath the earth the stars (a term which it must be remembered often includes the planets, the modifying participle *errantes* being dropped) "have much strength and efficacy." [76] It is said that a star has increased influence when in conjunction with the moon; but it has less, as can be seen from the diminishing of the sun's light when the moon intervenes between it and the earth.[77] As for the "mixing" of rays, *illud asseveramus: radios omnes miscere semper,* all rays are constantly mixed, but not as the aspects are pretended to determine.[78] Beyond such radiation, falling always from the visible sky and varying only with the angle from which it comes,

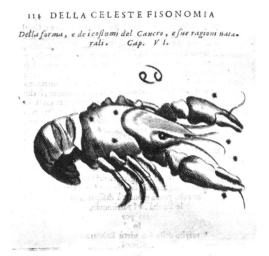

114 DELLA CELESTE FISONOMIA

Della forma, e de i costumi del Cancro, e sue ragioni naturali.   Cap. VI.

H ALI dice. Il Cancro è dimesso, & humile, di membra
grosse, le membra di sopra ha più grosse di quelle
da basso, di gran corpo, di dentatura corta, e diuersa, di ca-
pelli crespi, d'occhi piccioli, e di spalle ampie, fa gl'huo-
mini soaui, e dotti, le sue facoltà haurà da cose publiche, e
saranno occupati in negotij publichi. Mà il Bonato dice, che fa
il corpo dell'huomo scomposto, la pelle di tutto il corpo gros-
sa, & lo fa di sopra sottile, e di basso grosso, che ha i denti
torti, e gl'occhi piccioli. Leopoldo dice: Il Cancro è tutto
buono, la sua gola è nodosa, per abondanza d'humori. Il Materno dice: se l'horoscopo farà trouato nel Cancro, fa sempre
d'acuto ingegno, ma che fa tutte le cose sue con vna modera-
tione

Gio[vanni] Battista Dalla [sic.] Porta, *La Fisonomia dell'huomo, et la celeste* (In Venetia: Sebastian Combi, & Gio. La Noù, 1652), p. 114.

A description of the zodiacal sign of Cancer and its effects. "Ali says that the native of Cancer is dejected and humble, has thick limbs, the upper being heavier than the lower, is large in body, has short and irregular teeth, curly hair, small eyes, and broad shoulders, is affable and learned, has a capacity for public business, and will engage in public affairs. But Bonatus says that Cancer makes the human body disproportioned, the skin over the whole body thick, causes him to be delicate in the upper parts and heavy in the lower, and to have crooked teeth and small eyes. Leopoldo says that the native of Cancer is wholly good and, because of abundance of humors, has a knotty throat. Maternus says that if Cancer is in the horoscope it causes the native to have a sharp wit but to act moderately . . ."

Ali (Hali) is probably Ali-Ibn-Younis, a famous Arabian astronomer who died in 1008; but there are other possibilities. Bonatus (Bonato) is Guido Bonatti, a thirteenth-century Florentine. I have been unable to identify Leopoldo. Maternus (Materno) is Maternus Julius Firmicus, who lived in the fourth century.

astrological doctrine is *vana prorsus et irrationabilis:* the houses, the aspects, the zodiacal signs, and all the rest.[79]

The tendency of all this is clear. For a cosmic universe which was conceived animistically, in which planets "rejoiced" and were "dejected," "looked at" each other with friendly or unfriendly feelings, and varied from "benevolence" to "malevolence" in their attitudes toward men, Pico wanted to substitute one in which the heavenly bodies performed quite dispassionately and without consciousness roles assigned them at the beginning by a Creator-God who allowed the evil initiated by men to cause suffering but did not place in the skies forces which would dispose them to act well or badly. *Si sua cuique sideri et propria vis concedatur, esse tamen illam universalem:* if every star has its proper force, the influence acts universally, not selectively.[80] As an example let us take Aristotle. His soul did not come from the stars because, as he himself proved, it was immortal and incorporeal. His body, fit to serve his soul, did not come from the sky, *nisi tamquam a communi causa,* but from his parents. As a result of the power of choice inherent in his mind and body he elected to philosophize. His progress came from his plan and his industry, and that it was especially great was a consequence of his teacher's doctrine and the good fortune of his age, when a good beginning had been made and materials were at hand to bring philosophy to perfection. He was superior to his disciples and contemporaries because he had not a better star but a greater genius, the source of which was God. Similarly, the greatest of all philosophers, Socrates, ascribed his wisdom not to the luminaries but to a god or daemon who kept him company (*assistenti numini*).[81]

This is the gist of the whole treatise. Other telling arguments are added. Astrologers often claim as a cause what is posterior to the effect, as when they ascribe sex, which has been determined long before, to the moment of birth.[82] Elections are ridiculed. How can a fortunate hour for beginning a journey make the way soft to the feet, drive off bandits, clear away clouds, and make the sky serene? How does

128   DELLA CELESTE FISONOMIA

Del corpo, e costumi, che da Aquario, e sue cause naturali.
Cap.   XIII.

Dice Hali. L'Acquario dà l'vna gamba maggiore dell'altra, di sangue apparente nel corpo, e nel colore. Stima assai se stesso, di buona fama, libero, di gran spesa, dissipatore del suo patrimonio. Il Bonato dice: Fa l'huomo bianco, che ha bella faccia, e colorita, l'vna gamba maggiore dell'altra. Leopoldo: Acquario nel mezzo è buono, nel fine huomo vile, donna meretrice. Il Materno: L'Horoscopo nell'Acquario: ciò che haurà acquistato, in qualunque maniera, al fine lo dissiparà, & ciò che haurà, ò acquistarà, di nuouo perderà, ma ciò, che haurà perduto, facilmente per lo più raccoglie, molti riceuerà sotto il suo fauore, & a molti darà
da

Gio[vanni] Battista Dalla [*sic.*] Porta, *La Fisonomia dell'huomo, et la celeste* (In Venetia: Sebastian Combi, & Gio. La Noù, 1652), p. 128.

The zodiacal sign of Aquarius and its effects. "Ali says that Aquarius causes one to have one leg larger than the other and to be clearly sanguine in body and complexion. The Aquarian thinks well of himself, has a good reputation, is generous, spends freely, and dissipates his patrimony. Bonato says that Aquarius makes a man white, with a handsome, well-colored face, and to have one leg larger than the other. Leopoldo says that in the middle [of the first house] Aquarius is good; at the cusp he makes a man base and a woman a prostitute. Maternus says that a person with Aquarius in his horoscope will finally squander what he has acquired in any way and will again lose what he may have or acquire but, having lost it, will regain more; that he will receive many into his favor . . ." (The proper names have been identified in the note to the preceding figure.)

HIER. CARDANI LIB.
VII.

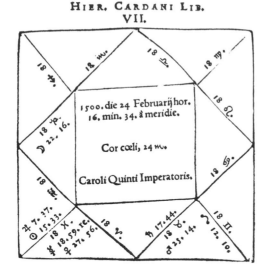

1500. die 24 Februarij hor.
16. min. 34. à meridie.

Cor cœli, 24 ♏.

Caroli Quinti Imperatoris.

Iupiter cũ tertia aquæ aquarij, magnitudinis quartæ, naturæ Saturni, parum Iouis.
Mars cum latere dextro Perſei, magnitudinis ſectidæ, naturæ Saturni & Iouis, in initio lacteæ uiæ.
Sol cum dorſo Pegaſi, magnitudinis ſecundæ, naturæ Martis & Mercurij: & cum uentre piſcis, naturæ Iouis & Mercurij, magnitudinis quartæ.
Mercurius cum alia uentris piſcis, magnitudinis & naturæ præcedentis.

Luna

Hieronymus Cardanus (Jerome Cardan), *Libelli quinque, quorum duo priores, iam denuo sunt emendati, duo sequentes iam primum in lucem editi, & quintus magna parte aucta est* (Nuremberg: apud Iohan. Petreium, 1547), sig. 109*v*.

Horoscope of the Emperor Charles V, said to have been born on February 25 (as we should say), 1500, at 4:34 a.m. (*à* being equivalent to *post*). A peculiarity is the noting of stellar magnitudes within named constellations. In book I, the *Supplementum almanach,* Cardan had discussed the names and powers of some forty-six stars. Here he apparently finds significance in their magnitudes and "natures," which are described in terms of the known natures of planets. So far as can be told at this distance of time, such data, probably intended to "correct" astrological theory by bringing it abreast of current astronomy, were innovative. In the translation which follows I have supplied "star" at what appeared to be appropriate points.

"Jupiter is with the third star in the water of Aquarius, a star of the fourth magnitude and of the nature of Saturn, with very little of that of Jupiter.

"Mars is with a star in the right side of Perseus, of the second magnitude and of the nature of Saturn and Jupiter, at the beginning of the Milky Way.

"The sun is with a star in the back of Pegasus, of the second magnitude and of the nature of Mars and Mercury; and with a star in the belly of Pisces, of the nature of Jupiter and Mercury and of the fourth magnitude.

"Mercury is with another star in the belly of Pisces, of the same magnitude and nature."

It will be noted that not all the stars are in the zodiacal signs. Apparently Cardan was attempting to meet the criticism that stars not in the signs, although ignored in the traditional readings, also emitted rays of a strength varying with their magnitudes.

the influence of the chosen moment remain active throughout the whole time?[83] We are told that a city whose building was begun under the cruel rays of Mars will lose many kings by the sword: in what way do the foundation stones retain their malevolent influence and project it on successive rulers?[84] From time to time Pico grants the astrologers their assumptions and proceeds to examine the legitimacy of their inferences.[85] Again, he criticizes the system from without, as in some of the above excerpts, or when he denies that miracles are either caused or portended by the skies and affirms that they are simply miraculous, as natural events are natural.[86] Toward the end he recurs to basic problems. The claim is rejected that however astonishing they may seem the predictions have the support of experience. According to the astrologers themselves what counts is the total configuration, and this never repeats itself or does so only *post multa milia saeculorum,* so that empirical verification is impossible.[87] Neither is it credible that astrology was revealed directly. To whom was the revelation vouchsafed—the Chaldaeans? the Egyptians? the Jews? Ptolemy? the Arabs? The Christian God cannot be the source, for the Scriptures prohibit astrology; if the Devil, we should grant no faith to the father of lies (*nulla fides daemoni, quem mendacii patrem Deus appellavit*).[88] The Chaldaeans and Egyptians, who have the best claim to the discovery, were superstitious, as given to idolatry as to mathematics, and possessed of little aptitude for wisdom.[89] The true sources are rather mathematics (which was penetrated by numerological mysticism) and figurative analogies, than which nothing is more fallacious.[90]

Although much else in the *Disputationes* has interest, we can afford the document no more space. Not every part is wholly convincing; Pico, too, lived in the fifteenth century. Nevertheless the total effect is impressive. A modern reader who comes to the treatise from weeks or months of reading about astrological doctrines and practices feels suddenly much nearer home. That the attack was taken seriously is revealed by the counter-arguments inspired by it. We look next at several of these, remembering that what was peculiar about Renaissance thought is more apparent in what seems strange than in what requires little psychic stretching.

III. Pro-astrological writings

The first direct reply was made by the same Bellanti who is said to have forecast Pico's death. His *Liber de astrologica veritate* (1498, 1502, 1554) [91] begins with an apologetic *Ad Lectorem* in which, besides professing admiration for his opponent's gifts and suggesting that, had Pico lived, he would have burned his book, the author acknowledges faults in his own Latinity and apologizes for having had to rush his refutation into print. The reply itself is noteworthy for the straightforwardness with which Pico's objections are reported. The first page and a half, for example, might be cited without change for the purpose of calling the foundations of the art into question. We pass over these to come directly to the defense, which opens, significantly, with the sentence, "But a great number of wise men and the testimony of authority and experience are against this." [92] Authority is taken up before experience, as was usual in scholastic disputation, and the first authority quoted is Aristotle, the founder of the contemporary physics.

The intellect, as Aristotle said in *De anima, iii,* could not understand the body if it were not separate from it, as the judgment of colors is hampered by color in the pupil of the eye. Only the mind's spirituality allows it to transcend corporeal substance and qualities sufficiently to comprehend them. Now foresight of the future is divine; hence celestial causes of future events are easier for the human intellect to grasp than terrestrial ones.[93] If we are capable of learning something about God, who is utterly remote from our senses, we can identify celestial forces with comparative ease. Indeed, because the heavenly causes of sublunar effects are nearer the nature of mind than physical substance or even motion, which involves the movement of substance through space, they are less difficult to know than the stars' courses.[94]

This argument is sufficiently complex to reward brief scrutiny. For one thing, the subject is shifted right back into an intellectual ambience from which Pico had tried repeatedly, if not consistently, to detach it. Bellanti implies that because the intellect is "higher" than matter it moves ideally in the area of pure concepts; hence forces (*vires*) of a quasi-mystical nature are more properly an object of contemplation than, for example, epicycles, and *qualitates* more important than *substantiae*. The attitude was traditional from a time when, outside of warfare, hunting, and a few other activities, the manipulation of physical objects or any sort of close technical concern with them was the business of slaves, hence "illiberal." The result was a concern with high-level abstractions which inhibited the laborious observation of particulars. Bellanti, as an astrologer, of course worked with celestial phenomena, either observing them at first hand or, more probably, computing them from tables or an Ephemeris. In controversy, however, he feels it proper to move the discussion to a plane upon which the lofty contemplation of a force appears more dignified than the determination of a physical means by which it might operate. The means belonged among *inferiora,* the power itself among *superiora.*

Another associated quality of the passage deserves notice. When Pico fails to convince, the reason is often that his assumption has been exploded (planetary orbits must be circular) or that his collection of empirical data has been inadequate. Bellanti's argument, in contrast, is so self-contained that its internal consistency invites exploration. He has begun by saying that the intellect can understand the body because the two differ as thought differs from matter, but his conclusion is that astrological forces are more readily understood than physical causes for the reason that they are more like mind. Like the scholastics generally, he likes to "prove" the correctness of his opinions by trains of thought so highly conceptual that ideas must be measured rather against each other than against some extra-verbal reality. He is so ill-at-ease with substantive argument that even when he speaks of experience he continues to move chiefly within the area of concepts.

An example appears in his discussion of the reliability of ancient astrological doctrines. We do not, it is objected, possess the demonstrations by which early beliefs were supported. "Who can show why Mercury, when retrograde, causes men to be good musicians? Or why Cancer is cold and Sagittarius hot? Or for what reason

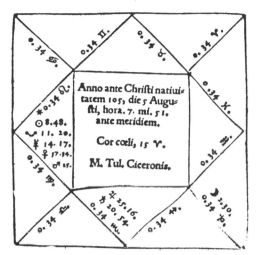

D Ecus eloquentiæ, os Romanum, cor leonis in horofcopo, Solem, caudam, Mercurium, Venerem, ac Martem cum eo habet: inde facundia & autoritas fumma decernebatur. Eadem fermè Petrarchæ affuerũt. Illi nihil deerat, huic nihil adijci poteft. Cauda cum Sole domino horofcopi, acutum ac uerfutũ, femper autem uiolentum decernit finem. Adiuuat decreta Saturnus Iupiterĉg in fcorpione triplicitatis figno, in qua tunc magna

Hieronymus Cardanus (Jerome Cardan), *Libelli quinque, quorum duo priores, iam denuo sunt emendati, duo sequentes iam primum in lucem editi, & quintus magna parte aucta est* (Nuremberg: apud Iohan. Petreium, 1547), sig. 113*v*.

Horoscope of Cicero, whose birth on August 5, 105 B.C., is said (sig. 113*v*) to be reported by "all" authorities and especially by Plutarch. But Plutarch says, in fact, that the birth occurred on "the third of the new Calends," or January 3, 107/106 B.C. Cardan knew that the time was "by no means certain" (*certum haud esse potest*); and he acknowledges doubt particularly about the moon's position.

The reading begins: "The ornament of eloquence and mouth of the Romans has in his horoscope (i.e., the first house) the heart of the Lion, and with it the sun, the Tail (the descending node of the moon), Mercury, Venus, and Mars: by these his fluency and high authority were determined. Almost the same things are reported of Petrarch. Nothing was lacking to him, and nothing could be added. The Tail, together with the sun's dominance in the horoscope, made him sharp and crafty but always decrees a violent end. These decrees are assisted by the fact that Saturn and Jupiter are in Scorpio . . ."

the eighth house signifies death rather than something else?" A true science ought to be clear and general, whereas astrology is *confusum & indistinctum* and also particular.[95] As elsewhere, the problem is honestly stated, and we look forward to replies to the specific questions.

Bellanti begins with the characteristic appeal to earlier writers: "But the authority and experience of excellent men is quite contrary." The early astrologers set down their canons and comments in books, and any diligent "experimenter" can himself see what struck them. Evidently the experimenter may as well read about experiences as have them. Zealous Christians, Bellanti continues, are put off by old errors: the belief that the will is wholly subject to the heavens, or that the world is eternal and had no efficient cause, or that nothing can be made of nothing, or that God has no care for worldly things. Again, the critic may misunderstand papal pronouncements. If a pope says that we ought to avoid running into danger, we ought to understand him as if he had warned us against praying with a beautiful woman, when he would not have meant that we should not pray at all.[96] The persons who offer such objections often want to appear learned, whereas in fact they are incapable of understanding the doctrines. The will cannot be constrained except *per accidens,* as a result of celestial influence exerted upon pre-existing inclinations.[97] Here comes another list of authorities: Aquinas, Damascenus, Aristotle, Ptolemy, Duns Scotus, and others. For example, Aquinas says that the heavens stream upon (*influant*) the body *per se,* the mind *per accidens.* As for the reliability of received doctrines, the ancients, having once understood the power of the heavens confusedly, began as lovers of truth to observe the movements of the luminaries with great labor and diligence, far above that of persons who observed the properties of bees and other animals, and, succeeding beyond the expectation of many, they discovered more, greater, and more startling powers, until at last they realized that the lower world was ruled by the higher. Thus Albumasar (ninth century) found the tides to be controlled by the moon. If some of their conclusions were mistaken, we should recall Aristotle's warning in the *Metaphysics* that we owe gratitude not only to those who discover truths but also to those who provoke doubts. This amounts to a general exhortation to faith qualified by an admission of the possibility of occasional error. *Est igitur dicendum: astrologiam esse scientiam cunctas habens conditiones ad scientiam requisitas.*[98] We can set aside our doubts and accept astrology as meeting all the conditions of a true science.

An addiction to scholastic thought-patterns is characteristic of the whole treatise but especially evident at certain points, as when the theory that Socrates was talkative because Mercury was in the house of Mars at his birth is tested syllogistically. A person at whose birth Mercury was in that position will have such-and-such qualities; Socrates was born with Mercury in that position; therefore Socrates had the qualities.[99] Realizing, perhaps, that the argument is less than decisive, Bellanti points out that astrology belongs among branches of knowledge which are not apparent to everybody but only to the *sapientibus,* upon whose opinions, he implies, we may rely. His conclusion does not bear upon the specific questions regarding Mercury, Cancer, and Sagittarius but upon the charge that astrology is not a true science: "In particular matters abstraction is not necessary even though possible; and of particulars which are incorruptible there can be knowledge."[100] The last stage in the preparation of this general principle has been the assertion that the effects of astrological forces are not uncertain because their operative modes are unknown.[101] A science (*scientia,* more properly "branch of knowledge") may concern itself with *what* but not worry seriously about *how,* and even the *what* need not be checked as a matter of course but can usually be accepted on authority. When Bellanti makes the familiar claim that "Nobody can deny that (the moon) increases the moisture in all bodies when it is waxing and decreases it when waning,"[102] no reader is likely to imagine him slicing stalks at all stages of the moon to verify the tradition. For Bellanti, as for most scholars of the period, "experience" often meant "reiterated report," as it still does for the general public. The attitude was so deeply founded that when Paracelsus made bold innovations in medicine on the basis that experience was more reliable than traditional doctrine he substituted folk remedies and old wives' tales for the pharmacopoeia and physiology of the authorities. Induction was a discipline not easily to be invented.

In 1512 another early reply to Pico appeared in Book XII of *De rebus coelestibus libri XIIII,* a posthumous work by Giovanni Pontano (?1422–1503), one of the most prolific writers of the fifteenth century and perhaps its most elegant stylist.[103] Pontano begins by expressing esteem for Pico and then laments the savagery of his attack. Other men, in antiquity and modern times, had tried to overthrow opinions they thought mistaken without subverting the entire discipline. What wonder if views differ when nature itself is so various? There are disputes about philosophy, natural science, medicine, government, even navigation and warfare; is it wonderful that astrologers think differently? Among those who had disputed about physics Democritus, Empedocles, Aristotle, and Plato might be mentioned; among those who had differed about the cure of diseases Herasistratus, Hippocrates, Asclepiades, Galen, and Avicenna. Yet accepted principles exist in both subjects, and both have been reduced to art and discipline. Pontano will refrain from mentioning also quarrels about theology.[104] In each of the disciplines errors can be laid to the complexity of the subject-matter. Who can know the specific workings of the stars when even earthly matters baffle us? "The mixtures of causes and things are infinite, and so also are the powers and efficacies of the stars." [105] So far objection would be difficult; but concession may appear to have gone too far. If the *effectiones* of the stars are unknowable, an astrological science would appear to be impossible.

In what follows, further admissions lead gradually to positive claims. The stars certainly do not build ships, or supply the axes by which criminals are punished, or settle kingdoms or prefectures, all these activities being determined by men.[106] Yet heavenly motions ferment or leaven the excretions necessary for generation. The consequence is an effect upon the mixture of humors, and through this upon the responses to sensations, so that pressure is exerted on total character and the use of the faculties. This happens most surely if the external situation is favorable: the region, the laws, the institutions, the parents' resources, and the like. If the environment is quite unsuitable, the innate predisposition will disappear like the skill of a sculptor who lacks materials upon which to work. If born in a rude country, a man with an aptitude for letters may turn to grazing or agriculture; if born to high station, he may become a magistrate. Such contingencies appear clearly in the variant forms of astrological predictions. A violent death portended by the stars may in one country be described as punishment by the axe, in others as punishment by crucifixion or stoning. Similarly a prediction of death by shipwreck or suffocation, if made of a man who lives in a waterless country, may indicate suffocation by snow, or hail, or rain, or even by overdrinking or some flooding of the brain (*cerebri exundatione*). Nowadays Syrians and Assyrians are forbidden by the Sultan to become soldiers; if the stars announced a military career for an Alexandrian, should we say that they lie? Can a man in a country where there is neither wool nor linen become a weaver, or an Egyptian, who as a Mohammedan must scorn all study and good letters, become a scholar? [107] The implication is that errors laid to the account of astrological theory often have some other source.[108] The basic doctrines are reliable.

This is the gist of Pontano's defense, which on its own terms is plausible and even graceful but shirks the task of making astrological preconceptions plausible. The remainder of the long treatise, which is not apologetic but explanatory, reveals with special clarity the analogical reasoning against which Pico had protested: a type of thought which before the birth of modern research methods almost necessarily projected upon nature the human structures and processes known to men through psychic experiences.

A good illustration appears in the early pages. Aristotle, the most skilled investigator of nature, has taught us that our beginnings flow from the heavens, which in contrast to lower things are *sempiterna*. *Superiora* act, *inferiora* suffer action, the roles of the two orders being, as it were, male and female. The parallel is developed in some detail. Motion is its own source, hence, like every progenitor, is male.[109] Its relation to terrestrial things is like that of the shipbuilder to the ship.[110] Thus the heavens procreate and pour down the heat which both makes generation possible and, through digestion, turns food into the blood from which men obtain their propensities, their interests (*studia*), and their habits. As a base metal is hammered out and formed by the strokes of the smith, so the agitations of the heavens play the chief role in procreating and terrestrial things the feminine role; or, again, as the male's seed insinuates itself into the menstrual blood of the woman and gradually affects and informs it, so the sun slips into the human body by means of its rays, its motions, and its heat, qualifies the body, warms it, and provides it with a soul. Indeed, one might say that the earth, covered as it is with water, is the world's womb, within which excretions fitted for generation are quickened and born by means of the sun's warmth. Together with the moon, which furnishes matter for the conception and, by moistening, prepares it, the sun is like one of the two major blood vessels from which spring the smaller ones that run to the uterus.[111]

After the argument we expect the authorities. Virgil is twice quoted,[112] but Pontano is now in full career and cannot long pause for corroboratory citations. If the earth is Parent and Nourisher, the sea has the office of imbuing the foetus with the senses by which the animal body will be dominated. Further, as the heart afterwards makes use of the digestive tract which it has itself produced (*officio utitur operáque praecordium, ab seipso autore ac magistro constitutorum*), so the sun uses the service of the planets for influencing and changing the qualities of lower things as may be necessary to strengthen and protect them against perishing. And as our beginning comes from the blood and the heart, our dispositions, inclinations, and interests will be determined by the qualities of the blood as this was tempered at the outset by the sun and stars. Hence knowledge of the actions and powers of the heavens, called by the Greeks *astrologia,* is what will be explained in the remainder of the treatise because the science is both noble and useful. If we foreknow events, we can evade misfortunes or prepare our minds for them, or, if they are to be favorable, we can encourage them, as a farmer cultivates vigorously a field which he knows to be fertile. So far as is possible, Pontano will explain the natural causes of celestial significations. Unfortunately, few ancient Latin books on the art except parts of Julius Maternus have been preserved. "If we had them all, I would be bold to say that not much of the discipline would be lacking for a complete knowledge of the significations themselves." [113] We may be confident that the ancients were wiser than we are but will make do as best we can.

No reader will have failed to perceive the "As . . . so . . ." structure of the preceding paragraphs. Similes have been drawn from human sexuality, shipbuilding, pottery, metalwork, the womb, blood vessels, nursing, the digestive tract, and farming. A premodern reader, being led in this way from the known to the unknown and finding no apparent discontinuities between them, might well feel himself enlightened. For unlettered men the reasoning process still consists largely of finding analogies. It had done so, in a noteworthy degree, for Socrates, and it continued to do so for Pontano.

Another characteristic of Pontano's thought—again shared with many contemporaries—appears in his explanation of why the zodiac "begins with" Aries. Of the four cardinal points in the sun's course, he tells us, the summer solstice is too hot for generation, the winter solstice is too cold and dry, and the autumnal equinox, "since it moves from dryness toward coldness, seems rather to look toward death than toward birth." [114] Because he accepts the implied equation of "beginning" with "birth" he restricts the inquiry within an area too small to contain the correct answer, which here would be that a continuous band like the zodiac has no beginning but that for the sake of convenience we imagine the year to begin with the vernal equinox, which coincides roughly (in the northern hemisphere) with the quickening of plant life. Further, he considers only the *cardines,* apparently not realizing even a theoretical possibility of selecting a point between them.

So elsewhere: what is argued is often inferences drawn from archaic premises.

Since fire, air, water, and earth *rerum sunt principia,* there must be in the heavens a force which can foster and increase them.[115] This was discovered in the signs, of which some were found to be fiery, others watery, and so on, until long observation had taught the qualities of all twelve.[116] The reasoning was assisted by another observation: when the great varieties of things were perceived to have a certain orderliness and the causes were sought, they were found to lie in these same origins (*principes*). Investigations by physicians at length settled the distribution of cold, heat, dryness, and moisture, which we know by experience to exist, just as we know that a magnet attracts iron. "Those who deny them deny the senses of sight and feeling." The qualities must be separated in the heavens just as white and black cannot coexist in the same place. We may be sure that the traditional conclusions are reliable, for "Daily observations of what frequently happens can give us satisfaction." [117] Thus we are reassured about a part of the total doctrine; but the long observation by the ancients appears to be taken for granted rather than known, and the choice of earth, water, air, and fire as "elements" had been made too long before to permit any question.

Pontano is by no means illimitably credulous. For example, he is skeptical of the reason usually given for the moon's moistness. If, as is said, the moon draws moisture from the earth, that could be expected to cool and fall back as rain. The sun, however, is not said to draw its heat either from the sphere of fire or from hot exhalations rising from the earth. Why may we not decide merely that "it is a property of the moon to moisten?" [118] In a later section the hypothesis is generalized: the planets also are "essentially" rather than materially hot, cold, moist, and dry.[119] In other places as well Pontano subtilizes the received beliefs without subverting them; but trustfulness is more congenial to him than doubt. He explains the doctrine of aspects by saying that opposing rays meet each other head on and quartile rays collide laterally, as winds sometimes do, but trine and sextile rays "mingle as friends and move forward together as if converging upon a single point," all the more because trine and sextile signs are of the same gender, whereas quartile signs are of opposite gender.[120] His discussion of the houses, although suave and attractive, is again substantially specious. The first house is "rightly" (*iure*) given to the newborn child because it is rising from beneath the earth and coming into the light.[121] The second, which lies next to it, is assigned to *lucrum* because "the body cannot perform its duties without provisions": money, furniture, and domestic substance generally. *Quid autem accommodatius?* [122] The third house, *fratres,* owes its identification to the fact that as a social animal man has born into him a desire for company; and the society of brothers and sisters is both prior to and stronger than that of friends (whose house is to come fifth, next after that of *parentes*).[123] The reasoning, which is typical of the usual defense (or explanation; the two are hardly distinguishable) of the houses, is of exactly the kind of *parabolica similitudo* against which Pico had protested.

Similarly with the rest of the long treatise. None of the objections likely to be offered by a modern skeptic is met, and few are envisaged as possible. One ought of course to remember that except in Book XII Pontano's aim is to give information. He did not anticipate a need to resist challenges; but for that reason the work reveals clearly intellectual habits which permitted an easy assimilation of astrological beliefs.

Although these early responses to Pico's attack were Italian, another reply, by the "mathematician and physicist" Jakob Schonheintz, published in 1502,[124] shows that Pico's treatise crossed the Alps rather quickly. If the mental habits shown by the *Apologia astrologiae* are not distinguished, they are perhaps typical of other practitioners who knew of Pico's work but disdained to reply. The tone of Schonheintz's book is angry and the apologetic method that of quoting authorities, especially Scriptural. The aim is evidently not that of contributing to a serious investigation but of safeguarding a prized activity.

No one, we are told at the outset, has written against astrology more strongly, more learnedly, or with greater energy and exertion than Pico, whose bites and barkings have deserved this retort. *Qui dicit quod vult, audit quod non vult.* Learn, reader, that astrology is useful and necessary to the human race because it raises its friends to the sky and teaches them heavenly matters.[125] It is a mark of the times that ignorant pretenders to scholarship (*indocti clericuli*) who can scarcely nibble at the bark of the Scriptures should dare to gnaw at their vitals. (So quickly does Pico cease to be "learned.") The reason why they vomit forth whatever comes into their mouths, even though it rises from the gorge, is that no one of authority has broken in upon their haranguing.[126] Schonheintz himself, plainly, intends to remedy this oversight.

The defense proper begins with praise of astrology as the most exalted of the human arts, its subject matter being the most powerful and least corruptible of created things, called divine by the ancients and having to do with the *atrium* or forecourt of God. The heaven itself, *caelum,* is named, as Pliny tells us, from *caelatura,* "the art of engraving." Naso (i.e., Ovid) sang that we were born to observe it; Crisippus and Posidonius praise it as the first part of the universe.[127] After this *exordium* we proceed to particulars. The writer of the attack—from this point the *Disputationes* and its author are not identified—has said "Do not turn to the mages" without adding "Lest, perhaps, following a temporary star, you should find the God who created the stars born and lying in a manger." No man who is *rudis & illustrium artium ignarus* is able to distinguish the superstitious from the natural. The real mage was the Gallic druid, the Egyptian prophet, the Indian gymnosophist, the Assyrian "Chaldaean," the Greek philosopher, the Latin wise man (*sapiens*); but mainly he was one who could predict the future by the stars and other means, as Jerome agrees.[128] Here follow definitions of "astronomy," "astrology," and "mathematician," which I skip; but the disciplines are all *honestissimae,* and, as mathematical arts, they are more reliable than the rest, *certiores reliquis.* The charge that they involve commerce with the demons is refuted by the Septuagint. Schonheintz next turns to what he describes as his opponent's first three conclusions.[129] We shall omit following the substance of his disproof to focus attention on his procedures. These consist, in large part, of accumulating passages from the authorities: Ovid, Juvenal, Petosiris, Michael Savonarola, Virgil, *Ecclesiastes,* St. Thomas Aquinas, Pliny, Cato, Varro, Columella, Palladio, Seneca, Vincentius, Augustine, Albertus Magnus, Bernardinus de Senis, Bonaventura, Antoninus, Ptolemy, Cicero, and Isidor within a few pages.[130] Although some distinction is made between pagan and Christian authors— for example, Virgil's *Georgics* are cited as proof of the agricultural uses of astrology— whatever is ancient tends to be treated respectfully. If a part of the outrage felt by Schonheintz derives from the insult to his profession, another part consists of resentment at what seems to him impudence.

No author able to invite a European reputation by writing in Latin is likely to be totally lacking in shrewdness, and Schonheintz occasionally makes a good point, as in speaking about free will. Although it is often possible to deliberate about the wisdom of yielding to the affections, certain acts which are caused *ex primis motibus animi* do not admit choice but precede it, as is evidenced by the legal principle that impulses are exempt from punishment. Other inclinations are extremely powerful, the planets to which bodily affections are ascribed being *motores spirituum.*[131] On the whole, however, to an even greater degree than Bellanti and Pontano, Schonheintz is incapable of centering his attention sharply on questions about "Why?" and "How?" and is happiest when controverting statements by multiple citations to the contrary. In this tendency he is probably representative of astrological habit, for the typical treatise of the period settles disputes by preferring one authority or set of authorities to others.

Throughout the entire period during which the controversy raged most astrologers apparently went about their work quite untroubled. Because our interest is in thought processes and not merely in argumentation, we shall notice a few documents not intended to be predominantly apologetic. We begin by glancing briefly at two books by Girolamo Cardano, a man of quite exceptional talents.

Cardan was one of the most brilliant and original men of his century—physician, astrologer, mathematician, and scientist—and in the book which brought him greatest fame might be expected to appear at his best. *Libelli duo: Unus, de supplemento almanach, alter, De restitutione temporum & motuum coelestium* [132] despite its title contains also a third section noted on the title page by the heading *Item geniturae LXVII. insignes casibus & fortuna, cum expositione.* The first two parts, although they fail to call basic astrological assumptions into question, come nearer to real science even than Pico in discussing celestial phenomena.

The *Supplementum almanach* is divided between astronomy and astrology. For the most part it discusses with mathematical sophistication such matters as the determination of the terrestrial and zodiacal poles, the colures, certain constellations, the use of observational instruments, and the names and magnitudes of some eighty-eight stars; but it also describes the influence of vertical stars—stars in the zenith—on customs and considers the fortunes of places and their changes. The *De restitutione* is predominantly astronomical. Considerable attention is paid to the true length of the year, which is set finally at 365 days 5 hrs. 48 min. 41 sec. 47 ter. 38 quar. 43 quin. 10 sex.[133] Other topics are the reason why Ptolemy thought the sun had a fixed apsis, why he erred about the moon's motion, and the true courses of Saturn, Mars, and the moon. The general impression left by all this is that Cardan, if he lived too early to be a major figure in the development of an inductive science, at least was moving in the right direction.

Thus we come to the *Geniturae,* with which we find ourselves back in the old quasi-mythological ambience. We learn from the horoscope of Petrarch that the elegance of his poetry was due to the presence of Jupiter in the house of Mercury, which stood in quadrant (this is odd) with Venus; of Pico, that he was made to have a confused mind (*turbidum ingenium*) by the presence of the moon in the eighth house, and that he lacked judgment because the moon was in quartile (*quia radiatio quadrata est*); of Cardan himself, that he was doomed to be plagued with a weak stomach and brain, plots, enemies, losses of property, abuse, extreme perils, and a bad reputation with the public. We put the book aside at last in a mood of mixed admiration and exasperation, wondering at an intellect which permitted Cardan to correct the ancients freely and yet left him credulous of their most dubious assumptions. Cardan evidently knew of Pico's attack but may not have bothered to read it.

The *Tractatus astrologicus* of Henricus Ranzovius,[134] a later work, suggests an awareness of skepticism but was written as a convenient handbook. The science is empirically founded, and although predictions may sometimes have proved wrong astrology "tends most often to truthfulness, provided the true time (of birth) is reported and the practitioners are skilled. For it has been repeated through many centuries within which almost numberless events have happened in the same way and been preceded by the same combinations of signs, so that by the frequent observation and registering of these the art has been established."[135] The art is so complex, however, that hitherto no one has explained it fully in a single book; and this Ranzovius has done to save his readers trouble and expense. The parts of his discussion treat five ways of casting horoscopes, the twelve houses, the zodiacal signs, the planets, the fixed stars, predictions, and a few special problems. All this is clear, detailed, and practical but not apologetic. If Ranzovius was aware of Pico's challenge he evidently thought it had long ago been adequately met.

Other practical treatises appeared from time to time: for instance, the *Astrologia gallica* of Jean-Baptiste Morin de Villefranche, published posthumously in 1661.[136] Morin was the last official astrologer of France and is highly regarded by Jean Hieroz, a vigorous modern propagandist, who saw in the work "rather the earliest treatment of scientific astrology than the last of traditional astrology." I have not read the entire work, which runs to many volumes, but the parts I have seen do not bear out this description. Morin might be described as an advanced traditionalist who accepted the basic postulates—as, indeed, any astrologer must—but modified them in the light of what he believed to be more accurate astronomical data, as Cardan had done. Thus he throws scorn on the attempts of Firmicus Maternus to draw horoscopes of Alexander the Great, Homer, and Achilles [137] and defines the length of the year "on the foundations of Tycho, revised by Kepler." [138] As late as 1717 Henry de Boulainvillier, in his *Traité d'astrologie,*[139] wrote with much the same purpose. Works like these, which are illustrative of a class, are interesting for the way in which traditional conceptions are modified and refined. For example, de Boulainvillier has a section called "Des Positions héliocentriques." [140] But the authors neither attack nor defend astrology at its roots, where it was most vulnerable. What appears to have been the latest work within the limits of our period to attempt this was the *Universa astrosophia naturalis* of Antonio Francesco de Bonatti (1687),[141] and on this we now pause before returning to other attacks which followed Pico's.

Bonatti, who was very earnest, intended to make his case for astrology by reason and authority in Book I and by *experientia* in Book II. He had studied the subject from early youth but discovered it to be obscured by so many errors and superstitions that *aliquid veritatis radius vix apparuerit,*[142] hardly any ray of truth appeared in it. At length, however, he decided that notwithstanding inaccurate comprehension of many causes and effects and of some of the heavenly motions, "something probably truthful and scientific could always be discerned." He has accordingly proceeded like the cultivator who carefully roots poisonous plants out of his stubborn fields lest the fruitful ones be spoiled. To be sure, the establishment of probable judgments requires from 200 to 300 years of observation; but we have accurate observations from former centuries, annotated and digested into tables, and he has used these in giving examples of accurate predictions about death. For the rest, he has treated astrology as a natural science which raises the mind to contemplation of God. Those who think he has attributed too little to the stars should know that although the heavens can control passions human freedom is secure, reason being in no way overcome by what is sensible or physical.[143] This principle, which hitherto has not been emphasized, was perfectly ordinary among pious men and necessary to the reconciliation of astrology with theology. Without it, Bonatti's book would certainly not have been approved by an Inquisitor as containing nothing contrary to Catholic faith, principles, or good customs.

The proof by reason and authorities contains much that is familiar but includes an admission that astrology is laughed at by most philosophers of the time. So far had things come by 1687. Nonetheless Bonatti remarks that the common people are hot to foreknow the future and that there is "universal recourse" to traveling fortune-tellers and disreputable jugglers (*circulatores . . . infames praestigiatores*).[144] He re-asserts the usual claim that the art began with the Chaldaeans and the Egyptians and accepts the view that the three kings who came from the East to worship the infant Christ were *sapientes seu magos*. The Emperor Hadrian was a skilled astrologer who foretold his own death; Diocletian was an *amator* who predicted to the Senate that he would be succeeded by a son or by nobody; and modern kings like Mathias of Hungary and the Emperor Frederick have also been believers.[145]

After more such citations and examples the author turns to *rationes* and urges first that if the heavens lacked stars and the sun never shone the world would be vastly different. The fact that we vary our clothing indicates that we feel alterations in the temperature; and he proceeds to relate the seasons to the sun's movements from one zodiacal sign to another. If the changes are laid wholly to the sun, the obvious reply is that not all springs are fruitful or all winters cold. Within the large regularities are differences caused by the planets. Thus a conjunction of Mars, Mercury, and Jupiter—three hot planets—in a certain aspect with the sun produces warmth in winter.[146] A further proof is the differences of people, some of whom are hot and clever, some religious, some acute, some dull. Must not the various speeds of the planets have some effect? And not by chance, since God's providence would then be denied. Moreover, the tides are known to be regulated by the moon. All these "reasons" are driven home by the usual batteries of prestigious names: at this point Julius Firmicus, Ptolemy, Manilius, Cicero, Fracastorius, Aquinas, and Du Hamel.[147] The opinion that celestial influences work on human beings by necessity is to be condemned as firmly as the madness of thinking they have no force. Yet, since they affect the passions without constraining absolutely, the Christian astrologer should not predict particular events, *ut Cardanus testatur,* and if he does not, he will avoid conflict with Holy Church and the Fathers.[148] In corroboration of the propriety of stargazing Bonatti quotes a Scripture especially favored by the apologists: "The heavens declare the glory of God, and the firmament showeth His handiwork." [149]

Here begins a refutation of thirty numbered objections to the science.[150] The retorts are sometimes commonsensical, as when Bonatti repeats a common argument that if the stars had no work to do God's creation of them would have been super-fluous.[151] He is much concerned by a familiar argument from the known contrasts between twins; the Biblical case of Jacob and Esau is a favorite. In combatting it he adds to the usual remarks that the times of birth normally differ by an interval of thirty minutes to two hours, other suggestions which are more ingenious than per-suasive: that not all the male's semen is received into the womb at the same instant and that because the two hearts are separated their astrological horizons are not identical.[152] To another conventional quibble, that of two infants born at the same place and moment one may become a king and the other a plowman, he cites Junctinus to the effect that no such births occur and adds that anyhow the stars operate *secundum materiam subiectam,* according to the receptive matter, and that similar fortunes would appear differently in men differently situated.[153] The objection that the animal names given to zodiacal signs are absurd is met by the claim, again borrowed from Junctinus, that the influences of the signs were determined first and appropriate names chosen later.[154] But we lack space to recapitulate all the answers, many of which are by this time standard, and must move on to a series of admissions introduced by the heading "What things are to be followed, and what rejected, in astrology." [155] What follows reveals the inroads made upon faith by nearly two centuries of disputation.

The errors in astrological practice, Bonatti says, are due to several causes: ignorance, avarice, a veiled or obscure way of writing, the alteration of sense from Chaldaean to Arabic and thence to Greek and Latin, the loss of valuable documents, and textual corruptions.[156] Further, the positions of the stars have changed since Ptolemy's time, and the lunar horoscope and the *fortunarum partes* were invented by money-minded Arabs.[157] The nodes are imaginary points and have no importance in themselves. The Dragon's head contains no antidote for a poison shed by its tail.[158] The next concession is startling: "Hence elections are stupid (*nugae*), and the dominions of planets over hours were invented rather by the magical art than by astrologers." [159]

Upon this point we must dwell briefly. A part of the total theory not hitherto explained has to do with the dominance of planets over every part of the day and night. The period between sunrise and sunset, no matter how long or short, was divided into twelve parts, and so also the period between sunset and sunrise. These were the "unequal hours." The first hour after sunrise was governed by the tutelary planet of the day (the sun on Sunday, the moon on Monday, Mars on Tuesday, Mercury on Wednesday, Jupiter on Thursday, Venus on Friday, and Saturn on Saturday), and the succeeding hours were governed by the other planets, in the order Sun–Venus–Mercury–Moon–Saturn–Jupiter–Mars, until the series was run through and begun again. Thus the sun governed the first, eighth, fifteenth, and twenty-second hours on Sunday, and, on Monday, every eighth hour beginning with the fifth. The moon governed the fourth, eleventh, and eighteenth hours on Sunday and the first of its own day, Monday. So throughout the rest of the week, as can be found by working out the system to the end.[160] Now "elections," or the choice of appropriate days and hours for the initiating or avoiding of activities, depended heavily on this system. A love-suit, for instance, could best be pleaded on Venus's day and in her hour, provided the positions of the other heavenly bodies were not inappropriate. Having decided that influence depended solely on position and that rays beat down most strongly from the zenith—a common realization at odds with the view that ascending planets and stars were most powerful—Bonatti not only rejected the whole tradition of planetary hours but courageously renounced along with it advice about elections, which formed the largest part of the professional astrologer's stock in trade and brought in most of his income. That he was willing to go so far illustrates the gradual encroachment of thought-ways which adumbrated a modern physics upon mythological and analogical reasoning.

Elsewhere he is less bold. Although suspicious of "friendly" and "unfriendly" aspects,[161] he does not exclude them from his own horoscopes. He gives qualified belief to the planetary domiciles (*non omnino fabulosae sunt*[162]) and to the "exaltations" and "dignities" of planets, but only because he finds some physical justification for them. He realizes that the retrograde movements of planets are only apparent.[163] We cannot, however, dwell longer on this section but must look briefly at his 329 pages of horoscopes, which are intended as experimental justification of astrological truths. This second part of his book comes nearer than anything else I have found to anticipating the attempts of Choisnard, Jung, and other modern investigators to offer an authentically inductive verification. The results support Bonatti's conviction that men's lives are connected with the stars because the superior world is bound to the inferior as a microcosm to the macrocosm from which it has derived.[164]

The horoscopes are grouped in sections which have to do with persons who died in infancy or early childhood, persons who died violently by the sword, fire, water, or falls, persons who met hazards but were still alive, and, finally, some sets of twins. The times of birth, we are told, have been accepted only from public registers (*a mortuorum matriculis*) or from trustworthy friends, and all can easily be checked.[165] The results are interesting and may impress some readers. A common source of possible error is present: since Bonatti is highly skeptical of the accuracy of clocks (*Incertitudo igitur omnis, ex Horologiorum fallacia emanat*[166]) and, moreover, suspects that most reported times are unreliable, he has "rectified" the moments of birth in the usual way. In casting his own horoscope he had to introduce a change of 44 minutes in order to put the moon into a position to facilitate the birth (*Luminare impulsum mei origini dedisse*).[167] One can approve Bonatti's determination not to meddle with hours as well as minutes[168] without being convinced that the chosen moments are correct; and when changes were made, they must inevitably have been in favor of positions and configurations which were more consonant with known facts of the life. Yet the safeguards were unusual for the period, and of all the defenses of astrology written during the Renaissance none may come so near to shaking a modern skeptic.

IV. Further attacks

With this document we conclude the sampling of pro-astrological documents and return to attacks, a number of which followed the appearance of Pico's *Disputationes*. The first in point of time appears to have been the *Contra L'astrologia diuinatrice* (1497) of Pico's friend Girolamo Savonarola, whose possible influence upon him has been noted.[169] The connection is specific: in a "Prohemio" Savonarola praises the *Disputationes* and says that his purpose is to make available to the unlearned public what Pico had demonstrated to the learned, that divinatory astrology is entirely false and superstitious. He will show first that judicial astrology is condemned by Christian doctrine, next that it is contrary to natural philosophy, and finally that in itself it is vain and fallacious.[170]

The first section is cogently argued but hardly surprising. Future events that do not proceed from necessary causes can be foreseen only by God, for whom the future is part of an eternal present. The Scriptures often denounce false prophets and diviners, and God's ability to predict is a proof of His godhead which would be weakened if the astrologer's pretense of foresight were well founded. The pride of the Babylonians in their astrology was scorned by God, who through Isaiah (47:10) said "Thy wisdom and thy knowledge, it hath perverted thee."[171] A reference to *Jeremiah* 10 is probably to verse 2: "Learn not the way of the heathen, and be not dismayed at the signs of heaven."[172] The assertion that Abraham taught astrology to the Egyptians, or that Moses was an astrologer, can be denied as easily as affirmed.[173] Further, astrology is opposed by Augustine, who says that astrologers make true predictions only with the help of demons and that the casting of children's horoscopes is a great error and a greater foolishness; by St. Jerome, St. Basil, St. Ambrose, St. John Chrysostom, Origen, St. Gregory, and Aquinas.[174] The section concludes with the citation of condemnations by the Church and by Roman law from the time of Tiberius to that of Theodosius and Justinian.[175]

The second division begins with a denial that support for astrology can be found in Aristotle, Plato, Pythagoras, or Democritus. Plotinus wrote on the subject but decided in the end that astrology was full of vanity and lies. Apuleius laughed at it; Averroës tore into it (*la lacera*); Ptolemy, in a Greek passage of the *Centiloquium* omitted from all translations, admitted that particular events can be predicted only by men granted divine light. Briefly, despite the false attribution of astrological books to Aristotle and Albertus Magnus, "we do not find that any learned men practised this astrology." Those who have believed in it were persons of little judgment and rather barbarians than wise men.[176] As for the prime ancient authority, Ptolemy, Savonarola shows in various ways that he had *poca philosophia*.[177]

From authorities Savonarola proceeds to reasoning. Cognition, he asserts, begins with sensation and passes through the imagination to the intellect; but future events, not having been sensed, can be guessed only on the basis of past experience, as when we say that a dry tree will blossom and bear fruit. In human affairs, moreover, free will permits a variety of developments, as the branch of a tree can be made into a table, a door, or a pillar. Hence a sharp distinction exists between, let us say, the prediction of an eclipse, which is certain, and that of an event which will befall a human being.[178] Where the connection between cause and effect is not necessary but *per accidens* there can be no certainty; and since astrology is continuously involved with accidents it is foolish.[179] Suppose, for example, an astrologer should say that a man is inclined to be a captain over soldiers. The effect can be prevented by in-firmity, or persuasion, or sensuality, or death at the hand of another, or lack of opportunity, or injury by a fall, and so on indefinitely.[180] Even should we grant, however, that all events were written in the stars, as in the Divine Mind, we could not read them accurately because our knowledge of the heavens is limited to what comes through one sense, that of sight, which can tell us nothing about such qualities as heat and dryness.[181] Again, how can the influence of the stars be separated from other forces? [182] Even if rays from the stars descend to us in straight lines they are diffuse by the time they arrive, as we see the sun's rays to be, so that isolation of them is impossible.[183]

To these reasons for skepticism Savonarola adds many others. The zodiacal signs are fictions, invented by man. The Lion could as well be called a dog, and all the twelve could be imagined as houses, or castles, or trees.[184] Aside from their silli-ness, horoscopes are inaccurate because astrologers do not await the moment of birth with astrolabes in their hands and clear skies always above them to be observed. If they did, the astrolabes are often imperfect, and rays may be refracted by vapors; as for the Ephemerides, they too are often faulty. Anyhow, why should not the moment of conception or—better still—that of the insertion of the intelligent soul (*anima intellettiua*) into the foetus by God be thought critical? Free will can prevent pre-dictions from coming true; or if freedom does not exist, what difference can be made by a visit to the astrologer? [185] It is better to follow caprice or imagination (*phantasia*) than a stargazer's advice; Caesar, who scorned astrology, was fortunate, and Julian the Apostate, who did not, was unlucky.[186] How stupid to choose auspi-cious astrological moments for mounting a horse, or entering a ship, or laying the first stone of a building, or putting on a new garment! Suppose, in the course of a journey, one must dismount; must one consult one's astrologer about a good moment for doing that too? Evil comes not from the skies but either from a bad disposition of matter or from the ill will of human beings.[187] Divine miracles do not result from favorable conjunctions but from the grace of the Holy Spirit.[188] The pretended science is refuted, too, by the failure of predictions. Albumasar said that Christianity would endure only 1460 years, although the current year is 1497; Abraham the Jew (*Habraam iudeo*) foretold the coming of the Messiah in 1444 or 1464, whereas instead the Jews have been evicted from Spain and have suffered worse than at any time since the destruction of Jerusalem. Arnaldo of Spain predicted the coming of Antichrist in 1345.[189] The tendency has been to remember only astrological successes, which often come by chance, and to forget the failures.[190] The unreliability of analogical thought is also noted passingly: Mercury is connected with Christianity because its movements are hard to understand, as Christian dogmas are difficult; might one not say as well that Mercury is contrary to Christianity, *laquale non e volubile come Mercurio?*[191] On its own terms, the little treatise is powerfully argued.

Gian-Francesco Pico, who had edited and published his more celebrated uncle's *Disputationes,* himself attacked astrology in Book V of *De rerum praenotione* (1506),[192] a work directed also against such other divinatory practices as geomancy (Book VI) and magic (Book VII). His basic preconception, like the elder Pico's, is that "Divine revelation comes only from good angels and from God but in no other way, either from bad angels or from nature."[193] Although his main purpose was to extend his uncle's argument into wider areas, his fifth book includes twelve chapters more or less correspondent to the twelve books of the *Disputationes,* sometimes repeating or varying his uncle's arguments but mixing in additional matter and observations of his own.[194] The first chapter after the introduction lists six reasons urged by astrologers for the reliability of their discipline. The first, from Aristotle, is refuted in Chapter iii and the second, an argument from the clear influence of the sun and moon, is taken up in Chapter iv. Succeeding chapters have to do with the scorn for astrology felt by mathematicians, the disapproval shown by divine and civil laws, the futility of elections,[195] uncertainties about the number of heavens and stars, and other discords between authors and principles. The discussion is not simplistic and by no means negligible, but since it largely parallels the *Disputationes* it need not detain us here. The survey of selected treatises will be brought to an end by consideration of three documents written by a theologian, a physician-theologian, and a humanist of ranging interests.

The first of these is a brief work by Jean Calvin, *Traité ou Avertissement contre l'astrologie qu'on appelle judiciaire et autres curiosités qui règnent aujourd'hui au monde* (1549).[196] Calvin's knowledge both of astrology and of astronomy was imperfect: for instance, he believed that the moon is full when it "approaches" the sun.[197] Also, he is willing to grant a good deal. Physicians, he says, use their knowledge of the heavens properly when they choose an opportune moment for bleeding or for dosing with pills and medicines, for we must confess that there is *quelque convenance* between the luminaries and our bodies.[198] Our temperaments, too, either owe something to the stars or have some correspondence with them;[199] the sky can cause not only tempests and tornadoes but also barrenness and pestilence; [200] and by watching the heavens farmers know when to plant.[201] Some of the objections—for example, that influence begins not at birth but at conception [202]—might by the mid-century seem tiresome, but Calvin wrote, like Savonarola, *pour les simples et non lettrés*.[203] For the rest, he reasons strongly against judicial or divinatory astrology, which he thinks to reveal a "silly curiosity" about the future,[204] and in favor of a divine dispensation administered directly.

Many of Calvin's arguments are by this time thoroughly familiar: that from the difference of twins, for example, although it is accompanied by the explicit claim that heredity has a hundred times the strength of astrological influences.[205] So too, although it has not previously been noticed here, is his question whether of 60,000 men in a single battle all who fall have the same horoscope.[206] Savonarola's objection to the choice of a favorable moment for beginning a journey is picked up: will not the condition of the heavens at the time of arrival have any effect? If the traveler is a king's counselor, will the horoscopes of his twenty attendants ever agree on a favorable instant? [207] Instead of summarizing the whole argument, however, we shall follow only two trains of thought, neither wholly new but both urged with considerable effectiveness.

The first is the involvement of other persons than the native in every horoscope. The astrologers

> will tell a man how many wives he will have. Yes—but do they find in his star the horoscope of his first wife, so that they know how long she will live? By this process the wives will be made to have no horoscopes of their own . . . In brief, by this reasoning the horoscope of every individual man will include a judgment of the whole disposition of a country, since (the astrologers) boast that they can judge whether a man will be happy in marriage, whether he will have fortunate or unfortunate meetings with other people in the fields, what dangers he may fall into, whether he will be killed or will die of a disease. Consider with how many people we have commerce during our lives.[208]

If developed, this notion leads to the perception of real difficulties. Must a man whose natal horoscope promises a happy marriage and good relations with his children inevitably be attracted to a woman destined by the stars to share happily in his vicissitudes and bear him dutiful sons and daughters? Are all the children, in turn, fated to be born at moments which will guarantee for them early lives compatible with his hopes? Nearly every prediction implies a relationship with other people, so that in the degree in which the stars compel, instead of merely inclining, the whole world of human experience must be an infinitely complex network of inevitable events. If a man is foreordained to perish by iron at a given time, he must meet the murderer forced to kill him; the murderer in turn must have opportunity, an adequate motive, and a weapon within reach; the victim's wife—if she loves him or is dependent upon him for support—must have an unlucky forecast for the day, as must all his friends, and his enemies lucky ones; and so on indefinitely. If the stars merely incline instead of forcing, the situation is not much improved, for the murderer's decision not to kill would falsify the horoscopes of victim, wife, friends, and enemies without allowing them the choices that would seem appropriate. All this is implicit in Calvin's comment.

The other effective argument is from theology, very common but urged here, not surprisingly, with special eloquence. Astrology is a diabolical superstition by which people are *quasi ensorcelés*.[209] God sometimes works with a grace which nullifies the influence of the sky, and people are often made new by the experience of conversion.[210] Many an event which befalls a man *gît en la volonté ou conditions d'autres que de lui:*[211] a conventional enough statement but unexpected from Calvin, as is his further observation that David "chose" plague among three possible scourges of God.[212] The famine in Elijah's time was a miracle and not caused by the stars; in such a divine punishment *toute constellation est exclue*.[213] The drying up of the Red Sea and the Jordan, similarly, was caused by God instantaneously,[214] not by stellar positions and angles contrived a long time in advance. To such affirmations as these are added the usual proofs from specific Scriptural texts. God rebuked the Chaldaeans, saying that the changes and falls of kingdoms cannot be read in the stars.[215] If *Genesis* says that the lights were put into the heavens for signs, we must understand the meaning to be that they are useful to farmers and physicians. The reading of nativities is to this as drunkenness is to wine—an excess, an abuse.[216] Joseph's prediction of plenty and famine to Pharaoh came from revelation, and Moses, although instructed in all the wisdom of the Egyptians, did not consult the heavens when deciding upon a time to lead the Jews from captivity.[217] The star that led the wise men to the manger was *dressé . . . par miracle*.[218] It is an abomination to lay the spread of Mohammedanism to the stars; its flourishing is a just vengeance for man's ingratitude.[219] Moses, in *Deuteronomy* 18, condemns diviners, observers of days—that is, makers of astrological elections—and other sorcerers and magicians.[220] The Ephesians, who had been given to *folles curiosités,* after their conversion to Christianity burned their books, as St. Luke tells us in *Acts,* to the value of 5,000 francs, and Simon the Magician was astonished that Christ found his arts valueless.[221] Let everyone *regarde à quoi il est appelé, pour s'appliquer à ce qui sera de son office,* and let the scholar abandon frivolities for good and useful studies.[222] The men of simple piety for whom the discussion was intended may well sometimes have found it convincing.

A collection of letters written by Thomas Erastus, who was a physician by pro-

Hieronymus Cardanus (Jerome Cardan), *Libelli quinque, quorum duo priores, iam denuo sunt emendati, duo sequentes iam primum in lucem editi, & quintus magna parte aucta est* (Nuremberg: apud Iohan. Petreium, 1547), *verso* of title page.

Portrait of Jerome Cardan. Around the edge of the medallion is a quotation from the *Helen* of Euripides (346–47) which means, "Whatever may happen, make the best of the future." I owe the identification to my colleague J. G. Keenan, of the Department of Classics. The implication is that astrological knowledge permits some guidance of one's future—a common notion which saved the Christian doctrine of free will.

fession but gave his name to a heresy, is interesting not so much for its content, which is sensible and enlightened, as for its occasion and tone.[223] When Erastus was called back from nine years of study in Italy to practice medicine at Schleusingen, he learned, much to his displeasure, that his patients had faith in almanachs which noted lucky and unlucky days for fertilizing, weaning children, cutting nails and hair, cupping, bleeding, purging, giving electuaries or pills, taking a journey, putting on new clothing, moving to another house, bargaining, and so on. Although he had known that such publications existed, he had been unaware that they were taken seriously. To his annoyance, he found that the calendars were an obstacle to his treatments: for example, a patient might refuse to be bled because the moon was in Scorpio. When no danger was involved Erastus had sometimes yielded to superstition, but he had also sometimes held out for the dignity of the science he had learned from the best teachers and had practiced with success. By means of an Italian book written by Savonarola, which he turned into simple German, he had, indeed, drawn some from their superstition; but although the learned approved the book, the ignorant condemned both it and its author, usually without giving reasons. Some persons, however, had offered arguments, and because these deserve a reply he will publish a correspondence which has already appeared in an unauthorized version, all the more because he has been driven from school and city by plague and has time on his hands.[224] (Might not a physician have been expected to remain?)

The development of the correspondence, which we know only by Erastus's contributions, is curious. For a long time the subject is the opinions of Hippocrates and Galen about astrology, and especially a work of the latter on critical days.[225] Strathmion—no doubt a pseudonym—insists that the text shows Galen to have believed in astrological medicine, Erastus that Galen attempted merely to explain why the third critical day of the lunar month was not the twenty-first but the twentieth. [226] What most engages interest is Strathmion's inability to attend to Erastus's assertions. "When I returned home yesterday evening from Thuringia," one letter by Erastus begins, "your letter was given me. Since I saw it was lengthy (*longiusculas*) I was moved to considerable pleasure, for I supposed I would receive some enlightenment. But when I began to read I perceived that you harped on the same old string." [227] In the next letter he returns to the theme: "You seem to write without reading my letter attentively." [228] The following letter makes the same complaint: "I have received your letter, in which you are like yourself (*tuas reperi literas, in quibus tui simile es*). I wonder that you can be content to reply twice by uselessly repeating the same arguments." [229] And once more: "The letter I received on March 15 contained nothing to which I have not already given an answer." [230] Although his patience is wearing thin and he quotes Galen to the effect that "False opinions make the minds of those who entertain them deaf and blind so that they can neither hear nor see anything," [231] he resignedly tries once more to clear the air, this time at special length. The job is hopeless, and later letters are addressed to other correspondents. In the meantime Erastus's tone has become that of a rather grim and exasperated impatience, as when a modern liberal persists in discussion about integration with an elderly Southerner whose convictions have arisen so early that their basis is prerational. That controversy occasionally involved persons unable or unwilling to listen is not, of course, surprising; what is remarkable is that the disputants so often met head on, as at the beginning Bellanti had met Pico. As for the content of the remaining letters, it is sufficient to observe that even for the skeptic the authorities remained important. Erastus shows no inclination whatever to say that the opinions of Galen and Hippocrates are of interest merely to the historian of ideas.

We may conveniently end the survey with comments about *Mantice, ou Discours de la verité de diuination par astrologie* (2nd ed. 1573), written by Pontus de Tyard, linguist, poet, scientist, churchman, royalist, and, for a time at least, proponent of the Hermetic *prisca theologia*. Its special advantage is that an assault on astrology by a speaker called Le Curieux is answered by an enthusiastic astrologer called Mantice (Diviner) and the dialogue concludes with a decision pronounced by the author in his own person. Because the arguments on both sides pick up many of the points made in three quarters of a century of controversy, the hundred-odd pages not only provide a compact summary but also end with a recommendation—early as the date is—of a conclusion which, despite the continued activity of astrologers, was to point toward the skepticism of responsible science.

The debate is preceded by a rejection of all divinatory practices other than astrological. Auguries, auspices, the study of entrails, and all the other superstitions nourished in Etruria are extinguished; *goëtia* or black magic has been destroyed along with other antiquities of Egypt; pythonesses and Euryclites or ventriloquists no longer prophesy; pyromantia and hydromantia—divination by fire and water—remain merely as names. Only astrology continues to have adherents.[232] In the present book the author will attempt to reproduce a lively recent discussion on the subject. The floor is given first to the antagonist.

After a preamble filled with citations a scornful résumé is offered of the qualities ascribed to the planets and signs. No exhalations from the earth can make the moon or Venus moist, and their presumed feminine gender is an inference from this quality. In fact, the planets are really *affranchies de noz sexes.* If the sun is especially hot in Cancer, why is Cancer thought to be cold and moist? and why is Sagittarius hot and dry if we suffer from cold when the sun passes through it? All such affirmations are *mensonges monstrueuses* and *menteries ridicules & fables,* so that prophecies made on such bases are false a thousand times to one.[233] Neither is the history of the art distinguished. The ancients raised statues or offered public praise to mathematicians, architects, physicians, emperors, soldiers, philosophers, and poets but never any to astrologers, who were condemned to death, banished, or otherwise punished by Tiberius, Vitellius, Diocletian, Maximian, Constantine, Valentinian, and Valens.[234] Plotinus, foremost among the Platonic philosophers, wrote against astrology.[235] Its absurdities are shown by contradictions in the horoscopes of a single family; that of the wife may predict her husband's death, and a man's fate cannot depend on his own stars if it is already determined by those of his father and elder brother.[236] Why do we have a police force and give praise to welldoers if actions are caused by the heavens? [237] The infant's conception or its endowment with a soul is as important as its birth; and what is to be said of a child who remains partly born for some time, now extruding a member and now withdrawing it, while the subtle diviner is all the while casting his figure? [238] If two princes choose a certain day for a battle it must prove unfriendly for one—he who, as even Guido Bonatti confessed, is less strong or has smaller forces.[239] Can there be enough cruel constellations to determine the deaths of a thousand men killed in a battle, or even of three or four destroyed by a single cannon shot? [240] Real astrological knowledge would require empirical observation of similar effects from similar configurations, but this is impossible because the return of all the heavenly bodies to identical situations may require as long as 49,000 years. The Babylonians' claim of 470,000 years of observation is contradicted by their identification of only 1,022 or, by another account, 1,476 stars. Can we believe that all the rest are *stériles, endormies, & paresseuses?* If it is claimed that planetary configurations, at least, are repeated, the proper retort is that the same effects have not recurred; empires, customs, laws, and religions have never been renewed.[241]

The energetic refutation continues. If it is true that the planets produce physical effects—the moon paleness, Mars redness, Saturn darkness—it is foolish to ascribe to the planets such traits as avarice, melancholy, cruelty, haughtiness, and lust, especially since these are determined not by substance but by position.[242] The relation of position to significance cannot derive from the place, since the exaltation of Mercury is the dejection of Venus; nor can it be due to the planet, since the influence is determined by the place.[243] The doctrine of aspects is also unacceptable. Aside from conjunction and opposition, why should Ptolemy have considered only trine, quartile, and sextile aspects, since 360° is equally divisible by 36, 40, 45, or 72? What actually counts can only be nearness. There can be no point in the comparison of stars to people dancing in a circle who can see someone two or three places distant better than the persons they are holding by the hand: *comme l'Estoille est illustrée d'vne rayonnante rondeur, autant luy seroit visible le ioignant, que l'eslongné.*[244] The whole system, indeed, is presumptuous and results in the profanation of what is holy, the setting of periods for religions and governments, and the assigning to the stars of the responsibility for impiety, the deluge, the final burning of the world, saintliness, miracles, original sin, and the Incarnation.[245] In fact, we can see from the example of crows and magpies, which so far as we can tell are identical although hatched at various moments during about a month, that human differences are due to the diversity of customs and rearing.[246]

Mantice now rises to speak and at first defends the tradition as having been established by scholars and confirmed by experience. What can we trust in high matters if not the authority of a famous person? It is irreverent to measure those who are greater by the ell of our own ignorance. In addition, the first men lived hundreds of years and profited from not being subjected to the dislocated stars under which later generations were born.[247] Ancient poetry is full of veiled wisdom: Orpheus was the first Greek astronomer; the flight of Daedalus symbolized his understanding of the stars; Bellerophon, Atlas, Phaëthon, Titan, Castor and Pollux, Orion, and many others are figures in astrological myths. Saturn, Jupiter, Mars, Apollo, Venus, Mercury, and Diana were "kings or other studious persons who by their toilsome industry learned the courses and influence of the planets which have since been called by their names." Tiresias was feigned to have changed sex because he distinguished the genders of the planets.[248] Roman laws against astrology were motivated by a wish to keep the people in ignorant submission; but the science was honored in Babylon,

Thebes, Ethiopia, and Egypt. The virginal priestess at Delphi served an oracle sacred to Virgo, and the python beneath the tripod was under the influence of the constellation Draco.[249] Next follow examples of rulers who heeded or, like Ariovistus, Pericles, and Xerxes, disastrously scorned astrological predictions.[250]

From historical proofs Mantice turns to natural ones. Knowing the ninth day of the moon to be unlucky, the ant never leaves his hill on that day. The scarab, having rolled together balls of cow or ass dung, buries them for a lunar period of twenty-eight days and then, on the twenty-ninth, digs them up and rolls them first from east to west in imitation of the firmament and then from west to east in imitation of the planets, doing this with thirty feet that signify the 30° occupied by each of the zodiacal signs. The male cynocephalus, or dog-headed ape, marks the equinox by urinating or barking sharply at each of the twelve diurnal hours.[251] Again, if the sea, which is the earth's humor, and the sap of trees and plants are affected by seasonal changes caused by the stars, why not also men?[252]

Next comes the rebuttal of negative arguments. The names of the zodiacal signs are defended as metaphorically suitable; the four Ptolemaic aspects, each divided

Typus Dodecamorij Tauri, quod domum Veneris, & exultationis Lunæ fignum dixerunt veteres, exhibens fitum Pleiadum, fiue Succoth Benoth, aliarumque ftellarum adiacentium.

Porrò quod Authores Hebræorum Pleiadum conftellationem confundant cum cauda Arietis, id factum effe putem ex vicinitate Pleiadum ad caudam Arietis, vti typus monftrat. Atque hinc quoque factum effe arhirror, quod Venerem Arieti inequitantem veteres Mythologi depinxerint, vel ob vicinitatem nimirùm Arietis ad Venereum fidus Pleiadum, vel quòd in fine Arietis Venus virtutem fuam exerere ftatim incipiat. Pleiades verò, Hyades, & Virgilias pafsim confundi videmus, vel ob congeries ftellarum, quibus fingulæ tres conftellationes dictæ conftant; vel quòd harum ortus, qui eodem ferè tempore fit, fimiles effectûs & operationes in inferiori mundo præftet. Mirum igitur non eft, fi Pleiades, Hyades, & Virgilias Authores vnam & eandem conftellationem intelligant.

Hanc itaq; congeriem ftellarum, fiue eæ fuerint Pleiadum, fiue Hyadum, aut Virgiliarum, antiqui Chaldæorum Aftrologi ob dictas rationes diuino honore fub ea, quæ fequitur, figura coluerunt.

Di-

Athanasius Kircher, *Oedipus aegyptiacus*, Vol. I (Rome: Vitalis Mascardi, 1652), p. 359.

"A figure of the zodiacal Taurus, which the ancients called the house of Venus and the sign of the moon's exaltation, showing the position of the Pleiades, or Succoth Benoth, and of other nearby stars."

The purpose is to explain one of the errors in which the admired ancients had been caught. A part of the Latin text can be translated as follows: "That the Hebrew authors confused the constellation of the Pleiades with the tail of the Ram was, I think, the result of the nearness of the Pleiades to the Ram's tail, as the figure shows. And I believe also that this was done because the ancient mythographers depicted Venus as riding on the Ram, or because of the great closeness of the Ram to the Venereal constellation of the Pleiades, or because Venus begins to exercise her influence at the end of the Ram." A similar excuse is found for the confusion of the Pleiades with the Hyades and the Virgiliae.

into three parts, parallel the four seasons with their beginnings, middles, and ends; and the four astrological angles are defended by a mathematical mysticism deriving ultimately, as we have seen, from Pythagoras. Planets in opposition are separated by six signs, planets in trine by four, planets in quartile by three, planets in sextile by two; and the proportions 6, 4, 3, 2 compose the whole harmony of the universe. "Thus sufficient reasons can be given for the foundations of astrology . . . Nothing appears in it without reason, order, and remarkable proportion."[253] As for the imputation of malice to the planets, that is an error; the majesty of Saturn, the benignity of Venus, and the warmth of Mars are worsened in human beings.[254] The horoscope is cast at birth instead of at some other time because it is then that the foetus becomes really human and begins both to absorb celestial rays and to breathe the air affected by these.[255] What has been said about crows and magpies can be answered by saying that all are engendered at about the same time but no doubt are as different from one another as men, although to men they seem identical, as perhaps men seem to them. Anyhow, because man has higher status and greater potentiality he is capable of greater individuation. The errors allegedly made by astrologers are no justification for the renunciation of the entire art. Everything else in the universe has some utility; are the heavens alone, the greatest and most dignified part of creation, to have none? By the line of argument espoused by Le Curieux we should have to reject also all medicine, all law, all theology, and all philosophy. Here Mantice stopped speaking, his face expressive of the disdain he felt for his opponent's reasoning.[256]

Although Mantice's speech is full of poetic conceptions, a modern reader is unlikely to be surprised that the palm is awarded to Le Curieux. De Tyard acknowledges having at one time been enthusiastic about daemons and spirits and later, after his experiments had had no more success than *l'espoir fumeux de l'Elixir aux Alchimistes,* having turned to astrology, about which he remained for a long time suspended between belief and disbelief. The practitioners he saw at work were ignorant of the true celestial movements because the Ephemerides they used could be seen by anyone who raised his eyes to the sky to be incorrect. The tables of Jean Stade, calculated on the basis of Copernicus and Erasmus Rheinhold, are badly in conflict with those of Alfonso, Blanchi, Pittate, and others, and judgments based on such uncertainties do not deserve faith.[257] In addition, competing doctrines about how to draw the twelve houses result in quite different horoscopal readings, though each has the support of respected authorities.[258] Equally chilling is the realization that the precession of the equinoxes must have invalidated many of the Ptolemaic practices still followed.[259] In sum, although de Tyard is much delighted by astronomical contemplation he "cannot with a clear conscience embrace judicial astrology before the movements are quite exactly known and a single method of constructing the houses has been proved by sound reasons and experience." At most he can confess that the stars do exert some influence.[260] The conclusion is modest but, if less sweepingly negative than some of the rejections noticed earlier, none the less basically skeptical.

V. Conclusion

By this time enough documents have been followed to make the general course of the controversy clear. Already most of the arguments have become familiar, and no purpose would be served by protracting the survey, which has been limited to documents written specifically about astrology. No attempt has been made to collect passing references to the subject wherever these might be found. Persons interested in English ideas and literature will find especially valuable Don Cameron Allen's *The Star-Crossed Renaissance: The Quarrel about Astrology and Its Influence in England*[261] and Paul Kocher's *Science and Religion in Elizabethan England*.[262] Chapter iii of A. J. Meadows' *The High Firmament: A Survey of Astronomy in English Literature*[263] contains a large number of literary allusions to astrology in the Middle Ages and Renaissance. An essay by Sanford V. Larkey discusses the danger created in the early years of Elizabeth's reign by the prophecies of Nostradamus and others.[264] And there have been other studies which are readily accessible. It remains here only to offer a brief summary aimed at pulling together strands of a very complex web.

The encouragement given to astrology by the Neo-Platonic renaissance which took its beginnings from Pletho and Ficino appears to have had connections with the *Corpus Hermeticum* brought to Florence about 1460 and translated into Latin by Ficino before he undertook a Latin rendering of the newly accessible Platonic dialogues. Since Hermetic theology is the subject of a separate chapter, we need only recall that it envisaged the whole universe as animate and as permeated with daemonic influences. Ficino himself, if a philosopher, was—like de Tyard's Mantice—the kind of philosopher who is drawn to poetic conceptions, especially if they invite the the mind to soar into the empyrean and entertain images of shining spirits. For him, accordingly, the Hermetic notion of a daemon sitting on every star and radiating influence blended easily with the mystical side of Plato as that had been developed in the Neo-Platonic school of Plotinus and others. His astrological treatise, *De vita triplici,* especially in the part called *De vita coelitus comparanda* ("On Guiding One's Life by the Stars"), called to the attention of the scholarly world a discipline which in the Middle Ages had occasionally been noticed by philosophers and theologians but was mostly a concern of physicians; and its influence was increased by Ficino's enviable mastery of Greek, as yet little known but the object of growing interest, and by his dominance of the Academy at Florence, then at the height of its brilliance under the patronage of the merchant-prince Cosimo de' Medici.

This interpretation may err on the side of too great specificity, for the nascent Humanism would undoubtedly have led to a rediscovery of the importance of astrology in antiquity without Ficino. In any event, astrology found an unlikely opponent in Pico, who at first promised to outdo Ficino in esotericism, and in the long run the effect was the destruction of the system. In 1586 Pope Sixtus V condemned judicial astrology in the bull *Coeli et terrae,* a judgment confirmed, with modifications, by Pope Urban VIII in *Inscrutabilis*—and this despite Urban's willingness to seek the aid of Tommaso Campanella in warding off the evil effects of eclipses.[265] On the whole, it is fair to say that the opponents reasoned more cogently, because less analogically and by authority, than the proponents. By 1700 the battle was essentially won for scholarship, science, and philosophy if not for the general public.

The human mind, however, is capable of strange vagaries. One of these is noted by Kocher, who observed that "of the six full-scale polemics published in England against astrology in the Elizabethan age, five—those by William Fulke, John Calvin, William Perkins, John Chamber, and George Carleton—came from ecclesiastics." [266] That theologians should oppose not only the determination of human actions but sometimes even the inclination to them by the stars is readily understandable. The concept of free will is logically inseparable from the allocation of praise and blame. What follows is more unexpected.

> And who, on the other side, spoke up for astrology? To the bewilderment of the modern analyst, chiefly the foremost scientific men of the age . . . an almost solid front of physicians, astronomers, and other natural philosophers, renowned for their achievements.[267]

We have noted the example of Cardan. The judgment of other astronomers is more problematic. Kepler is known to have cast horoscopes, and not, probably, as has sometimes been urged, merely to earn money. Yet his polemic against Robert Fludd is sometimes as tough-minded as could be wished: for example, he says, Fludd "takes over confusedly and inaccurately what he has received from a tradition of conflicting opinions; but I proceed by natural order, so that everything may be corrected by the laws of nature and confusion may be avoided." [268] The position of other men of science is similarly equivocal. On the whole, the tendency Kocher found in England is probably less marked on the continent—except, perhaps, among physicians, among whom the use of astrology had a long history. Yet one can appreciate without difficulty why scientists often were prejudiced in favor of determinism. It has never been easy for persons bent on the discovery of laws to admit interference by human will; and as yet the full importance of heredity and environment was seldom, if ever, recognized. Were a choice necessary, causation might, after all, be better laid to physical rays emanating from planets and stars, which at least were subject to observation, than to mystical numbers, cabalistic verbal formulas, and devils.

NOTES: CHAPTER ONE

1. Quoted in Franz Boll and Carl Bezold, *Sternglaube und Sterndeutung: Die Geschichte und das Wesen der Astrologie*, 4th ed. (Leipzig: B. G. Teubner, 1931) p. 58.

2. Since each zodiacal sign occupies 30° of the heavens, Saturn will have moved beyond Aries into 3° 23′ of Pisces, Mars to 22° 48′ of Taurus, and Mercury into 11° 44′ of Sagittarius. Degrees are counted from the right-hand margins or cusps as the observer faces outward from the earth: i. e., counter-clockwise.

3. See Alan Leo, ed., *Casting the Horoscope*, 10th ed. (London: L. N. Fowler & Co. Ltd., 1969), pp. 110–11.

4. Jean Hieroz, *L'Astrologie mondiale et météorologique de Morin de Villefranche*, traduction intégrale du 25ᵉ livre de *L'Astrologia Gallica*, "Des Constellations universelles du ciel" (Paris: Les Éditions Leymarie, 1946), p. 34. The calculations from the horoscope are my own.

5. Adapted from Christopher McIntosh, *The Astrologers and Their Creed: An Historical Outline* (London: Hutchinson & Co., 1969), p. 123.

6. Another horoscope of Edward VII, differing only slightly, is printed by Leo, *Casting the Horoscope*, in the front pages.

7. McIntosh, *Astrologers and Their Creed*, p. 27.

8. Cf. J. D. North, "Kalenderes Enlumyned Ben They: Some Astronomical Themes in Chaucer," *Review of English Studies*, New Series, Vol. XX (1969), 138, n2.

9. McIntosh, *Astrologers and Their Creed*, pp. 133–34.

10. Occasionally one hears of "occult powers" as well, as in Antonio Francesco Bonatti, *Universa astrosophia naturalis* (Patavii: Apud Petrum Mariam Frambottom, 1687), p. 48 (I, xii). But the vehicle of these was regularly thought to be *motus, lumen,* and *calor.*

11. Cf. Robert Eisler, *The Royal Art of Astrology* (London: Herbert Joseph Limited, 1946), p. 162.

12. Eight because 30°, 60°, and 90° can each be counted in two directions.

13. These details are drawn mostly from Eisler, *Royal Art*, p. 96.

14. Cf. *ibid.*, p. 87. The facts, however, are commonplace.

15. Aldebaran, in Taurus, is 57 light years away; Pollux, in Gemini, 32; Regulus, in Leo, 56; Spica, in Virgo, 230; and Antares, in Scorpio, 380. See Eisler, *Royal Art*, p. 205.

16. Boll and Bezold, *Sternglaube*, p. 2.

17. —*ist kaum eine Spur von Vorherberechnung der Schicksale eines einzelnen gewöhnlichen Menschen zu finden, ibid.*, p. 3.

18. Some linguistic patterns, however, suggest Sumerian sources (*ibid.*, p. 8).

19. A. Sachs, "Babylonian Horoscopes," *Journal of Cuneiform Studies*, VI (1952),), 54–56 (for the dating of the Babylonian text) and 51 (for the dating of the Greek horoscope).

20. *Ibid.*, 53 and 51.

21. Paris: Librairie Félix Alcan, 1927.

22. Choisnard, *Preuves*, p. 46.   23. *Ibid.*, pp. 46–47.

24. Jean Hieroz, *L'Astrologie selon Morin de Villefranche, quelques autres et moi-même*, 2d ed. (Paris: Les Éditions des Champs-Élysées "Omnium Littéraire," 1962), pp. 15–16.

25. *Ibid.*, p. 17.

26. Lucius Bellantius Senensis, *Liber de astrologica veritate, et in disputationes Ioannis Pici adversus astrologos responsiones* (Venetiis: Bernardinum Venetum de Vitalibus, 1502), sig. A4*v* (I, ii).

27. Leo, *Casting the Horoscope*, p. 61.   28. *Ibid.*, p. 62.   29. *Ibid.*, pp. 131 and 59n.

30. With the foregoing brief account cf. Gustav Braunsperger, *Beiträge zur Geschichte der As-*

trologie der Blütezeit, vom 15. bis zum 17. Jahrhundert (München: H. Murauer, 1928), pp. 10–12.

31. Ioannis Pici Mirandulae Concordiaeque Comitis, *Opera Omnia* (Basiliae: Ex Officina Henricpetrina, 1572), I, 266.

32. Ed. Eugenio Garin (Lexington, Kentucky: The Anvil Press, 1953), p. 36.

33. Bonatti, *Astrosophia*, p. 10 (I, iii).

34. Tycho Brahe, *De disciplinis mathematicis*, in *Opera*, ed. I. L. E. Dreyer (Havniae: 1913ff., I, 167ff.); cited by Braunsperger, *Beiträge*, p. 59.

35. G. Pico della Mirandola, *Disputationes adversus astrologiam divinatricem*, ed. Eugenio Garin, 2 vols. (Firenze: Vallecchi, 1946–1952), I, 40. There is an Italian translation on facing pages.

36. *Ibid.*, I, 44.   37. *Ibid.*, I, 46.   38. *Ibid.*, I, 46–54.   39. *Ibid.*, I, 58.

40. *Ibid.*, I, 60.   41. *Ibid.*, I, 100–102 (II, i).   42. *Ibid.*, I, 104–106 (II, i).

43. *Ibid.*, I, 106–108 (II, ii).   44. *Ibid.*, I, 108 (II, ii).   45. *Ibid.*, I, 112–16 (II, iii).

46. *Ibid.*, I, 116–24 (II, iv).   47. *Ibid.*, I, 126 (II, v).   48. *Ibid.*

49. *Ibid.*, I, 128 (II, v).   50. *Ibid.*, I, 132 (II, v).   51. *Ibid.*, I, 134 (II, v).

52. *Ibid.*, I, 136–42 (II, vi).   53. *Ibid.*, I, 140 (II, vi).   54. *Ibid.*

55. *Ibid.*, I, 144 (II, vii).   56. *Ibid.*, I, 154–56 (II, vii).   57. *Ibid.*, I, 156 (II, viii).

58. *Ibid.*, I, 162 (II, ix).   59. *Ibid.*, I, 164 (II, ix).   60. *Ibid.*, I, 168–70 (II, x).

61. *Futura multo post tempore a praesenti constellatione effici non posse.—Ibid.*, I, 462 (IV, vi).

62. —*tot annis, quot signorum partibus a tali loco planeta distabat.* Although the passage is unclear, the "parts" may be three "faces" in each sign of 10° each, which sometimes were given special names. For the passages just summarized, see *ibid.*, I, 462–64 (IV, vi).

63. *Ibid.*, II, 360–62 (X, iii).   64. *Ibid.*, II, 370 (X, iv).   65. *Ibid.*, II, 378 (X, v).

66. *Ibid.*, II, 378–84 (X, v).

67. *Perbella magis . . . quam naturalis et vera.—Ibid.*, I, 296 (III, xiv).

68. *Ibid.*, I, 348–50 (III, xvii).   69. *Ibid.*, I, 194 (III, iv).

70. For the discussion see *ibid.*, I, 304–320 (III, xv).   71. *Ibid.*, I, 286–88 (III, xiii).

72. *Ibid.*, I, 178 (III, i).

73. —*ostenditur caelum causam esse universalem neque ad ipsam individuorum varietatem referendam.—Ibid.*, I, 188 (III, iii).   74. *Ibid.*, I, 190–92 (III, iii).

75. *Ibid.*, I, 242 (III, x).   76. *Ibid.*, I, 256–60 (III, xi).   77. *Ibid.*, I, 262 (III, xi).

78. *Ibid.*, I, 264 (III, xi).   79. *Ibid.*, I, 260 (III, xi).   80. *Ibid.*, I, 390 (III, xxv).

81. *Ibid.*, I, 408–10 (III, xxvii).

82. —*iacta alea erat priusquam e matris, ut ait Lucilius, bulga infans committeretur.—Ibid.*, I, 458 (IV, v).   83. *Ibid.*, I, 466–68 (IV, vii).   84. *Ibid.*, I, 470 (IV, vii).

85. He seems, in fact, to believe that this is his usual method. For example: *Qui mos in disputando servatus est et deinceps servandus; tum si detur astrologis quod maximum dant theologi, astrologiam tamen nihil esse.—Ibid.*, I, 420 (IV, i).   86. *Ibid.*, I, 506 (IV, xiv).

87. *Ibid.*, II, 458–60 (XI, i).   88. *Ibid.*, II, 484–86 (XII, i).   89. *Ibid.*, II, 490–92 (XII, ii).

90. *Ibid.*, II, 504–506 (XII, iv).

91. See note 26, above.

92. Bellanti, *De astrologica veritate*, sig. a1v.

93. *Praeuidere autem futura . . . diuinum quoddam est, ergo facilius & conuenientius per caelestes quam per inferiores consequi poterit.—Ibid.*

94. *Ibid.*, sig. a1v–a2r.   95. *Ibid.*, sig. a3r.   96. *Ibid.*, sig. a3r–a3v.

97. *Ibid.*, sig. a3v.   98. *Ibid.*, sig. a3v–a4r.

99. —*eam sententiam sic syllogice figurari potest. cuiusque natiuitatis mercurius sic se habuerit &c. natus eius &c. huius natiuitatis predicta sic se habent: igitur &c.—Ibid.*, A4v.

100. *Ibid.*, A5r.   101. *Ibid.*, A4v.   102. *Ibid.*, B3r.

103. Ioannis Iovianus Pontanus, *Opera: De Rebus coelestibus libri XIIII, eiusdem de luna frag-mentum, item commentariorum in centum Claudij Ptolomæi sententias libri duo* (Basiliae: ?1556).

104. *Ibid.,* pp. 2526–29 (XII—which consists solely of a "Prœmivm").

105. *Ibid.,* pp. 2530–31 (XII).   106. *Ibid.,* p. 2534 (XII).

107. *Ibid.,* pp. 2534–35, 2538–39 (XII).

108. *Neque igitur ubique incessendus est Mathematicus* (i. e., astrologus), *cum praedictiones euentorum euismodi minimè succedent.—Ibid.,* p. 2540 (XII).

109. *Siquidem motus ipsius principium, omnisque autoritas penes marem existit, cui ut autori, quod dictum est, ratio inest ac forma, cuius ipse moueatur gratia.—Ibid.,* pp. 1963–64 (I, "Prœmivm").

110. "—or the mould to the flagon" (*—& sigulo in fingendis amphoris*). But the meaning of *sigulo* is doubtful.—*Ibid.,* p. 1964 ("Prœmium").

111. *Ibid.,* pp. 1964–66 ("Prœmium").   112. *Ibid.,* pp. 1966–67 ("Prœmium").

113. *Ibid.,* pp. 1967–70 ("Prœmium").   114. *Ibid.,* pp. 1971–72 (I, i).

115. *—necesse est etiam in caelo, a quo mouentur, eiusmodi uim inesse, quodammodo foueat, & tanquam astruat materiam in qua sese exerceat.—Ibid.,* p. 1975 (I, iii).

116. *Ibid.,* pp. 1975–76 (I, iii).

117. *Quotidianae quoque obseruationes eorum quae subinde contingunt, docere haec satis queunt. —Ibid.,* pp. 1976–77 (I, iii).   118. *Ibid.,* pp. 1983–84 (I, vii).

119. *Ibid.,* p. 2104 (II, viii).   120. *Ibid.,* p. 2007 (I, xv).   121. *Ibid.,* p. 2081 (II, iv).

122. *Ibid.*   123. *Ibid.,* p. 2082 (II, iv).

124. Jacobus Schonheinz, *Apologia astrologiae* (Nurmberga: 1502).

125. "Jacobus Schonheinz mathematicus et Phisicus Lectoribus Salutem," unpaginated.

126. *—quod eos perorantes nemo interpellet e sede celsa, tumetsi guttere* (sic), *quicquid in buccam venit euomunt.—Ibid.,* sig. a2r.   127. *Ibid.,* sig. a2v.

128. *Ibid.,* sig. a3r–a3v.   129. *Ibid.,* sig. a3v–a4r.   130. *Ibid.,* sig. a4v–a6v.

131. *Ibid.,* sig. a5v.

132. Norimbergae: Apud Io. Petreium, 1544.   133. *Ibid., De motu solis,* iv.

134. Henricus Ranzovius, *Tractatus astrologicus de genethliacorum thematum iudiciis pro singulis nati accidentibus, ex vetustis et optimis quibusque auctoribus . . . collectus* (Francofurti: Typis Wolffgangi Richteri, 1602).   135. *Ibid.,* "Ad lectorem."

136. For the edition, see note 4, above.   137. *Ibid.,* p. 17 (XXV, iii).

138. *Ibid.,* p. 22 (XXV, iv).

139. Garches (S. & O.): Aux Éditions du Nouvel Humanisme, 1947.

140. *Ibid.,* pp. 58–71 (I, iii).

141. See note 10, above.

142. *Ibid.,* "Praefatio."   143. *Ibid.*   144. *Ibid.,* pp. 1–2 (I, i).

145. *Ibid.,* pp. 2–3 (I, i).   146. *Ibid.,* pp. 4–5 (I, i).   147. *Ibid.,* pp. 6–7 (I, i).

148. *Ibid.,* pp. 7–9 (I, ii).   149. *Ibid.,* p. 10 (I, iii).

150. For all thirty see *ibid.,* pp. 10–22 (I, iii).   151. *Ibid.,* p. 10 (I, iii).

152. *—in locis maternis, non eodem momento totum semen recipitur, tum etiam centrum cordium amborum geminorum cum non sit idem: sed varia varijsque in locis, esse quoque orizontes varios necessum* (sic) *est.—Ibid.,* pp. 15–16 (I, iii).

153. *Ibid.,* pp. 16–17 (I, iii).   154. *Ibid.,* p. 18 (I, iii).   155. *Ibid.,* p. 25 (I, v).

156. *Ibid.,* pp. 25–26 (I, v).   157. *Ibid.,* p. 26 (I, v).   158. *Ibid.,* p. 28 (I, v).

159. *Ibid.*

160. The French names of five days give a better clue here than the English: *lundi, mardi, mercredi, jeudi, vendredi.* The first hours of these days are governed, respectively, by Luna, Mars,

Mercurius, Juppiter, and Venus. A literary use is in Chaucer's *Knight's Tale,* in which Palamon, Emily, and Arcite pray to Venus, the moon, and Mars "in their hours," the first, third, and sixth after sunrise on Friday.

161. Bonatti, *Astrosophia,* pp. 28–29 (I, v): *Illud autem alterum quod inconsonum est, radiationum amicitias, ac inimicitias notant. . . . Nescirem autem qua ratione, ita definierint de adspectuum inimicitijs, quae nulla prorsus existit.*   162. *Ibid.,* p. 29 (I, v).

163. —*contraritates, implicationesque esse minimè credendas.*—*Ibid.,* p. 35 (I, vii).

164. *Constat ergo mirabili consensu mundum superiorem, cum inferiori colligatum esse, & ex corpore animaque, quasi ex caelo, & terra homo ortum suum duxisse . . . Quamobrem cum mundus magnus minorem regat, patet etiam hac de causa hominem quasi minorem quendam Universum, ab illis corporibus luminosis, quae illum constituunt secundarie, post Optimum Deum gubernari.*—*Ibid.,* p. 65 (I, xvii).   165. *Ibid.,* p. 70 (II, i).

166. *Ibid.,* p. 39 (I, viii).   167. *Ibid.,* p. 40 (I, viii).   168. *Ibid.,* p. 70 (II, i).

169. Hieronimo Sauonarola, *Opera singolare del Reuerendo Padre F. Hieronimo Sauanarola contra l'astrologia diuinatrice in corroboratione delle refutatione astrologice del S. conte Ioan. Pico de la Mirandola, Con alcune cose dil medemo* (sic.) *di nuouo aggionte* (In Vinegia: 1536).   170. *Ibid.,* pp. 2r-2v. There are page numbers, but only on the right-hand pages.

171. *Ibid.,* pp. 3r-4v (I, i).   172. *Ibid.,* p. 5r (I, i).   173. *Ibid.*

174. *Ibid.,* pp. 5v-6r (I, ii).   175. *Ibid.,* pp. 7v-9r (I, iv–v).   176. *Ibid.,* pp. 9r-9v (II, i).

177. *Ibid.,* pp. 10r–10v (II, i).   178. *Ibid.,* pp. 11v-12r (II, ii).

179. *Ibid.,* pp. 12r-12v (II, iii).   180. *Ibid.,* p. 18r (II, vii).

181. *Ibid.,* pp. 18v-19r (II, viii).   182. *Ibid.,* p. 19v (II, viii).

183. *Ibid.,* p. 20v (II, viii).   184. *Ibid.,* pp. 23r-23v (III, i).

185. *Ibid.,* pp. 23v-24v (III, ii–iii).   186. *Ibid.,* p. 25r (III, iii).

187. *Ibid.,* pp. 25r-26r (III, iii).   188. *Ibid.,* p. 26v (III, iv).

189. Or perhaps 1314; the Roman numerals are unclear. *Ibid.,* p. 27r (III, iv).

190. *Ibid.,* p. 31v (III, v).   191. *Ibid.,* p. 28r (III, iv).

192. Ioannis Francisci Pici, Mirandulae Domini, Corcordiaeque Comitis: *Opera omnia* (Basiliae: Ex Officina Henricpetrina, 1573), II, 366–709. Book V occupies pp. 504–92.

193. *Ibid.,* II, 428 (II, vi).   194. *Ibid.,* II, 505 (V, i).

195. —*nec mores hominum, nec bonas aut malas leges a coelo pendere, corporeas quoque dispositiones ab eo non effici.*—*Ibid.,* II, 566 (V, ix).

196. I use a modern version reprinted from the 1842 edition of Calvin's *Oeuvres françaises,* ed. P. L. Jacob: Jean Calvin, *Avertissement contre l'astrologie; Traité des reliques; suivis du Discours de Théodore de Bèze sur la vie et la mort* (Paris: Librairie Armand Colin, 1962).

197. *Ibid.,* p. 6.   198. *Ibid.,* p. 7.   199. *Ibid.,* p. 8.   200. *Ibid.,* p. 15.

201. *Ibid., p.* 21.   202. *Ibid.,* p. 8.

203. *Ibid.,* p. 5. No one of *moyen savoir,* he says, will need his warning—an obvious error.

204. *Ibid.,* p. 4.   205. *Ibid.,* pp. 8–9.   206. *Ibid.,* p. 12.   207. *Ibid.,* p. 13.

208. *Ibid.,* p. 11. Historically, the casting of women's horoscopes seems to have begun with the migration of astrologers to Roman territories, where women had not only a better status than in Greece and the Middle East but also money.   209. *Ibid.,* p. 4.

210. *Ibid.,* pp. 9–10.   211. *Ibid.,* p. 11.   212. *Ibid.,* p. 15.   213. *Ibid.,* pp. 15–16.

214. *Ibid.,* pp. 16–17.   215. *Ibid.,* p. 18.   216. *Ibid.,* pp. 20–22.

217. *Ibid., p.* 23.   218. *Ibid.,* p. 25.   219. *Ibid.,* p. 26.   220. *Ibid.,* p. 30.

221. *Ibid.,* pp. 32–33.   222. *Ibid.,* p. 34.

223. Thomas Erastus, *De astrologia divinatrice epistolae . . . iam olim ab eodem ad diuersos scriptae, & in duos libros digestae* (Basiliae: Per Petrum Pernam, 1580).

224. *Ibid.,* pp. 1–3.

225. Days on which a disease was expected to take a decisive turn for better or worse.

226. The explanation is that the seven-day lunar periods consist really of six days and a fraction each, so that the three periods add up to fewer than twenty-one days.

227. *Ibid.*, p. 18 (Letter III).   228. *Ibid.*, p. 30 (Letter IV).   229. *Ibid.*, p. 41 (Letter V).

230. *Ibid.*, p. 51 (Letter VI).   231. *Ibid.*, p. 58 (Letter VII).

232. Pontus de Tyard, *Mantice, ou Discours de la verité de diuination par astrologie* (Paris: Galiot du Pré, 2d ed. augmentée, 1573), pp. 5–6.   233. *Ibid.*, pp. 18–21.

234. *Ibid.*, pp. 22–24.   235. *Ibid.*, pp. 29–30.   236. *Ibid.*, pp. 30–31.

237. *Ibid.*, p. 31.   238. *Ibid.*, pp. 33–34.   239. *Ibid.*, pp. 34–35.   240. *Ibid.*, p. 36.

241. *Ibid.*, pp. 37–38.   242. *Ibid.*, pp. 39–40.   243. *Ibid.*, p. 42.   244. *Ibid.*, p. 50.

245. *Ibid.*, p. 54.   246. *Ibid.*, pp. 55–56.   247. *Ibid.*, pp. 64–65.   248. *Ibid.*, pp. 66–70.

249. *Ibid.*, pp. 71–74.   250. *Ibid.*, pp. 74–75.   251. *Ibid.*, pp. 79–80.

252. *Ibid.*, p. 84.   253. *Ibid.*, pp. 85–89.   254. *Ibid.*, pp. 91–92.

255. *Ibid.*, pp. 95–96.   256. *Ibid.*, pp. 97–104.   257. *Ibid.*, pp. 105–107.

258. *Ibid.*, pp. 107–108.   259. *Ibid.*, pp. 109–112.   260. *Ibid.*, pp. 113–14.

261. Durham, North Carolina: Duke University Press, 1941.

262. San Marino, California: The Huntington Library, 1953.

263. Leicester University Press, 1969.

264. "Astrology and Politics in the First Years of Elizabeth's Reign," *Bulletin of the History of Medicine,* Vol. III (1935), 171–86.

265. For the bulls see D. P. Walker, *Spiritual and Demonic Magic from Ficino to Campanella* (London: The Warburg Institute, 1958), pp. 205–206. Frances Yates discusses the astrological magic of Bruno in detail in *Giordano Bruno and the Hermetic Tradition* (London: Routledge and Kegan Paul, 1964).

266. Kocher, *Science and Religion,* p. 202.   267. *Ibid.*

268. Cited by Eugenio Garin, ed., *Testi umanistici su l'ermetismo* (Roma: Fratelli Bocca, 1955), p. 11.

CHAPTER TWO

⚛ Witchcraft

I. The human impact

Of all the varieties of occultism, witchcraft has the most depressing history. The expenditure of human energy and wealth in the alchemist's search for the Stone or the Elixir, although sobering, is trivial in comparison to the torture and execution of supposed witches. And this suffering reached its height not during the Dark Ages but in the High Renaissance.

The Renaissance persecutions of witches, conducted in Catholic Europe at first by the Inquisition and other ecclesiastical courts but later, as in England, by the secular authority, for the sake of convenience may be said to have been initiated by the promulgation on December 5, 1484, of Pope Innocent VIII's bull, *Summis considerantes affectibus,* which called upon both the Church and the secular power to aid the Inquisition in extirpating witchcraft. The same bull appointed Jakob Sprenger and Heinrich Kramer (or Institoris), subsequently to become famous as authors of the *Malleus maleficarum,* or "Hammer Against Witches," as "inquisitors of those heretical practices." The trials continued throughout the sixteenth century and most of the seventeenth, rising sometimes to horrifying crescendos. In Lorraine a single judge, Nicolas Remy, with his assistants sent no fewer than 800 persons to death in sixteen years; and *Daemonolatreiae libri tres* (1595), the treatise in which he explained his legal assumptions and procedures, for a while replaced the *Malleus*

as the most authoritative textbook on the subject.[1] In Westphalia, about 1630, another
judge was responsible for nearly 500 executions.[2] According to Henri Boguet, writing about 1590 concerning trials in Burgundy, Germany was "almost entirely occupied with building fires for [witches]. Switzerland has been compelled to wipe
out many of her villages on their account. Travellers in Lorraine may see thousands
and thousands of the stakes to which witches are bound."[3]

Estimates of the total number of victims in Europe between 1484 and the
gradual dying down of fanaticism toward 1700 run as high as 300,000. The *Encyclopedia of Witchcraft and Demonology,* an authoritative work by Rossell Hope Robbins, suggests 200,000 as a conservative figure. The number of deaths in England
is estimated at numbers running from 1,000—perhaps approximately accurate—to
70,000.[4] Contrary to widespread opinion, trials appear to have been more numerous
under Elizabeth than under James I, who expressed severe views in his *Daemonologie* (1597) but gradually became skeptical about specific accusations.[5] The practical meaning of these figures for everyday life is suggested by a remark in George
Gifford's *A Dialogue Concerning Witches and Witchcraftes* (1593) to the effect
that a white witch at "R. H.," whose trade was the removal of charms by counter-
magic, "by report hath some weeke fourtie come vnto her, and many of them not of
the meaner sort."[6] At a time when England was still thinly populated, enough
persons in a country village might think they were bewitched to provide full-time
work for a "wise-woman."

Witches, indeed, were suspected everywhere—on the next farm, in the village,
within the family, among the clergy. Cardinal Wolsey was accused by Tyndale of
having "bewitched the king's mind, and made the king dote upon him more than
ever he did on any lady or gentleman."[7] The Scottish Earl of Bothwell, who might
have claimed the throne of Scotland if James VI had died without an heir, was
implicated in an attempt to wreck James's ship by raising a storm as the King
returned from his wedding to Anne of Denmark.[8] An attempt of the Countess of
Somerset to procure her husband's impotency by charms and drugs, made public by
a sensational trial in 1616, clearly involved sorcery, often thought to depend on an
implied and perhaps unconscious pact with the Devil, and suggests the prevalence
of superstition in high places as well as in the populace. The history of witchcraft
has, however, often been written, and I do not intend to repeat it here.[9] My concern
is rather with the intellectual habits which made the long frenzy possible.

Of course not everyone shared the common delusions. In the contemporary
literature of the subject attacks are sometimes made on skeptics, and a number of
treatises, although never, so far as they can be judged by explicit assertions, totally
incredulous, show a healthy tough-mindedness. One of these, the *Cautio criminalis*
(1631), by Friedrich von Spee, a Jesuit confessor of accused witches whose hair is

said to have been turned prematurely white by his experiences,[10] is worth looking at because it offers appalling insights into the unreliability of the evidence used to convict.[11]

Who, von Spee asks, would not confess to witchcraft if put in the prisoner's place? Torture Capuchins, Jesuits, religious of all orders; if they refuse to acknowledge their crimes at once, exorcize them, shave all the hair from their bodies lest they protect themselves against pain by a hidden charm, and have at them again. In the end all will confess. Do the same to prelates, canonists, professors of theology, and the same thing will happen. Ultimately, we will all turn out to be witches.[12] He himself is so unable to endure physical suffering [13] that he would accuse himself of anything if tortured, all the more because theologians agree that in those conditions the sin is not mortal.[14] It is said that many prisoners are insensible to torture and laugh at it, but this is nonsense. If the victim endures the pain with clenched teeth, contorted lips, and held breath, witnesses cry out that she feels nothing but amusement. When the apparent insensibility called "sleeping" under torture is not a faint it is, in fact, the result of a stiffening intended to assist endurance. "This is what the poets meant in their stories about Niobe, when they say that because of her suffering she hardened into stone." [15] How terrible the agony was is suggested by the discovery that when a confession is said to have been obtained without torture the accused has sometimes been subjected "only" to a broad iron press with sharp teeth which crushed the shinbones to the point where blood spurted out on both sides and flesh was mangled. "And yet they call that 'Confessed without torture! . . .' What kind of insight can those have who lack all understanding of such pains? How can outstandingly learned men judge and discriminate when they cannot understand the language, the specialists' jargon, of the inquisitors?" [16]

What made the situation hopeless for the accused was the lack of any means of proving innocence. A failure to confess was an indication of guilt, for without magic the witch would have been unable to stand the suffering.[17] What purpose, von Spee inquires, does the torture serve if the prisoner is equally guilty no matter how she behaves under it? And why, if some of the accused may conceivably be innocent, may not God instead of the Devil have strengthened them? Anyhow, if no merely human resources could have availed her, the torture must have been illegally cruel; and that it was so the claim that she must have had supernatural help itself testifies.[18] How, indeed, can the accused *not* be executed? Von Spee once heard the question put to a group of court officials: how can an innocent prisoner be released? After reflecting for some time, the officials said finally that they would think about the matter overnight. But in fact no answer was possible: "If anybody thinks he has found a means, he reveals that he knows nothing about what goes on." [19] Evidently judicial methods were especially tyrannical in Germany, for Remy says that nearly as many as the 800 he condemned "saved their lives by flight or by a stubborn endurance of the torture." [20]

What actually happened in the proceedings which von Spee witnessed can be summarized as follows. The accused person, usually but not always a woman and often elderly, was called before the inquisitor and informed of the charges; she denied them, and was told to go back to her cell and consider for a couple of hours whether she wished to hold to her lie—all this "as if she had spoken to the wind or told stories to stones." Upon being brought back she was asked whether she still intended to be obstinate and tell falsehoods. If the answer was in effect "Yes," she was led off directly to the torture chamber. [21] Once she was there her guilt continued to be taken for granted, and often the executioner's assistants informed her what she was expected to say, telling her things would go easily with her if she made the same admissions as others who had already been tortured. "Thus it comes about that in the end she makes known the same particulars that others have confessed earlier." [22] Eventually it turned out that what the torturer wished to be true was true. [23]

Even then the cruelty was not intermitted, for the desire of pious princes and churchmen to "root out" the terrible iniquity of witchcraft made them wish her to implicate others. "Don't you know Titia too? Haven't you seen her at your witches' Sabbats?" If the answer was "No," the examiner said to the hangman, "Tighten the ropes." When at last, by unbearable agony, a "Yes" was drawn from the victim, the next question was about Sempronia; and so on until three or four were implicated. "The reader may himself judge how it comes about that we have so many witches in Germany." [24] In the same way the prisoner was told what crimes she had committed—what cows she had caused to run dry, what crops she had destroyed by hailstorms, what children she had killed and eaten. And so on in every detail, with the result that the testimony of various witches coincided to produce the irrefragable evidence of evildoing so triumphantly cited by the theorists whose writings we shall examine.

The admissions so extorted usually stuck. A confessor sent to the condemned heretic—for on the continent the basic charge included heresy as well as crime— would tell the witch that she could not be shriven preparatory to her burning until she had released from danger those against whom she had brought false charges. The reply was usually that she could not for fear of facing additional torture; and when the confessor urged that she would incur eternal damnation if she left innocent persons under suspicion, she might say that she would help the guiltless in any way except by risking more suffering—and this despite her realization that going to death with lies on her soul would mean endless Hell fire. [25] To von Spee, who because of his noble compassion must have been confided in more than most priests who undertook this unhappy ministry, it seemed that out of fifty who went to the stake scarcely five—indeed, scarcely two—were guilty.[26] At several points he appears to be on the verge of denying the very possibility of guilt, for he hints at the possession of a secret he dares not tell; but the official theory was too strong for him, and in his first *quaestio* he admits that witches exist.

Sometimes—apparently rather often—a confession evoked by torture would be denied when the ropes or screws were loosened, and the denial itself, perhaps, retracted when torture was renewed. This tendency did not, apparently, suggest to many theologians or legal philosophers the unreliability of statements wrung from prisoners under duress, although some show awareness of the problem. The most succinct comment is that of Johann Georg Godelmann, rather a fair-minded legal theorist than an extraordinarily empathetic person: "He lies who can endure much, and he who can endure nothing. The former does not want to confess what he has done, and the latter confesses he has performed more things than he ever dreamed of." [27] The usual view was that the relaxation of torture had encouraged a resurgence of impudence; so the witch was again submitted to the engines. How many times this practice might be repeated was a subject of dispute, but in general it appears that after the third repetition of torture—which von Spee thought to become more exquisitely agonizing as the body was further broken—no further effort to renew the confession was proper. (A convenient fiction that the torture was being "continued" instead of "renewed" offered a way out of the difficulty.) Since conviction for heresy required an admission of guilt, judges not especially eager to condemn might then discharge the sometimes permanently maimed prisoner. More often the charge of criminal acts was thought to have been proved, and the accused was "relaxed" to the secular authority for execution. If, however, repeated torture evoked a second or perhaps a third confession and the witch once again professed innocence before she was led to the faggots, she was regarded as "relapsed" [28] and was refused the preliminary strangling earned by acknowledging guilt. In general, although not always and everywhere, it was felt, as Parrinder has remarked, that "The confessions proved that the Church was right, and so exculpated her from charges of cruelty": exactly the motive for similar practices in certain Communist states in our own century.[29]

In England, where except in cases involving treason torture was illegal, the proceedings were of course milder; and after the breach with Rome in the 1530s the Inquisition, which had never persecuted English witches, had no further opportunity to act. Also, the proportion of executions to indictments was lower: according to Parrinder, "the percentage of hangings to accusations never passed forty-two per cent in England, and was usually about half that figure." [30] It should not, however, be assumed that from 58 to 79 per cent were cleared, for we often hear of reputed witches escaping before or during imprisonment; some died in their cells or committed suicide; others were given lesser punishments; and a released suspect might later be retaken and executed. Also, treatment just short of torture was not unusual. Matthew Hopkins, an infamous witch-finder of the 1640s, admitted having kept witches awake for two or three nights running.[31] The cells were often freezingly cold, the food might be inadequate, and severe psychological pressures were exerted. The age was pre-humanitarian. Although a few persons might think that physical suffering was the worst of all evils, in general people were less tender-minded than now. Jean Bodin spoke for many when he said that although witches are burned, "the punishment is far lighter than that which Satan causes them in this world, not to speak of the eternal punishments which are prepared for them."[32] The Italian Francesco Guazzo was able to say that a man who had often publicly blasphemed the Virgin Mary was "mercifully" punished when Mary touched him while he slept, so that when he awoke "he found himself without hands or feet, lying there wretched, maimed and useless. . . . He was thus mercifully punished for his blasphemy; for so do the Blessed Saints mete out gentle punishment."[33]

The severity of the persecutions on the continent was justified by legal arguments to the effect that witches had to be treated more harshly than other evildoers because witchcraft was treason to God as well as to the state. The *Malleus maleficarum* of Sprenger and Institoris laid down the basic premises as early as 1484.[34] Various deceits might be practised. The judge might promise that he would be merciful, "with the mental reservation that he means he will be merciful to himself or the State." He might arrange for some friend or patron to spend the night with the accused on the excuse that it was too late to go home, and hidden spies would take notes of the conversation. Again, the authors say, let her be put in a castle and told that the castellan is going on a journey, and then let the visitors promise her freedom if she will teach them some of her magical practices.[35] More important, witnesses who were ordinarily barred by law from testifying might give evidence against a witch: excommunicated persons, accomplices, notorious evildoers and criminals, heretics, the wife, sons, and other kindred of the accused, her servants, and repentant perjurers.[36] Although the usual requirement for proof was the concurring testimony of two or more witnesses to the same action or fact, in cases of witchcraft the evidence of six or eight or ten persons who concurred that the prisoner was a witch—one might say, "She bewitched my child," another "She bewitched my cow"—might be accepted as conclusive provided the witnesses were not mortal enemies of the accused, she was generally reported to be a witch, and there was some visible or tangible evidence.[37] It was not required that the witnesses be identified to the accused.[38] Counsel for the defense, if one was admitted, was not to use "pretentious oratory," introduce any "legal quirks or quibbles," bring any counter-accusations, or defend heresy. (Doing so would make him not merely himself a heretic but a heresiarch.) [39]

Much of this was regularly justified on the ground that since witchcraft is practised in secret or among other malefactors no condemnations could be obtained without a relaxation of the customary legal safeguards against injustice. The propriety of concealing the identity of witnesses, however, was defended, not altogether insincerely, by the principle that the names of accusers might be kept secret when a likelihood existed that the prisoner might take revenge on them. Witches were especially malicious and might be assumed to possess extraordinary means of retaliating.

Much subsequent writing about witchcraft was aimed at supporting, extending, or qualifying these principles. Only a few documents can be mentioned here, and those only as illustrative. Boguet's *Examen of Witches* (1590) described "the procedure necessary to a judge in trials for witchcraft" in seventy "Articles" which, according to Montague Summers, were "actually adopted in general practice by most local Parliaments and puisne (petty) courts." [40] Imprisonment might follow upon a single accusation or upon common rumor, "for this is almost infallible in the matter of witchcraft" (Art. III). Stool pigeons might give false testimony or pretend also to lie under the same charge in order to induce confession (Articles XII and XVIII). A presumed witch might be tortured even on a holy day (Art. XXV). Child-witches too should be executed, but more gently than adults, as by hanging (Art. LXIII). Jean Bodin, in other areas a rather advanced thinker, in *Daemonomania,* also a work which had considerable influence, asserted that every witch might be assumed to be a parricide, since witches do murder, and that the murders were all malicious, since it could be taken for granted that "sorcerers have done nothing by mistake, but always by malice and impiety." [41] Indeed, it was to be supposed that every sorcerer had committed every possible kind of depravity.[42] "When a woman is reported to be a witch (*sagam*), there is a most grave presumption that she is one"; hence she might be put to the torture if there was any corroborating evidence, although this was not to be allowed if the case was not one of witchcraft.[43] Moreover, the special severity of the punishment meted out to witches was not aimed primarily at castigating vice but at mollifying God's wrath, since the crime was against His majesty.[44] It was further aimed at bringing God's benediction upon the whole land and at striking others with fear and terror, so that the number of the wicked would be diminished and good men might pass their lives in security.[45] Indeed, no punishment could be great enough for witches,[46] since they were guilty of many crimes which singly merited death: they denied religion, blasphemed, gave faith to the Devil, consecrated their children to Satan, sacrificed infants to the Devil, invoked the Devil and swore by him, committed incest and murder, ate human flesh, killed secretly by poison and fortune-telling (*sortilegiis*), and so on through a list of fifteen items.[47] Yet Bodin takes some pains to be scrupulous and reminds his readers that the concurring testimony of fifty people that Peter was charmed to death could be refuted by the appearance of Peter alive and well.[48]

Such principles of course met some resistance. In Reginald Scot's *The Discoverie of Witchcraft* (1584), which along with Jean Wier's *De prestigiis daemonum et incantationibus ac veneficiis* (1564; French translation, 1579) is an early retort from what seemed to the orthodox to be the Devil's party, Bodin's procedural advice is treated with contempt.[49] Johann Godelmann, however, because although a Protestant he came nearer to sharing the legal pre-assumptions of Bodin, Boguet, and the *Malleus,* was more likely to effect reforms. He begins by acknowledging in a preface that crimes of *lèse-majesté,* among which blasphemy, heresy, magic, hurtful incantations, and divinatory predictions and consultations are to be reckoned, "offend eternal majesty far more gravely than temporal," [50] and he agrees that the punishment for injury caused by enchantment is death. The purpose of his treatise, however, is to secure a more faithful observation of existing laws, and he proceeds to draw careful distinctions.[51] Ordinary criminal procedures should be followed, not extraordinary. The accuser should be questioned and required to show evidence and give reasons for his suspicions.[52] The proofs should be *liquidissimae* and *luce, sicuti dicitur, meridiana clariores,* quite transparent and clearer than noonday light.[53] The significance of the Devil's mark, thought to have been made by his claw at the time the pact was entered into and strongly emphasized by Bodin, is denied: "These indications are empty, absurd, and frivolous and are to be rejected, not admitted, as contrary to our laws." [54] Imprisonment ought to follow, not precede, the examination of witnesses.[55] The accused should be allowed counsel (*procurator*).[56] A confession of impossible actions proves nothing.[57] The implication of others by confessions is not always to be believed,[58] and the confessions extracted must be made seriously (*serio, non autem iocose*), circumstantial (*specialis*), and confirmed by two witnesses.[59] Although a long road had yet to be trodden toward justice, a few preliminary steps had been taken.

The effectiveness of such tracts as Godelmann's is hard to estimate. Many later treatises which were frequently reprinted and accepted as authoritative—for instance, Remy's *Demonolatry* and Martin Delrio's *Disquisitionum magicarum libri sex* (Louvain, 1599)—continue to show horror at the enormity of witches' crimes. That procedures remained improper in some areas, at least, is clear from von Spee's *Cautio* (1631), at which we have glanced. No doubt individual judges on the continent too sometimes did their best to be scrupulously fair and pronounced adverse judgments sorrowfully, as in the famous Lancashire trials of 1612.[60] Nevertheless the situation of any person accused by malicious neighbors was regularly desperate. As C. H. Lea has said, all too often the only real defense was to show that the witnesses were mortal enemies and therefore disqualified from giving testimony.[61] Often, however, they were not identified; or, if they were to be named, the investigator might very early ask whether the prisoner knew them, and, if he did, whether they were friends or enemies. If the answer was "Friends" because as yet no ground for enmity was known, no later claim of mortal enmity was possible.

The courts seem usually to have had fixed ideas about incriminating *indicia.* In the trials at which Hopkins cooperated a special emphasis was placed on the witches' "teats," bodily abnormalities at which a devil was thought to have sucked blood, and on the Devil's mark, any peculiar area of skin which appeared to be insensible to pain. (We do not hear much of teats on the continent.) Boguet, in his *Examen,* regards as virtual proof of guilt an inability to weep and a tendency to keep the eyes on the ground.[62] Almost anywhere the discovery in the witch's house of unguents, clay images, or other implements of sorcery told heavily against her, as did also, in England, the ownership of pets which might be thought familiar spirits. Although certainly many of the victims used charms and some thought themselves to be witches—what proportion it is impossible to estimate—von Spee's belief that their confessions were not to be trusted is confirmed by regional differences in expectations. The witches condemned by Remy almost all admitted that when they entered houses to spread poison they took the form of cats,[63] a detail not common elsewhere; and whereas in England the rare witches' Sabbats were presided over by Satan himself, often in the form of a black goat, in certain parts of the continent the chief figure was regularly a woman, the *Donna,* identified as Diana or Herodias.

The modern reader of the treatises is further afflicted by their cool, reasonable tone and by clear implications that the authors were not abnormally evil men. In general, they reason cogently according to their lights and aim not at producing maximal human suffering but at the relief of mankind from a grievous plague. How their minds worked we shall attempt presently to see; but first it will be useful to suggest what kinds of persons were accused and the reasons why they were indicted. Here again there is a significant difference between England, where the typical witch was poor and illiterate—of 590 suspects in the home counties during one period all but four were laborers or tradesmen or, usually, their wives [64]—and the continent, where the property of a condemned witch was confiscated by the court. The English witch, at whom we shall look shortly, was typically a woman, poor, uneducated, something of a social outcast, "queer" and perhaps partly demented, and usually old. The presumption that she was a sorceress was enormously strengthened if she was also physically repulsive, afflicted by some such evident abnormality as a drooping or crooked eye, and given to unintelligible but ominous muttering.

Exactly such a description is offered by Scot. "One sort of such as are said to bee witches, are women which be commonly old, lame, bleare-eied, pale, fowle, and full of wrinkles." Being ignorant and stupid and consequently unable to provide adequately for themselves, they go from house to house asking "for a pot full of milke, yest, drinke, pottage, or some such releefe; without the which they could hardlie live"; and when they are refused they may utter curses on "the maister of the house, his wife, children, cattell, &c. to the little pig that lieth in the stie. . . . Doubtlesse (at length) some of hir neighbors die, or fall sicke; or some of their children are visited with diseases."[65] The mutterings are remembered, and an accusation follows. This is the basic situation, illustrated by hundreds or thousands of stories in the contemporary literature of witchcraft—for the neighbors too are often illiterate and suspicious, unaware of the nature of actual causality and ready enough to lay to the charge of an enemy any of the innumerable misfortunes to which people who live constantly on the verge of disaster are subject.

A case history or two may be useful, for I am attempting to describe the implications for real human beings of the theory of witchcraft soon to be examined. For example, the son of John Ferrall, vicar of Brenchlie in Kent, according to Scot passed one day by the house of a certain Margaret Simons, and by chance her little dog barked at him,

> which thing the boie taking in evill part, drewe his knife, & pursued him therewith even to hir doore: whom she rebuked with some such words as the boie disdained, & yet neverthelesse would not be persuaded to depart in a long time. At the last he returned to his maisters house [he was apprenticed to a clothier], and within five or sixe daies fell sicke. Then was called to mind the fraie twixt the dog and the boie.

The boy's father, as it happened, already suspected the presence of a witch in the parish, because "when he desired to read most plainlie, his voice so failed him, as he could scant be heard at all. Which hee could impute, he said, to nothing else, but to hir enchantment." Actually, Mrs. Simons told the author whose report we are following, "at all times his voice was hoarse and lowe," so that he was suspected to have the French pox and "divers" parishioners refused to take communion from him until he produced a certificate from two physicians which said that he suffered from lung disease.[66] Happily, the case was dismissed.

In some such way as this suspicion was aroused, and if at the time the magistrates were proceeding actively against witchcraft in the region an accusation might be made and the trial begun, with results of the kind already suggested. A sow might die, a promising crop come to nothing, two cows fall sick, the butter not come, and too often some reason was found to lay the blame on a neighbor. In George Gifford's *Dialogue Concerning Witches and Witchcraftes* (1593, 1603), another skeptical document, a man called Samuel, when asked about his health, replies that he is pretty well but "me thinke my meate doth me no good of late." Having heard of the activities of witches in the neighborhood, he is afraid now and then when he sees a hare stare at him, or a weasel run across his yard; and "there is a foule great catte sometimes in my Barne, which I haue no liking unto." One old woman especially makes him uneasy. Moreover, an apparently well hog has died suddenly, and "My wife hath had fiue or sixe hennes euen of late dead." He is thinking of seeking the help of counter-witchcraft. Later, when the discussion is continued in Sam's house, his wife says that another hen has died, the good woman R. last week couldn't make the butter come until she used charms, and this morning an old woman looked "sowerlie" on her and mumbled.[67]

Thus it went. A peddler might be mumbled at because he refused to undo his pack to sell a few pins. A bored husband might find himself impotent. A boy coming home late with the cows might invent a story about having been delayed by witches in the form of animals. The image gradually produced in a modern mind is that of impoverished communities of jealous and surly countryfolk given to backbiting and predisposed by their ignorance—like savages—to believe that every natural misfortune was willed.

II. The theory of witchcraft

Innumerable stories could be cited to support this generalization. When the witch-fever was on a community, every misfortune might be laid on a witch: "adversitie, greefe, sicknesse, losse of children, corne, cattell, or libertie. . . . a clap of thunder, or a gale of wind is no sooner heard, but either they run to ring bels, or crie out to burne witches; or else burne consecrated things, hoping by the smoke thereof, to drive the divell out of the aire." [68] Suspicion generated suspicion, and shortly the whole area was in an uproar. Scot, who has just been quoted, is one of the atypical doubters: "But if all the divels in hell were dead, and all the witches in *England* burnt or hanged; I warrant you we should not faile to have raine, haile and tempests, as now we have. . . . I am also well assured, that if all the old women in the world were witches; and all the priests, conjurers: we should not have a drop of raine, nor a blast of wind the more or the lesse for them." [69] Few contemporary writers even among the skeptics would have risked so sweeping a generalization, for there were— it seemed—all too many solid reasons for believing that witchcraft existed and was sometimes, however rarely, practised. We turn now to the intellectual processes by which the belief was established, attempting, as far as possible, not to let modern convictions interfere with an understanding of earlier thought-ways however detestable they may seem to us.

Especially, but not merely, in Protestant countries, total skepticism usually foundered on Scripture. "Thou shalt not suffer a witch to live" (*Exodus* 22:18): this most

Martin Delrio, *Disquisitionum magicarum libri sex,* London, 1604, title page.

The author is identified as a Jesuit priest, a Doctor of Theology, and professor of sacred theology at the University of Graz, in Austria.

Proceeding to the left and downward from the upper center, the pictures illustrate God speaking to Moses and Aaron and then the ten plagues described in *Exodus* 7–11: the rivers of blood, frogs, lice, flies, the murrain of beasts, boils, hail, locusts, and darkness. The last picture (upper right) presumably shows Pharoah grieving over the threatened death of the first-born. The intent of the series is perhaps to suggest the superiority of miracles to magic.

quoted of all Biblical texts left little ground for maneuvering. True, Scot attempted plausibly to show that the Septuagint's φαρμακούς, for the Latin *veneficos* or *maleficos,* meant not "witches" but "poisoners"; and he quoted "Josephus an Hebrue borne" as having said that the word designated a person who possessed "any poison that is deadlie, or prepared to anie hurtfull use." [70] Such a person should "suffer that which he meant to doo to them, for whom he prepared it." [71] For the most part, however, even those most passionately opposed to the executions acknowledged the reality of witchcraft and confined their arguments to the thesis that many or most of those convicted were innocent and the legal practices unjust.

Many other Biblical texts contributed to the admission. The visit paid by Saul to the Witch of Endor, who raised or—as others thought—pretended to raise the spirit of Samuel is almost as frequently cited. And what could be urged against the many passages in the Gospels which described the casting out of devils by Christ? "And these signs shall follow them that believe; In my name shall they cast out devils" (*Mark* 16:17). The long argument about "transvection," or the ability of demons to transport witches through the air to their Sabbats, was sometimes, as in the *Malleus,* decisively resolved by the question, "Did not the devil take up Our Saviour, and carry Him up to a high place, as the Gospel testifies?" [72] *Leviticus* 20:6 declared that the Lord would set His face against "the soul that turneth after such as have familiar spirits" and would "cut him off from among his people"; and the twenty-seventh verse of the same chapter said flatly, "A man also or woman that hath a familiar spirit, or that is a wizard, shall surely be put to death: they shall stone them with stones: their blood shall be upon them." The prescription of means was ignored, the sentence of death honored.

Many other passages encouraged the popular superstition. Sorcerers are mentioned in *Revelation* 21:8 and 22:15 along with whoremongers, murderers, idolaters, and liars. The mention in *Ephesians* 2:2 of "the prince of the power of the air" might, with a little violence, be interpreted as meaning that power over the air is given to demons. *Job* 41:33, written of the Leviathan, could be cited as proof that efforts to make innocent use of demonic power were hopeless: "Upon earth there is not his like, who is made without fear." The Devil was certain to get the better of any mortal who tried to control him. *Psalm* 78:49, "He cast upon them the fierceness of his anger, wrath, and indignation, and trouble, by sending evil angels among them," supported a generally accepted doctrine that all the evil performed by devils was done either with God's permission or by his explicit order. *Leviticus* 18:3 (*Leviticus* was an especially rich source), "After the doings of the land of Egypt, wherein ye dwelt, shall ye not do: and after the doings of the land of Canaan, whither I bring you, shall ye not do," could be understood as referring to the magical operations to which those abominable peoples were addicted. But indeed any literalist reading of Scripture necessarily entailed a belief both in the unceasing evil machinations of devils and in sorcery. The miracles of Christ, so often described as involving the casting out of devils, alone would have sufficed to produce a conviction that demons often "possessed" human beings. From this incontrovertible truth to a belief that the Devil might bargain with mortals and promise them effective enchantments in exchange for their souls after death was so easy a step that theorists often seem not to have realized they took it.

For witchcraft, it is important to recognize, was everywhere and always understood to involve a pact with the Devil. The pact, indeed, was its defining characteristic. Conjuring without demonic assistance belonged in a different category which cannot be described more than roughly in the present context. On one level, white magic was no more than a primitive physics and chemistry which utilized real but occult forces hidden in nature itself. Much that appeared wonderful to the uninitiated might be performed by it. On another but overlapping level was a magic or science which appears superstitious to moderns but in the Renaissance might be indistinguishable from the former. This is described by Guazzo as "no more than a more exact knowledge of the secrets of Nature, which by observing the courses and influences of the stars in the heavens, and the sympathies and antipathies subsisting between separate things, compares one thing with another and so effects marvels which to the ignorant seem to be miracles or illusions." [73] Between both these kinds of operations and witchcraft was something else which might either be condemned as witchcraft or exalted as the highest level of active wisdom. This involved the powers not of devils (διάβολοι) but of daemons (δαίμονες). The existence of such spirits, intermediate between men and gods, had been vouched for by the newly recovered Hermetic *corpus,* but the spirits were in fact vestigial from paganism, which had sensed *numina* everywhere, and perhaps the Christian consciousness had never totally lost contact with them. Such daemons might be friendly, indifferent, or hostile, the hostile ones being no doubt identical with the fallen angels or devils, the friendly ones good angels (for example, the Intelligences or tutelary angels of the planets), and the indifferent ones quasi-automatic forces which differed from the natural energies known to modern science chiefly in being somewhat personalized. Whether attempts to constrain the help of good or indifferent daemons were licit was vigorously debated, but traffic with the unfriendly daemons was almost universally condemned as *goëtia,* or black magic. No matter what protestations of innocence might be made by the black magician, the consensus of informed opinion was that he entered into an implicit pact with the Devil, however unwittingly, just as the white witch or "wise-woman" did. If so, he too was a witch. Usually, however, the witch made an explicit pact, agreeing to yield his soul ultimately to the Devil in exchange for extraordinary powers during his lifetime.

The connection between witchcraft and the pact is, so far as I know, accepted by all modern students of the subject and is such a commonplace in the Renaissance treatises that no purpose would be served by massive documentation. "Magicians use superstitious and diabolical arts and add the evocation of demons to their practices, as Proclus has witnessed." [74] Or, again, in an especially comprehensive and authoritative tract, *prohibita Magia* is defined as "a faculty or art by means of which, through the force of a pact entered into with demons, wonders are performed which surpass the common apprehension of men." [75] And so everywhere. To be sure, complications are created by technicalities in the vocabulary. Such words as *magi, lamiae, sagae, praestigiatores, fascinatores, striges, venefici,* and *malefici* vary in significance from tract to tract, so that attention must be paid to the ways in which they are differentiated. The link between the witch and the Devil, or a devil, is, however, regularly taken for granted and was the chief basis for the savage attempts made to destroy the offenders against God and men.

No understanding of the way minds worked over the subject is possible without some realization of what scholarship was like in the Renaissance. The unexceptionable authority of the Scripture has been noticed; what remains to be considered is the nature of non-Scriptural "proof."

First, many of the authors of treatises on witchcraft are extremely learned men, but learned in a way that requires description. To the modern scholar it may at first appear that Renaissance savants had limited responsibilities which he may contrast enviously with his own. For them Latin did duty also for German, French, Italian, and English, or whichever of these languages were not native to them, and because they paid little attention to secular literature (except the classics) they felt no need to study such historical vernaculars as Old French, Middle High German, Anglo-Saxon, and Middle English. Further, whole areas of intensive modern research were unknown to them—for example, psychology in its modern forms, the exact sciences apart from a rather elementary mathematics, even history as that is now understood. Most important of all, they were necessarily unaware of whatever has happened since the Renaissance, to which modern students must devote an immense proportion of their schooling. We realize, of course, that their mastery of Latin was far greater than ours; we know that Greek had come in (though real competency in it was less widely diffused than is generally thought); and we are aware that theology and the scholastic philosophy were complex, if possibly not very rewarding, disciplines. Specialists have learned also that Hebrew and Rabbinical studies were beginning to be undertaken.

What we cannot know until we actually immerse ourselves in the Neo-Latin writings of the period is how enormous the literature was and how thoroughly, in course of time, ancient and medieval texts were combed for citations bearing upon special interests. A typical list of "authorities"—many, no doubt, second or third-hand—may help to suggest both the gradual accumulation of scholarly resources and the impact upon modern readers. Leonardo Vairo, in an interesting and ultimately rather skeptical document about enchantments (including the evil eye) called *De fascino libri tres* (1583), supports his assertions that "nearly all authors, not merely Latins and Arabs but also Greeks," accepted the reality of *fascinum* by citing Aristotle, Alexander Aphrodisiensis, Plutarch, Heliodorus, Isigonus, Pliny, Nymphodorus, Apollonides, Philarchus, Algazel, Avicenna, Pomponatius, Solinus, Philostratus, Virgil, Ioannes Franciscus Ponzinibius, and Petrus de Tarantasia at one burst before slowing down in order to bring in others more at leisure.[76] The list is in no way unusual. According to H. C. Lea, Guazzo's *Compendium,* already several times quoted here, cites 322 sources.[77] Scot cites 224 "forren authors" and 23 English.[78] Jean Wier's *De prestigiis* cites 342 authors.[79] In reading a treatise by Delrio or Bodin or Lavater or Remy one has the impression of following the processes of a mind which is not only (usually; Remy is perhaps an exception) highly intelligent and responsible but also impressively well-read.

And Saul perceived that it was Samuel, and he stooped with his face to the ground, and bowed himself. —1st Samuel. Chap: 28. v. 14.
W. Faithorne. fecit.

Joseph Glanvil, *Saducismus Triumphatus: or, Full and Plain Evidence Concerning Witches and Apparitions,* 2d ed. [London]: S. Lownds, 1682, frontispiece.

Samuel appearing to Saul when called up by the "woman that hath a familiar spirit," the Witch of Endor. For the story see *I Samuel,* 28: 7–25. The Witch stands at the right; Samuel, although he appears to be kneeling, is presumably "rising." ("And the woman said unto Saul, I saw gods ascending out of the earth. And he said unto her, What form is he of? And she said, an old man cometh up; and he is covered with a mantle. And Saul perceived that it was Samuel . . ." —Ibid., 13–14.) An oddly inconsistent detail is the gauntlets on the table, placed in such a way as to suggest a common fraud: the subject is made to believe he is holding the medium's hands when in fact they are free to ring bells, knock on the table, etc.

What marks a critical difference from modern scholarship is a set of distinct presumptions about evidence. In part the Renaissance scholar used his sources exactly as his modern counterpart does, balancing one set against another or supporting his own views by multiple citations of writers who agreed with him. Again as in modern scholarship, references might be given in the text (*secundum Isidor. 8 Ety. c. 9*) or put into the margin (*Aug. Civ. Dei XIV cap. iij*); or they might be general—for instance, "If you read *Artemidorus,*" or *uti Peripatetici asseruerunt,* or the remark that although the origin of magic is often ascribed to Zoroaster there were several men of that name—four (Arnobius), five (Suidas), or six (Pliny). Nothing of this causes the modern student acute intellectual distress despite the fact that he would often appreciate a more exact reference, is unable to expand the abbreviations, or feels a galling sense that he is expected to be far more learned than he is. The real differences lie elsewhere.

One simple, although inadequate, explanation would be that the modern historical scholar tends rather to use the assertions of remote authors as source materials for an understanding of their periods than to think of basing his own serious opinions on them. In the search for objective truth his ultimate commitment is not to distinguished minds but to the empirical evidence on which they have based their conclusions. In the Renaissance too some weight was given to "experience." Indeed, many of the tracts on witchcraft put primary emphasis on what someone claimed to have witnessed directly. What is lacking is the concept of controlled experiment; and, for the rest, statements were taken seriously that the twentieth-century mind would not dream either of believing or of finding it necessary to refute. The two halves of this sentence may be developed briefly, the latter half being considered first.

The taking of an opinion seriously does not, of course, require agreement with it. When Delrio denies to rings, seals, "characters," and images a magical power attributed to them by Ptolemy, Porphyry, and others [80] he does nothing in the least unusual. After all, views were often contradictory, and it was impossible then, as now, to credit all of them. In the same way the assertions of more recent men are often denied, as when the same writer advises us to be wary of Cornelius Agrippa, the unknown author of the *Picatrix,* Paracelsus, Roger Bacon, the Arabian alchemist Geber, Raymond Lull, Arnold of Villanova, Thomas Bungey (*sic*.), and George Ripley.[81] And yet the faith given to mere statement is not merely astonishing but sometimes shocking. Although the Renaissance intelligence might be sharply critical, its grounds of belief were not those accepted today.

How this worked can be seen, for example, in Gian-Francesco Pico's *La Strega, ovvero Degli Inganni de' Demone,*[82] a work written in Latin but now hardly accessible except in translation, where a discussion of the possibility that a witch might copulate with a demon is settled by a reminder that Anchises, Semele, Tiresias, and others were punished for having had sexual union with pagan gods.[83] Similarly, Ulric Molitor, in *De lamiis et phitonicis mulieribus,* gives as evidence for the power of witches to transform men into animals the turning of Ulysses' men into beasts by Circe and the metamorphosis recorded in *The Golden Ass* of Lucius Apuleius.[84] If the treatises were self-consciously belletristic one might imagine such citations to be intended as mere showmanship or perhaps as wit or irony, but they often stand side by side with equally incredible evidence drawn from popular rumor or the lives of the saints and appear to be similarly credited. Sometimes the use of an authority is curious in a different way, as when Boguet, in a passage about the lenient treatment of a young witch, says, "This is in agreement with the words of Lucan: 'But we forgive him for his tender age.'"[85] Is this no more than a rhetorical flourish? Apparently not; the consideration that Lucan was a pagan, a poet, and no "authority," for any reason that can readily be imagined, in matters pertaining to ethics or the law is apparently thought to be irrelevant.

It does not, I think, follow that for Renaissance scholars poetry was indistinguishable from factual history or that because they accepted the reality of witchcraft they must have had literal faith in everything Apuleius and Homer and Virgil had written. The epistemological situation was a good deal more complex. A hint of the

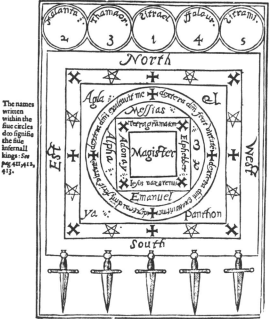

414 15.Booke. The difcouerie Necromancie.

A figure or type proportionall, fhewing what forme muft be
obferued and kept, in making the figure whereby
the former fecret of inclofing a fpirit in chriftall
is to be accomplifhed, &c.

The names
written
within the
fiue circles
doo fignifie
the fiue
infernall
kings: See
pag.411,412,
413.

Reginald Scot, *The Discouerie of Witchcraft* (London: 1584), p. 414.

A conjuring circle to be used while imprisoning a spirit in· a crystal (which could easily be carried in a pocket). The magician of course is to stand at the center. In the inner square are inscribed four of the divine names, and between the square and the circle are four more, "Alpha" "and Omega" counting as two. In the rim of the circle are the repeated phrases "The right hand of the Lord has created strength" and "The right hand of the Lord has exalted me." In the corners outside the circle are four additional names of God; the border of crosses and stars suggests Christ and astrological influences. The circles at the top contain the names of "the fiue infernall kings," Melanta, Thamaor, Zitrael, Falaur, and Zitrami. The daggers at the bottom presumably imply a threat to devils who may wish to take advantage of the conjuror.

contemporary attitude toward such citations is given us by Pico when, toward the end of his dialogue, he causes his skeptical disputant, Apistio or Faithless, to come round to a better conviction with these words: "Do you think that I believe to be mere jests what is agreed on by all the ancients and moderns, to which assent is given by poets, rhetoricians, stoics, jurists, philosophers, theologians, prudent men, soldiers, and peasants, and taken also from experience?" [86] Although by themselves such pagan fictions might have proved little, they corroborated other evidence and hence in some degree contributed to persuasion. Even in this diminished role, however, they had an importance which would be denied them by modern thought. And authors like these are quoted often enough without external parallels to qualify somewhat the degree of skepticism toward them which has just been implied.

The other difference from modern scholarship, that having to do with the weight accorded first-hand observation, is also complex. As has been said, the importance of experience is granted, especially by Sprenger and Kramer, Boguet, Remy, and others who drew on a rich fund of testimony given at actual trials. Guazzo is particularly full of stories—so much so that for the student of literature his treatise is likely to be the most interesting of all, partly but not merely because it contains parallels for incidents encountered elsewhere—for example, in Marlowe's *Doctor Faustus*. Like the citations of "authorities," however, the arguments from experience would carry little or no conviction in a modern court of law.

The reason is that the evidence is seldom critically evaluated, or not carefully enough questioned to satisfy the modern intelligence. So far as I can recall, the only attempts at a real experimental corroboration involved the observation of sleeping witches to see whether they actually left their beds at times when they reported having attended nocturnal Sabbats. (It was regularly discovered that they did not.) For the rest, when it was not limited to seeing—for example—whether a prisoner really had an odd patch on her skin or the patch really was insensitive to pain, "proof" often consisted in accumulating additional stories of a similar kind, the assumption being that where there was a great deal of smoke there must necessarily have been fire.

One explanation of the tendency to avoid tests no doubt is to be found in the illicit and horrible nature of the witch's magical practices. It was unthinkable that an inquisitor should smear himself with a salve which was said to permit flying through the air, sometimes in the form of an animal, or perhaps even that he should try out on a cat the effect of an allegedly magical powder made from the body of a murdered child. But, indeed, the Baconian method had not yet been distinctly formulated during much of the period, and when it was clearly stated it had to wait a long time for acceptance. So the accusations of hysterical or malicious or superstitious neighbors were allowed to pile up until they created a presumption of guilt encouraged by the whole tenor of theological and scholarly thought and sealed finally by a confession wrung from the prisoner by torture or other pressures. "Experience" thus consisted largely of old wives' tales, the marvels connected with the immediate situation being accepted as probable because they resembled others reported by the "authorities" from different times and places.

An extreme illustration appears in the relatively early *Malleus*, where we read that "as William of Paris says in his *De Uniuerso,* it is proved by experience that if a harlot tries to plant an olive it does not become fruitful, whereas if it is planted by a chaste woman it is fruitful." [87] Here, surely, experimentation could have done no harm; but no disposition appears to test the belief by watching, let us say, twenty trees set out by known harlots and twenty others set out by women in whose virtue trust was felt. Reiterated report is enough. The same author offers as proof that devils can produce visual illusions a commonplace story originally told by St. Gregory of a woman who thought she was eating lettuce but instead ate a devil in the form of a lettuce or, possibly, invisible within it. [88] Here a generalization is corroborated by a case history, reassurance being supplied to the incredulous by an acknowledgment of the source (St. Gregory's first dialogue). The doubter could check the story for himself. He was not expected to ask "How do you know it was the lettuce?" or "May she not merely have been crazy?" If one such story was thought insufficient, a second and third and fourth were added, until at last acceptance could no longer be withheld. When the emphasis was on modern instances the scholarly method was similar. Guazzo illustrates the Devil's habit of giving his votaries money which changes into coal, or charred clay, or pig's dung, or a rusty pebble by four stories dated 1586, one dated 1585, and one dated 1587, all six being vouched for, he says, in the courts of justice.[89] For the rest, "experience" is sometimes claimed as the basis for a truism: "It is also a matter of common experience that the tongue of one prudent man can subdue the wrangling of a multitude." [90] No wonder the Archduke Sigismund of Austria, one of the speakers in Molitor's *De lamiis,* preferred argument to evidence: "I myself do not believe in public rumors, for common people easily credit whatever is said." He asked that the existence of witches be "demonstrated by authorities and by the force of reason, since a well-handled discussion ought to lead to a rational conclusion." [91] Alas, "authorities" and "proofs from experience" were all too often ultimately indistinguishable because the latter included stories borrowed trustingly from the former.

What has been said should not be understood to imply that no skepticism can be found in the documents. On the contrary, there is a great deal: so much, in fact, that one realizes only a sound investigative method was needed to initiate an era of brilliant intellectual progress. And that was to come, but not quickly. In the meantime, the writers on witchcraft might be placed fairly accurately on a scale ranging from very credulous to hard-headed. At one end we find, for example, Guazzo, who was capable of writing, "We often find lying about the shrines of the Saints fragments of thunderbolts which are believed to have been wielded and hurled by some demon." [92] In the same half of the spectrum appear Sprenger and Kramer, Boguet, Remy, Bodin—despite his distinction in other intellectual areas— Gian-Francesco Pico, who nevertheless wrote a slashing attack on astrology, and Hopkins. In the other and more honorable half are von Spee, Vairo, Johann (or John, or Jean) Wier, George Gifford, and Reginald Scot. Somewhere between come James I of England, Giovanni Anania, Delrio, Thomas Erastus, Joseph Glanville, Godelmann, Lavater, and Molitor. Notwithstanding what now seem to have been lapses into fideism, the members of the intermediate group often show intellectual power, and some of them are attractive writers. The tonality of many, as has been said, is cool and reasonable. Attention must be paid to the intellectual milieu when rendering moral and intellectual judgments. Not even the most bloodthirsty—the authors of the *Malleus,* Remy, Boguet, Bodin—appear to me, at least, as benighted as the Rev. Montague Summers, who although a modern was ready to credit almost

400 15.Booke. The discouerie Art of coniuring.

The characters of the angels of the seauen daies, with their names: of figures, seales and periapts.

The seuenth Chapter.

Michael.

Gabriel.

Samael.

Raphael.

Sachiel.

Anael.

Cassiel.

These figures are called the seales of the earth, without the which no spirit will appeere, except thou haue them with thee.

Reginald Scot, *The Discouerie of Witchcraft* (London: 1584), p. 400.

The seven days of the week are assigned to the seven angels whose names appear. The "figures, seales and periapts" (periapts are charms worn about the body) are given, and after them the names of planets and zodiacal signs: for Michael, the sun and Leo; for Gabriel, the moon and Cancer; for Samael, Mars, Aries, and Scorpio; for Raphael, Mercury, Gemini, and Virgo; for Sachiel, Jupiter, Sagittarius, and Pisces; for Anael, Venus, Taurus, and Libra; for Cassiel, Saturn, Capricorn and Aquarius.

The circle at bottom left contains some of the innumerable Hebrew and Greek names of God. The triangle symbolizes the Trinity, with other magical words along the sides. The figure at bottom right also contains obscure words, although "Alpha and Omega" and, opposite, "Aries, Leo" present no difficulty. The figures are "seales of the earth, without the which no spirit will appeere"; but skepticism emerges in "except thou haue them with thee."

any story, no matter how absurd, which tended to justify his spiritualistic preassumptions. The worst is Matthew Hopkins, the notorious witchfinder; but since his interest was financial, his intellect hardly comes into question.[93] How the skepticism operated will become clear as we proceed.

The means to the acquisition of magical powers, as has been said, was the making of a pact with the Devil, who might appear, in theory, because he was invoked, as in the Faust legend, but who in the documents himself almost always initiated the conversation. What the pact involved is explained with special fullness by Guazzo. The witches (1) deny Christ, (2) undergo a mock baptism, (3) receive a new name, (4) deny their godparents and are given new ones, (5) give the Devil a piece of their clothing, (6) swear allegiance to him, (7) pray to be struck out of the book of life and inscribed in the book of death, (8) promise sacrifices to the Devil, (9) make yearly gifts to him, (10) receive his mark—at least many do—and (11) vow not to honor the Eucharist, to blaspheme, to abstain from holy water and blessed salt, and to attend the Sabbats. All this is prepared for by "some sympathy in wickedness between the witches and the devil."[94]

Other descriptions, when not briefer, vary in detail but agree in essentials. According to Godelmann, for instance, magicians (a common synonym for "witches") "knowingly turn to daemons, enter into a pact with them, worship them as GOD, beg their help and counsel, and evoke and attract them by magical ceremonies and the recitation of words, whether barbarous and meaningless to them or understood by them, together with monstrous figures (*characteribus*), images, prayers, and execrations." In making the pact the witch must "First, horrible though it is to say, renounce GOD his Creator and rescind the treaty made with Him in holy baptism, deny the Son of God, curse His good deeds (*beneficia*), attack His name with blasphemies, reproaches, and contumely, adore the Devil alone, place all faith and hope in him, follow his commands zealously, and use things created by GOD only for the injury and destruction of men. Afterwards, having died at the appointed time, he must grant his body and soul to the Devil: some swearing all this by the name of a familiar demon, whereas others are driven to make the promise in handwriting, using their own blood." The Devil, in return, agrees to come when called, give counsel, offer help in wrongdoing, answer questions, free his follower from dangers and prisons, give him riches, satisfy his desires, and, finally, serve his will like a slave, doing diligently whatever is required. Once the ceremonies are completed the Devil instructs his new convert either himself or through practised magicians and books, revealing to him how he should perform his operations, draw monstrous figures, carve seals (*sigilla*), fashion images of wax and metal, and make evil uses of roots, stones, metals, earths (*terras*), bones, hairs, and the like.[95] As was said earlier, the pact might be implicit instead of explicit. A magician who thought he had used the Devil might find in the end that the Devil had used him, that in accepting help he had unknowingly made a commitment of his soul. In one form or another, however, the pact was an—indeed, *the*—essential part of witchcraft.

Curiously—the discovery may be quite unexpected—the greater the theorist's skepticism the more emphasis he is likely to put on the Devil's part in all the mischief. Thus Vairo, who makes a sudden change of direction in Book II after seeming almost illimitably credulous in Book I ("I would have fallen into the reader's hate and ill will if on the threshold of this work I had wished to call into doubt an opinion of enchantment accepted by men, including common people"),[96] affirms that everything is done by demons and nothing at all by any other power. What makes this possible is the demons' exceptional knowledge: "They have very great understanding of all things, for they are acquainted with the virtues of the heavens, the stars, birds, fish, trees, plants, metals, stones, and especially the elements and are aware what can help or injure man. . . . Thus the demons do by means of natural poisons what the enchanters think they accomplish by means of their eyes or other instruments."[97] Similar explanations appear in other treatises. Such skills, we are assured, result from the devils' former status as angels and from their studies of the universe during the long ages since their fall. In this way magic becomes a kind of natural science which produces its effects not by mumbo-jumbo but by expert manipulation of the hidden properties of objects.

The appearance of the Devil, whether invoked or voluntary, might be in the form of a speaking animal—a dog, a goat, a cat, or some other—but more usually was that of an imperfect man. According to Remy, his features were dark and shapeless, his eyes deep-set and flashing, his mouth wide and smelling of sulphur, his hands and feet deformed: "for Demons can never so completely ape the human shape but that the deception is apparent to even the most stupid." [98] The hands may be claw-like, the feet hoofs. Their voices, we are told by the same expert, are thin and indistinct. A witch's testimony taken on March 28, 1588, was that they spoke "as if their mouths were in a jar or cracked pitcher." [99] One reason is that they must manipulate air without the use of lungs, throats, palates, or "sides"; but they always speak idiomatic vernacular.[100] We are sometimes informed that the indistinctness is deliberate, its purpose being the same as the ambiguity of oracular pronouncements. The stench is said by Remy to be invariable, and he adds that witches are instructed to avoid cleanliness and not to wash their hands lest the efficacy of their incantations be obstructed. Indeed, hand-washing is often an effective protection for an intended victim.[101]

The existence of demons and their motives for tampering with men are usually taken for granted in the treatises but occasionally explained. Anania, in *Natura daemonum,* gives in some detail particulars which were too well known to need constant repetition. In the beginning all the angels were created on the first day along with the heavens (*sub caeli nomine*), as is shown by the text *quando facta sunt sydera, laudauerent me angeli.* All the angels were perfect and all were content; but they differed among themselves in qualities without any of them suffering from insufficiency of a kind to induce a fall. Of the three classes, none was so inferior to the others in excellence, wisdom, or freedom of the will that it was unable to stand. The fall therefore was voluntary. Moved by instability of mind and swollen with pride, Lucifer said, "I will place my seat in the north, and I will be like the highest." His sin was the most execrable of all possible sins because it was committed wholly without occasion. A battle ensued, Michael acting as leader of the good angels, though where it was fought, or how long, is uncertain. The event was the expulsion of the demons from heaven. Some fell to Tartarus, but others of greater strength (*pars uero altera eaque potior*) to "this dark and icy air which surrounds us." Hence the Devil's temptation of Eve and Adam in the form of a serpent and the constant interference of demons in human affairs ever since.[102] The story is familiar to students of English literature from Milton's *Paradise Lost* and would not require even a quick summary if in this age of secular education and a dying,

Ulricus Molitor, *De lamiis et phitonicis mulieribus* (Strassburg: J. Prüss, ca. 1488–1493), p. 174.

Witches causing hailstorms and thunder. Opposite, in black letter type, appears the question, *An possint provocare demones grandines et tonitrua* ("Can demons cause hailstorms and thunder?"). The demons do not appear in the drawing but would be responsible for the effects. The witch on the right is putting a snake into the conjuring pot, that on the left what appears to be a cock.

"existentialist" Christianity knowledge of it was not rapidly disappearing—even, one fears, among the clergy.

In a longer discussion it would be interesting to follow with some care theories of the beginnings of human magic—magic, it will be remembered, being often synonymous with witchcraft. Here space allows only the offering of a few hints. Wier attributes the earliest practice of sorcery to Mizraim, son of Ham, whom Noah had cursed after having been seen naked in his drunkenness. Mizraim was "the first who discovered the impiety, full of blasphemies, of an execrable magic," and from him the black art descended to the Egyptians, the Babylonians, and the Persians.[103] The *Malleus* quotes Vincent de Beauvais as having reported in his *Speculum historiale* that Zoroaster, "who is said to have been Cham, the son of Noe," was the first magician and astrologer.[104] Other authorities emphasized the importance of Moses, who according to the *Cabala* had been given esoteric knowledge as well as the Law on Mt. Sinai, or, in another version, learned magic of the Egyptians, known from the story of their competition with Moses before Pharaoh to have been able to perform marvels. In either account it was assumed that Moses's magic was white and

Pierre de Lancre, *Tableau de l'inconstance des mauvais anges* (Paris: Nicolas Buon, 1613), facing p. 118.

Portrayal of the witches' Sabbat. At *A* Satan, in the form of a ram, is seated on a throne. Beneath, a witch and a subsidiary demon present a child to him. In the foreground, two witches about to chop up a frog preside over a cauldron which sends up a smoke in which witches and perhaps a warlock are arriving, on broomsticks or animals, for the obscene ritual. In the left margin initiates are dancing back to back, naked; in the opposite margin devils and human beings are dancing together. At the banquet in the lower righthand corner a dismembered child appears in a dish.

that the perversion of it came later. King James, who in his *Daemonologie* often reasons shrewdly, rejects vigorously the opinion that the mature Moses practised forbidden magic.

> For first, that that generall proposition; affirming *Moyses* to be taught *in all the sciences of the Ægyptians,* should conclude that he was taught in *Magie,* I see no necessity. For we must vnderstand that the spirit of God there, speaking of sciences, vnderstandes them that are lawfull. . . . Secondlie, giuing that he had bene taught in it, there is great difference, betwixt knowledge and practising of a thing (as I said before). For God knoweth all thinges, being alwaies good. . . . Thirdlie, giuing that he had both studied and practised the same (which is more nor monstruous to be beleeued by any Christian) yet we know well inough . . . that suppose he had beene the wickeddest man in the worlde before, he . . . became a changed and regenerat man.[105]

In one way or another the beginning of magic is, however, regularly pushed back to a remote antiquity. The presence of Satan in the Garden of Eden implied the activity of devils among men from the time of the first parents.

Since discussions of the origin of magic never, so far as I am aware, speak explicitly of the appearance of the Devil and the swearing of a pact with him, further discussion of them would be digressive. It may be added, however, that the fall of the bad angels was sometimes said to be corroborated by pagan stories: "Not only do our theologians and those of the Hebrews show us this fall, but the Assyrians, the Arabs, the Egyptians, and the Greeks confirm it in their writings. . . . Trismegistus describes the same fall in his *Pimander*." [106] Non-Christian literature thus corroborated Christian truth and threw additional light on it. Guazzo probably drew from Hermetism when he listed six distinct kinds of daemons—fiery, aerial, terrestrial, aquatic, subterranean, and lucifugous or light-fleeing.[107]

III. Witches' activities

Once the pact had been entered upon, what kinds of sorcery did the witches perform? The *Malleus* gives a convenient list:

> They raise hailstorms and hurtful tempests and lightnings; cause sterility in men and animals; offer to devils, or otherwise kill, the children whom they do not devour. But these are only the children who have not been reborn by baptism at the font, for they cannot devour those who have been baptized, nor any without God's permission. They can also, before the eyes of their parents, but without being seen, throw into the water children walking by the water side; they make horses go mad under their riders; they can transport themselves from place to place through the air, either in body or in imagination; they can affect Judges and Magistrates so that they cannot

Ulricus Molitor, *De lamiis et phitonicis mulieribus* (Strassburg: J. Prüss, ca. 1488–93), p. 180.

A witches' feast. The subtitle on the opposite page reads *An super lupum vel baculum unctum ad convivia veniant et mutuo comedant et bibant et sibi mutuo loquantur ac se invicem agnoscant* ("Can [witches] come to feasts on a wolf or an anointed stick, eat, drink, speak together, and recognize one another?"). Here all that is shown is the eating.

hurt them; they can cause themselves and others to keep silence under torture; they can bring about a great trembling in the hands and horror in the minds of those who would arrest them; they can show to others occult things and certain future events . . . ; they can see absent things as if they were present; they can turn the minds of men to inordinate love or hatred; they can at times strike whom they will with lightning, and even kill some men and animals; they can make of no effect the generative desires, and even the power of copulation, cause abortion, kill infants in the mother's womb by a mere exterior touch; they can at times bewitch men and animals with a mere look, without touching them, and cause death; they dedicate their own children to devils.[108]

Of such actions as these one reads constantly in the treatises.

But there are others too; comprehensive as it may appear, the description is incomplete. I add details from an account given by Scot in his *Discoverie*. Witches can

> pull downe the moone and the starres. . . . send needles into the livers of their enimies. . . . transferre corne in the blade from one place to another. . . . cure dis-

eases supernaturallie, flie in the aire, and danse with divels. . . . plaie the part of *Succubus,* and contract themselves to *Incubus.* . . . transsubstantiate themselves and others, and take the forms and shapes of asses, woolves, ferrets, cowes, apes, horsses, dogs, &c. . . . keep divels and spirits in the likenesse of todes and cats . . . raise spirits (as others affirme) drie up springs, turne the course of running waters, in-hibit the sunne, and staie both day and night, changing the one into the other. . . . go in and out at awger holes, & saile in an egge shell, a cockle or muscle shell. . . . bring soules out of the graves. . . . teare snakes in peeces with words, and with looks kill lambes. . . . bring to passe, that chearne as long as you list, your butter will not come.[109]

With these supplementations the explanation is reasonably full.

The actual ceremonies by which malicious intentions were carried out need not be dwelt on. The reports of trials give us vivid, if untrustworthy, glimpses of witches, in nine cases out of ten women (because of the widely asserted weakness and special ignorance of their sex), muttering curses, fashioning and then mutilating images, planting charms beneath doorsills, causing rainstorms by beating water in a bowl or stream or their own urine evacuated into a hole dug in the ground, spreading powders, boiling the bodies of children preparatory to drinking the broth and mak-ing an unguent out of the "more solid parts," mixing poisons, injuring by touch, fascinating by the evil eye, murdering infants with needles, sending toads or cats or other small animals on evil errands, or, very frequently, merely assenting to a demon's offer to bring trouble upon an enemy, or his family, or his cattle. The formal invocation of the Devil by the drawing of a magic circle, the inscribing within it of triangles whose corners are filled with cabalistic figures and the names of de-mons, and the uttering of Latin formulas, as in Marlowe's and Goethe's versions of the Faust story, is rarely heard of and never, I think, confessed. Evidently the learned tradition of black magic existed quite separately from the practice of vulgar witches, whose illiteracy in any case would have made it inaccessible to them. In this respect modern stories of witchcraft—for example, Charles Williams's in *All Hallows' Eve*— are quite unfaithful to the records of actual prosecutions, which in England involved almost without exception, and on the continent very often, persons whose social status was low. In the same way modern Satanist cults, as in San Francisco, draw upon late and imaginative, rather than historical, sources. But in one respect there is contact: the treatises have much to say about the witches' Sabbats, which with elegant additions like the use of a naked girl's belly as an altar appear to be imitated by modern covens. These deserve separate consideration.

For two reasons at least, a prurient interest and a desire to implicate additional persons (together, on the continent, with greed to seize more property), the inquisi-tors or examining magistrates seem to have inquired into their prisoners' attendance

Ulricus Molitor, *De lamiis et phitonicis mulieribus* (Strassburg: J. Prüss, ca. 1488–1493), p. 164.

Witches transformed into animals. The subtitle on the opposite page is *Utrum possit facies hominum in alias formas immutare* ("Can the human form be changed into other shapes?"). Such transformations were thought to occur especially when, as here, witches mounted sticks to fly to their Sabbats.

at the Sabbats with special eagerness. Although witches may occasionally have met to trade secrets and boast about their achievements—some kind of actual conference is strongly implied by Thomas Potts' report of the testimony at the Lancashire trials in 1612 [110]—most of the accounts are purely imaginary, the details having been suggested to the accused women in the way von Spee has described. The fact, already once mentioned, that in Latin countries, and particularly in Italy, the central figure was Diana or Herodias, the *donna* or *signora*,[111] whereas in other places it was the Devil or a devil, is significant. The witches confessed what their judges expected to hear because doing so promised an end to their sufferings. It is in fact precisely such agreements on matters now regarded as impossible that bring the findings at the trials most strongly into doubt. Of the 800 or 900 witches sent to the stake by Remy, "some two hundred persons, more or less," admitted meeting with other witches at some pool or stream, raising clouds from it by which they were borne aloft and carried wherever they would, and at last causing the clouds to fall as hail.[112] Elsewhere the raising of storms was separate from transvection.[113] However obtained, the descriptions of the Sabbat all have a family resemblance.

The Sabbats seem not to have been very enjoyable. Having arrived at the meeting place by flying through the air on sticks, or on the back of a devil transformed into an animal, or by changing themselves into animals, the witches performed obscene rites of worship, often kissing the Devil's buttocks beneath his tail. They reported on the evil they had accomplished and were praised or scolded in proportion as it was great or small. They danced, usually naked, back to back, and moving to the left, no one being excused because of age or infirmity. They ate a disgusting meal which gave them no sustenance. Finally, they engaged in promiscuous sexual intercourse.

Details are provided richly. Remy says of the banquet, in a typical description, that the food is loathsome and nauseating and fails to satisfy hunger. Sometimes it is mere illusion; again it is real but is made from animals which have died or are otherwise unclean. But bread (used in the Eucharist) and salt (used in Old Testament sacrifices and apparently also in baptism and in holy water) are always lacking.[114] The dances were terribly fatiguing,[115] and we sometimes learn that after the Sabbats witches spent several days in bed recuperating. A popular modern belief that the number of witches in every group or coven was twelve or thirteen is quite

Ulricus Molitor, *De lamiis et phitonicus mulieribus* (Strassburg: J. Prüss, ca. 1488-1493), p. 170.

A devil making lubricious advances to a woman. The subtitle (overleaf) is *Utrum diabolus in forma hominis apparere et cum huiusmodi maledictis mulieribus incubando possit commisceri* ("Can a devil appear in the form of a man and, by lying with cursed women of this type, have intercourse with them?"). The devil is identified by his tail, his feet, and his grotesque mouth; otherwise the picture is decorous.

unsubstantiated by the documents. On the continent we hear of very large numbers; Pico, for example, affirms that as many as 2,000 might be present,[116] and nowhere, to my knowledge, is a standard number distinctly mentioned.

An issue raised into prominence by Margaret Murray's *The Witch-Cult in Western Europe* (Oxford: Clarendon Press, 1921) is commented on by Pico: is Christian magic continuous with pagan (in England, perhaps, with Druidic)? Dicaste, an inquisitor, is asked whether the "games" of Diana or of the Herodiades were the same as those heard of in the sixteenth century. The reply is, "Some people say yes, and others prefer the view that they are a new heresy." The questioner then gives his own opinion, that some of the games are ancient and some the result of a new superstition, so that one might say that on the whole they are "antique in essence and new by accident (to speak in the modern idiom)." [117] So far as it goes, the judgment is commonsensical: sorcery has certainly been practised in all societies, and no doubt because at bottom the human psyche is always the same its forms tend to be similar. But to argue that *in detail* Renaissance witchcraft was identical with pre-Christian, or even that, in any very meaningful sense, pagan sorcery—which did not know the Christian Devil—was its source, is to assert as fact what in the absence of sufficient evidence can, at most, be no more than hypothesis.

These, then, are the essentials of witchcraft: a meeting with the Devil (or a devil; the lack of an article in Latin, together with different conventions of capitalization, makes the distinction often impossible), a pact to deny God, the performing of evil deeds, and occasional or regular attendance at the Sabbat. From the reports of trials one gathers that most of the witches really acted in secret, muttering their charms, mutilating their clay images, and dispensing their powders or potions without the knowledge of anyone except, perhaps, their own children, who could be forced by orders or threats to help. (Hence it was concluded by the inquisitors that every child of a witch was almost certainly also a witch.) Occasionally two or more witches might co-operate to bring harm upon a common enemy, and more rarely still a larger number might congregate to cackle together, but as social outcasts— "loners"—no doubt they usually hated and feared their rivals as well as their victims. In the main, they were probably poor old women with foggy minds who felt themselves abused and tried to strike back at oppressors by hexing them. Nevertheless the Sabbats were firmly established in the official theory and receive much attention in the documents.

IV. Steps toward the denial of witchcraft

Instead of dwelling longer on the practices, which unless poisons were used or the victim suffered psychological damage must have had no influence on the results thought to have been achieved, I turn to elements of the official theory which by implying skepticism were finally to lead to a denial of witchcraft itself.

First, it was essential that the charms themselves be thought ineffectual, that doubts arise about a universe so structured as to make enchantments operative. This step was taken with the emergence of a conviction that devils were the real agents of all the mischief. The demon was not constrained by the witch's rigamaroles but seized upon her ill will as an excuse to do injuries by which, because she had assented to them, his claim to her soul would be established. At the same time, of course, he would gain satisfaction from the exercise of his malevolence upon the immediate victims.

The conviction was shared even by so credulous a writer as Remy. That there is efficacy in the mere words of a curse or charm, he declared, "seems to me just as ridiculous and absurd as the similar belief in the virtue of written characters and letters. . . . How can it be possible for a mere vocal noise to act so powerfully?" [118] The power's true source was the demon.[119] Similarly, in the medicines and bewitched objects which apparently cause hurt or healing there is "no inherent or natural power either of hurting or of healing." However prodigious the result may seem, "it is all done by the Demons through some power of which the source and explanation is not known." [120]

The same belief appears in James I, whose insistence that witches exist and must be punished was qualified by a Scottish toughness of mind.

> . . . it is no power inherent in the circles, or in the holines of the names of God blasphemouslie vsed: nor in whatsoeuer rites or ceremonies at that time vsed, that either can raise any infernall spirit, or yet limitat him perforce within or without these circles. For it is he onelie, the father of all lyes, who hauing first of all prescribed that forme of doing, feining himself to be commanded & restreined thereby, wil be loath to passe the bounds of these injunctiones; aswell [*sic*] thereby to make them glory in the impiring ouer him (as I saide before:) As likewise to make himselfe so to be trusted in these little thinges, that he may haue the better commoditie thereafter, to decieue them in the end with a tricke once for all; I meane the euerlasting perdition of their soul & body.[121]

"The father of all lyes": the phrase was useful, since it encouraged the belief that, like nearly everything else the Devil said, his explanations of charms were deceptive. The causal result of enchanting was merely damage to the witch's soul. The rest of the evil was done not magically but quasi-naturally, by means known to devils though seeming marvelous to the more limited human intelligence.

The same explanation appears in other writers whose minds were even less critical. Guazzo, whose *Compendium* in long stretches is a compilation of the mostly wildly impossible stories, nevertheless affirms that demons are never constrained by rites or incantations but pretend to be in order to deceive and catch men.[122] The less gullible Gifford, whose *Dialogue Concerning Witches and Witchcraftes* throws gentle scorn on many current beliefs, says of the Devil that

> God giueth him power sometimes to afflict both men and beastes with bodily harmes: If he can, he will doe it, as intreated and sent by Witches, but for Vs to imagin either that their sending doth giue him power, or that he would not doe that which God hath giuen him leaue to doe, vnlesse they should request and send him, is most absurd.[123]

Boguet, although convinced like Remy and Guazzo that witch trials must be prosecuted vigorously, asserts that "For the most part the witch has only the intent to harm, whilst Satan actually performs that which he would have done." [124] Although witches' poisons are sometimes really harmful,[125] Satan "only works by secondary and natural causes." [126] The beating of water or the throwing of powder either does not produce hail or does so naturally, as a mixture of saltpeter with alum produces clouds and causes thunder and lightning.[127] Ointments and unguents do not cause transformations into the forms of beasts or permit flight through the air but merely stupefy.[128] The words of a conjuration "are no more than a symbol of the pact between the witch and Satan." [129] No injury can be caused merely by "looking," [130] by touching,[131] or by maltreating an image.[132] Among the relatively fideist authors, once more, Thomas Erastus concurs. Although the sorcerers are wrong in believing that conjurations have intrinsic power to constrain and in thinking that devils can give potency to materials and actions which by nature have no malevolent force, nevertheless they deserve to be punished because they furnish occasions to real devils to do ill.[133] The comparatively measured and sensible Delrio, who belongs to the middle group of limited believers in witchcraft, is also in accord. Thaumaturgy can "do nothing which is repugnant to the nature of things." If a bronze head of Albertus Magnus spoke, as rumor reported, "he spoke in the head who established oracles in the statues of idols: who was only an evil spirit." [134] The authors were, indeed, virtually unanimous on the point. Gian-Francesco Pico, who read thoroughly before writing his attack on astrology but had not done his homework on witchcraft, is one of the few exceptions.[135] And when so much was granted, the whole elaborate mythology was undermined at the base and would topple as soon as belief in the Devil ceased.

A second denial which formed part of the sophisticated theory had to do with delusions. Tricksters (*praestigiatores*), said Godelmann, "charm and deceive the eyes of men, by Satan's help, with incantations and illusions, so that they do not see things as they really are but think they see what is not there. These are properly called enchanters (*Zauberer*)." [136] Once achieved, this insight too spread through the whole area of inquiry and threatened to convert all the occult phenomena into sleight-of-hand or a kind of hypnosis.

How this worked can be seen in the discussions of physical transformation and of transvection. The two subjects will be considered separately.

The popular belief was that witches often turned themselves into cats, wolves, and other animals, sometimes in order to enter houses undetected, sometimes to make aerial voyages to the Sabbats, and sometimes for the purpose of killing or injuring their enemies' livestock. The theologians and jurists mostly agreed that the changes were only apparent. According to Guazzo, "no animal's soul can inform the human body, and no human soul an animal's body."[137] The transformation of Diomede's companions into birds was really a rapid substitution, as when a hind was made to replace Iphigenia.[138] Scot quotes in the margin *"Hermes Trismeg. in suo Periandro"* (for *Pimandro*) and writes in the text: "And yet *Hermes Trismegistus* thinketh he hath good authoritie and reason to saie: *Aliud corpus quàm humanum non capere animum humanam; nec fas esse in corpus animae ratione carentis animam rationalem corruere."*[139] Molitor demonstrates by means of authorities and a wild story that transformations of people into animals are mere appearance; and he gives as an instance the deluding of our senses in dreams and delirium.[140] Boguet gives a long series of tales about transformations[141] and then reverses his field to say, "Nevertheless it has always been my opinion that Lycanthropy is an illusion, and that the metamorphosis of a man into a beast is impossible." The reasoning soul given to man by God cannot enter an animal, and it is impossible to believe that the soul is restored when human shape is resumed because in the interval the soul would have no residence. What really happens is either that Satan "leaves the witch asleep behind a bush, and himself goes and performs that which the witch has in mind to do," causing her afterwards to think that she has done it, or, more frequently, "it is the witch himself who runs about slaying: not that he is metamorphosed into a wolf, but that it appears to him that he is so."[142] Hence the fatigue which the witch feels afterwards.[143] Nevertheless the witch is guilty, for he either has committed the crime or has wished to; and he never would have had the wish if he had not first renounced God and heaven.[144]

The same arguments appear in other treatises. Remy affirms that "it is not in the power of the Demon to effect any such matter. . . . For what madness it is to believe that anything which has been formed and created can destroy and overturn as it pleases the most excellent work of Him who created it."[145] The man can believe himself changed, and so will act as if he were the animal; or the demon can deceive the observer. At most Remy will admit that a witch can have the swiftness, strength, and ravenous appetite of, say, a wolf, so that the appearance may "differ but little from actuality."[146] Yet even this admission comes hard. The opinion of Joannes Althusius is the same: "I ask whether we shall think the deeds done by themselves or by the Devil when they confess that they have transformed themselves into wolves or other savage beasts?" The answer is that only God can change forms and essential properties.[147] Even Pico sides with the majority here. His Fronimo, who can swallow a great deal, at last gets round to admitting that such transformations as those described by Homer and Apuleius are devilish deceptions and not actual.[148]

Skepticism about transvection, or the power of witches to fly to distant places through the air, was less common. Remy says that witches sometimes really travel to the meetings either on foot or supernaturally, but sometimes they only dream or imagine they have been present. What is impossible is that the witch's soul should attend while her body remains in bed. (That this could be done was an article of the popular faith—a product, no doubt, of the fact that husbands rarely found themselves sleeping alone.) Whether the soul could leave the body, or the witch, by some "glamor" or illusion, could make a pillow or an armful of straw impersonate her during her absence, is frequently discussed in the treatises. On the whole, Remy concludes, "The commonest practice of all witches is to fly up the chimney," notwithstanding the smallness of the aperture, and to proceed in a basket, or on a reed, or broom, or pig, or bull, or dog, or forked stick, to the rendezvous.[149] The authors of the *Malleus* have no doubts at all. In a passage already quoted they ask, "Did not the devil take up Our Saviour, and carry Him up to a high place, as the Gospel testifies?" They counter the argument that a spirit is unable to move a physical body by reminding readers that "the highest bodies, that is, the stars, are moved by spiritual essences" (the Intelligences).[150] Boguet also cites the incident of the pinnacle and mentions transvections of "St. Philip, Ezekiel, Habakkuk, Elijah, Enoch, St. Antide Archbishop of Besançon, St. Ambrose, Pythagoras, the Philosopher of Tyana, and countless others." [151] Guazzo too is on the side of faith. The witch transports herself "on a cowl-staff, or a broom, or a reed, a cleft stick or a distaff, or even a shovel" after she has anointed herself with an ointment made "chiefly from murdered children"; or she may ride on an ox, a goat, or a dog. He also believes in the simulacra.[152] Those who doubt all this, he remarks severely, "certainly sin in lack of reverence to our Mother the Church." [153] Yet some did doubt, and by doing so contributed further to the final breakup of the entire conceptual syndrome.

Molitor, with Sprenger and Kramer one of the earliest writers, is already skeptical: quick journeys over great distances to the Sabbats are illusions even if shared by the witches.[154] Godelmann's view is the same: he thinks that stories of flights through the air are fables, and the unguents which are said to make transvection possible merely put the magicians to sleep. Further, witches cannot pass through cracks and crevices.[155] The best summary of attitudes is perhaps that although confessions drawn from accused persons by torture or heavy psychological pressure inhibited disbelief in the Sabbats themselves, and the Sabbats, being large assemblies,

P[ierre] Boaistua (or Launay): *Histoires prodigieuses extraictes de plusieurs fameux auteurs, Grecs & Latins* (Paris: Charles Macé, 1575), sig. 19*r*.

A portrait of a monster said to have been born at Cracow either in 1543 or in 1547 on the day of St. Paul's conversion. The eyes were fiery, the mouth and nose ox-like; there was a horn like an elephant's trunk; the back was hairy; monkeys' heads substituted for teats; there were cats' eyes above the navel and dogs' heads at the elbows and knees; the hands and feet were a monkey's. Since the monster lived only four hours, the picture must have been drawn from a verbal description. It is wrong, Boaistua says, to think such a monster a devil's child, for devils cannot engender on human beings. The cause is rather divine judgment, a "heated and obstinate imagination of the woman" while she conceives, "superabundance, or defect and corruption, in the seed," or some other such natural circumstance. (pp. 20-22, 14-16).

could not be held near every witch's home, so that some means had to be accepted of rapid transportation over distances, doubt of transvection had begun and was to spread along with disbelief in the rest of the alleged phenomena.

Another subject often discussed in the treatises is copulation between enchanters and demons. As succubus—the term *succuba* is rarely used, presumably because devils were thought actually to be sexless—the devil might receive a warlock's semen. Afterwards he became an incubus and discharged the semen into the body of a witch. Few theorists believed that devils themselves produced semen. They were disembodied spirits without corporeal substance. (Hence the generation of a true devil's child in a recent film, *Rosemary's Baby,* runs quite counter to informed Renaissance opinion.) At most, accordingly, the devils helped in the generation of illegitimate children. Even so much as this is frequently denied, for reflection tended to raise serious questions.

Sprenger and Kramer, writing at the beginning of the witchcraft scare, credit the popular belief.[156] Guazzo proves the reality of succubus in his usual way by citing Plato's *Cratylus,* Philo, Josephus and "the Old Synagogue," St. Cyprian, St. Justin

Ludwig Lavater, *De spectris, lemuribus, variisque praesagitionibus* (Leyden: Henry Verbiest, 1659), title page of a late edition.

The author is called a "distinguished theologian," and the book is said to be "truly golden." The witch in the picture is stirring a mischievous brew while a demon, her instigator and instructor, squats nearby. Other animal-headed demons fly in the background, and Death, with his scythe, reminds the viewer that a time will come when the Devil will claim the witch's soul.

Martyr, Clement of Alexandria, Tertullian, and others. "But a more substantial proof," he adds, "is to be found in S. Jerome on *Ephesians* vi, and S. Augustine (*Civ. Dei.* xv, 23), who is followed by the consensus of all Theologians, and especially by S. Isidore, chap. 8. The same belief is championed in the Bull of Pope Innocent VIII against witches." [157] How could a good Christian doubt? The Devil, however, cannot produce semen but can only carry it, keeping it warm during transportation.[158] Other authorities accept the reality of copulation but deny the power even of second-hand generation. According to Boguet, the icy coldness of the Devil's semen prevents conception.[159] Remy cites the coldness of the Devil's penis and the witch's fear and pain as preventing fertility. Moreover, the mind derives not from the semen but from God, whose co-operation would be necessary to the generation of a human being.[160] The birth of monsters, often thought to result from such unholy unions, he believes a consequence of "some excessive activity" of the mother's imagination, as in the case of the spotted sheep produced by ewes which had had Jacob's wands before their eyes.[161] As for the body used by the demon in coitus, Remy thought it was probably "either the corpse of a dead man, or else some concretion and condensation of vapours."[162] Boguet opts for the second possibility, which, he explains, should "not seem strange, if it is considered that the vapours which rise from the earth very often seem to us to take the form of men or animals."[163]

Although a few writers, among them Godelmann,[164] thought that the intercourse with demons was imaginary, opinions like these dominate in the treatises. The witches admitted intercourse with demons, in the later documents often professing it to be acutely painful; popular opinion supported it, the Fathers affirmed it. And yet there were problems. The notion that a dead body was resuscitated for the purpose apparently was not found attractive, and the alternative hypothesis involving the "concretion and condensation of vapours" may have led to or corroborated the notion that the Devil's penis and his semen were icy cold and therefore unsuitable for generation. In any event, most of the theorists agree that demons are infertile. Molitor urged this view as early as 1489.[165] The magician Merlin, often thought to have been a devil's child, was, he says, an ordinary infant who was stolen from his parents and made to appear as the child of a woman in whom a false pregnancy had been induced. Had not Galen said that semen is unproductive if it is not accompanied by "an emanation from the heart" which "measures the fire of love"?[166] The English dramatist Thomas Heywood, in his *Life of Merlin,* makes the same suggestion but qualifies it in a way he might not have found necessary if he had been better read in witchcraft. Merlin's father is doubtful, his mother certain; probably he was conceived normally, his mother concealing the father's identity in order not to endanger him. But some believe that Merlin "was conceived by the compression of a fantastical spiritual creature, without a body," and this is not impossible. Plato's mother is said by Speusippus, Elearchus, and Amaxilides to have conceived after "congression with the imaginary shadow of Apollo," and in the *De Socratis Daemone* it is affirmed that spirits inhabit the moist air between the earth and the moon and sometimes, in envy of men, take human shape as incubi and generate children called by the Romans *Fauni* and *Sicarii,* as Augustine has remarked in his *De Civitate.*[167] On the whole, however, the tendency was to preserve faith in demonic intercourse while denying the possibility of issue. And this again marks a stage in the development of incredulity.

Similarly quasi-rationalistic explanations were evolved for fortune-telling in all its permutations. Predictions of the future do not depend on instruments or cabalistic rites but on demons. Vairo stated the principle succinctly: "Certain hidden and future things are foreknown not through the power of keen imagination but with the help of daemons."[168] As Remy pointed out, only God knows the future. Demonic predictions are presentiments or conjectures, or foretell events the demons themselves will produce, or are early pronouncements of happenings which have occurred at a distance. The demon sees the event, rushes at superhuman speed to another locality, and announces it as about to happen.[169] Gifford extends the explanation to weather-magic: this is performed not in order to produce a tempest but when a tempest is known to be impending.[170] Oddly, I have run across no extended discussion of predictions in relation to free will. One would have supposed that this problem, so painfully argued out in connection with God's foreknowledge, would have been relevant also to fortune-telling. The reason it was not thought so may have been the limited credence granted by scholars to all the varieties of predictions. Because devils had possessed extraordinary knowledge as angels and had not forfeited all of it by their fall, and because also they had been able, individually, to watch human beings and observe the universe from the beginning, they were better able than men to guess what might occur in the future. Further, they had shrewd insights into human intentions, they could announce as impending some action they had themselves determined to perform, and by reason of their swift motion they could pretend to foretell events that had already happened, just as by scouting about invisibly they could discover the whereabouts of a lost object and enable a witch to predict where it would be found. They did not, however, really foreknow. Hence the riddling nature of many of their pronouncements.

Much the same line was followed in discussions of apparitions of the dead. Guazzo, as usual less doubting than most of the theorists, insisted that "the souls of the departed can and do at times appear to the living." He instances the appearance of Christ to Peter when that disciple was fleeing persecution and adduces the authority of Ambrose, Dionysius the Areopagite, Justin Martyr, Tertullian, Origen, St. Gregory of Nyssa, St. Cyprian, Surius, Pope Adrian I, St. Gregory of Tours, St. Gregory of Neocaesarea, Nicephor, St. Basil, St. Gregory of Nazianus, and St. Augustine. "To conclude shortly," he adds, "there is unlimited authority on this matter"; and he ends by citing theologians like Richard de Middleton, Peter of Palude, Scotus, Denys the Carthusian, Dominic Soto, Peltanus, St. Peter Canisius, and Gregory of Valencia. But we need not believe that the appearances are frequent.[171] None the less his opinion was not that of the majority.

The more usual view was stated by Remy when he affirmed that except by the special permission of God devils do not really raise the dead but impersonate them or make their corpses move as if alive.[172] Godelmann agrees that Satan is incapable of performing resuscitations, an act of which only God is capable.[173] Even Guazzo advises his readers that apparent spirits are often phantoms: "In S. Clement of Rome we also read much concerning Simon Magus: that he made a new man out of air, whom he could render invisible at will."[174] An English reader may think of such Spenserian spirits as the false Una contrived by Archimago. In Protestant countries an indisposition to believe in the return of dead souls was strengthened by a promulgation of the London convocation in 1562, that "The Romish Doctrine concerning Purgatory . . . is a fond thing vainly invented, and grounded upon no warranty of Scripture but rather repugnant to the word of God."[175] If the souls of the dead were at once received into Paradise or Hell their return to earth was unlikely.

The longest and most heavily documented treatment of apparitions is by Ludwig Lavater, a German Lutheran who first wrote in the vernacular and then produced an expanded version in Latin. An English translation by "R. H." to which I have not had access was published in 1572. The book is learned, intelligent, but, on the basis of innumerable authorities, affirmative, only insisting that the spirits, although sometimes real, are not usually those of dead men but are "good or evil angels, or other arcane and occult operations of God."[176] The reason they appear is that by means of them God exercises the faithful and punishes the faithless. Yet they are often illusions—the fantasies of melancholics or madmen,[177] misapprehensions of imperfect senses,[178] the result of a fright induced by other men,[179] or impersonations by priests or monks undertaken for some such ulterior purpose as access to a desirable woman.[180] Common people, again, often mistake natural objects for specters.[181] Since the work is rather about apparitions than about witchcraft it cannot detain us longer. Yet it connects with tractates on witchcraft and in its skepticism as well as in its credulity is a typical product of its time.

V. Conclusion

It must be understood that, like the appearance of bad angels as specters, all the activities of demons are "permissive." This thesis runs through virtually all the treatises. Molitor insists that devils can do nothing without God's will.[182] Godelmann tells us that the imprecations, charms, and poisons used to injure or destroy cattle and men are sometimes effective through God's permission.[183] Remy explains the turning to worthless objects of gold given to witches by demons as resulting from God's denial to devils of the power actually to enrich.[184] Guazzo, in a passage more than usually difficult for a modern reader to follow, gives this as the last of seven reasons why God allows the Devil to "Busy Himself with witchcraft": "It shows His power. For although He allows the demon to effect the greater marvels, such as turning water into blood (Guazzo is thinking of the competition between Moses and Pharaoh's magicians), He does not permit him to accomplish smaller things, such as the generation of gnats."[185] One gathers, rather uncertainly, that the greater feats are allowed for special purposes but that, contemptuously, the devils are frustrated in trivial undertakings that might give them pleasure. The general lines of speculation about infernal power are nevertheless clear. Admission that the devils performed evil against God's will would have implied a Manichaean dualism, a heresy which had long been refuted. Although I do not recall that they were often cited, the Bible also contained a number of texts about how God had hardened the hearts of bad men in order to drive them further into iniquity. Divine rulership over the universe had to be maintained at all costs.

Much else in the treatises might form part of a longer analysis. Was it, for example, or was it not, legitimate to obtain the help of white witches or "wise men" in resisting charms and curses? Opinion was divided. Godelmann urged, against Paracelsus and others, that magical cures were also of the Devil and therefore illicit.[186] Delrio believed that all magical effects required a pact with the Devil, either explicit or implicit, and hence were forbidden.[187] On the other side, Remy argued that countermagic used by a witch against her own charms was licit if instead of being cajoled or bribed she was forced by threats or violence to help. The Devil would not then be honored but forced to work against his own ends.[188] Boguet agreed with the majority: "It was therefore well said by St. John Chrysostom that it is better to die than to seek the help of the Devil or witches to be cured."[189] There is also protracted discussion of the efficacy of the sign of the Cross, naming Christ, sprinkling holy water, and using other rites of exorcism. In general, the Protestants thought such practices "Popish" and superstitious; but among the Catholics too there were many who believed them to be rather aids to faith than magically efficacious. Again, a separate section might be written on the disputed question whether a witch's powers ceased upon her arrest. Their disappearance would of course have encouraged justices and torturers and was often affirmed, but many instances are reported of visitations to the prisoner by demons and even of cohabitation with them in the cells. The present summary of the official theory is, therefore, very far from exhaustive. My intention has been partly to offer a general overview of what witchcraft was thought to be like but more centrally to illustrate the mental processes embodied in the scholarly documents.

The basic weakness of the reasoning, obviously, is the reliance placed upon "authorities," which made the rooting out of misconceptions a slow and difficult undertaking. The oftener the traditional stories were repeated the stronger the "proof" became. If Sprenger and Kramer, for example, picked up a tale from the life of one of the early saints and Guazzo borrowed it from them, it acquired the support of a fourth author. The next user became a fifth, a still later writer a sixth, and so on indefinitely, until the list acquired an apparent solidity that made disbelief next to impossible. The essential step of doubting the initial witness, of asking "How did he *know?*" and "Didn't he perhaps misinterpret the evidence?" began gradually to be taken—we have noticed honorable instances—but could not quickly become widespread and almost instinctive. In the typical treatise a belief in the theoretical possibility, if not the next-door actuality, of witchcraft was forced both by the theological premises and by the feeling, still far from uncommon, that what has been repeated throughout all history and over the whole of the known world could not be wholly false. So the long delusion not only continued but, as the prosecutions multiplied, grew in intensity and practical consequences. Yet the beginnings of a healthier attitude are clearly visible in the treatises, superstitious as many of them are, and in the long run was to lead to the abandonment of stupidities which only now, in the backwash of an anti-rationalist rebellion against hard factual knowledge, are once again beginning to be credited by people who should know better.

In the meantime writers whose minds we continue to find attractive shared the deplorable errors. Sir Thomas Browne's acceptance of the existence of witches is well known: and this despite his *Pseudodoxia epidemica,* a long work directed against popular beliefs. Martin Luther's credulity about witches was unbounded: it cannot be denied, he said, that the Devil lives and reigns in the whole world.[190] According to K. M. Briggs, Thomas Fuller was a believer, and Sir Walter Raleigh distinguished between theurgy and witchcraft by asserting that whereas the theurgist or necromancer commanded the Devil, witches obeyed him.[191] Joseph Glanville's *A Blow at Modern Sadducism in Some Philosophical Considerations about Witchcraft* (4th ed. 1668) is *"concerned for the justification of the* belief of witches, *it suggesting* palpable, *and current evidence of our* Immortality."[192] Richard Baxter's *Certainty of the World of Spirits* (1691) shows that at the end of the seventeenth century a reasonable and charitable man could persevere in the delusion. As late as July 11, 1711, Joseph Addison was able to write, "I believe in general that there is, and has been such a thing as Witch-craft; but at the same time, can give no Credit to any particular Instance of it."[193] We are reminded of Dr. Johnson's attitude toward ghosts. As for popular interest in witches during the High Renaissance in England, its extent is suggested by Robert Reed's discovery that more than seventy Elizabethan and Jacobean plays have to do with the supernatural.[194] Although the occult of course includes more than witchcraft, the role of witchcraft in the plays is important enough to justify Reed's inclusion of a chapter on "Origins of English Witchcraft and Demonology."

Other men of course took a different view. Jerome Cardan, who believed in demons and was an enthusiastic astrologer, nonetheless was essentially skeptical about witchcraft.[195] John Selden refused faith.[196] So too did Gabriel Harvey.[197] Montaigne objected to the prosecutions: "How much more naturall and more likely doe I finde it, that two men should lie, then one in twelve houres, passe with the windes, from East to West? . . . When all is done, it is an over-valuing of ones conjectures, by them to cause a man to be burned alive."[198] Less well-known men also refused assent to the prevailing opinion. Arthur Wilson, steward to the Earl of Warwick, says of eighteen witches condemned in Essex in 1645, "I was at Chensford at the trial and execution of eighteene women. But could see nothing in the evidence which did perswade me to thinke them other than poore, mellencollie, envious, mischevous, ill-disposed, atrabilus constitutions." [199]

Such disavowals, when public, no doubt did something to help sway opinion. No real substitute existed, however, for hard intellectual argument. This was begun and carried on, all over Europe, in treatises like those we have looked at; and ultimately, except in cultural backwaters, the battle for sanity was won. For a very long time, however, a faith in witchcraft remained possible for wise, learned, and well-intentioned men. It disappeared only when the skepticism which pushed back the responsibility for magical results from formulas and operations to the Devil himself left to be denied only a single pre-assumption. "Gut responses," where the delusion had its ultimate source, then began to be distrusted, if not by everyone, at least by the fashioners of a modern world which, for all its imperfections, is free at least from the blood-chilling cruelties sketched at the beginning of this discussion.

NOTES: CHAPTER TWO

1. For a modern translation see Nicolas Remy, *Demonolatry,* transl. E. A. Ashwin, ed. Montague Summers (London: John Rodker, 1930). For the number of executions see p. 56 (I, xv). For the book's authority see, e. g., Henry Charles Lea, *Materials Toward a History of Witchcraft,* ed. Arthur C. Howland (New York and London: Thomas Yoseloff, 1957), II, 604. This is a reprint of the original (Philadelphia: University of Pennsylvania Press, 1939) edition and appears to have identical pagination.

2. Friedrich von Spee, *Cautio criminalis, oder Rechtliches Bedenken wegen der Hexenprozesse,* transl. Joachim-Friedrich Ritter (Weimar: Verlag Herm. Böhlaus Nachf., 1939), intro., p. xx. I have not had access to the Latin version of 1631.

3. Henry Boguet, *An Examen of Witches Drawn from Various Trials,* transl. E. Allen Ashwin, ed. Montague Summers (London: John Rodker, 1929), p. xxxiii.

4. For the figure of 200,000 see Rossell Hope Robbins, *The Encyclopedia of Witchcraft and Demonology* (New York: Crown Publishers, Inc., 1959, 7th printing 1970), p. 17.

5. See Geoffrey Parrinder, *Witchcraft* (Harmondsworth, Middlesex: Penguin Books, Ltd., 1958), p. 87. In the five home counties of Essex, Hertfordshire, Kent, Surrey, and Sussex there were 455 indictments under Elizabeth and 103 under James. Thereafter the number decreased: under Charles I, 108; during the interregnum, 72; under Charles II, 44; under James II, 1; under William III, 7. Parrinder's source was Cecil Henry L'Estrange Ewen, *Witch Hunting and Witch Trials* (London: Kegan Paul & Co., 1929).

6. I use the facsimile edition, with an introduction by Beatrice White, published for the Shakespeare Association (London: Oxford University Press, 1931), sig. Hr.

7. Christina Hole, *Witchcraft in England* (London: B. T. Batesford Ltd., 1945), p. 119.

8. Cf. *ibid.,* p. 88.

9. Besides the authoritative works by Robbins and Lea (see notes 4 and 1, above), there is a rich English bibliography of scholarly and semi-scholarly works, of which the best known in this country is perhaps G. L. Kittredge, *Witchcraft in Old and New England* (Cambridge, Mass.: Harvard University Press, 1929). Among continental works the following deserve special mention: Jules Baissac, *Les grands Jours de la sorcellerie* (Paris: 1890), and Wilhelm Gottlieb Soldan, *Soldan's Geschichte der Hexenprozesse* [Stuttgart: 1843], neu bearb. von dr. Heinrich Heppe (Stuttgart: J. H. Cotta, 1880).

10. Cf. Robbins, *Encyclopedia*, p. 479.

11. For information about von Spee see *ibid.*, pp. 479–84, and Michaud's *Biographie universelle*, nouvelle éd. (Paris and Leipzig, n. d.), art. "Spé ou Spee, Frédéric de." The *Cautio* was several times reprinted at Frankfurt and Cologne and was translated into French (Lyons: 1660). I have not had access to the Latin text.

12. Von Spee, *Cautio* (German transl. cited in Note 2, above), pp. 95–96 (XX, xvi).

13. He is said, however, after a murderous attack made on him in a wood, to have attempted to preach despite seven serious wounds. 14. *Ibid.*, p. 81 (XX, v).

15. *Ibid.*, pp. 119–20 (XXVI, i–ii). 16. *Ibid.*, pp. 84–85 (XX, ix).

17. *Ibid.*, pp. 113–14 (XXV, intro.). 18. *Ibid.*, pp. 114–15 (XXV, ii, iii).

19. *Ibid.*, p. 95 (XX, xvi).

20. Remy, *Demonolatry*, p. 56 (I, xv).

21. Von Spee, *Cautio*, p. 69 (XVIII, xv). 22. *Ibid.*, p. 91 (XX, xiii).

23. *Ibid.*, p. 93 (XX, xiv). 24. *Ibid.*, pp. 87–89 (XX, xii).

25. *Ibid.*, pp. 80–81 (XX, iii). 26. *Ibid.*, p. 135 (XXIX).

27. Ioanne Georgio Godelmanno, *Tractatus de magis, veneficis et lamiis, deque his recte cognoscendis et puniendis* (Francoforti: Ex Officina Typographica Nicolai Bassaei, 1591), III, 104 (III, x).

28. Cf. Lea, *Materials*, I, 337.

29. Parrinder, *Witchcraft*, p. 80. 30. *Ibid.*, p. 31.

31. Matthew Hopkins, *The Discovery of Witches*, ed. Montague Summers (London: At the Cayme Press, 1928)—a reprint of the rare original edition of 1647, which runs to only thirteen small pages. See pp. 54–55.

32. Joannes Bodinus, *De magorum daemonomania . . . libri IV, seu detestando lamiarum ac magorum cum Satana commercio* (Francofurti): Typis Wolffgangi Richteri, 1603), pp. 372–73. This is a reprint; the work was first published in French (Paris, 1580) and then translated into Latin (Basel, 1581).

33. Francesco Maria Guazzo, *Compendium maleficarum*, transl. E. A. Ashwin, with notes by Montague Summers (London: John Rodker, 1929), p. 115 (II, ix).

34. For a modern rendering see the translation by Montague Summers (London: John Rodker, 1928). I have checked this with an edition of 1490 and found it generally trustworthy. The work was reprinted in 1487, 1489, ?1490, 1494, 1496, ?1510, 1511, 1519, 1520, 1574, 1576, 1580, 1582, 1584, 1588, 1595, 1598, 1600, 1604, 1614, 1615, 1620, 1620–21, 1660, 1666, and 1669. Copies were once so abundant that a 1912 sale at Leipzig of a "unique collection of books dealing with witchcraft" included no fewer than twenty-nine copies (bibliographical note, pp. xli–xlii). 35. *Ibid.*, pp. 231–32 (III, xvi). 36. *Ibid.*, p. 209 (III, iv).

37. *Ibid.*, p. 213 (III, vii). 38. *Ibid.*, p. 216 (III, ix). 39. *Ibid.*, pp. 217–18 (III, x).

40. Boguet, *Examen*, long title and p. vii. The "Articles" are on pp. 211–38.

41. Bodin, *Daemonomania*, p. 422 (IV, iv). 42. *Ibid.*, p. 423 (IV, iv). 43. *Ibid*.

44. *Ibid.*, p. 436 (IV, v). 45. *Ibid.*, pp. 436–37 (IV, v). 46. *Ibid.*, p. 438 (IV, v).

47. *Ibid.*, pp. 439–45 (IV, v). 48. *Ibid.*, p. 387 (IV, ii).

49. Reginald Scot, *The Discoverie of Witchcraft* [1584]. With an introduction by the Rev. Montague Summers (London: John Rodker, 1930), pp. 11–18 (II, i–viii).

50. Godelmann, *Tractatus,* "Praefatio," p. 2.

51. Since Godelmann's ambience is German, he cites especially German laws, quoting them some-times in German; but many of his arguments are supra-national, and he draws from writers of all periods and places.   52. *Ibid.,* III, 10 (III, ii).   53. *Ibid.*

54. *Ibid.,* III, 18–19 (III, iii).   55. *Ibid.,* III, 46ff. (III, vi).   56. *Ibid.,* III, 11 (III, ii).

57. *Ibid.,* III, 59 (III, vii).   58. *Ibid.,* III, 88 (III, ix, *Summae,* 1).   59. *Ibid.,* III, 112 (III, x).

60. See Thomas Potts, *The Wonderfvll Discoveries of Witches in the Covntie of Lancaster* (London: Printed by W. Stansy for Iohn Barnes, 1613). A facsimile of this edition can be found in G. B. Harrison, *The Trial of the Lancaster Witches* (London: Peter Davies, 1929). For the judgment see p. 163ff.

61. Lea, *Materials,* I, 361.

62. Boguet, *Examen,* pp. 121–23 (XL–XLI).

63. Cf. Lea, *Materials,* II, 612.

64. Parrinder, *Witchcraft,* p. 32 (figures taken from C. L'Estrange Ewen, *Witch Hunting and Witch Trials*).

65. Scot, *Discoverie,* pp. 4–5 (I, iii).   66. *Ibid.,* pp. 3–4 (I, ii).

67. Gifford, *Dialogue Concerning Witches,* sig. Ar-B2*v.*

68. Scot, *Discoverie,* p. 1 (I, i).   69. *Ibid.,* p. 2 (I, i).

70. *Ibid.,* p. 64 (VI, i). On p. 71 (VI, viii), however, he quotes the word as φαρμακεῖς; and indeed Liddell and Scott give "poisoner" for φαρμακεύς.   71. *Ibid.,* p. 64 (VI, i).

72. Sprenger and Institoris (or Kramer), *Malleus,* p. 106 (II, i, 3).

73. Guazzo, *Compendium,* pp. 3–4 (I, ii).

74. Godelmann, *Tractatus,* I, 17, (I, ii).

75. Martin Delrio, *Disquisitionum magicarum libri VI* (Mainz: 1603), p. 4 (I, ii).

76. Ioannes Vairo, *De fascino libri tres* (Parisiis: Apud Nicolaum Chesneau, 1583), pp. 2–3 (I, i). Vairo was an Italian Benedictine, at one time prior of Santa Sophia at Benevento and later a bishop.

77. Lea, *Materials,* II, 489.

78. Scot, *Discoverie,* intro., p. xxxi.

79. See Jean Wier, *De prestigiis daemonum et incantationibus ac veneficiis* [1564], transl. into French in 1579 and reprinted in *Histoires, dispvtes et discovrs des illvsions et impostvres des diables* (Paris: A. Delahaye et Lecrosnier, Éditeurs, 1885), II, 392–98 (*"Avtevrs allegvez"*).

80. Delrio, *Disquisitiones,* p. 39 (I, iv, 1).   81. *Ibid.,* p. 10 (I, iii).

82. Gian-Francesco Pico, *La Strega, ovvero degli inganni de' demone* (Milano: G. Daelli e C., Editori, 1864). This is of course a reprint: the first edition, in Latin, was published probably at Bologna in 1523 and is very rare. The Italian translation I have used is by Turino Turini.

83. *Ibid.,* pp. 112–13.

84. Ulric Molitor, *Des Sorcières et des devineresses* (*De lamiis et phitonicis mulieribus*) (Paris: Librairie Critique Emile Nourry, 1926), pp. 19–20 and 21 (Chap. IV). This edition contains a facsimile of the Latin edition published at Cologne in 1489. Although another speaker at first objects to this proof, in the end he says (p. 27), "Tu m'accables de tant d'histoires et d'autorités que je ne sais plus quel parti adopter." These two classical instances of transformation are favorites among the authors.

85. Boguet, *Examen,* p. 170 (Chap. lii).

86. Pico, *La Strega,* p. 135.

87. Sprenger and Institoris, *Malleus,* p. 35 (I, v).   88. *Ibid.,* p. 60 (I, ix).

89. Guazzo, *Compendium,* p. 26 (I, ix).

90. Sprenger and Institoris, *Malleus,* p. 42 (I, vi).

91. Molitor, *Des Sorcières,* p. 8 (Chap. I).

92. Guazzo, *Compendium*, p. 124 (II, xi).

93. The treatises not hitherto cited are the following: Giovanni Lorenzo Anania, *De natura daemonum libri IIII* (Venetiis: 1581); Thomas Erastus, *Deux Dialogves de Thomas Erastvs, Tovchant le povvoir des sorcieres*, etc., Novvellement tradvits de Latin en François, reprinted with Wier, *De prestigiis*, etc., II, 399–553; Joseph Glanville, *A Blow at Modern Sadducism, In some Philosophical Considerations About Witchcraft*, 4th ed. (London: 1668); Ludovicus Lavaterus, *De spectris, lemuribus et magnis atque insolitis fragoribus* (Genevae: Apud Eustatium Vignon, 1580); James the First, *Daemonologie* (1597); *News from Scotland, declaring the Damnable Life and death of Doctor FIAN, a notable Sorcerer* (London: John Lane, The Bodley Head, Ltd., 1924). Although many more treatises than these exist—see, e.g., Lea's three volumes of *Materials* for titles—these not only provide a representative sample but include many of the really capital tracts.

94. Guazzo, *Compendium*, pp. 13–17 (I, vi).

95. Godelmann, *Tractatus*, I, 18–20 (I, ii).

96. Vairo, *De fascino*, p. 204 (III, i).   97. *Ibid.*, p. 207 (III, i).

98. Remy, *Demonolatry*, p. 28 (I, vii).   99. *Ibid.*, p. 30 (I, viii).   100. *Ibid.*

101. *Ibid.*, pp. 38–40 (I, x).

102. Anania, *Natura daemonum*, pp. 10–28.

103. Wier, *De prestigiis*, I, 14 (I, iv).

104. Sprenger and Institoris, *Malleus*, p. 15 (I, 2).

105. King James, *Daemonologie*, pp. 24–26.

106. Wier, *De prestigiis*, I, 3 (I, i).

107. Guazzo, *Compendium*, p. 73 (I, xviii).

108. Sprenger and Institoris, *Malleus*, p. 99 (II, i, 2). I have corrected one mistranslation ("without being seen"—*nullo vidente*—for Summers's "when no one is in sight").

109. Scot, *Discoverie of Witchcraft*, p. 6 (I, iv).

110. Potts, *Wonderfvll Discoveries* (see note 60, above).

111. Cf., e.g., Pico's *La Strega*, pp. 59, 63, and 127.

112. Remy, *Demonolatry*, p. 74 (I, xxv).

113. That aerial turbulence should lift bodies is, however, natural.

114. Remy, *Demonolatry*, pp. 57–60 (I, xvi).   115. *Ibid.*, pp. 60–61 (I, xvii).

116. Pico, *La Strega*, p. 83: "Riferiscano eglino stessi, che sono da due milia uomini quelli che frequentano il giuoco."   117. *Ibid.*, pp. 59–60.

118. Remy, *Demonolatry*, p. 127 (II, ix).   119. *Ibid.*, p. 128 (II, ix).

120. *Ibid.*, p. 118 (II, viii). Cf. also, about medicines, p. 148 (III, iii).

121. King James, *Daemonologie*, pp. 16–17.

122. Guazzo, *Compendium*, pp. 80–81 (I, xix).

123. Gifford, *Dialogue Concerning Witches*, "The Epistle," sig. A2v-A3r.

124. Boguet, *Examen*, p. xliv ("Author's Preface").   125. *Ibid.*, p. 67 (Chap. xxiii).

126. *Ibid.*, p. 49 (Chap. xvii).   127. *Ibid.*, p. 66 (Chap. xxii).

128. *Ibid.*, p. 69 (Chap. xxiv).   129. *Ibid.*, p. 79 (Chap. xxvi).

130. *Ibid.*, p. 81 (Chap. xxviii).   131. *Ibid.*, p. 84 (Chap. xxviii).

132. *Ibid.*, pp. 86–87 (Chap. xxx).

133. Erastus, *Deux Dialogves*, II, 404 and 417.

134. Delrio, *Disquisitiones*, p. 35 (I, iv).

135. Pico, *La Strega*, p. 26, "Mi par cosa de ridere. . . ," and the announcement of a changed point of view, p. 135, "Pensi tu che io stimi burle . . ."

136. Godelmann, *Tractatus*, I, 23 (I, iii).

137. Guazzo, *Compendium*, p. 50 (I, xiii).   138. *Ibid.*, p. 9 (I, iv).

139. Scot, *Discoverie of Witches*, p. 56 (V, v).

140. Molitor, *Des Sorcières*, pp. 63–67 (Chap. xi).

141. Boguet, *Examen*, pp. 136–43 (Chap. xlvii).   142. *Ibid.*, pp. 143–46 (Chap. xlvii).

143. *Ibid.*, p. 151 (Chap. xlvii).   144. *Ibid.*, pp. 154–55 (Chap. xlvii).

145. Remy, *Demonolatry*, p. 110 (II, v).   146. *Ibid.*, pp. 112–13 (II, v).

147. See Godelmann, *Tractatus*, "Ad Iudicem" (address at beginning of Book II, written by Althusius), sig. R2v-R3r.

148. Pico, *La Strega*, pp. 131–32.

149. Remy, *Demonolatry*, pp. 51–53 (I, xiv). On pp. 43–44 (I, xii) he acknowledges belief in the ability of witches to charm their husbands into a deep sleep during their absences or to leave convincing simulacra of themselves.

150. Sprenger and Institoris, *Malleus*, pp. 106–108 (II, i, 3).

151. Boguet, *Examen*, p. 42 (Chap. xiv).

152. Guazzo, *Compendium*, p. 34 (I, xii).   153. *Ibid.*, p. 39 (I, xii).

154. Molitor, *Des Sorcières*, pp. 68–72 (Chap. xii).

155. Godelmann, *Tractatus*, II, 36–37, 46 (II, iv).

156. Sprenger and Institoris, *Malleus*, pp. 21–28 (I, 4).

157. Guazzo, *Compendium*, p. 30 (I, xi).   158. *Ibid.*

159. Boguet, *Examen*, pp. 37–38 (Chap. xiii).

160. Remy, *Demonolatry*, pp. 13–16 (I, vi).   161. *Ibid.*, pp. 22–25 (I, vi).

162. *Ibid.*, p. 12 (I, vi).

163. Boguet, *Examen*, p. 16 (Chap. vii).

164. Godelmann, *Tractatus*, II, 32–48 (II, v *in toto*).

165. Molitor, *Des Sorcières*, pp. 73–78 (Chap. xiii).   166. *Ibid.*, pp. 75 and 78 (Chap. xiii).

167. Thomas Heywood, *A True History of the Strange Birth of Ambrosius Merlin, and his Wonderful Prophecies* [c. 1620]. In [Thomas Heywood], *The Life of Merlin, Surnamed Ambrosius* (Carmarthen: J. Evans, 1812), p. 40.

168. Vairo, *De fascino*, p. 80 (headnote to II, v).

169. Remy, *Demonolatry*, pp. 170–73 (III, x).

170. Gifford, *Dialogue*, sig. K2v-K3r.

171. Guazzo, *Compendium*, pp. 59–60 (I, xvii).

172. Remy, *Demonolatry*, pp. 87–88 (II, i).

173. Godelmann, *Tractatus*, I, 38 (I, iv).

174. Guazzo, *Compendium*, p. 7 (I, iii).

175. Quoted by Montague Summers in his introduction to Scot's *Discoverie*, p. xxix.

176. Lavater, *De spectris*, "Epistola" (unpaginated).   177. *Ibid.*, p. 9 (I, ii).

178. *Ibid.*, pp. 15–20 (I, iv).   179. *Ibid.*, p. 20 (I, v).

180. *Ibid.*, p. 22 (I, vi).   181. *Ibid.*, p. 47 (I, xi).

182. See, e. g., Molitor, *Des Sorcières*, pp. 57–62, especially pp. 59–60 (Chap. x).

183. Godelmann, *Tractatus*, I, 65–66 (I, vii).

184. Remy, *Demonolatry*, pp. 7–8 (I, iv).

185. Guazzo, *Compendium*, p. 111 (II, ix).

186. Godelmann, *Tractatus*, I, 87 (I, viii).

187. Delrio, *Disquisitiones*, p. 112 (II, iv).

188. Remy, *Demonolatry*, pp. 152–53 (III, iii).

189. Boguet, *Examen*, p. 113 (Chap. xxxvi).

190. Cf. Lea, *Materials*, I, 422–23.

191. K. M. Briggs, *Pale Hecate's Team: An Examination of the Beliefs on Witchcraft and Magic*

Among Shakespeare's Contemporaries and His Immediate Successors (London: Routledge and Kegan Paul, 1962), pp. 42 and 43–44.

192. Glanville, *Blow at Modern Sadducism,* sig. A4*v* and A5.

193. Hole, *Witchcraft in England,* p. 145.

194. Robert R. Reed, Jr., *The Occult on the Tudor and Stuart Stage* (Boston: The Christopher Publishing House, 1965), p. 9.

195. Cf. Lea, *Materials,* II, 435ff.

196. Briggs, in *Pale Hecate's Team,* p. 47, cites the *Table Talk* (Oxford: 1892), p. 195, as evidence.

197. Cf. *ibid.*

198. Montaigne, *Essais,* transl. Florio (London: 1603), III, xi, 615-16 (quoted by Briggs, *Pale Hecate's Team,* p. 33).

199. Quoted by Briggs, *Pale Hecate's Team,* p. 13 and note, from Arthur Wilson, *Account of his Life by Himself,* in Peck's *Desiderate Curiosa* (London: 1779), II, xii, chap. xvi, p. 476.

 # White Magic

I. Preliminary distinctions

In one of its two main senses, white magic is *magia naturalis,* a pre-modern form of natural science. Natural magic is Giovanni Baptista Della Porta's subject in the first of the three treatises we shall examine. Not only is there no question of an explicit or implied pact with a devil but no daemonic powers whatever are solicited. What Della Porta describes is magic because it operates through occult properties and qualities, but it is natural because the forces through which it achieves its effects are objectively present in nature: elements, qualities, properties, "virtues" of several kinds, "forms," proportions, and intrinsic sympathies and antipathies. No invocations are offered, no implorings made; whatever consciousness exists in non-human nature is not constrained by ceremonies to be helpful. If *magia naturalis* is not continuous with modern science, the reason is that its preconceptions, like those of alchemy—as we shall see in a later chapter—were subsequently abandoned.

At its opposite extreme, white magic is allowable spiritual magic, something different from black magic or *goëtia* only because it stays clear of bad daemons and does not endanger the operator's soul. It uses rites, incantations, cabalistic names, mystical characters and symbols, fumigations, and significant objects of various kinds, and the magician may invoke not merely the members of the Holy Trinity but also other "gods" through whom the High God was supposed to perform His will.

The operator's state of mind may be of crucial importance, so he may prepare himself by repentance, expiation, fasting, ablutions, solitary meditation, and other ceremonies. Indeed, he must sometimes "sacrifice." Not surprisingly, opinions differed about the legitimacy of such behavior, and in time the English Puritans were to regard as culpably superstitious the sign of the cross, the use of a ring in marriage rites, and even kneeling for communion. We shall not, however, follow the controversies as in the preceding chapter but instead will give the available space to explication and commentary. The third of the three treatises, Cornelius Agrippa's *De occulta philosophia libri tres,* covers the whole range of possibility from natural magic to ceremonial or religious magic and will receive much attention in the pages to follow. Beyond it, but verging on, and almost certainly falling into, the area of black magic were the efforts of such men as Tommaso Campanella and Giordano Bruno to constrain bad daemons without incurring guilt. This has been discussed by Frances Yates and D. P. Walker [1] and will not concern us because it is implicitly covered in the discussion of witchcraft.

Between ceremonial magic and natural magic was still a third kind, celestial or astronomical magic. This is not excluded from natural magic, since astrological forces could be construed as a part of nature, but its emphasis might shift toward ceremony if the heavens were thought—as Ficino thought them—not merely to exert influence by means of rays and heat but also to be endowed with intelligence and will. Celestial magic is the subject of Agrippa's second book but will be studied here as presented in Ficino's *De vita coelitus comparanda,* a section of his *De vita triplici* which focuses wholly upon it.

In the present chapter we shall consider Della Porta, Ficino, and Agrippa in that order for the purpose of moving steadily from pseudo-science toward deeper and less "natural" *occulta.* Since nothing can be achieved without the deepest possible submersion in outmoded thought-patterns, the discussion will again be highly, and perhaps fatiguingly, explicit; and once again, because the subject is not accurately understood by most general readers and the sources of information are not widely accessible, much space must be given to summary. We turn first to the *Magiae naturalis libri viginti* of Della Porta, a work first published in four books in 1558 and reissued in an enormously expanded version in 1589.[2]

II. Natural magic and Giovanni Della Porta's *Magiae naturalis libri viginti* (1589)

Della Porta explains in his preface the sources of his knowledge. He has "consulted with all Libraries, Learned Men, and Artificers" as he traveled through France, Italy, and Spain and has written letters to "Those places and men, I had not the happiness

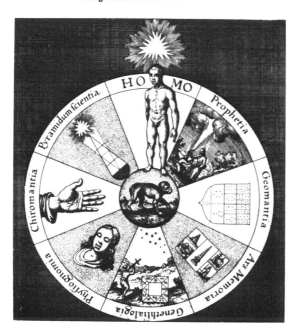

TOMI SECVNDI
TRACTATUS PRIMI,
SECTIO SECVNDA,
De technica Microcosmi hiftoria,

in

Portiones VII. divifa.

AVTHORE
ROBERTO FLVD aliàs de FLVCTIBVS
Armigero & in Medicina Doctore Oxonienfi.

Robert Fludd, *De supernaturali, naturali, praenaturali et contranaturali microcosmi historia* (Oppenheim: Hieronymus Gallerus, 1619), following p. 277, title page of Vol. II.

The human arts. Man, again stretching from the earth toward God, is represented at the center as the *simia naturae,* or ape of nature, because in his sciences he follows the nature which God has created. The segments of the larger circle represent certain of his arts: prophecy, shown here as depending on divine revelation; geomancy; the art of memory (on which Frances Yates has recently written); astrology; physiognomy, an art of reading character from the face; chiromancy or palmistry; and "the science of pyramids," evidently to be taken as representative of the mathematical and geometrical arts generally. All these arts are discussed *in extenso* in writings of the period.

to see," so that "whatsoever was Notable, and to be desired through the whole World, for Curiosities and Excellent Things, I have abundantly found out." He has left nothing "unassayed"—that is, unchecked in one way or another, since he could not actually have tested all his claims by experiment—and in the process has expended his "narrow Fortunes in a large magnificence." In the enlargement of what had been a much briefer work he has been helped by "an Academy of curious Men," who also incurred expenditures. In speaking of matters which are "Magnificent and most Excellent" he has, he says, "veil'd" his subjects "by the Artifice of Words, by Transposition and Depression of them; And such Things as are hurtful and mischievous, I have written obscurely; yet not so, but that an ingenious Reader may unfold it." The practice was common in all writing about *occulta.* He denies vigorously that the information offered in his book is in any way illicit. He has suffered from "the Calumnies of detractors and envious men, that most immodestly wound me, calling me a Sorcerer, a Conjurer, which names from my tender Youth I have abhorr'd. . . . I never Writ here nor elsewhere, what is not contain'd within the bounds of Nature." [3]

Nothing of all this is consciously dishonest. Della Porta has gathered his materials, with some help from other men, by "research"—as we should say—into his subject; he has done what experimenting he found convenient; and he is confident that what he has set down in print is in accord with what a modern would call natural law. We are to expect not conjurations but "science," an account of surprising ways in which forces really work. In no treatise of the Renaissance can we examine more favorably what natural magic was like at its least mystical level. Also, perhaps, in none will we so quickly find reasons for disbelief. The very sobriety of the author's purpose and the limitation of his perspectives to phenomena that involve no traffic with spirits make exceptionally apparent fundamental contradictions between his view of physical nature and one likely to be credible to educated modern persons.

As was usual in all such disquisitions, the author begins with a capsule history of his subject. Magic originated in Persia, as Porphyry and Apuleius say. According to Pliny the first magician was Zoroaster, son of Orimasius or, perhaps, a different Zoroaster called Proconnesius, and the first writing about magic was by Osthanes, a contemporary of Xerxes. Men called *magos* or magicians by the Persians were called *sapientes* by the Latins, *philosophos* by the Greeks, *Brachmanes*—that is, *gymnosophistas*—by the Indians, *Chaldaeos* by the Babylonians and Assyrians, *Druydas, Bardos,* and *Semnothes* by the Celts, *sacerdotes* by the Egyptians, *prophetas* by the Cabalists. The discovery of such identifications was a mark of Renaissance syncretism. Among the most excellent magicians were the Persian Zoroaster, the Roman Numa Pompilius, the gymnosophist Thespion, the Thracian Zamolxis (or Zalmoxis), the Hyperborean Abbaris, the Egyptian Hermes, and the Babylonian Buddha.[4] Although subject to fluctuation, the names and details are in an accepted tradition. Since the ancient authorities differed, a treatise might use several large pages in an anxious weighing of competing claims to precedency and distinction, but there was general agreement that the lines of the art had been laid down in the remote past and that the title "magician" in the beginning was roughly equivalent to "wise man." We have met with similar recapitulations in earlier chapters and will meet with others in chapters to come.

After this introduction Della Porta proceeds to answer the question "What is the Nature of Magick?" The art has two divisions, of which "one is infamous, and unhappie, because it hath to do with foul spirits, and consists of Inchantment and wicked Curiosity; and this is called Sorcery." Such magic, in short, is witchcraft, about which Della Porta is skeptical: it "stands meerly upon fancies and imaginations." Although heretical if taken literally, the assertion implies that Della Porta ranged himself among the realists as opposed to the dreamers. The second magic "is natural; which all excellent wise men do admit and embrace, and worship with great applause": for example, Pythagoras, Empedocles, Democritus, Plato. It is, in fact, "the very highest point, and the perfection of natural Sciences," or, again, "the practical part of natural Philosophy." According to the Neoplatonists, "as *Plotinus* imitating *Mercurius*"—that is, Hermes Trismegistus—it is "a Science whereby inferiour things are made subject to superiors, earthly are subdued to heavenly." In Della Porta's opinion, however, the art "is nothing else but the survey of the whole course of Nature." By its aid men "do strange works, such as the vulgar sort call miracles," although in fact "the works of Magick are nothing else but the works of Nature." Magic is, indeed, so far from being really miraculous that "Superstitious, profane, and wicked men have nothing to do with this Science" and should be driven "out of Cities, and out of the world, to be grievously punished, and utterly destroyed." [5] Della Porta had himself fallen under suspicion and had had to defend himself against a denunciation made to Pope Paul V.[6] His indignation, however, is probably sincere, for *Natural Magick* is remarkably free of suggestions that the author liked to dally with incantations and spirits and was restrained from writing about them only by fear of the authorities.

This reading is confirmed by the following chapter, entitled "The Instruction of a Magician, and what manner of man a Magician ought to be." Nothing is said about the necessity of piety, or acquaintance with the cabala, or a visionary temperament, or knowledge of the orders and special capacities of daemons. The magician must be "a very perfect Philosopher" who knows the qualities and effects of the four elements; he must also be a skilled physician, an herbalist, and a minerologist. He must understand distillation, know mathematics and particularly astrology, and understand optics, since "sleights" depend usually on the tricking of sight. Finally, "the professor of this Science must also be rich: for if we lack money, we shall hardly work in these cases." [7] No encouragement is offered poor men who may wish to use their knowledge of the science to acquire wealth. The mention of illusions is not accidental, for Della Porta enjoyed practical jokes and gives instructions about how to play them; but he was thinking also about mirrors and the *camera obscura,* which in a later chapter [8] he describes in some detail and which itself illustrates clearly the "wonders" attainable through his science.

So far our concern has been with his general view of his subject; we turn next to his conception of the universe. Natural substances, we are informed, are composed of matter and form (*nam substantiam voco id, quod ex utraque compactum est*), and although the matter is not altogether without force "the Form has such singular vertue, that whatsoever effects we see, all of them first proceed from thence," everything else—the elements and their qualities, for example—being used as the "instruments" of form.[9] This is to say that Aristotle's material cause is vastly inferior in potency to his formal cause; and it means also that in Della Porta's opinion the emphasis of many contemporaries on the four elements and their four qualities was misguided. The pre-eminency of form over matter is explained in the answer given to the question, "Whence the Form cometh." It comes "from a most excellent place; even immediately from the highest heavens, they receiving it from the intelligences, and these from God himself" (*a suprema igitur vertigine proxime, huic ab intelligentiis, illis denique ab ipso Deo*).[10] These intelligences, as every contemporary reader would have known without explanation, are spiritual beings intermediate between God and men: in the Christian view angels, in the Neo-Platonic view daemons. If Della Porta would not have us invoke the intelligences directly and, after this passage, ignores them, they nonetheless are brought into his account of the sources of energy. Hence, "seeing that formes come from heaven, they must needs be counted Divine and heavenly things." The Form-giver "doth not make it of any thing, as though it were but some frail and transitory substance, but fetcheth it meerly out of himself, and bestows it first upon intelligences and stars, and then by certain aspects informeth the Elements, as being fit instruments to dispose the matter. . . . Thus hath the providence of God linked things together in their rankes and order, that all inferiour things might by their due courses be derived originally from God himself, and from him receive their Operations."[11] Because of their high origin in the mind of God, the forms are what the magician will work with. Corroboration, the author adds, is provided by the "rings" of Plato and the "golden chain" of Homer.[12]

How these forms are to be conceived and used appears in what immediately follows. There are, we are told, sympathies and antipathies, or consents and disagreements, among creatures, "For some things are joyned together as it were in a mutual league, and some other things are at variance and discord among themselves." The only explanation necessary is that this is "the pleasure of Nature"; but from the consents and disagreements we can "gather many helps for the uses and necessities of men."[13] Although nothing is said at this point about forms, I believe I am not mistaken in thinking that the connections through sympathy and antipathy are to be referred to the discussion just preceding. As will be seen, similar shapes imply close relationships, and the examples to be given of plant and animal behavior may involve less obvious aspects of the Aristotelian and scholastic concept of form.

The illustrations, once begun, are profuse. "There is deadly hatred, and open enmity betwixt Colewarts and the Vine; for whereas the Vine windes it self with her tendrils about every thing else, she shuns Coleworts only." Hence Androcides learned that colewort is an effective antidote against drunkenness. Ivy is bad for all trees, but worst for the vine, so that it too is "good against drunkennesse." The same antagonism exists between cane and fern: "a Fern root powned (*contusa,* "crushed," "pounded"), doth loose and shake out the darts from a wounded body, that were shot or cast out of Canes." Hemlock and rue are similarly at enmity: if the gathering of rue in bare hands raises blisters, hemlock juice will remove them. According to Zoroaster, a wild bull tied to a fig-tree becomes gentle; so wild fig-stalks, if added to

VERA EFFIGIES.
IOANNIS BAPTISTÆ
PORTÆ.

Gio[vanni] Battista Dalla [*sic.*] Porta, *La Fisonomia dell'huomo, et la celeste* (in Venetia: Sebastian Combi, & Gio. La Noù, 1652), following title page.

Portrait of Della Porta.

water, make beef cook quickly. The next example is a name-magic which appears to imply the understanding of Latin by animals: "The Elephant is afraid of a Ram, or an engine of war so called . . . hence the Romans by these engines put to flight the Elephants of *Pyrrhus* King of the Epyrotes, and so got a great victory." Since the ape, a creature inclined to drunkenness, "cannot abide a Snail," "a Snail well washed is a remedy against drunkennesse." "A Dog and a Wolfe are at great enmity; and therefore a Wolves skin put upon any one that is bitten of a mad Dog, asswageth the swelling of the humour." [14]

The catalogue continues, sometimes offering consequences which appear not to relate to the details, or to relate to them in unexpected ways. "Those living creatures that are enemies to poisonous things, and swallow them up without danger, may show us that such poisons will cure the bitings and blows of those creatures." Where the emphasis might have been upon compatibility it is put upon destruction, as though the eating were motivated by hatred. Sometimes the lack of practical utility shows disinterested curiosity: "the breath of Elephants draws Serpents out of their dens, and they fight with Dragons; and therefore the members of Elephants burned, drives (*sic*) away Serpents." Finally, "the Morehenne loves the Hart, which is given to lust; both of their members are inciters to venery." [15]

Experimental testing of such precepts is not regularly easy. Where, for instance, can elephants be found demonstrating their enmity toward dragons? Even when it might be attempted—as by shooting a dart from a cane bow into an animal and then trying to dislodge it by applying fern root, or by obtaining a Roman battering ram from a museum and displaying it to zoo elephants to see whether they fall into panic—it is seldom likely to have been undertaken. The source of the beliefs must have been, very often, folklore, the unreliability of which is notorious; for the rest it was "scientific" treatises like the *Historia naturalis* of Pliny and other works which derived from or paralleled it, like the bestiaries, herbals, and lapidaries which played so important a role in the "unnatural natural history" of the Middle Ages. Sometimes implications are clearly drawn from what might be called "behavior," a word which I choose deliberately to imply some degree of consciousness. The shunning of cole-wort by the grapevine is illustrative. Again, the qualities are thought to inhere in parts as well as in the whole, so that eating a "member" of the moorhen or the hart transfers lubricity.

The treatise next turns to astrology, which had been especially prominent in Ficino's *De vita coelitus comparanda*. "I suppose," Della Porta writes, "that no man doubts but that these inferiour things serve their superiours, and that the generation and corruption of mutable things, every one in his due course and order, is over-ruled by the power of those heavenly Natures." The Egyptians, who lived under clear skies, realized "that all things took their destiny from them," an insight supported by citations from Ptolemy, Aristotle, Plato, Iamblichus, Orpheus, Plotinus, Albumasar, Hermes, Lucilius, Athenaeus, Democritus, and Vitruvius. The greatest power is the sun's, the next greatest the moon's. Some examples are given of the moon's influence. "When the moon passeth through those signs of the Zodiak which are most peculiar to the earth, if you then plant trees, they will be strongly rooted in the earth: if you plant them when she passeth through the signs of the Air, then the tree so planted, will be plentiful in branches and leaves." The earthy signs were Taurus, Virgo, and Capricorn, roughly equivalent to May, September, and January; the aerial signs were Gemini, Libra, and Aquarius, roughly equivalent to June, October, and February. No importance is attached to season, to heat or moisture, the effect of both being accepted as subsidiary to the position of the moon in a sign. [16]

Other illustrations are borrowed from the animal kingdom. The pismire or ant "worketh by night about the full of the Moon, but she resteth all the space betwixt the old and the new Moon. The inwards of mice answer the Moons proportion; for they encrease with her, and with her they also shrink away." Again, "The Beast

Robert Fludd, *De supernaturali, naturali, praenaturali et contranaturali microcosmi historia* (Oppenheim: Hieronymus Gallerus, 1619), title page.

The emblem relates the subject of the work, man or the microcosm, to the universe or macrocosm. With "Reason" written above his head, man stands with his hands and feet touching the rims of the visible universe: a symbol, perhaps, both of the range of his rational faculties and of their limitations. Beyond the sphere of the fixed stars, marked with the zodiacal signs, are three further areas, those of the Lower, Middle, and Higher Hierarchies. At the bottom each of these is divided in such a way as to assign three orders of angels to each of the three hierarchies. We thus have, reading from within outwards, the Angels, Archangels, Virtues, Powers, Principalities, Dominations, Thrones, Cherubim, and Seraphim. Inside the fixed stars are the planetary orbits in the usual order: those of Saturn, Jupiter, Mars, the Sun, Venus, Mercury, and the moon. Inside these, again, moving inwards, are the realms of fire, air, water, and (the black ball in the center) earth. Above "Reason" (which is correlative with the Lower Hierarchy) is "Intellect" (correlative with the Middle). Although illegible here, "Mind" (Mens) should appear above "Intellect" (to be correlative with the Higher Hierarchy). Between the man's legs are the humors: "Phlegm" (correlative with the realm of water), "Blood" (correlative with that of air), and the two *cholerae,* red and black (correlative with the realm of fire). The three words at the right which balance the faculties of the mind and the hierarchies present difficulties. The outermost means "Appearances" or "Epiphanies." The next seems to contain the Greek roots for "light" and "law" but may conceivably be patterned on ἐπιφώνημα, a rhetorical term for "interjections." If so, an allusion may be intended to *Rev.* 4: 6–8, where "beasts" full of eyes are described who chant "Holy, holy, holy" to Divinity. *Ephiona* is completely puzzling. If Greek, its form is incorrect; and it appears not to be Hebrew. Above all, surrounded by darkness (mystery) is brilliant light emanating from Deity, figured as brightness within a partly darkened (because not easily comprehensible) Trinity. The books on either side of the title signify that what appears on the pedestal will be explicated in the text.

Such an emblem offers a visual equivalent of the ambivalence of man's position in the universe. He is "low," because excellence diminishes from the outermost sphere inwards; but he is also the center, hence very far from despicable.

Cynocephalus (a dog-headed ape) rejoiceth at the rising of the Moon, for then he stands up, lifting his fore-feet toward heaven, and wears a Royal Ensign upon his head"; but when the moon is dark he hangs his head and refuses to eat, and his female "all that while pisseth blood." Such phenomena suggest to "whoever is rightly seen in all these things" that he should "ascribe all these inferiours to the stars as their causes; whereas if a man be ignorant hereof, he loseth the greatest part of the knowledge of secret operations and works of nature." [17]

This being so, how are we to "draw forth and fetch out the vertues and forces of superiour Bodies"? According to the (Neo-)Platonists it is precisely through magic that "the attraction or fetching out of one thing from another, by a certain affinity of Nature," is accomplished, the bond being love. This is why fire is drawn to the moon's sphere, earth drawn down to earth, iron drawn to the lodestone, chaff to amber, water to the moon. The "Indian Wisards" say that the whole world is alive and that male and female parts couple everywhere in it. Orpheus called Jupiter and Nature man and wife. "The very order of the Signs (which alternate in gender) declareth, that the World is everywhere male and female." Vegetation has both sexes, fire is male to air's female, water is male to earth's female. The magician profits from all this "when once he knows which and what kinds of matters Nature hath partly framed, and partly Art hath perfected." He prepares and compounds his substances "at such a time as such an influence raigneth; and by this means doth gain to himself the vertues and forces of heavenly bodies." The principle of affinity involved is similar to that which causes the flame of a candle to bend down and ignite a heated piece of paper which has been placed beneath it, the candle representing the "superiours," the planets and zodiacal signs, the paper representing "inferiours," the earthly things upon which the magician wishes to operate.[18]

Because all the parts of the universe are thus related, natural magic "depends upon the contemplation and view of the face of the whole world." We can be instructed by living creatures, which "though they have no understanding, yet their senses are far quicker then ours. . . . they teach us Physick, Husbandry, the art of Building, the disposing of Houshold affairs, and almost all Arts and Sciences." In physic, for example, we learn that bay leaves placed in doves' nests protect against enchantments; that wild olive is an antidote to a chameleon which an elephant has eaten by accident; that ants are a remedy against mandrakes, apes' blood against agues, staring at geese and ducks a remedy against stomach cramp, sow-thistle effective against dim-sightedness.[19] In the discussion of such lore Della Porta does not raise, and probably never thought of, such obvious questions as how we know, while watching a lion eat an ape, that the lion has been suffering from a quartian ague, or that the hawks which are observed to eat sow-thistle had bad vision before and good vision afterwards. The principle is none the less abundantly clear: animals and birds know by instinct natural sympathies and antipathies which we can discover by watching their behavior.

Certain sympathies are signaled by visual likeness. The herb *scorpius,* or walwort, is "like" a scorpion, therefore "good against the sting of him." *Testiculus,* or "Ragge-wort," is double and has a greater and a smaller part; "the greater helps generation, the smaller hinders it." The area of reference is determined by the suggestion of testicles; the smallness of the lesser part implies constriction, a failure to develop, hence antagonism to fertility. The herb called dragon "is full of speckles like a Serpents hackle, and is a remedy against their hurts." "The Lark hath a crested crown, of the fashion of the herb Fumitory." "An herb which grows in the head of an Image, being wrapt in a cloth, is good for the Head-ach." "Christal is like unto water; if one sick of an Ague keep it, and roul it in his mouth, it quenches his thirst." [20] Such associations derive not from the profounder wisdom of sages who lived in less degenerate times or from meticulous empirical study but from naive thought-processes not searchingly questioned because of a reverence for traditional wisdom.

So with the rest of Della Porta's doctrine, or most of it. A further guide to physic is the recognition that "All parts of the body, are nourished by their like, the brain by brains, teeth by teeth, lights (i. e., lungs) by lights, and the liver by the liver." The principle is that known as imitative magic and has been found in premodern cultures all over the globe. "A man's memory and wit is holpen by a Hens brain" despite the unmistakable stupidity of chickens; because the hare multi-plies rapidly its "womb and curd" make a woman fruitful, and its stones increase a man's potency. Carrying the skin or eyes of a lion or a cock—which was believed to terrify a lion if the two came face to face—makes a man bold and fearful to his adversaries; the tongues of talkative creatures like frogs, wild geese, and ducks, which chatter most in the evening, will make a woman "utter her night-secrecies" if placed in her bed.[21] The acceptance of such superstitions by a man of wide reading and at least moderate intelligence should not evoke astonishment, for modern scientific knowledge came late and was hard-won. The value of the *Magiae naturalis libri viginti,* indeed, is that because of the author's exceptional clarity and concreteness intellectual habits are revealed which in more pretentious documents are veiled by generalities, rhetoric, and even more frequent appeals to authorities whose works were impressive because of their antiquity.

A few additional principles may be noted more briefly. "A Harlot is not only impudent in her self, but she also naturally infects therewith, all that she touches and carries about her; so that if a man do often behold himself in her glasse, or put on her garments, it will make him impudent and lecherous as she is." [22] The qualities acquired by objects through use are contagious: what lies near something else comes to resemble it. A related principle is that things once connected continue to exercise an influence when separated. The particular example cited here has to do with the fact that the soul "is a chief help, and strikes a great stroke in those qualities which are in living creatures," so that if you can remove a creature's testicles, or tongue, or eyes without killing it the medicinal usefulness of the organ will be enhanced. Disseverment from the body and removal to another place does not interrupt a flow of energy into the part from the *anima*. In general, "virtues" possessed by living creatures tend to disappear at death but sometimes continue after it, as is demonstrated by the ability of a drumhead made of a wolf's skin to frighten sheep and the refusal of a harp strung with the guts of various animals to be tuned into harmony.[23]

Here Della Porta's theoretical book, the first of his twenty, comes to an end. We need do no more than glance at the remaining nineteen, which contain directions for magical operations without speculation about why they work. The plan is to begin with the natural sciences, those having to do with animals, plants, minerals, and "other works of Nature," and then, by way of a digression on fountains and

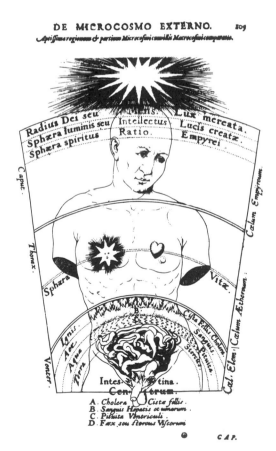

Robert Fludd, *De supernaturali, naturali, praenaturali et contranaturali microcosmi historia* (Oppenheim: Hieronymus Gallerus, 1619), p. 105.

"A very appropriate comparison of the divisions and parts of the microcosmos with those of the macrocosmos."

The highest part of the mind, *mens*, is a "ray of God, or uncreated light." The middle part, *intellectus*, lies within the "sphere of brightness or of created light." The lowest part, *ratio*, is within the sphere of the empyreal spirit. The whole head is in the empyreal heaven. The middle heaven, the aethereal, is divided by a "sphere of life" within which the human heart is shown as the microcosmic equivalent of the macrocosmic sun. In the lowest of the three heavens, the elemental, each of the elements is equated with one of the "humors": fire with cholera and the gall-bladder, air with the blood of the liver and the veins, water with phlegm and the stomach, and earth with the dregs or excrement of the bowels. The body centers on the sex organ.

springs, to proceed to the mathematical sciences.[24] Like all his contemporaries, Della Porta believed in generation from putrefying substances.[25] He also gives examples of mixed breeding—from a dog and a tiger, or a lion, or a wolf; from a dog and an ape; from a camel and a boar (the result is the two-humped camel); from a man and a mare, or an ass, or a goat.[26] A hare-lip, he tells us, comes from the mother's sight of a hare during pregnancy. A woman with child who longs for something will "imprint the likeness of the thing mused upon, in the tender substance of the child."[27] (This is the reason why, in Ben Jonson's *Bartholomew Fair* and many other writings, it is assumed that such a yearning must be gratified quickly.) Now and then the analogical thought-ways fundamental to most magical processes are obscure, as when we are informed that if a hen's egg is exactly round it will yield a cock but if elongated a hen,[28] but they can usually be guessed at. Here the connection probably turns on the "perfection" of the sphere as a geometrical shape and the superiority of the male to the female. The discussion of plant husbandry resembles that of the management of livestock and even begins with another section on generation by putrefaction. In later books the tone is sometimes jocular, as in a section on how to roast a goose without killing him: "you shall almost eat him up before he is dead."[29] Everywhere, however, the assumption is that "a Magician being furnished with Art, as it were another Nature, searching throughly [*sic*] into those works which Nature doth accomplish by many secret means and close operations, doth work upon Nature, and partly by that which he sees, and partly by that which he conjects and gathers from thence, takes his sundry advantages of Natures instruments, and thereby either hastens or hinders her work."[30] Occasionally he shows that he has actually experimented, as in writing about the lodestone or burning-glasses. On the whole, however, the treatise is backward–looking. We may profitably abandon it here and turn to Ficino.

III. Astrological magic and Marsilio Ficino's *De vita coelitus comparanda* (1489)

De vita triplici, written about 1482–89 and first published in 1489, consists of three parts. The first, called variously *De vita sana* and *De Studiosorum sanitate tuenda,*[31] is consistently medical. Ficino had been trained as a physician and continued to the end of his life to think of himself as a medical man despite the application of the greater part of his energy to a Platonizing philosophy. The emphasis is upon the diseases to which scholars are peculiarly subject, as in Burton's *Anatomy of Melancholy:* phlegm or *pituita,* atrabiliousness, *distillatio* or catarrh, headaches, and the like. The remedies prescribed are syrups, pills, electuaries, and other treatments outwardly not strikingly different from medicines or diets that might be prescribed today but derived from conceptions subsequently destroyed by such discoveries as those of the periodic table and of bacteria and viruses as the causes of infection. For

Ficino, as for the typical physician of his period, chemical analysis turned largely on the four elements and the four qualities, all having relations, which might be stressed or virtually ignored, with the planets, the zodiacal signs, and other celestial phenomena. The second part, *De vita longa* (1497) or *De vita producenda* (1576), is also chiefly medical but from time to time edges toward the occult, as in Chapter xiii, *Quae adminicula senes a Planetis accipiant ad omnia membra fouenda,* where attention shifts from pharmacopoeia to astrology; and in other places the subject is helpful odors and songs. Chapter xix salutes the mages who brought gifts to the infant Christ and urges old men to profit from such wisdom as theirs. The third section, however, is most pervasively magical and will repay most richly the study of persons attracted to the history of superseded ideas and attitudes. Its substance is best suggested if we translate the title, *De vita coelitus comparanda* (thus in both 1497 and 1576) as "On Guiding One's Life by the Stars" or, perhaps but not certainly more accurately, as "On Obtaining Life from the Heavens." [32]

The whole of Part III has to do with ways of attracting benevolent celestial influences—chiefly but not exclusively planetary—and repelling maleficent ones. The means include the making of talismans (*imagines*) to be worn on the body, the eating of foods made from plants in which the desired influences are especially concentrated, the breathing of appropriate odors, the hearing or chanting of songs whose tones and modes are accommodated to specific planets, the wearing of planetarily appropriate clothing, the selection of a proper spot for a dwelling, the choice of astrologically propitious ways of moving, and other behavioral patterns suited to the absorbing of desirable rays and protection against harmful ones. The first three chapters lay the groundwork for what follows by explaining in general terms how the influences work; and because in the present study theory is regarded as the grammar of practice we must pause on them.

The intellect and the body could not, we learn, be unified without the soul, since pure intellect lacks what might be called psychological drive (*affectus*), which is the principle of motion, and the body by itself is indisposed to activity.[33] The *anima* or soul is, however, *utrique conformis,* a suitable intermediary which shares the qualities of both, and is inclined to movement by its nature (*ex se, & sponte mobile*). It stands midway between divine and fallen nature and is drawn by *affectus* to each. The method so far is a traditional one of introducing between two incompatible terms a third which will permit communication between them. But there is also an *anima mundi* or World-Soul, and this is crucial to the train of thought.

The World-Soul, we are told, possesses as many "seminal reasons" or active principles as there are ideas in the Divine mind. By means of these it creates the species or varieties of material existences. When a specific form decays, it can be reconstituted by the absorption of appropriate matter even though this may be scattered (*sparsa*), the guiding force in the process being the seminal reason, which presses the matter into conformity with the "idea." *Mox in materiam hanc ita opportune paratam, singulare munus ab idea trahes, per rationem uidelicet animae seminalem.*[34] Powers or energies (*numina*) which are completely separated from matter cannot, however, become attached to it. Again we need a middle term to unite incompatibles, and this time the resolution is found in daemons and the *mundus animatus* or vital nature, especially the living stars. The whole world in fact is alive and filled with soul: *Neque in mundo uiuente toto quicquam reperitur tam deforme, cui non adsit anima, cui non insit & animae munus.*[35]

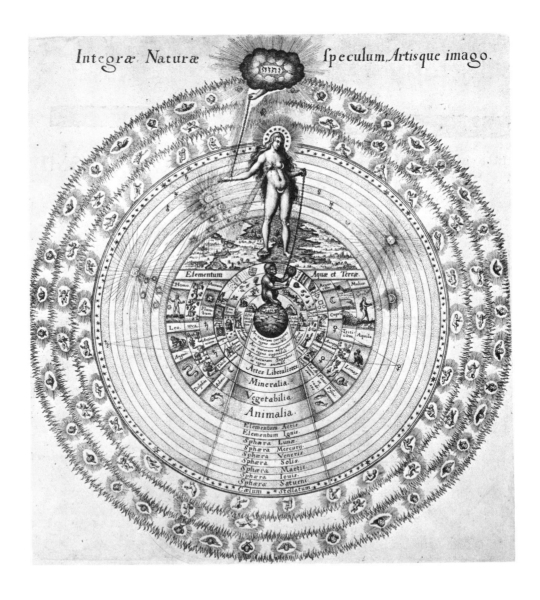

This Hermetic principle is exactly what Ficino needs for his purpose. The gifts made by soul to matter are of course always appropriate, just as we ourselves offer to men things suitable to them rather than to fish or birds. Alternatively, each material form may be thought of as attracting an appropriate soul, as firewood treated with sulphur draws flame. The union is accomplished partly through the rays of a star associated with a co-operating daemon and partly through the omnipresent World-Soul, from which both daemon and star acquire their rationality (*in qua & cuiuslibet stellae daemonisque ratio uiget*).[36] This rationality has two aspects: it is

---

Robert Fludd, *Utriusque cosmi maioris scilicet et minoris metaphysica, physica atque technica historia* (Oppenheim: Hieronymus Gallerus, 1617–1619), Vol. I, frontispiece.

The relationship of man's arts to nature. Interpretation is assisted by an "Emblematis . . . Explicatio" on I, 7. The outer three circles, which contain symbols that represent cherubim, seraphim, and archangels, surround the sphere of the fixed stars, the spheres of the planets, and two additional spheres of fire and air. At the top, God's hand holds a chain which descends to the figure of a nude virgin, Nature, pictured with starry hair in order to prevent identification as a pagan goddess. From her left hand, in turn, the chain descends to an ape, a symbol for Art; along the chain God's powers and effects are transmitted. Nature guides the *primum mobile* and turns the fixed stars (the draftsman has found no pictorial equivalents of these functions); also, influences from the fixed stars pass through her hands to generate material substances, and the planets act as *marculi,* or "little hammers," to produce earthly metals. Although pictured on one of her breasts, the sun is Nature's heart, and her belly is filled with the moon's body *(corpore lunari repletur).* The life and vitality of elemental creatures are born from her breast, which also feeds *(lactat)* the creatures constantly. The earth under Nature's right foot stands for sulphur, the water under her left foot for mercury; the joining of these through her body symbolizes their union in whatever is generated or grows. The ape, Art, is "born from man's talents" and helps Nature by means of secrets learned from diligent observation of her ways.

The seven innermost circles represent animals, vegetables, minerals, the "more liberal" arts, "Art Supplementing Nature in the Animal Kingdom," "Art Helping Nature in the Vegetable Kingdom," and "Art Correcting Nature in the Mineral Kingdom." The animals shown are, on the right, the fish, the snail, the eagle, and woman; on the left, the dolphin, the snake, the lion, and man. In the same order, the vegetables are flowers and roots, wheat; trees, grapes. The minerals are sal ammoniac, orpiment (Mercurial), copper (Venereal), and silver (Lunar); talc (if *taleum* is a mistake for *talcum,* glossed by Ruland as a "transparent, brilliant material"— again Lunar), antimony (Jovial), lead (Saturnian), gold (Solar). The more liberal arts are fortification, painting, perspective, geometry, music, arithmetic; motion, time, cosmography, astrology, geomancy. (The usual list included grammar, dialectic, rhetoric, arithmetic, music, geometry, and astronomy.) The arts which supplement or otherwise assist or correct nature are the following: in the animal kingdom, medicine, egg-production, bee-culture, sericulture; in the vegetable kingdom, tilling and tree-grafting; in the mineral kingdom, distillation by means of retorts and distillation by means of cucurbits (gourd-shaped vessels).

Much of this is peculiarly Fluddian, and much appears arbitrary—for example, the inclusion of "Time" and "Motion" as liberal arts. "The measurement of time and motion" is certainly intended. Other ambiguities and omissions may also be determined by spatial limitations.

seminal in breeding and exemplary in cognizing (*partim quidem seminalis ad generandum, partim etiam exemplaris ad cognoscendum*).[37] In other words, the star-daemon both acts and knows that it acts, and it has an intelligence which permits it to recognize formal categories. According to the older Platonists, among whom Plotinus is especially mentioned in the brief summary which heads the page, the World-Soul has built in that part of the heaven which lies beyond the stars "figures" that resemble the seminal reasons or generative powers mentioned earlier and has impressed special properties on them. There are forty-eight of these altogether, twelve being associated with the zodiacal signs and thirty-six, apparently, either with the "faces" of the signs or with the decans, who in Egyptian astrology ruled 10-degree sections of the sky.[38] Some awkwardness is evident here, since the seminal reasons have already been said to be equal in number to the ideas in the Divine mind; but I think we need not infer that the Divine ideas are limited to forty-eight. When the specificities offered by one ancient authority conflict with a general statement offered by another, both are kept as valuable.

After further remarks on stellar configurations Ficino returns to the *anima* or World-Soul. When this generates the lower (sublunar, terrestrial) forms and powers it does so, as has been seen, with the help of the stars and their figures. Individual differences (*Singulares uero indiuiduorum dotes*) have, however, rather a planetary origin, although the positions of the planets relative to the stars may be significant. As the human heart spreads vigor through the organs and limbs through the medium of the spirit, so the World-Soul radiates its energy from the sun, using as its instrument a fifth essence which flourishes everywhere as the spirit of the world's body. We can absorb more of this essence if we learn to separate it from impurities mixed with it. It is concentrated in subtle substances which have a "warm, damp, and clear quality"—for example, wine and white sugar, especially if to these we add gold and the odor of cinnamon and roses. A further principle, alluded to by Della Porta, enables us to direct the energy to any desired party of the body: food to help the brain, or liver, or stomach can be found in the brain, liver, or stomach of an animal as like a human being as possible. Not all solarian objects can be eaten, however, and those which cannot may be "exhibited" externally: metals, stones, and the like. This should be done especially in the day and hour of the sun, *Sole in figura coeli regnante;* and similar practices can be used to attract Jovial influences, provided only that we remember the necessity of introducing gold, wine, mint, and saffron into cold things.[39]

In illustration Ficino first offers a list of solarian things: all gems and flowers which are called "heliotrope" because they turn toward the sun; gold, orpiment, and whatever is golden in color; chrysolite, carbuncle, myrrh, frankincense, moss (*muscus*), amber, balsam, yellow honey, sweet calamus (*calamus aromaticus*), saffron, and cinnamon. Solar also are the cock, the swan, the lion, the beetle or Spanish fly (*cantharis*), and the crocodile. Men who are yellow-haired, or curly-haired, or, indeed, bald can "accommodate superior things to their use partly by eating them, partly by means of unguents and suffumigations." The favorable influence of other planets can be attracted in similar ways: for example, that of Jupiter through silver, hyacinth, the topaz, coral, crystal, beryl, sapphire, "green and bronze colors," wine, white sugar, honey, and thoughts or emotions which are steady, equable, religious, and regulative (*legiferis,* possibly "law-giving"). Among men, those are primarily Jovial who are sanguine in temperament, handsome, venerable. Among animals the lamb, the pea-cock, the eagle, and the bullock are Jovial. Venereal influences are treated more briefly: "Modesty does not allow me to explain how the virtue of Venus is attracted by turtle-doves, pigeons, the white water-wagtail (*motacillis*), and other things." Cor-nelian, sapphire, and lapis lazuli are Venereal, as are also copper of a saffron or red color, coral, all colors and flowers which are beautiful, variegated, or green, also harmonious sounds (*concentus*) and agreeable odors and tastes.[40] Some overlapping is noticeable among the categories, perhaps because of a similar overlapping of planetary *virtutes.*

Although the bases of such associations are too complex to work out in detail, clearly they have developed not from patient inductive research but from sensed or felt relationships. The peacock and the sun are both dignified, regal. Gold and the sun are primates or chieftains in their different orders and have a similar color. Frank-incense was offered by the mages to the infant Christ, a king like the sun. Amber, yellow honey, saffron, and cinnamon are yellowish, mellow, and "warm." The croco-dile was associated with the Nile, from the mud of which the sun generated living creatures. The lion too was a primate, and his mane perhaps suggested the sun's rays. From time immemorial the belief that he feared the cock indicated that the cock could be no less lordly; also the cock strutted and saluted the sun by crowing. And so with the rest. Such correspondences were extended by lore having to do with the pagan gods after whom the planets had been named: for example, the "love" of turtle-doves and the supposed lecherousness of pigeons made them Venereal.

Such explanations as these are of course partly guesswork, although partly not. I offer them to discourage once more a possible supposition that ancient wisdom is reliable in such matters, which the seers could have understood only by Divine reve-lation. Anthropologists can offer parallels from an astonishingly broad range of other cultures outside the Graeco-Roman sphere which are not credited with possessing a red line directly to God; nor do the details always coincide. Neither can importance be found in the documented "working" of the Graeco-Roman system. In Melanesia men are effectively charmed to death; in Africa a criminal falls instantly to the ground when he tastes a magical potion. All magical formulas have roughly equiva-lent potency: they succeed in the proportion in which they are believed in and the situation is one in which mental states are decisive.

Ficino's explanation is different: "preparations" of solar, Jovial, and Venereal plants, stones, and animals can be used without fear "Because they are made in heaven (*coelitus*), are under constant control (by God and His ministers), and are antecedently prepared there for such uses. What is most important is that the world is an animal which is more highly integrated (*animal in se magis unum est,* reading *unum* (1497) for *uinum* (1576)) than any other animal, even the most perfect. Accordingly, as the quality and movement of any one of our principal members extends to things other than itself, so the actions of the world's principal members move everything, and the members of lower things easily receive from the higher ones what they are prepared to offer."[41] Thus a Western intelligence offers as grounds for a world-wide belief an analogy between the structure of a man or other animal and that of the entire universe. In the long run Western rationality was to arrive at notions which would first undermine, and later destroy, the older mythical thought-patterns; and because it had from antiquity a greater potentiality than non-Western thought to achieve such a development even its older manifestations are precious. Before this could happen, however, it was necessary that millennia pass during which it accepted "natural" views characterized by the projection of man's self-consciousness and purposiveness upon what did not possess them.

A theoretical justification having thus been provided, Ficino continues with a discussion of the choices of planetary influences. The Arabian astrologers consider man principally solar, and Ficino agrees because of man's erect and attractive posture, his subtle humors, the clarity of his spirit, the sharpness of his imagination, and his zeal for truth and glory. But man also has a Mercurial quality "because of the strenuous mobility of his native versatility." He is born naked, weaponless, and lacking in everything but acquires what he needs by industry, *quod est Mercurij proprium.* He is also partly Jovial: in his "complexion" or temperament, in his laws, and because the second month, when the foetus receives life, and the ninth, in which it is born, are under the domination of Jupiter. For the rest, the influence of Saturn is equivocal and causes men to be solitary, divine or inert (reading the *brutum* of 1497 for the *bruta* of 1576), blessed or miserable; and Mars, the moon, and Venus have to do with emotions and acts which are common to men and other animated creatures. Let us therefore turn to the sun, Jupiter, and Mercury: *Ad Solem igitur & Iouem atque Mercurium reuertamur.*[42] This conclusion is qualified later, when the coldness and austerity of Jupiter are said to be benevolently qualified by the warmth and softness of Venus; but on the whole we are to obtain strength, dignity, and justice from Jupiter, wit, activity, and inventiveness from Mercury, and everything good from the sun, which, however, because of its intensity may usefully be tempered by a judicious admixture of the cooler Jovial influences and the moister Venereal ones.

Chapter ii also contains, for the sake of completeness, a list of Mercurial, lunar, Saturnine, and Martial stones, plants, animals, and colors but reminds us that influences are to be attracted when the planet "is dominant, as has been said, in its day and hour if possible, but also when it is in its domicile, or exaltation, or at least in its triplicity, at its terminus, or in an angle of the sky in which it is not retrograde (*directus*) or combust, or, most often, in the east, if placed higher than the sun; or, again, when it is in apogee and in aspect with the moon." [43] We must bear in mind, too, that we are exposed to and dominated by the planet whose qualities we share. We become subject to Saturn through listlessness (*otium*), solitude, constancy (*firmitatem*), theology, occult philosophy, superstition, magic, agriculture, and sadness; to Jupiter through civil and competitive business, natural philosophy, civil piety, and concern with the law; to Mars through anger and strife; to the sun and Mercury through zeal for eloquence, song, and adroitness in pursuit of the truth and of glory; to Venus through pleasure, music, and festivity; to the moon through plant-like food (*uictum plantis similem*). Certain fine discriminations must be made. For instance, the public and large-scale (*amplam*) exercise of talents is solar, the private and cunning exercise Mercurial. Or, again, grave music is Jovial or solar, light music is Venereal, and that between is Mercurial.[44] But the principle by now is clear.

The third and last of the three introductory chapters having to do with general theory adds little that is new. We are told again that the *mundanum corpus* is alive, as Indian philosophers proved by its generation of living things—a notion finally to be disproved by Pasteur—and are reminded that the agency of its life is the *anima*. Between the *anima* and the tangible world, which is partly fallen, the medium of communication is spirit, as between our souls and bodies; and this spirit, through which generation is accomplished, may be called either "heaven" or "fifth essence." It exists both in the world's body and in ours; only the world does not draw it from the four elements, as if from its humors, in the way ours does. Instead it is procreated by the world's "generative virtue" *quasi tumens,* as if from its spontaneous swelling, and with it the stars and the four elements. The spirit is a *corpus tenuissimum, quasi non corpus, & quasi iam anima,* a body so fine that it is almost a soul; it contains very little earth, more water, more air still, and most of all stellar fire. This is the immediate agent (*proximus author*) of all generation and motion; hence the saying, *Spiritus intus alit,* "The spirit nourishes within." It is bright, warm, moist, life-giving, and the source of higher endowments in the soul.[45] If all this is mostly recapitulation, it tends at least to fix in our minds an outline of Ficino's most basic conceptions.

The remainder of *De vita coelitus comparanda* can be skimmed more hastily. We shall, however, notice some of the most characteristically Ficinian emphases in Chapters iv–xxvi, paying special attention to the recommendations which are most unmistakably magical.

Repeatedly Ficino discusses the use of talismans or *imagines:* medals or rings made of appropriate astrological materials and sometimes inscribed with the symbols of planets or constellations. Much has been made of these by D. P. Walker in *Spiritual and Demonic Magic from Ficino to Campanella* and by Frances Yates in *Giordano Bruno and the Hermetic Tradition*,[46] and Ficino is obviously fascinated by them. In the background, probably, is a famous passage in the Hermetic *Asclepius* (discussed in Chapter V of the present study) which has to do with the ability of the ancient Egyptians to induce daemons to dwell within images made to attract them. It should be noted, however, that Ficino is cautious in his treatment of the subject. He denies that daemons can be forced [47] and says plainly that he himself does not use images: *Ego enim medicinis ad coelum temperatis, non imaginibus utor.*[48] Medicines are far preferable because powders, liquors, unguents, and electuaries are not only more apt to absorb astrological influences than are stones and metals but may be taken directly into the body and, moreover, can be compounded of many ingredients.[49] Yet the talismans are repeatedly recurred to, as if Ficino could not keep his mind off them, and Chapters xiii, xv, xvi, xviii, and xx are given over to them almost wholly.

Chapter xiii is partly historical. Ptolemy mentioned images in the *Centiloquium,* saying that they were to be made at astrologically appropriate times. Haly says that an image of a snake can be useful if it is made when the moon enters the constellation Serpent or is in a favorable aspect to it, and an image of a scorpion made when the moon is in Scorpio or in aspect with it. The passage from the Hermetic *Asclepius* is cited: not only daemons, but even the souls of ancestors—Hermes, Isis, Osiris— were drawn into the Egyptian images. Zoroastrian magicians evoked the spirit of Hecate with the aid of a golden pillar (or ball? *aurea quadam pila*) inscribed with heavenly characters and set with a sapphire. Porphyry asserts the power of images and says that proper incensing of them at the right astrological moments will draw aerial daemons into them; and so also Iamblichus, Proclus, and Synesius. Such images can be good for the health, if less wonderfully so than medicines. Because hard substances absorb energy only with difficulty it is, however, important to choose the right materials, as, for example, gold if solar influence is in question.[50]

In chapter xv, where the superiority of medicines is again insisted on, we are told that a (solar) stone can be hung about the neck with gold bound to it by saffron-colored threads of silk while the sun is ascending under Aries or Leo—two solar signs—or is in the middle of the sky and in aspect with the moon. For attracting lunar influence the best stone is selenite, "which not only imitates the moon in its shape but, by its motion, accompanies (*circumeat cum . . .*) the moon." If you find this, suspend it, surrounded with silver, from your neck by means of a silver thread when the moon is entering Cancer or Taurus or is at suitable angles with them. Warmed by your body, it will introduce its virtue continuously into you. But we do not know the solar stone, Pantaurus, found by Apollonius Theanaeus in India, which shines like fire and has so much spirit that it breaks the earth where it is conceived and draws other stones to it as a magnet draws iron.[51] The chapter includes an account of some experiments made by Ficino with stones during his youth: for example, he engraved a bear on a magnet to obtain the influence of the celestial Ursa Major and hung the medal round his neck on an iron thread, but desisted because he had discovered that the influence was mostly Saturnian and Martial. Another passage has to do with a Persian charm against snakebite made by incising on the stone emathite an image of a man girded with a serpent who holds the serpent's head in his right hand and its tail in the left, his knees bent, his head thrown a little back. This is enclosed in a gold ring with the symbol of the constellation Serpent inserted between the metal and the stone. In such ways as these the principle is confirmed that heavenly things are closely connected with earthly.[52] Ficino himself is none the less inclined to think that nature works best without too much forcing (*soleat tenore quodam progredi naturali*). He does not deny some efficacy in images and believes that something may be accomplished by them if the materials are chosen with care, but he repeats that more power inheres in astrologically prepared medicines and unguents.[53]

Chapter xvi once more explains the theory behind all this. The occult virtues of things have not an elemental source but a celestial one. Stellar and planetary rays are alive; [54] they shine, as it were, from the eyes of living bodies, and offer wonderful gifts from the imaginations and minds of celestial beings. The effects of the rays are produced very rapidly, as when a person is fascinated by a glance; Ficino has explained this phenomenon in his book on love.[55] Chapter xviii describes planetary and zodiacal images: for instance, Mercury can be represented as a throned man with a cock's crest and eagle's feet, holding a cock or fire in his left hand, winged, with a pen in his right hand, and dressed in vari-colored garments.[56] Such representations appear also in the iconological treatises which are so important for the interpretation of Renaissance art and need not detain us. Other uses of images are mentioned: to bring minds together or to separate them, to bring happiness or calamity to a single person, to a household, or to a city.[57] Campanella was later to equip his imaginary *Città del sole* with images apparently intended to protect the entire population against misfortune. Nevertheless Ficino continues to show uncertainty, his mind evidently being divided: "I do not assert that such things can be done. Astrologers think they can be done, and teach how, but I dare not explain such matters." [58] He says that Thomas Aquinas was fearful of images, and that Iamblichus believed that the users of them were often deceived by daemons who pretended to be good. In any event, in Ficino's opinion the power, if it exists, has its source not in the carving but in the materials, which may at most be warmed into slightly greater activity by the engraver's tools. *Praeter enim id quod inanes esse figuras suspicor, haud temerè uel umbram idolatreiae debemus admittere.* It is better to avoid the suspicion of idolatry by omitting figures.[59] Chapter xx recurs once more to the subject but adds little new except the suggestion that the working of images will be assisted, like most other magical operations, by a strong faith.[60]

Throughout these sections Ficino's tone wavers. He is interested but doubtful, attracted but troubled by scruples. So might any deeply pious magician at times wonder about the limits of the permissible. The observation that, in any event, metals absorb celestial influences less readily than other substances, and that medicines not only can be taken directly into the body but also can be skillfully compounded, offers some relief. The theory underlying the construction and use of talismans is, however, already familiar and may fairly be described as an adaptation to minerals of practices described elsewhere by Ficino in relation to astrological medicine.

Other sections of the *De vita coelitus comparanda* offer the picture of a man enamoured of astrology trying additional ways of inviting beneficent celestial influences and discouraging maleficent ones. In Chapter xi, for instance, we are advised how best to absorb vital energy from the World-Spirit. We should be nourished and warmed by things recently alive which were close to Mother Earth— among other things, the fragrance of plants and trees, which refreshes and invigorates as if *flatu spirituque uitae mundanae*. Because the World-Spirit is midway between body and soul it is wonderfully good for both. High, serene, and temperate places are most suitable for absorbing it. The sun's rays are stronger there, and the constant motion of the air, even if barely perceptible, will bathe and penetrate you as you walk about in daylight or dwell in suitable quarters, lending motion and vitality to your spirit. You should choose odorous places for your walks but should

SCALA NOVENARII.

Nomina Dei novem literarum.	Tetragrammaton Sabaoth. יהוה צבאות			Tetragrammaton Zidkenu. יהוה צדקנו			Elohim Gibor. אלהימגיבר			In Archetypo.
Novem chori angelorum.	Seraphim.	Cherubim.	Throni	Dominationes.	Potestates.	Virtutes.	Principatus.	Arhangeli.	Angeli.	In mundo intelligibli.
Novem angeli praesidentes coelis.	Metanon.	Orphaniel.	Zaphkiel.	Zadkiel.	Camael.	Raphael.	Haniel.	Michael.	Gabriel.	
Novem sphaerae mobiles.	Primū mobile.	Cœlum stellatū.	Sphara Satur.	Sphara Iovis.	Sphara Martis.	Sphara Solis.	Sphara Veneris.	Sphara Mercurii.	Sphara Lunae.	In Mundo coelesti.
Novem lapides, repraesentantes novem choros angelorum.	Sapphyrus.	Smaragdus.	Carbūculus.	Berillus.	Onyx.	Chrysolithus.	Iaspis.	Topazius.	Sardius.	In mundo elementali
Novem sensus, cùm extimi tum intimi.	Memoria.	Cogitativa. *	Imaginativa.	Sensus cōmunis.	Auditus.	Visus.	Odoratus.	Gustus.	Tactus.	In minore Mundo.
Novem ordines Cacodaemonum.	Pseudothei.	Spiritus mendacii.	Vasa iniquitatis.	Vltores scelerū.	Praestigiatores.	Aereae potestates.	Furiae seminatrices malorū	Criminatores sive exploratores	Tentatores sive insidiatores.	In Mundo infernali.

change them frequently and move about gently. The mind must avoid Saturnian tedium and cultivate instead the *voluptas* of Venus, which will be aided by the fancy that you are walking in the Paradise described by Moses.[61] Foods should be chosen because of their special relationship to the planets whose influences we wish to receive. We are reminded also of the planetary affinities of tastes, odors, and musical sounds. Pleasing and seductive sounds and songs belong to Jupiter, the sun, and Venus, or sometimes to Mercury, threatening and mournful ones to Mars and Saturn.[62]

The advisability of keeping oneself in maximal contact with solarian or, less frequently, Jovial, Mercurial, and Venereal things is developed elsewhere. "Wear, dwell in, look at, hear, smell, imagine, think about, and desire solarian things. Imitate the sun's dignity and services in your life. Move among solarian men and plants and touch laurel constantly." But it will be best, as has already been noted, occasionally to mix in Jovial and Venereal things.[63] In a word, having learned the planetary affiliations of plants, animals, and minerals, we are to associate ourselves in appropriate ways—by eating, drinking, smelling, touching, looking at, or hanging them about our bodies—with whatever objects are in sympathy with, or under the influence of, the planet or planets we think most beneficent to us. So far as may be possible, account is to be taken of the astrological situation, as by walking in the sun on the sun's day and in its hour, or making a Jovial talisman when Jupiter rules the sky. Even our companions may be chosen with regard to celestial considerations. A Saturnian like Ficino—or any other serious philosopher—should avoid other Saturnians, who will increase his tendency to melancholy and bodily inertia, and consort instead with solar, Jovial, or, occasionally, with Mercurial or Venereal persons, whose cheerfulness and alacrity will tend to lighten his spirit. Although the system's details are complex, its basis is easily grasped.

One further set of considerations causes the minutiae to fall into a neat struc-

---

Henry Cornelius Agrippa of Nettesheim, *Opera* (London, ?1531), I, 152.

The scale of nine. The headings in the left-hand column read "Names of God in Nine Letters," "The Nine Choirs of Angels and the Nine Angels Who Preside over the Heavens," "The Nine Moving Spheres," "The Nine Stones Which Signify the Nine Orders of Angels," "The Nine External and Internal Senses," and "The Nine Orders of Bad Daemons." Balancing these, in the right-hand column, are the headings "In the Archetype," "In the Intelligible World," "In the Heavenly World," "In the Elemental World," "In the Lesser World" (man, the microcosm), and "In the Infernal World." Much of the rest consists of names or is readily intelligible. "Iaspis" and "Sardius," in the third horizontal line, are jasper and carnelian. The orders of bad daemons include "False Gods," "Lying Spirits," "Vessels of Iniquity," "Avengers of Crimes," "Deluders," "Aerial Powers," "Furies Who Sow Evil," "Accusers or Examiners," and "Tempters or Layers of Ambushes."

ture. "As the number of the planets is seven, so there are seven degrees or stages (*gradus*) through which inferior things are attracted to superior." The lowest degree, that of stones, metals, and hard things, belongs to the moon. The Mercurial grade includes herbs, fruits, gums, and animals' members. The Venereal grade involves subtle powders and their vapors and the smells of herbs and flowers. The order of Apollo, or the sun, is that of words, songs, and sounds. Mars's grade includes "powerful concepts of the imagination, forms, movements, and desires." The Jovial grade consists of rational deliberations and consultations, the Saturnine grade of *secretiores simplicioresque intelligentiae, quasi iam a motu seuinctae, conuinctae diuinis,* or the more secret and uncomplicated ideas which are disjoined from motion but allied to divine matters.[64] Because this schedule contradicts much that we have already been told, it is difficult to take seriously. We have heard about solarian, Jovial, and Venereal plants and animals, and the long discussion of medals and rings has been misleading if stones, metals, and all hard things belong to the moon. Ficino's mind lacked tough precision, so that a fondness for systematization leads him to find attractive, despite its incompatibility with other parts of his treatise, an organizing principle which at once enhances the parallelism of sublunary things with celestial and creates a progression which moves from hard materiality, in the lowest sphere, through such intermediaries as vapors and odors to words and concepts of increasing abstractness. The passage appears, however, in a context having to do chiefly with songs, and upon these we may pause finally.

Words, we have been told, have the power to affect images when pronounced with special feeling, *acriore quodam affectu.*[65] The agency is probably Venereal daemons who rejoice in such works and words, or perhaps *daemones simpliciter seductores.* (Since we are to hear of songs appropriate to several of the planets, once more awkwardness is apparent.) At any rate, the power of words is attested by Origen, Zoroaster—who, together with Iamblichus, forbade the changing of barbarous words—Pythagoras, ancient Hebrew sages, and poets generally. At this point Ficino again feels a scruple and says, "It is best to leave incantations alone" (*Sed praestat dimittere cantiones*);[66] but not all songs are incantations, and after the passage already summarized about the seven planetary *gradus* he proceeds to describe how tones, or compositions of tones, can be discovered which belong to specific heavenly bodies.

The method requires, first, that we find out the power or effects of a star, a constellation, or even an aspect and what things are repelled by it, or attracted. The next step is to consider what star dominates what place and what men, and to observe the tones and songs used there so that you will be able to use the same ones and the meanings implicit within them. (For example, India was known to be Saturnian, Spain Jovial, Britain Martial, Egypt solar.) Finally, we must study the daily positions and aspects of the stars, and, under these, find out the speeches, songs, motions, and leapings (*saltus*), together with the customs and actions, to which men are moved by them so that we may be able to imitate these in the songs which we will address to a given part of the sky. Song is the most powerful of all imitations because it reflects the intentions and moods of the spirit and stirs up those who hear it. Harmony is purer than matter and more like the sky than medicine, for it is warm, breathing air and, in a way, alive, composed of articulations and joints (*articulationibus artubusque*) like an animal, and possessed of a feeling and significance to which the sky will respond, as will the singer himself, especially if his nature is Phoebean (Apollo being the god of song). If rays from the eyes can infect, so much more can a spirit flowing richly from the imagination and heart, more fervent and stronger in motion, so that it can remove or inflict diseases of the body and spirit. The Pythagoreans and Platonists, indeed, say that the sky is a spirit which rules everything by its movements and tones. All music comes from Apollo ultimately, but Jupiter is a musician in so far as he is *cum Apolline concors,* and Venus and Mercury when near Apollo (the sun). The remaining planets have not songs but voices (*uoces*). Jovial harmonies are grave, eager, sweet, and joyful. Venus's are lascivious, soft, voluptuous. Those of the sun and Mercury are intermediate between these. Our task is to conciliate each of these planets with our songs: to make them respond as one zither does to a note struck on another. Prayers, too, if full of feeling and sense and spoken vehemently, work like songs. But this has been spoken of "a certain natural power of speech" and is not to be misunderstood as the invocation of pagan deities (*de numinibus adorandis*).[67]

All this is written with a special fervor, as though Ficino's sympathies were strongly engaged. The section allows us to add to an image of the author wearing solarian garments, eating solarian foods, drinking solarian liquids, and walking in the sun at astrologically appropriate times—though without the dubious solarian medals hanging from his neck or solarian rings on his fingers—another image of the same man, no doubt similarly accoutered, strumming a musical instrument in solarian rhythms and intoning solarian words while dancing or posturing, if this could be done simultaneously, in a solarian way and making solarian gestures and leaps. Or, again, we can imagine him inviting Jovial, or Venereal, or Mercurial influences in comparable ways. A program of this sort, if followed earnestly, might absorb a large part of one's waking energy. Nevertheless we must do Ficino the justice of recognizing that his intentions were innocent of malice and that his "magic"—for magic it certainly was—was guarded anxiously against idolatry and, like Della Porta's, was conceived as "natural."

IV. Spiritual or ceremonial magic and Cornelius Agrippa's
De occulta philosophia libri tres (1531)

With the *De occulta philosophia libri tres* of Cornelius Agrippa of Nettesheim (an early version completed about 1510; first printed version apparently 1531, first dated edition 1533) we are in the intellectual universe of a man who although at times somewhat aggressively pious [68] was suspected of forbidden arts and popularly believed to have a familiar spirit in the shape of a black dog that plunged into a river at his death.[69] Like Paracelsus, he had a prickly character that embroiled him with his associates and kept him moving restlessly about Europe; but he was capable of writing modestly, and the *De occulta philosophia* is calmly declarative rather than combative. Nowhere is there a fuller compendium of all the kinds of magic which stopped short of witchcraft. Discussion of it has been postponed here because of the intention to work up to it through more skeptical or limited treatises; [70] but it might have engrossed our attention throughout the whole chapter, and no single work is a better introduction to the subject.

A doubt is raised about Agrippa's commitment to occultism by a work called *De incertitudine et vanitate omnium scientiarum et artium* and published in 1531, either simultaneously with the *De occulta philosophia* or a little earlier. Since the latter was written about 1510 and the former, presumably, much later, the *De incertitudine* can easily be interpreted as a recantation. The problem, however, is complicated. If the magical work had come to be regretted, why did the author permit its publication? and if for money only, why did he not add a warning at the beginning or end? Further, the *De incertitudine* is by no means directed wholly, or even chiefly, against magic. It attacks also grammar, poetry, history, oratory, disputation, the art of memory, arithmetic, music, dancing, dueling, the arts of courtly and domestic economy, ethics, metaphysics, and much else. Indeed, it appears to be indiscriminately skeptical: all human knowledge is riddled with error. (From this point of view, magic may be as "true" as anything else.) Again, in Chapter XLVI we are told that theurgy, or the invoking of superhuman powers other than devils, is not forbidden. This is not to say that the two works do not often conflict directly. For example, astrology, assumed in the earlier work to be trustworthy, is strongly attacked in the later. Nevertheless it may be doubted that Agrippa ever really abandoned faith in magic. For one thing, the denunciatory tone appropriate to diatribe tends, by an internal momentum, to distort actual beliefs. Everything drawn into discussion must be treated as contemptible; and the occult sciences could not be omitted from a treatise intended to seem exhaustive. The result is less a sober confession than a massive rhetorical achievement. A second reason is the strong possibility that Agrippa wanted to safeguard himself against accusations of heresy (which were in fact made) by providing himself in advance with a defense. If criticized, he could point out that his orthodoxy was on record. But in any event *De occulta philosophia,* which was much reprinted, was not in its own century regarded as a compendium of exploded superstitions. It was rather a *summa* of esoteric wisdom, and as such we shall consider it here.

The three books are given over, respectively, to natural, celestial, and ceremonial (or religious) magic. Of these, the first is much like Della Porta's *Magia naturalis* and Ficino's *De vita coelitus comparanda* together but more orderly, more specific, and less defensive. It discusses the elements; the occult virtues in things; sympathies and antipathies; the dominance of *superiora* over *inferiora;* the powers and influences of the planets, the signs, and certain fixed stars; how to attract "the divinities who rule the world, and their ministers the daemons"; poisons; fumigations; unguents and philters; rings; lights and colors; fascination; divination and auguries; presages and prodigies; geomancy, hydromancy, aeromancy, and pyromancy (one divinatory skill for each of the elements); the revival of the dead; dreams; passions and their effects on the body; the virtues of words, including proper names; incantations and enchantments; the relations of letters in several languages (Hebrew, "Chaldaean," Greek, and Latin) to signs and planets; and much else. Although parts of this go beyond Della Porta and Ficino and not all the magic seems "natural," some of the new themes are taken up later in the books upon which we can most usefully focus our attention.

We shall begin with a consideration of numbers, which had been highly significant in Plato's *Timaeus,* almost the only writing by Plato known in the Middle Ages, and the subject matter—though the emphasis there was different—in the entire *quadrivium* of arithmetic, astronomy, geometry, and music. The subject had already been introduced in Book I, in which we are informed that the order, the numbers, and the shapes of letters "are not arranged by chance or accident (*non fortuito, nec casu*) or by the caprice of men, but are formed divinely, so that they relate to and accord with the heavenly bodies, the divine bodies, and their virtues." Of all languages Hebrew is *sacratissima* not only in its shapes (*figuris*) but also in its vowel points and accents, "as if consisting in matter, form, and spirit, having been produced in God's seat, which is Heaven, by the positions of the stars."[71] Aspects in the correspondence of the Hebrew letters with planets and fixed stars are determined by such qualities as forms, separations, reversals, twistings, directions, sizes, openings, closings, and order.[72] Briefly, the letters are not, as is understood today, conventional symbols chosen from an almost unlimited range of possibility but are so representative of the actual structure of the universe, or its parts, that manipulations of them have intrinsic power. The belief requires no explanation.

It is still common among illiterate people and among children, who, if told that "eau" means "water," may say, "But it's *really* 'water,' isn't it?" With what degree of seriousness I do not know, C. S. Lewis plays with a similar idea in his cosmic trilogy, *Out of the Silent Planet, Perelandra,* and *That Hideous Strength,* in which the "Old Solar" spoken beyond the sphere of the moon not merely expresses but contains the real nature of things. A primitive awe of letters is testified not only by anthropological reports but also by Homer's sole reference to writing (*Iliad* vi, 168–70). Accordingly, we are to be instructed first in that part of the total science of numbers which is described by the term "numerology."

The Hebrew alphabet has three parts: twelve letters are simple, seven double, and three are *matres,* "mothers," "parents," or "sources." The simple letters correspond with the twelve zodiacal signs, the double ones with the seven planets, and the *matres* with the three elements (excluding air, which the Hebrews regarded as a bond and spirit of the others). In a way which is not explained, the vowel points and accents also fit into the system. The result is that the characters are like

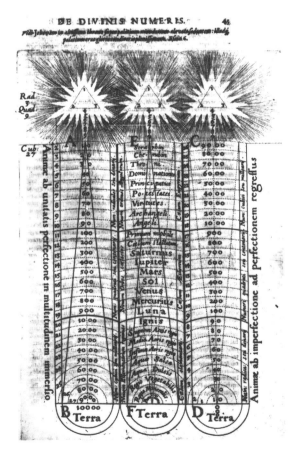

Robert Fludd, *De supernaturali, naturali, praenaturali et contranaturali microcosmi historia,* (Oppenheim: Hieronymus Gallerus, 1619), p. 45.

Numerology and the heavens. This figure is badly printed and hard to reproduce clearly. On the facing page, the decades (10, 20, 30, etc.) are said to be like lines, the hundreds like surfaces, and the thousands like solid bodies. "For this reason the composition of the highest heaven is simple, like a line drawn out from a divine point, or like a decade—a number equal to that of simple fingers flowing from superessential unity. The composition of the middle heaven is like a surface, related to the higher as a surface is related to a line or a square to its root. The lower heaven is related to the middle, from which it proceeded, or to the composition of the middle, as to a square, or as a body is related to its surface, by the multiplication of which it has been produced." That is to say, a line moving laterally produces a surface, and a surface moving forward or backward produces secrets or sacraments and are vehicles, as it were, of their material referenda and of the "essences" and powers these contain (*rerum explicatarum, illarum essentiam & vires ubique secum ferentes*).[73] For this reason Origen believed that Hebrew names lost their force when translated.[74] "Accordingly the twenty-two letters are the basis of the world and of all the creatures which exist and are named by them." [75] The Chaldaean alphabet has the same three divisions, and the alphabets of other languages have also been related to signs, planets, and elements. The equivalences are explained in a table; but the Hebrew letters, we are reminded, are most efficacious and have deepest meaning.[76]

Book II, in which numerology is especially developed, opens with praise of mathematics and a claim that "everything which is done in terrestrial affairs by natural energies is accomplished, led, or governed by number, weight, measure, harmony, movement, and light." [77] This is proved by Aristotle's mention of self-moving effigies and by descriptions elsewhere of speaking statues of Mercury, a flying wooden pigeon, and a hissing serpent of brass. All these and similar wonders, of which vestiges still exist, were produced through a knowledge of natural science and of mathematics.[78] Further, the Pythagoreans, other pagan philosophers, and Hebrew sages agree that because mathematical concepts are more "formal" than physical ones they have greater actuality: [79] a notion compatible with philosophical realism and a preference for stable concepts over mutable physicality. Through numbers "we succeed in discovering and understanding everything knowable.

---

a solid body. "Thus the third heaven is the height and length of constructed objects, the middle heaven their breadth, and the lowest heaven their depth. And this is what the Sacred Scriptures testify when they say, 'All things are established by number, weight, and measure.' . . . In the supersubstantial world, the Two have emerged in this way from the One, and from the Two, the Third; which Three, indeed, by their ineffable disposition, look down from their supersubstantial world and burst forth as a joyful harmony into the material world. . . . In this way everything was produced from nothing by number, measure, and weight."

In the left-hand column of the figure we read, from the top downward, "Radicals or tens," "squares or hundreds," and "cubes or thousands." These same phrases reappear in reverse order at the right of the third column. At the left of the middle column appear "The nine orders of angels," "The nine celestial spheres," and "The nine elemental regions." The last are those of fire; higher, middle, and lower air; salt and fresh water; and the vegetable, mineral, and earthly kingdoms. Along the left margin is written, "The immersion of the soul from the perfection of unity into multiplicity"; along the right, "The return of the soul from imperfection to perfection."

Apparently the three columns are to be thought of as superimposed, not as separate. For example, the soul descends from heaven and in due time, if all is well, reascends to it, passing, as it does so, through the elementary regions, the celestial spheres, and the spheres of the orders of angels.

Through it we come nearest to natural prophecy; and Abbot Joachim himself arrived at his prophecies in no other way than through formal numbers." [80]

These assertions are immediately supported by more authorities: Jerome, Augustine, Origen, Ambrose, Gregory Nazianzenus, Athanasius, Basil, Hilary, Rabanus, and Bede, all Catholic doctors whose opinions coincided with those of the pagan authors already named. The fundamental principle can be seen in the herb *pentaphyllon,* or cinquefoil, which by virtue of its five leaves resists poisons, drives away demons, and assists expiation. One of its leaves taken twice daily in wine cures the ephemeral or one-day fever, three cure tertian fever, and four cure quartian fever, the cause being a "proportion" of numbers with "things." Simple numbers—those from one to nine—signify divine things, the tens heavenly things, the hundreds terrestrial things, and the thousands things of ages to come.[81] Here follow chapters on the numbers from one to ten (Chaps. iv–xiii), one on the numbers eleven and twelve, and one on numbers above twelve. We shall be able to afford space only to one of the simpler chapters and the *Scala,* or ladder, which accompanies it, that which treats of the number two.

Two signifies knowledge, memory, light, man (the microcosm), charity, weddings, and society. Although the first three of these equivalences are partly obscure, the remaining four offer no difficulty. The microcosm is the second and lesser of the two *mundi;* in charitable actions one person extends loving help to another; a marriage is the union of two souls, also of male with female; society begins with the association of two persons. Two also represents sex (there are two sexes); a middle place marked by man's capacity to participate in good and evil; the principle of division (as Adam, by a divine act, produced Eve from his side); also, sometimes, discord and confusion (division again), misfortune, impurity, and matter. Jerome observed that God did not say the second day's creation was good, and Pythagoras and Eusebius also thought two a bad number. On the other side, there were two tables of the law, two cherubim regarding the mercy-seat of the Ark, two olive-trees distilling oil in Zachariah, two natures in Christ, two Mosaic visions of God—one of His face, one of His back parts—two testaments, two precepts of charity, two *primae dignitates*, two first parents, two kinds of daemons (good and bad), two intellectual creatures (angels and human beings), two great heavenly luminaries, two solstices, two equinoxes, and two poles. Moving from the text to the table, we discover a series of additional equivalences. Archetypally, two stands for Iah and El, names of God written with two Hebrew characters each. In the elemental structure of the universe, two of the four kinds of matter, earth and water, produce living souls. In the lesser universe, the microcosm, the two principal locales of the soul are the heart and the brain. In the infernal world, the two chief daemons are Beemoth (Behemoth) and Leviathan; and the two punishments predicted for the damned by Christ were weeping and the gnashing of teeth.[82]

The significances of other numbers are more elaborate. The *Scala* for two has only four columns; that for nine has eleven columns and that for twelve has fourteen. For example, nine represents the nine orders of angels, the nine celestial spheres, nine precious and semi-precious stones, nine internal and external senses (the five usual ones plus memory, thought, imagination, and common sense), nine orders of devils, and three nine-letter names of God.[83] The numbers above twelve must be considered in terms of their origins and parts: the numbers of which they are the sum or the product, and also the numbers these are less than or exceed.[84] Extraordinary knowledge of Biblical history is displayed. The star which led the

LIBER SECUNDUS.   179

Tabula Martis in abaco   In notis hebraicis.

Signacula five characteres.

Martis.   Intelligentiæ Martis.   Dæmonii Martis.

Tabula Solis in abaco.   In notis hebraicis.

Signacula five characteres.

Solis.   Intelligentiæ Solis.   Dæmonii Solis.

M 2   Tabula

Henry Cornelius Agrippa of Nettesheim, *Opera* (London: ?1531), I, 179.

The square of Mars appears at the top in Arabic and Hebrew numerals. Beneath it are "Symbols or Characters"—of Mars, of the intelligence or planetary angel of Mars, and of the daemon of Mars—which, since the good daemon is the intelligence, must be evil. The lower part of the illustration gives similar information about the sun.

Both the difficulties and the ingeniousness of numerologists are illustrated here. In the upper square, the total of each vertical and horizontal column and of the two diagonal columns which contain five figures is 65, and each of the numbers between 1 and 25 appears only once. The lower square—of the sun—is less successful. Although ten of the fourteen columns total 111, two (the bottom horizontal column and the second vertical column from the left) total 131, and two (the top horizontal column and the fourth vertical column from the left) total 80. Also, the numbers 3 and 25 are repeated, and 5 and 34 do not appear.

Wise Men to the manger appeared thirteen days after Christ's birth; the crucifixion occurred on the fourteenth day of the first lunar month.[85] Other curious information appears. We learn that the human foetus becomes a perfect body, ready to receive a reasonable soul, on the fortieth day; women require forty days to recover from a

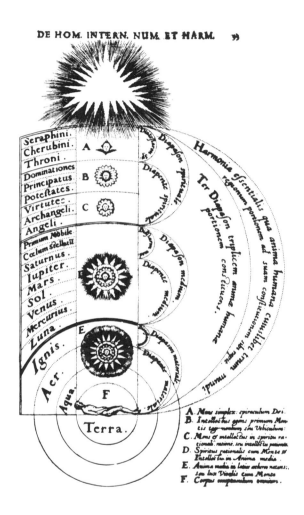

DE HOM. INTERN. NUM. ET HARM.

Robert Fludd, *De supernaturali, naturali, praenaturali et contranaturali microcosmi historia* (Oppenheim: Hieronymus Gallerus, 1619), p. 93.

Another visual explication of harmonies. The earth, at the bottom, is surrounded by the regions of water, air, and fire; these again by the planetary spheres, the fixed stars, and the *primum mobile;* and finally by the nine orders of angels, above whom divine light, surrounded by the darkness of mystery, emanates from the Trinity. In the center column *A* represents simple mind, which is the breath of God; *B* is active intellect, the first shelter or vehicle of mind; and *C* is mind or intellect in the rational spirit—reason or the receptive intellect. Each of these parallels three of the angelic hierarchies. *D,* the sun, represents "rational spirit, in the middle soul with the mind or intellect." *E,* which spans the regions of fire, air, and water, is the middle soul floating in ethereal fluid, or the vital light within mind. *F,* the recumbent human figure, is "the body which is the receptacle of all."

The arcs drawn at the right show harmonic relationships among all these. The largest arc represents "The essential harmony by means of which any human soul procures for its own nature a portion of the three regions of the world." The next is "The threefold diapason which constitutes a triple share of the human soul." Inside this, in turn, come three diapasons or octaves, one spiritual, one material, and one intermediate. Last of all come the diatesseron (fourth) and diapente (fifth) in the spiritual, material, and intermediate realms.

The mathematics of all this is puzzling; but many minds besides Fludd's resonated strongly to efforts to show that both materially and spiritually everything existent possessed musical harmonies—usually, as here, expressed as musical chords—founded on a numerical mysticism derived from Pythagoras and the Platonic *Timaeus.*

Henry Cornelius Agrippa of Nettesheim, *Opera*, (London: ?1531), I, 193.

LIBER SECVNDVS.   193

Quòd fi fuper eodem centro circulus fabricetur per fummum caput, demifli brachij, quoufque extremi digiti circuli illius circumferentiam contingant, paffique pedes in eadem circuferentia, quantum extrema manuum à fummo vertice diftat, tunc circulum illum fuper imi pectinis centro ductum in quinque æquas partes dividunt, perfectumque pentagonum conftituunt, ipfique pedum extremi tali ad umbilicum relati, triangulum faciunt æquilaterum.

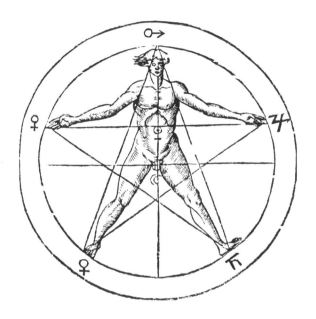

Proportions of the human body. The superscription reads as follows: "If a circle is drawn on the same center through the top of the head, the arms being stretched so that the tips of the fingers touch the circumference of the circle and the feet spread to the same circumference so that the distance between them and the hands is the same as that between the hands and the top of the head, then the circle drawn upon the center of the stomach is divided into five equal parts and makes a perfect pentagram, and the bottoms of the feet are related in such a way to the navel as to make an equilateral triangle" (which is not, however, shown). The planetary symbol over the head is that of Mars; in a clockwise direction, the other four are Jupiter, Saturn, Venus, and Mercury. The sun's symbol appears on the stomach and the moon's beneath the sex organ.

birth; an infant does not smile for forty days; Christ preached forty months, was in the tomb forty hours, mounted into the sky forty hours after His resurrection. Sixty was holy to the Egyptians because the crocodile lays sixty eggs in sixty days and hatches them for sixty more, and it also lives sixty years and has sixty teeth.[86] Interested minds had been at work for centuries on the problems, and by Agrippa's time an industrious compiler was able to accumulate masses of data of the most surprising kinds.

As yet we are only on the threshold of the subject, which exfoliates in both expected and unexpected directions. For example, a chapter describes at some length ancient ways of expressing numbers by gestures: ten thousand by the left hand turned backwards on the middle of the chest, the four fingers raised skyward; sixty thousand by grasping the front of the left thigh with the curved left hand.[87]

The implication appears to be that there is a natural connection between the gestures and the numbers, not merely arbitrary association.

After three succeeding chapters on Roman, Greek, and Hebrew and Chaldaean letters we come to a discussion of what may be called numerology proper: the assigning of numerical values to letters of the alphabet and the uses of these in finding mystical values in words. In the Roman alphabet the letters A—I have values running from one to nine; the letters K—S stand for ten, twenty, and so on through ninety; and a final group, consisting of T, V (for U), X, Y, Z, together with consonantal I and V, HI (as in *Hieronymus,* "Jerome"), and HU (as in *Huilhelmus,* "William") represent one hundred, two hundred, and so on through nine hundred.[88] The computations performed on the basis of this system can be illustrated by the finding of a child's star—i. e., planet—from his name. The numerical values of the letters in his name, his father's name, and his mother's name are totaled and divided by nine, the remainder—one through nine, zero being no number—being interpreted as follows: one and four indicate the sun, two and seven the moon, three indicates Jupiter, five Mercury, six Venus, eight Saturn, and nine Mars. The child's zodiacal sign can be determined by arriving at the same total and dividing by twelve: a remainder of one designates Leo, of two Aquarius, and so on through the others, but not, of course, by taking the signs in simple succession.

Robert Fludd, *De supernaturali, naturali, praenaturali et contranaturali microcosmi historia* (Oppenheim: Hieronymus Gallerus, 1619), p. 62.

Still another diagram meant to interpret the cosmic harmonies. The large triangle represents the Triune Godhead, which extends beyond materiality. *Hyle,* or unformed matter, surrounds the structured universe, along the outside border of which three diapasons or octaves are indicated, the corporal, the spiritual, and the double. The smaller triangle at the center contains the four Hebrew letters of the Tetragrammaton, the ineffable name of God. The angelical world, the elemental world, and the stellar or celestial world, pictured as circles which touch at the center, produce two diatesserons or fourths and a repeated diapente or fifth. Three hemispheres which border on the inner triangle are unlabeled except for the names of chords: again the diapason, the diatessaron, and the diapente. The meanings of the numbers within these arcs is obscure.

(Surely this notion could have been checked easily against horoscopes. That it was not, or that the discrepancies were somehow rationalized, reveals a general tendency to avoid empiricism.) The justification is that "The Most High created all things with weight, number, and measure, from which, as from its origin, the truth of letters and names derives, these not being imposed haphazardly but in accordance with a certain reason that we do not know." [89] Nonetheless we are informed that one is identified with the sun and with Jupiter because both are kings, two with the moon and with Saturn and Mars because they are maleficent, and three with Jupiter, the sun, and Venus—all fortunate planets—and with Vesta, Hecate, and Diana. Also, eight is equated with air, four with fire, six with earth, and twelve with water, so that the elements as well as the planets, signs, and pagan divinities are absorbed into the structure.[90]

A succeeding chapter offers "Planetary Tables," which consist in squares of numbers so arranged that addition downward, across, and diagonally produces identical sums. Although some of the tables are extremely complicated, producing totals adding up (for the moon) to figures as large as 369, the simplest table, that of Saturn, will illustrate the principle.

4	9	2
3	5	7
8	1	6

Here the total in each direction is fifteen. Each such square is accompanied by another containing Hebrew letters instead of numbers, these presumably having equivalent values. A tablet representing Saturn, thus engraved on a lead plate—lead being the metal associated with Saturn—helps in childbirth, confers safety and power, and causes requests made of princes and other men of authority to be granted, provided only the tablet is dedicated to the planet's beneficent aspect. If the planet's maleficent powers are invoked, the tablet will be inimical to buildings and plantings, destructive of honors and dignities, provocative of quarrels, and dispersive of armies. Further, the numbers and letters are associated with divine names. In the given case, the names are "Ab," "Hod," "Iah," "Agiel," and "Zazel." Finally, along with each pair of tables appear certain "Signs or Characters"—odd, and sometimes elaborate, designs impossible to describe and expensive to reproduce—which, in the simple example we have chosen, stand for Saturn itself, "The Intelligence of Saturn," and "The Daemon of Saturn." [91] All this, although once more suggestive of the wastage of enormous quantities of human energy and of time, shows the mythologically oriented mind diligently following up the detailed implications of fundamental preconceptions.

The remainder of Agrippa's second book has to do with geometrical figures, musical and other sounds, and similar harmonies and proportions in the human body and soul. The geometrical figures, we are told, "have no less power than the numbers themselves." The circle is equivalent to unity as the center and circumference of everything, and to ten because "by accumulation it returns to unity, as to its principle, being the end and the summit of all numbers." (Is this an inference from Arabic numerals?) Accordingly the circle is the perfect figure, and magicians who invoke devils stand within it as a protection. The pentagram, which has all the qualities of five because it possesses five obtuse angles, five acute angles, and five triangles, has wonderful force against demons. The quadrangle, the hexagon, the heptagon, and the octagon similarly have qualities and virtues which depend

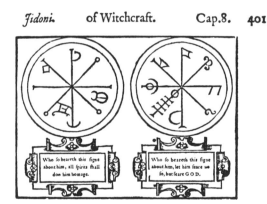

Reginald Scot, *The Discouerie of Witchcraft* (London: 1584), p. 401.

Magic seals. The seal at upper left enforces the obedience of "all spirits"; that at upper right is a protection against foes.

The passage which follows—from another chapter—gives instructions for the conjuring up of a dead man's spirit. This is best done at a suicide's grave; or a pact can be made with a criminal about to be hanged. The conjurer is to go to the grave "about eleven a clocke in the night" accompanied only by a servant, who is to hold a candle in his left hand and a crystal stone in his right hand; the conjurer himself is to hold in his right hand a staff on which are written several names of God, beginning with the Tetragrammaton. Further instructions are given overleaf.

on their differing lines and intersections. The cross, so sacred to Christians, was valued also by the Egyptians and Arabs because it is the most right-angled of all figures (*figura omnium rectissima*) and is the simplest figure with breadth and height (*longitudinem & latitudinem*). Its force derives from the heavens because the luminaries shine from four principle angles, the *cardines,* and it is related also to the powerful numbers five, seven, and nine. Hence for the Egyptians it was holy, signified allegorically safety in the future, and was imprinted on the breast of Serapis. The Greeks too venerated it. All these figures may be inscribed on cards or plates, where they work "by a certain sympathy produced by aptitude and natural likeness." Similarly with the regular solids—the sphere, the tetrahedron, the hexahedron, the octahedron, the icosahedron, and the dodecahedron. For instance, the cube, with eight solid or three-dimensional angles, twenty-four planes (apparently the three projecting from each of the eight corners regardless of overlapping), and six bases represents earth. The pyramid represents fire, perhaps because of association with πῦρ; the octahedron represents air, the icosahedron water, and the dodecahedron the sky or heaven.[92]

The discussion of harmony, music, and concords (*concentus*), which turns mainly on proportions, develops the numerical theme further. We hear again of the harmony in heaven itself; of the power of music to attract beasts, serpents, birds, and dolphins, to hold fish immobile in an Alexandrian pond, to make elephants gentle and to please even the elements; also of a Halesian fountain frequently mentioned in connection with music, which leaps at music as if in joy and overflows its bounds. Music can remove or inflict disease, heal persons stunned by the tarantula, and cure the bites of vipers.[93] The celestial harmony not only governs the universal whole but is creative.[94] As we have already been informed by Ficino, three of the planets have voices, the other four *concentus*. The ancient tetrachord corresponded to the four elements, the lowest tone representing earth and those of water, air, and fire being successively higher. Later, when Terpander of Lesbos increased the number of strings (on the harp or lyre) to seven, the notes corresponded to the planets. Of the four classical modes, the Dorian related to water and the first of the humors, phlegm; the Phrygian to fire and cholera; the Lydian to air and blood; and the Mixolydian to earth and black bile. Again, an instrument of nine strings had affinities with the muses and the celestial spheres, no inconsistency being felt in the recognition that Thalia had no *concentus* but was assigned to silence and earth. Finally, the distances between the planets are described in tones and half-tones, as though their orbits were equivalent to frets on the neck of a stringed instrument.[95]

The proportions, measure, and harmony of the human body, since man is a microcosmos, resemble those of the universe. Temples, houses, theaters, ships, machines, even such parts of these as columns, capitals, and pedestals were anciently built on the model of the body, as was Noah's Ark. Every part or member of man corresponds to "some sign, some star, some intelligence, some divine name." (One remembers astrological diagrams in which parts of the body are connected by lines with signs in an encircling zodiac.) [96] The suggestion is not developed, a transition occurring here to a series of curious diagrams showing a naked man inside various geometrical figures: in a circle with arms spread; similarly in a square; in a circle again with arms and legs stretched in such a way as to make a pentacle centering on the sex organ; in a square with his fingers and toes touching the corners; and others. All of these are explained elaborately in terms of proportions, some of them most ingenious; and planetary symbols are occasionally put in the circumference. The chapter, which is unusually long, ends with remarks about the proportions of the humors in a healthy body (blood eight, phlegm four, cholera two, black bile one), the responsiveness of the pulse to the sun and hence to years, months, days, hours, and minutes, and other rather miscellaneous topics.[97] In following pages we are informed about numerical correspondences in the departments or subdivisions of man's soul. The proportion of reason to concupiscence is that of the diapason or octave, the proportion of reason to irascibility that of the diatessaron or fourth, and the proportion of anger to concupiscence that of the diapente or fifth. Again, the soul corresponds to earth by its sense, to water by its imagination, to air by its reason, and to the heavens of fire by its understanding. If the proper relationships are in any way disturbed, they can be restored by music, as the sound of David's harp put to flight a devil which had possessed Saul.[98]

We must skip the little that is new in the remainder of Book II—for example, an explanation of the twenty-eight houses of the moon, geomancy, and a long list of alternative names for each of the planets [99]—in order to approach ceremonial or religious magic. The first division of Book III, which is concerned generally with the necessity of piety in the operator if the magic is to succeed, observes that the body cannot be healthful without health in the mind and spirit (*animus*) and that this, in turn, is accessible only through integrity of life, piety, and holy religion. A trust in nature alone often leads to deception by bad daemons.[100] The basic principle of success in magic, in fact, is the "dignification" of the operator by avoidance of too much concern with the flesh and the senses and by the elevation of his mind to pure intellect.[101] The magician must also observe silence in order to keep the mysteries from unfit persons [102] and must perform all his marvels in the name of the Lord Jesus Christ and with thankfulness to Him and to God,[103] taking as his guides love, hope, and faith, of which the last is the greatest and the source of all miracles.[104] The introductory section ends with Chapter ix, after which we move to an explication of the "divine emanations," or "numerations," or "attributes" of God implied by the Sephiroth, His ten most holy names. On these we must pause, for the cabala came in

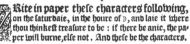

408   15.Booke.   The difcouerie *To go inuifible, &c.*

andbuelie of all things, my will quicklie to be fulfilled. *Vade in pace, in nomine patris, & filij, & fpiritus fancti.* And the holie ✛ croffe ✛ be betwéene thée and me, or betwéene vs and you, and the lion of Iuda, the roote of Ieffe, the kindred of Dauid, be betwéene thée & me ✛ Chriff commeth ✛ Chriff commandeth ✛ Chriff giueth power ✛ Chriff defend me ✛ and his innocent bloud ✛ from all perils of bodie and foule, fléeping or waking: *Fiat, fiat,* Amen.

To know of treafure hidden in the earth.

The tenth Chapter.

This would be much practifed if it were not a coufening knacke.

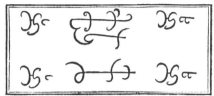

Rite in paper thefe characters following, on the faturdaie, in the houre of ☽, and laie it where thou thinkeft treafure to be : if there be anie, the paper will burne, elfe not. And thefe be the characters.

This is the waie to go inuifible by thefe three fifters of fairies.

IN the name of the Father, and of the Sonne, and of the Holie ghoft. Firft go to a faire parlor or chamber, & an euen ground, and in no loft, and from people nine daies; for it is the better: and let all thy clothing be cleane and fwéete. Then make a candle of virgine waxe, and light it, and make a faire fier of charcoles, in a faire place, in the middle of the parlor or chamber. Then take faire cleane water, that runneth againft the eaft, and fet it vpon the fier : and yet thou wafheft thy felfe, faie thefe words, going a-bout the fier, thrée times, holding the candle in the right hand ✛ Panthon ✛ Craton ✛ Muriton ✛ Bifecognaton ✛ Sifton ✛ Diaton

Reginald Scot, *The Discouerie of Witchcraft* (London: 1584), p. 408.

Charms for the discovery of hidden treasure. On the day of Saturn, in the hour of the moon, a paper bearing the symbols, if placed on a spot where treasure is buried, will burst into flame.

Directions for achieving invisibility follow. The nine-days' preparation is not unusual, nor is the isolation. The "fairness" of the chamber and the cleanliness of the clothing are protections against evil spirits, which reveled in filth. The water to be used in the ceremony must be both fair and clean, and the charcoal fire must also be fair (i.e., must burn cleanly, without much smoke). The washing is a form of purification and further implies the innocency of the operation (white magic).

strongly with the elder Pico and thereafter, although sometimes looked on askance, played an important, if occasional, role in esoteric thought at least through the period of Robert Fludd.

According to Orpheus, wisdom was "Pallas," intelligence was "Mercury," love was "Venus," and so on. Other pagan names were also in use. The Hebrew *mecubales,* or masters of tradition, who were most learned in divine things, accepted, however, ten principal divine names as powers (*veluti numina quaedam*) or members of God, and by these, which they called Sephiroth, as by emanations, God comes into relation with the finite, influencing it "as if through garments (*vestimenta*), instruments, or examples of the archetype," affecting everything from the highest heaven down to the lowest depth.[105] Each of the names has its *numeratio,* or numerological equivalent, and both name and equivalent have a number of verbal significations. With the exception of the last, each name sheds its influence by means of one of the orders of angels and one of the celestial spheres and the planet it contains; and each also has connected with it at least one intelligence, or angel, which "governed" or "guided" at least one Biblical personage. We cannot afford space for the complete list but may notice three names and then speak more generally about the remaining seven.

The first name is EHEIE, or "divine essence," "the being of the most simple Divinity," "what the eye has not seen." It is attributed to God the Father. Its numeration is "Keter," which means "crown," "diadem." This first name works through the seraphim and by means of the primum mobile gives existence to everything in the universe. Its intelligence is called "Metattron," or "Prince of Faces," since his duty is to introduce others to the Prince's face; and through him God spoke to Moses.

The second name, IOD, means "Divinity filled with ideas" and also "First-born" and is attributed to the Son of God. Its numeration is "Hochmah," which signifies "wisdom." It works through the cherubim upon the sphere of the fixed stars, "constructing there as many figures as there are ideas contained in it." Its intelligence is Raziel, who was governor or protector of Adam.

The third name, ELOHIM, signifies "jubilation," "remission," "rest," "penitence," "great trumpet," "redemption," and "the future life." Its numeration is "Binah," meaning "providence" or "intelligence." The name is applied to the Holy Spirit and works through the Thrones and Saturn. Its special intelligence is Zaphkiel, who governed Noah; but it has also a second intelligence, Iophiel, who governed Shem.

These names are the "three sovereign numerations, and the highest," by whose order all things are done. The remaining numerations—a word used, apparently, because of the calculation by which an alternative name is generated—perform the commands of these three and are called the *numerationes fabricae,* or constructive numerations. They are EL (Haesed), ELOHIM GIBOR (Geburah or Pachod), ELOHA (Tiphereth), SABAOTH or ADONAI SABAOTH (Nezah), ELOHIM SABAOTH (Hod), SADAI (Iesod), and ADONAI MELECH (Malchud). Except for the last, these work, in turn, through descending orders of angels and descending spheres: the Dominations and Jupiter, the Powers and Mars, the Virtues and the sun, the Principalities and Venus, the Archangels and Mercury, the Angels and the moon. Each has work of a special order to perform, and each has its intelligence or intelligences associated as governors or guides with Old Testament personages. The tenth numeration, ADONAI MELECH, works through the souls of the blessed (*ordinem anamasticum, animarum videlicet beatarum*) and of heroes, about whom we shall shortly hear more, and governed Moses. The special works of the seven spheres and orders are, respectively, in simplified summary, the making of bodily forms, the punishing of faults in the dishonest, the vivifying of the sun and the producing of metals, the producing of vegetables, the producing of animals, the producing of growth and decay, and the bestowing on men of understanding, industry, and the gifts of knowledge, industry, and prophecy.[106]

If all this seems more than adequately complete, we must adjust ourselves to the realization that these names are only a beginning. Denys the Pseudo-Areopagite collected forty-five names of the Father and as many of the Son (*tum Dei Patris, tum Christi*). From a single text of *Exodus* the Hebrew doctors derived seventy-two names of God and of angels; and according to other experts there are so many divine names in Scripture that we have no idea of them all. A large number are drawn from the Bible *per artem Cabalisticam, Calculatoriam, & Notariacam, & Gimetriam*: cabalistically, by numerology, by a kind of shorthand compression, and by gimetry or *gematria*, the substitution of another word having the same numerical value.[107] Again, a name may be drawn from the first letters of a Scriptural verse which speaks of God, or from the last letters, or from the center read backwards, or by a change from one alphabet to another. All the names are "sacraments and vehicles of the Divine omnipotence, not fixed by men or by angels but by the great God Himself in a certain way (*certo modo*), according to a number and figure which are unchangeable by reason of their eternal stability; they breathe the harmony of Divinity and are sanctified by God's help," so that "the heavenly powers fear these Divine names, Hell trembles at them, the angels worship them, the bad daemons dread them, all creatures revere them, and all religions hold them in veneration." By their aid, if we use them piously, we can produce marvelous effects on nature; but they must not be changed in one iota or translated.[108] In deriving the names men have not played with letters or ideas, have not dabbled in cryptography with the aim of producing symbols to be used as fancy or piety may direct. The names are "real" and were hidden in Scripture by an art so complicated that the encoding attributed by cranks to Bacon is, in comparison, childishly simple. Each has intrinsic power of a specialized kind, and knowledge of it confers power on the magician.

Some of the ways in which the magic can be performed are described. For instance, four four-letter names of God (in Hebrew) can be written in a square on the front of a round medal in such a way as to produce four additional names or seals read vertically, the square being circled by other Hebrew letters which express the names' "intention." On the reverse side the seven-letter Hebrew name "Ararita" is written straight across, and around it is engraved the Scriptural verse in which the name appears. The medal must be made of pure gold or virgin parchment; if the latter, the ink is to be made from the smoke of a consecrated candle, or incense, and from holy water by an artist purified from sin, filled with unshakable hope and firm faith, and with mind raised to the Most High. The medal will then protect against all infirmities and afflictions. Another medal, also illustrated, will guard the wearer against bad daemons and men and against all dangers of the road, of water, of enemies, and of arms. It bears on its front the first five Hebrew characters of the first five verses of *Genesis* and on its back the last five characters, hence is a "symbol of the entire creation of the world."[109] For the rest, we are assured that God's will is carried out by angels, the sky, and the celestial bodies, so that all things—including, evidently, the mystical energies which inhere in proportions, harmonies, numbers, and letters—work together in His service. Corroboration is cited from St. Augustine, from Origen, and especially from the *Apocalypse,* in which numbers play a noteworthy role.[110]

Of all the names, IESV, which has four letters, is by far the most efficacious because it has been given power over all things by the Father, whose name is also a tetragrammaton. This name sheds its influence upon the angels, and they, in turn, impart its energies to the sky, twelve angels being deputed to perform this duty for the zodiacal signs and seven more for the planets. From these, in turn, the power is distributed to all the other instruments and ministers of God. Christ said, "Whatsoever you ask of my Father in my name He will give you," and again, "In my name they shall cast out devils." Accordingly—the conclusion appears to make otiose much of what has preceded—the single name IESV is the only one we need. In fact, we cannot now receive any grace or favor from heaven without the consent of the name, as is clear from the inability of Jews and cabalists to perform marvels with the other names since Christ's incarnation. Also, it is known that no Hellish power can resist that name if it is pronounced to honor Him; and even insensible things (what has happened to the conviction that the whole world is alive?) revere it and tremble when the name is spoken faithfully and truly and accompanied with the sign of the cross made by innocent hands.[111]

From the subject of God's names Agrippa proceeds to a consideration of His members, which are specified in Biblical texts. In *The Song of Songs* we read, "Thy head is like . . ." "The hair of thy head . . ." "Thy throat . . ." *Isaiah* says, "You have not questioned my mouth." From the *Psalms* we learn that "The eyes of the Lord are on the just." God has nostrils with which He savors burnt offerings. He has shoulders ("The principality is founded on His shoulders"), arms ("Who knows the force of the Lord's arms?" and hands ("Thy hands, O Lord, have made and formed me"). He also wears garments: "The Lord is clothed with beauty, and covered with light as with a garment"; "I have extended my cloak over thee." He carries symbols of royalty: "Thy rod and thy staff they comfort me." It follows that "our members, clothing, adornments, and whatever is on or about us is ruled, directed, preserved, governed, and judged by these divine members and adornments, according to the saying of the Prophet, 'He has put my feet upon the stone and has directed my steps.' And He says elsewhere, 'Blessed is the Lord my God who directs my hand in battle and my fingers in war.'" If something is needed for one of our members, we can often obtain help by invoking the name on which the member depends.[112]

The treatise continues to dwell on the subject of God's ministers. The heavenly bodies are possessed of souls, as is testified by *Ecclesiastes,* Jerome, Origen, Job, Eusebius Pamphilus, Augustine, Albertus Magnus, Aquinas, John the Scot, Nicolaus Cusanus, Aureolus, Plotinus, and William of Paris.[113] Some of the souls are intelligences, which are intelligent substances free of the weight of a solid body subject to decay and are immortal, without senses, present in and exerting influence upon everything. Their nature is the same as that of spirits and daemons.[114] They are of three sorts: *supercoelestes,* which are wholly without body and, as it were, intellectual spheres who serve and adore the One God but have nothing to do with the lower world; the celestial intelligences or worldly daemons which preside over the skies and luminaries, including the signs, triplicities, and segments of the heavens consisting of ten, five, and single degrees; and the *daemones quasi ministros* which govern the lower world, some of these being fiery, other aerial, watery, or earthy.[115] Of this last order, some are assigned to the cardinal directions, some to the day, noon, or night; or, again, the ministering daemons are situated in special places—the forests, the mountains, the fields, houses—and were anciently called fauns, satyrs, Pans, nymphs, naiads, nereids, dryads, muses, genii, and lemurs. According to the Platonists there are as many of this third order as of the others: as many as there are stars in the sky.[116]

After further discussion of angels (Chapter xvii) and of daemons and their bodies (Chapters xviii–xix), Agrippa turns to the subject of guardian angels and the bad daemons it is their duty to combat (Chapters xx–xxii). Next follows consideration of the language used by angels in speech among themselves. It is certainly Hebrew, but the use of it does not involve the lungs, tongue, or lips. Instead thought is passed from mind to mind silently, as a corporal body produces an image in the eye or in a mirror (Chapter xxiii). Much else is added. Because the animation of the entire universe was so basic to the mythical world-view we are examining, and because magic relied so heavily on the inviting or repelling of the conscious or half-conscious energies with which both physical and spiritual universes were permeated, a compilation such as Agrippa's required a thorough canvassing of nonhuman spirits in a book devoted to supernatural magic. Chapter xxiv lists the names of the spirits which preside over signs, stars, the twenty-eight houses of the moon, the four winds and the four parts of the world, the elements, and much else. Chapters xxv–xxviii concern ways of deriving the names of angels from Scripture, again, and from celestial bodies, cabalistic calculations of various kinds, and the names of the objects over which the spirits preside. In Chapters xxix–xxxi the subject is the characters and seals of spirits: hieroglyphs or symbols, geometrical shapes, a special alphabet left by Petrus Aponus or Aponensis and transmitted by Honorius of Thebes, and other alphabets, characters, and marks drawn from revelation (by Constantine, Judas Maccabaeus, and even by pagans, from oracles).

After this exhaustive survey we are ready to learn how good daemons can be attracted and bad ones repelled, a topic which owes its importance, as would be clear by this time even without assertion, to the fact that "The efficacy of religion has its effects by means of the presence of daemons."[117] Although good daemons cannot be forced, we can invoke them by sacred things like stars, infernal deities (this verges on being, or is, illicit), the elements, the silence of night, the overflowings of the Nile, the mysteries of Memphis, and the sacred rattles (*sistra*) of Pharos. If the daemons come, they do so "willingly, through a kind of habit." Bad daemons can be fought through the agency of good daemons provided we are in a state of grace and combat them with sacred words and terrible incantations, or through the Divine power, or by the names and character of supernatural virtues, or by the naming of miracles, sacraments, and mysteries.[118] The lesser powers—fauns, naiads, lemurs, and the rest of the pagan semideities—can be drawn by going to their haunts and soliciting them with perfumes, songs, poems, and incantations, the mind all the while being kept innocent, credulous, and quiet.[119]

At this point we return to the *ordo anamasticus* of blessed spirits and heroes. This includes the *Issim,* or *viros fortes & robustos,* called heroes by the gentile mages. Fulgentius included among them Priapus (a Roman god of fertility, depicted lewdly at Pompeii and elsewhere), Hippo, and Vertumnus. Many, or perhaps all, were the offspring of a daemon and a human being, like Merlin and, perhaps, Plato, who was said to have been born of a virgin and the phantom of Apollo. Such beings have no less power over the lower world than the gods and daemons, as appears from the dedication to them of temples, images, altars, sacrifices, and vows.[120] Our own Christian heroes are, of course, the saints, whom Jesus uses to distribute the gifts of His grace in the lower world. Each saint has his own special gifts, benefits, and graces to confer, and these are bestowed by them not only more promptly than by the angels but also more abundantly, since the saints have a nature more like our own. Of these the twelve principal ones are the Apostles, who are seated on twelve tribunals judging the twelve tribes of Israel at twelve "foundations" situated at the twelve gates of the celestial city; and they also preside over the twelve zodiacal signs and are represented by twelve precious stones.[121] After the Apostles come the seventy-two disciples, who govern each a five-degree segment of the sky (one wonders often about overlappings; it will be recalled that identical segments are ruled by the celestial intelligences or worldly daemons) and also tribes, peoples, nations, and languages (the number of which after the confusion at Babel was seventy-two). Beneath these, in turn, come innumerable other saints, each with his peculiar assignment of office, place, nation, and people.[122]

We are not yet at the end, for there remain to be considered kings, princes, and pontiffs, "by whom this world is ruled, and by whose laws it is disposed." God said to Moses, "I have made thee as a god over Pharaoh," and again, "If the thief is hidden you shall take the master of the house before the gods" or—apparently—the judges. In *Psalms* we read, "The princes of the people are assembled with the god Abraham, for the powerful gods of the earth are raised very high." This is the reason why "all antiquity treated its princes as gods and honored them as divinities." Cities, provinces, mountains, rivers, seas, and isles have been named after them (the name, we recall, contains something of the object); pyramids, colossi, arches of triumph have been raised to them; their names too have been given to stars, days, and months. They can sometimes cure diseases merely by touch. Joshua commanded the sun and moon to stand still, Moses the Red Sea to divide, Joshua the Jordan; and Alexander did as much for his army. Accordingly we should obey, supplicate, honor, respect, and revere the Supreme God in their persons.[123]

In the final chapter of Book III, "Conclusion to the Whole Work," Agrippa remarks that the structure of his treatise is in some places orderly and in others not.[124] Whether the discussion of how God made man in His own image follows in an orderly way here is not certain, for Agrippa's perceptions were sometimes strangely unlike ours; but the succeeding chapter, on man's soul, grows naturally enough out of such comments as that memory, understanding, and will are the image of the Trinity.[125] The soul, we are told, is "a number which is substantial, uniform, returning upon itself, and rational. . . . It is not a quantitative number but a number independent of all corporeal laws, wherefore it is not subject to division or to multiplication by its parts." The substance of the soul is divine and emanates from divine sources, bringing its number with it: "not the number by which the Maker (*opifex*) has disposed all things, but a rational number which allows it to understand everything by the proportion it has itself with all things." In other words, although man's faculties are several his soul is a unity, and its rationality derives from the unity and indivisibility which is God. The soul is "clothed with a little celestial and aerial body" and is infused into the middle of the heart, which itself is the middle of the body, and from thence it spreads throughout all the corporeal members and parts, the bond being that between its own natural heat and the heat of the body and the medium being the humors. Illness or evil causes it to retire to the heart again; and if the heart loses its warmth the man dies and the soul flies away with its ethereal vehicle under the guidance of its genius and its guardian daemons, who take it before its judge. It is then conducted, quietly, either to glory or to punishment.[126] Agrippa does not believe in the reincarnation asserted or implied by many of his Oriental sources.

Here we return to the planets, the intelligences, and the angelic choirs. Gifts and virtues are bestowed on man through the seven planets acting as instruments: for example, through Saturn high contemplation, profound intelligence, the ability to judge weights, a firm rationality, stability and fixity in keeping resolutions; through

Jupiter, unshakable prudence, temperance, benignity, piety, modesty, justice, faith, grace, religion, equity, clemency, and regality.[127] But these gifts are derived more distantly from the seven intelligences who stand before the face of God, the function of the planets being that of making the body receptive by affecting its "complexion" or the mixture of humors within it. As for the angelic choirs, these too are deeply involved. The angels make man a messenger of the divine will and an interpreter of the divine mind; the archangels give him domination over animals, fish, and birds; and so on through the intermediate ranks up to the cherubim, who give him "light of the mind and energy of wisdom regarding the high images and figures by which divine things themselves can be contemplated," and, finally, the seraphim, who bestow upon him a burning love.[128] Persons who do not understand these mysteries but rely wholly on things of the lower world do so in vain;[129] but if we do understand the mysteries and yet fail to obtain the gifts, the fault is sin, which is an unruliness and intemperance of spirit.[130]

The remainder of Book III can be summarized still more quickly. Living creatures lower than man are struck by a kind of terror when they see him and recognize him instinctively as their master. This is because of a seal (*signaculum*) impressed upon man by God, called "Pahad," or "left hand," "sword of God," by the Hebrews. But man also inspires love because of his "Haesod," which means "clemency," "right hand," and "scepter of God." These numerations use the ministry of the intelligences and the stars and were stronger before the Fall; but a good man, like Daniel among the lions, or like many hermits, receives no hurt from animals.[131] After death man's soul remains near his body if it loves the body beyond the grave, or if the corpse is unburied, or if death has come by violence, and it can be evoked by vapors, liquors, and smells together with chants, sounds, and other means of reawakening its native imaginative and spiritual harmony. The fumigations used in such ceremonies should include eggs, milk, honey, oil, water, and flour to provide a medium within which a semi-material body can take shape.[132] The soul's power resides in its three parts, thought, reason, and imagination (*mente, ratione & idolo*). By the force of intense thought a soul can transport its body into a distant place, cause it to pass through doors as Peter did in escaping from prison, impress its conceptions or desires on other minds, and cause the face or body to become luminous, as did those of Moses, Socrates, Zoroaster, Elijah, Enoch, Alexander, and even Theodoric, who threw out sparks.[133] Of the three parts of the soul only thought is immortal. Reason is long-lived, but the imagination or *idolum* is material and mortal, being the sensible and animal soul. Nevertheless the entire soul is immortal in so far as it is united with thought. Unfortunately some men have not acquired thought, which comes only through struggle, and these die utterly until the resurrection. Middling souls, which are not devoid of thought but have not been wholly absorbed into it, are relegated to secret places at death, where they rejoice or suffer through the imagination and the irascible and concupiscent "virtues." [134] All this bears in one way or another on man's soul and places it firmly above animal nature and above the body but recognizes within it a hierarchy of faculties or principles of which thought, *mens,* is highest.

Agrippa is nothing if not thorough, and a series of chapters follows on the four furies (*furores*), fury being defined as "an illumination of the soul coming from gods or daemons." [135] The first fury is that of the muses, who are the souls of the celestial spheres and appear not to have much in common with the familiar muses of the arts. The muse of the moon governs vegetal creation, that of Mercury animals, and so on through the other seven according to a scheme like one already noted.[136] The second fury is that of Dionysus and purifies the mind while agitating it; the third is of Apollo, "the mind of the world"; and the fourth is of Venus, who is ardor or love.[137] There is also another kind of abnormal mental state called ravishment (*raptus*) or ecstasy, in which the spirit is withdrawn from the senses and sometimes from the body. This happens to epileptics and sometimes to people suffering the extreme of some passion.[138] Dreams are often prophetic: their source is then a union of the "phantastic spirit" with the understanding in a pure and quiet mind, or else simple revelation. Preparation for such dreams should include fasting and other rites of purification, expiation, and sacrifice.[139] Still another kind of divination —the implicit subject also in the chapters on the furies—is by the drawing of lots, the throwing of dice or bones, and other similar sporting with chance.[140]

What remains has to do with purifications, expiations, adorations, vows, sacrifices and oblations. Abstinence, fasts, chastity, solitude, and tranquillity are recommended,[141] and much is said about the proper way of presenting sacrifices and offerings. We hear of many pagan practices, including sacrifices to deities other than God, and even—described quite factually and without any suggestion of horror—of the killing of an especially bad man as a communal scapegoat.[142] The Jewish detestation of idolatry is missing from Agrippa, and like many other scholars of the period he tends to accept everything ancient as true and right. If we sacrifice to God, we should commemorate some "work, miracle, sacrament, or promise drawn from the Holy Scriptures." For example, if we wish to destroy enemies—no implication is offered that this is improper—we may remember how God destroyed the giants by the flood, ruined Babel, Sodom and Gomorrah, and engulfed Pharaoh's army in the Red Sea. If our desire is to avoid perils by water, we may recall the saving of Noah from the flood, the passage of Israel through the Red Sea, and Christ walking on the waves, saving the imperiled boat, and rescuing Peter from drowning. Also, it is well to use all the divine names, or at least those which are related to the object of our petition.[143] Objects sanctified by the preference of God or of daemons should be used in the ceremonies: the cross, images, idols, paintings. For example, Christ may be represented as a lamb, or the four evangelists as a lion, a bull, an eagle, and a man. Genuflections, barings of the head, ablutions, aspergings, incensings, processions, music, candles, and temple and altar decorations are also sacred, being like "pacts between the gods and us, under the form of praise, respect, and obedience." Spoken or written enchantments, names, figures, characters, and seals are recommended; and there is efficacy also in barbarous words and in Hebrew, Egyptian, Greek, and Latin words.[144] The times of the sacrifices must also be chosen with care. Lucky days should be used for petitions, unlucky ones—as, to illustrate, June 17, when Moses broke the tablets—for *piacula* or sin-offerings. Magicians observe such times in the same way they observe the days and hours of the planets and other celestial circumstances. Jesus Himself encouraged a choice among times by saying, "Are there not twelve hours in the day?"[145] And at last, with a "Conclusion to the Whole Work" in which Agrippa asserts that mysteries he has not explained clearly will be understood by readers of discerning minds, the extended and astonishing farrago of superstitions from all the known countries and religions comes at last to an end.

V. Conclusion

Whether the reader will have been disappointed by the foregoing pages I am unable to foresee. On one side, the magician's circle and the pentagram have been mentioned only once, and then allusively; and no specific charms have been offered for removing warts, or quieting storms, or averting bad luck incurred by breaking a mirror. Neither has anything been said about the sticking of pins into images, or the ruining of a neighbor's crops by hail, or the drying up of his cow—operations which belong within the sphere not of white magic but of witchcraft. On the other side, white magic appears sometimes to be simply misunderstood physics and chemistry and botany and zoology, sometimes to be identical with astrology, and sometimes to be like elaborately ceremonialized prayer. It may be any of these; but parts of it occupy an intermediate area between natural science and religion, and these may be looked at more closely.

What intervenes between purely physical forces which, like the sympathies and antipathies described by Della Porta, work automatically and purely spiritual forces like those of the higher angels and of the Trinity is a whole range of more or less "natural" phenomena in which the dissociation of matter and spirit is difficult. In the heavens, for instance, are luminaries which radiate light, heat, and perhaps moisture or dryness. Insofar as they do no more, the magic which turns their energies to human uses was conceived to be "natural." Even Della Porta, however, the least mystical of the three authors, believed that the "forms" he regarded as crucially important derived immediately from the sky, medially from the intelligences, and finally from God, and both Ficino and Agrippa write fairly consistently as though nothing in the entire universe lacked soul, or at least nothing above the vegetable kingdom. The nine celestial spheres are intimately connected with the nine orders of angels; the planets are "gods"; spirits preside over the signs, the poles, and the elements; and responsibilities are assigned also, by Agrippa, to demi-gods like the pagan fauns and satyrs, to "heroes" like Priapus and Vertumnus, and to legions of Christian saints. The three orders of spirits, supercelestial, celestial, and mundane, are, indeed, innumerable, even the lowest containing incalculable numbers of spirits. What is at work might be called the Hermetic principle that no part of the world is devoid of consciousness, but it is, I think, more accurate to call it a primeval tendency, still operative in savage cultures and among very young children, to imagine everywhere a consciousness very like our own. The phenomenon, I suggest once more, is what psychologists call "projection." But because an enormous literature had developed and the educated mind was still backward-looking, the formulations given animistic religion by "Chaldaeans," Egyptians, Greeks, Romans, and other less influential nations, like India, which were known about chiefly by allusions, were all poured into a mixing bowl with Christianity and consolidated into the preposterous but fascinating *mélange* we find in Agrippa.

NOTES: CHAPTER THREE

1. See Frances Yates, *Giordano Bruno and the Hermetic Tradition* (London: Routledge and Kegan Paul, 1964) and D. P. Walker, *Spiritual and Demonic Magic from Ficino to Campanella* (London: The Warburg Institute, University of London, 1958).

2. For Latin excerpts I use Io. Baptista Porta, *Magiae naturalis libri viginti* (Rothomagi, i. e., Rouen: Sumptibus Ioannis Berthelin, 1650); but I quote usually from an anonymous English translation of 1658, John Baptista Porta, *Natural Magic,* ed. Derek J. Price (New York: Basic Books, Inc., 1957). The early Latin edition in four books was published at Naples in 1558, ran through six editions within ten years, and was translated into Italian, French, Dutch, Spanish, and apparently Arabic; but the later edition is not only enormously expanded but resulted from the assistance of an academy of "Men of Leisure" called the "Otiosi." (See Price's preface, pp. v–vi.) This version ran through twenty-seven editions in Latin and translation.

3. "The Preface to the READER," unpaginated. Unless otherwise noted, references will be to the English translation mentioned in the previous note.

4. *Ibid.,* I, i (1). Here and elsewhere, the Latin quotations are from the Rouen edition mentioned in Note 2.   5. *Ibid.,* I, ii (1–2).   6. See "Editor's Preface," *ibid.,* p. v.

7. *Ibid.,* I, iii (3–4).   8. See *ibid.,* XVII, vi (363–64).   9. *Ibid.,* I, v (6).

10. *Ibid.,* I, vi (7).   11. *Ibid.*   12. *Ibid.,* I, vi (8).   13. *Ibid.,* I, vii (8).

14. *Ibid.,* I, vii (8–9).   15. *Ibid.,* I, vii (10).   16. *Ibid.,* I, viii (10–11).

17. *Ibid.,* I, viii (10–13).   18. *Ibid.,* I, ix (13–15).   19. *Ibid.,* I, x (15–16).

20. *Ibid.,* I, xi (16–17).   21. *Ibid.,* I, xii (17–18).   22. *Ibid.,* I, xiii (19).

23. *Ibid.*, I, xiv (19–20).   24. "Proeme" to Book II (26).   25. *Ibid.*, II, i–iv (26–33).

26. *Ibid.*, II, v–xii (33–43).   27. *Ibid.*, II, xix (51).   28. *Ibid.*, II, xxii (56–57).

29. *Ibid.*, XIV, ix (321).   30. *Ibid.*, III, viii (73–74).

31. I use primarily Marsilius Ficinus Florentinus, *Opera* (Basiliae: Ex Officina Henricpetrina, 1576), I, 493–572; but the text is not consistently reliable, and I have sometimes emended readings from a separate edition of the *De vita triplici* published at Basel in (?) 1497. The longer part-titles are from the *Opera*, the shorter ones from the separate edition. In citing the *Opera* I omit the volume number (always Vol. I) in order to avoid an excessively long string of figures. The best discussion of Ficino's total philosophy is Paul Oskar Kristeller's *The Philosophy of Marsilio Ficino* (New York: Columbia University Press, 1943); but the book is organized by topics rather than by documents and makes only a few passing references to *De vita triplici*.

32. Walker, in *Spiritual and Demonic Magic* (p. 3), besides offering the second of these renderings suggests also a punning meaning, "On Instituting Life Celestially"; and either translation is certainly possible.

33. —*ad motum per se inefficax & ineptum*, Ficino, *Opera*, III, i (531).   34. *Ibid.*

35. *Ibid.*   36. *Ibid.*   37. *Ibid.*   38. *Ibid.*, III, i (531–32).

39. *Ibid.*, III, i (532–33).   40. *Ibid.*, III, i–ii (532–33).   41. *Ibid.*, III, ii (533).

42. *Ibid.*   43. *Ibid.*   44. *Ibid.*, III, ii (534).   45. *Ibid.*, III, iii (534–35).

46. See Note 1, above.

47. *Nam et natura superior ab inferiore conciliatur quidem aliquando, sed cohiberi nequit.—Ibid.*, III, xxvi (571).   48. *Ibid.*, III, xv (552).   49. *Ibid.*, III, xiii (549).   50. *Ibid.*

51. *Ibid.*, III, xv (551).   52. *Ibid.*, III, xv (551–52).   53. *Ibid.*, III, xv (552).

54. Reading *uiui* (1497) for *uini* (1576).   55. *Ibid.*, III, xvi (553).

56. *Ibid.*, III, xviii (557).   57. *Ibid.*, III, xviii (558).   58. *Ibid.*

59. *Ibid.*, III, xviii (558–59).   60. *Ibid.*, III, xx (561).   61. *Ibid.*, III, xi (544).

62. *Ibid.*, III, xi (545—misprinted as 546—46).   63. *Ibid.*, III, xiiii (550).

64. *Ibid.*, III, xxi (562).   65. *Ibid.*, III, xxi (561).   66. *Ibid.*, III, xxi (562).

67. *Ibid.*, III, xxi (561–64).

68. As, e. g., in his *Oratio habita Papiae* (*Oration Delivered at Pavia*), 1515, toward the end of which he submits everything he has written or may write and whatever he has said or may say to *omnibus ejus negotii censendi et iudicandi potestatem habentibus* and especially to *sacro episcoporum collegio, ejusque capite summo Pontifice* for correction. See Eugenio Garin, ed., *Testi umanistici su l'Ermetismo* (Roma: Fratelli Bocca, 1955), p. 126.

69. See, e. g., Henry Morley, *The Life of Cornelius Agrippa von Nettesheim* (London: Chapman and Hall, 1856), II, 318–19. But the story is a commonplace.

70. There is an excellent French translation, by A. Levasseur, first published in 1727 and *revu, corrigé et complété* by F. Gaboriau (Paris: Librairie Générale des Sciences Occultes, Bibliothèque Chacornac, 2 vols, 1910). Books I and II are in Vol. I of this edition, Book III in Vol. II; but I have again omitted volume numbers in the notes in order to avoid confusing strings of figures. The translation is quite reliable; but wherever the text seemed ambiguous or doubtful I have checked it against Henricus Cornelius Agrippa ab Nettesheym, *Opera*, Vol. I (Lugduni: c. 1650?). A recent critical edition of the Latin text, edited and annotated by Karl Anton Novotny (Graz, Austria: Akademische Druck u. Verlagsanstalt, 1967) has just come to my attention, and I have been able only to reassure myself about the reliability of the London edition by spot-checking.

71. Agrippa, *La Philosophie occulte* (the French translation described in the preceding note), I, lxxiv (205–206).   72. *Ibid.*, I, lxxiv (206).   73. *Ibid.*, I, lxxiv (206–207).

74. *Ibid.*, I, lxxiv (207).   75. *Ibid.*   76. *Ibid.*, lxxiv (207–208).

77. *Ibid.,* II, i (213). It must be remembered that page references to Books I and II are to Vol. I, and references to Book III are to Vol. II.   78. *Ibid.,* II, i (214-16).   79. *Ibid.,* II, i (217).

80. *Ibid.,* II, ii (219).   81. *Ibid.,* II, ii (219-21).   82. *Ibid.,* II, v (225-27).

83. *Ibid.,* II, xii.   84. *Ibid.,* II, xv.   85. *Ibid.,* II, xv (275).

86. *Ibid.,* II, xv (277-78).   87. *Ibid.,* II, xvi (283).   88. *Ibid.,* II, xx (292).

89. *Ibid.,* II, xx (293-94).   90. *Ibid.,* II, xxi (294-95).   91. *Ibid.,* II, xxii (297-308).

92. *Ibid.,* II, xxiii (309-11).   93. *Ibid.,* II, xxiv (312-15).   94. *Ibid.,* II, xxv (315).

95. *Ibid.,* II, xxvi (317-22).   96. *Ibid.,* II, xxvii (322-24).   97. *Ibid.,* II, xxvii (337-38).

98. *Ibid.,* II, xxviii (339-41).   99. *Ibid.,* II, xxxiii, xlviii and li, and lix.

100. *Ibid.,* III, i (1-2). I remind the reader that from this point on the references are to Vol. II.

101. *Ibid.,* III, iii (8).   102. *Ibid.,* III, ii (3-7).   103. *Ibid.,* III, iv (12).

104. *Ibid.,* III, v (16-17).   105. *Ibid.,* III, x (33-35).

106. For the entire passage see *ibid.,* III, x (35-39).

107. "A cabbalistic method of interpreting the Hebrew Scriptures by interchanging words whose letters have the same numerical value when added" (*OED*). The spellings in English also include *gematry*. An immediately following passage in Agrippa reads as follows: *ubi unum nomen, aut multae dictiones, per certas earum literas retractae colligunt: aut unum nomen per singulas suas literas dispersum, plura significat sive restituit.* (Text edited by Novotny.)

108. *Ibid.,* III, xi (39-43).   109. *Ibid.,* III, xi (46-48).   110. *Ibid.,* III, xii (50-51).

111. *Ibid.,* III, xii (51-53).   112. *Ibid.,* III, xiii (55-57).   113. *Ibid.,* III, xv (64-65).

114. *Ibid.,* III, xvi (66).   115. *Ibid.,* III, xvi (66-68).   116. *Ibid.,* III, xvi (69-70).

117. *Ibid.,* III, xxxii (138).   118. *Ibid.,* III, xxxii (138-39).

119. *Ibid.,* III, xxxii (141-42).   120. *Ibid.,* III, xxxiv (146-47).

121. *Ibid.,* III, xxxiv (147-48). The relevant passage is in *Revelation:* 21:10-14; but there is confusion about the judgment of the twelve tribes, which has been described differently in 7:4-8.

122. *La Philosophie occulte,* III, xxxiv (148-49).   123. *Ibid.,* III, xxxv (150-53).

124. *Ibid.,* III, lxv (286).   125. *Ibid.,* III, xxxvi (157).

126. *Ibid.,* III, xxxvii (163-64).   127. *Ibid.,* III, xxxviii (165).

128. *Ibid.,* III, xxxviii (166-67).   129. *Ibid.,* III, xxxviii (167-68).

130. *Ibid.,* III, xxxix (168-169).   131. *Ibid.,* III, xl (173-74).

132. *Ibid.,* III, xlii (196-97).   133. *Ibid.,* III, xliii (201-204).

134. *Ibid.,* III, xliv (207-208).   135. *Ibid.,* III, xlvi (212).

136. *Ibid.,* III, xlvi (212-15).   137. *Ibid.,* III, xlvii-xlix.

138. *Ibid.,* III, l (224-26).   139. *Ibid.,* III, li (227-30).

140. *Ibid.,* III, lii (233-35).   141. *Ibid.,* III, lv.

142. See *ibid.,* III, lix (257).   143. *Ibid.,* III, lvi (265-66).

144. *Ibid.,* III, lxiii (271-75).   145. *Ibid.,* lxiii (276-78), lxiv (281).

 # Alchemy

I. Introduction

Like astrology, alchemy is dauntingly, and indeed at first sight hopelessly, complex. Mrs. Charles Singer's *Catalogue of Latin and Vernacular Alchemical Manuscripts in Great Britain and Ireland, Dating from Before the Sixteenth Century*,[1] runs to three volumes, and a *Catalogue des manuscrits alchimiques grecs*[2] to eight. The Greek sources have been studied with special care by M. Berthelot in *Les Origines de l'alchimie*,[3] the Arabic ones, or some of them, by E. J. Holmyard and others.[4] The Arabic texts, which were directly responsible for the reintroduction of alchemy into Western Europe in the twelfth and thirteenth centuries—long after the decay of the Alexandrian culture from which they had derived—are very numerous and still, in large part, untranslated. There is also an extensive modern scholarship, again in a number of languages; and a sophisticated understanding of the alchemical operations demands a knowledge of chemistry far beyond that possessed by the typical literary scholar. In the circumstances, the temptation is strong to abandon the whole subject to the historians of science. Yet some glimpse of the basic assumptions and the patterns of thought which guided the art's development can be obtained by persons other than scientists; and it is worth attaining, because efforts to produce the Philosopher's Stone and the Elixir absorbed immense quantities of energy and wealth and fitted well into an intellectual ambience now almost totally destroyed. The better we understand the patterns, the less likely we are to misread the past in terms of our own preconceptions.

For the most part, it has been taken for granted that alchemists were the direct precursors of modern chemists. In one sense this is true, for the alchemist's laboratory contained furnaces, glass and ceramic vessels of several kinds, and other equipment which chemists were later to use. Further, a millenium, more or less, of experimentation with mercury, sulphur, arsenic, antimony, orpiment, cinnabar, copper, lead, iron, and other metals, not to mention organic substances—eggs, hair, blood, marrow, and much else—resulted in the discovery of byproducts, as Donne observed in *Love's Alchemy:*

> . . . no chymique yet th'Elixar got,
> But glorifies his pregnant pot,
> If by the way to him befall
> Some odoriferous thing, or medicinall.

For example, the distillation of alcohol led, about 1510, to the manufacture of the first liqueur (Benedictine).[5] Again, the use of such processes as sublimation, calcination, coagulation, and distillation, as well as the stimulation of chemical reactions by heat, looked forward to operations still performed in the laboratory. In every other way the discontinuity is nearly complete, for the physical theory of the alchemists was incapable of transformation into a modern theory and had to be rejected in its totality before chemistry could be born. The "elements" of the alchemists were the Aristotelian fire, air, water, and earth; the substances thought necessary to produce gold or the philosopher's elixir were at first mercury and sulphur and at other times a still simplistic triad which added salt; and alchemical manipulations were based, as will be seen, on the assumption that the behavior of matter imitated, or could be made to imitate, that of plants, animals, men, and of God Himself in His work of creation and redemption. This is to say that the principles were animistic, voluntaristic, and even dramatic. Except in the most primitive fashion, the alchemist did not analyze but analogized.

Since the human mind is prone to vagaries, we ought not, perhaps, to be astonished that in fairly recent times both indirect and direct attempts have been made to affirm the possibility of the transmutation of base metals to gold. Berthelot himself, a sensible man, thought in 1885 that we might ultimately pass beyond the periodic table and the certainties it appears to offer: "nul ne peut affirmer que la fabrication des corps réputés simples soit impossible *a priori.*"[6] Later still Fritz Paneth, in a lecture delivered at Cornell University, said that "the trend of modern chemistry is toward rather than away from the theories which were condemned by the official science of the last century" and urged that the positive and negative particles of hydrogen might be primordial matter of the kind sought by the alchemists.[7] A few years earlier H. Stanley Redgrave, also assertedly a chemist, suggested that the *prima materia* of the alchemists was identical with the modern Ether of Space—a concept since abandoned—and was inclined to justify efforts at transmutation on the ground that elements can in fact be altered by radioactivity.[8] An occultist like A. E. Waite, whose attitude toward alchemy resembles that of Montague Summers toward witchcraft, is temperamentally inclined to assume the possession of profound wisdom by our ancestors. The most extended modern defense known to me was offered, however, by C. Théodore Tiffereau, a Frenchman who thought he had made gold in Mexico in 1847 and 42 years later was still pathetically appealing for funds to discover ways of making his still uncertain processes economically viable. He spoke before, or sent *mémoires* to, the Académie des Sciences six times between June 27, 1853, and December 25, 1854, and then after a long

Basil Valentine His Triumphant Chariot of Antimony (London: 1678), p. 112 (opposite p. 101).

Alchemical vessels. The explanation on p. 101 reads as follows: "Of your Earthen Retort A. open the upper hole B. into which put your Matter by Parts, lest all together s[c]enting the heat, should act too forcibly; and presently Close the Hole with its proper Cover. To the Spirits received in the Vessel C. exit is given by the hole D. into the other opposit Receiver E. to which again is applied the other Receiver F. So, the more subtle Spirits ascending through the Hole D, settle in the Recipient F. But the more gross remain in the bottom G. of the Receiver C." The fire beneath the retort is taken for granted and not shown.

This edition is late but contains an English text.

period of silence surfaced for another lecture—this time not before the Académie—on March 16, 1889. His reports were received skeptically, although a preface by Jules Lermina to the book which he ultimately published suggested that chemistry is rising toward the verification of hermetic truths; and a concluding "Étude" by Gustave Itasse, a commercial chemist, affirmed that the gold Tiffereau claimed to have made in 1847 had "toutes les propriétés physiques de l'or natif, mais diffère de celui-ci par quelques propriétés chimiques, n'appartenant pas en propre à un autre métal."[9] In the meantime, like many another alchemist, ancient, medieval, or of the Renaissance, Tiffereau had run out of funds but supported himself by the new trade of photography. Although his sincerity is beyond question, in all probability—like earlier practitioners—he separated out gold associated with other metals as an impurity.

Several of the medieval and Renaissance authors whose treatises we shall examine also claimed to have succeeded in transmuting baser substances. "I did it myselffe *Thomas Charnocke*," we read in a sixteenth-century document called *The Breviary of Naturall Philosophy.*[10] The celebrated Nicolas Flamel (c. 1330–1417) is reported not only to have made projection but to have founded or endowed fourteen hospitals, to have built three chapels, and to have made gifts to seven churches from his profits.[11] Significantly, this is the only alleged use known to me for the general good of a science which professed to explain its secrets darkly in order to keep them from men who would make a selfish use of their power. "I, who possess the Stone, and communicate to you this Book," writes the anonymous author of *The Glory of the World,* "would faithfully admonish and beseech you to keep this my TABLE OF PARADISE and GLORY of the WORLD, from all proud and unjust oppressors of the poor."[12] "I was almost on the point of giving up the whole thing in despair," confesses an unknown German who wrote *The Book of Alze* in the fifteenth century or thereabouts. "At length I communicated my discovery to a friend, who faithfully executed my instructions, and brought the work to a successful issue."[13] Basil Valentine, who called himself a Benedictine monk, tells us that his diligence and the prayers of a brother monk whose disease of the kidney he had cured "so prevailed with God, that there was revealed to me that great secret which God ever conceals from those who are wise in their own conceits."[14] Such explicit professions are uncommon, success ordinarily being rather implied than stated—if, indeed, it is not merely hoped to be imminent. Most of the claims are easily doubted, and a number of successes were produced by a fragment of the Stone received from somebody else, so that the secret remained a mystery.

One account, however, is puzzling both because of its circumstantiality and because its author was the well-known Helvetius (Johann Friedrich Schweitzer),

190 TRACTATUS I. LIB. VII.

Igne A. accensu super arulam B. C. D. subtiliatione expellit aërem grossiorem per tubam E. qua egrediendo flat, & ventos benigniores excitat.

Aut propter multitudinem aquarum in terræ viscera irrumpentem, integram aëris substantiam ex terræ ventre extrudentium, ut experimento sequenti declaratur, unde non modò venti, sed etiam terræmotus ut plurimum fiunt.

Experimentum.   II.

Aqua cadens in superiorem regionem vasis A. B. C. D. descendit in regionem ejus inferiorem per tubam E. & expellit aërem in ea contentum per foramen tubæ, F. qui transiens per orificium fistula. G. eam flatu suo resonare facit.

Aut quando magna terræ quantitas cadit in immensam terræ cavitatem seu specùm, aërem in ipsa retentum subitò & violenter ejiciens, ut in experimento sequenti declaratur, atque tunc semper ferè circa illam mundi plagam tremor terræ persentitur metuendus.

Robert Fludd, *Utriusque cosmi maioris scilicet et minoris metaphysica, physica, atque technica historia* (Oppenheim: Hieronymus Gallerus, 1617), p. 190.

Physical experimentation, once chiefly practised by alchemists, gradually became more "modern." Here a theory of earthquakes is illustrated by a simple apparatus intended to show that the irruption of water into "the earth's viscera" can expel air so violently as to cause earthquakes. The vessel has two parts, the upper filled with water, the lower with air; water—replenished from a spout—falls through the tube E to expel air through the tube F, with the result that the pipe G is made to whistle. "Or," the text continues, "when a large quantity of earth falls into an immense cavity or cave in the earth," the same thing happens, and an earthquake may be feared.

physician to the Prince of Orange in the seventeenth century and author of books on medicine and botany. The objection offered above to the "making" of gold by Tiffereau is irrelevant here. According to his *Golden Calf,* Helvetius was visited in December, 1666, by a stranger "of a mean Stature, a little long face, with a few small pock holes, and most black hair, not at all curled, a beardless chin, about three or four and forty years of age (as I guessed) and born in *North Holland."* The visit, the stranger said, was induced by the discovery from some of his treatises that Helvetius was skeptical about alchemy. The interview is reported in detail, and we learn that Helvetius, while being allowed to handle a piece of the Stone, surreptitiously removed a bit and experimented unsuccessfully with it. During another visit the stranger—who subsequently disappeared—gave him a somewhat larger sample of the Stone, and Helvetius then, with its aid, transmuted a half-ounce of lead to gold which was proved by tests made by a goldsmith and a silversmith to be "most pure." As Taylor remarked, "There seems in this account to be no room for any mistake or illusion: Helvetius either transmuted lead to gold or has lied prodigiously." [15]

If forced to choose, one must say that he lied: although not, perhaps, consciously. Given the analogical thought-patterns from which even the most advanced thinkers in the seventeenth century were not wholly free, he may have been too readily convinced. Certainly the chemical tests for gold were still relatively un-sophisticated. What is odd is not so much the claim as the character of the nar-rator, the specificity of the details, and a tonality which suggests, quite atypically, that a negative report would not have been unendurable to the narrator. Ordi-narily the writer of an alchemical document wants to be thought an initiate, the possessor of a rare and precious secret. His praise of the Stone or the Elixir is indirect praise of himself. Helvetius makes no pretense of expertness. He does not understand what happened or why, and he seems to feel no pleasure in his achieve-ment. The process, too, was of the simplest: aside from the fragment of the Stone he used only lead and merely heated the two together. Is it possible that the story was religious allegory, the Stone being a religious doctrine—Luther's dogma of justification by faith only, or another—and the lead a body of "base" theology which was transmuted by the new insight? Tonality is against such an interpretation. Yet since gold is an element it cannot possibly, by mere cooking, be made from other elements either by addition or by subtraction. The imaginative non-scientist may play, if he likes, with fancies about radioactivity, atomic fusion or fission, or with other more soaring concepts as unclear as he may find them attractive; but at present the best possible judgment of Helvetius' report is that something went wrong.

A melancholy which may afflict the modern student of alchemy arises from a vivid realization that, in fact, all the attempts were useless. No amount of per-severance, or study, or expenditure of wealth, or prayer and self-discipline, could possibly have led to success. The futility was, if anything, greater than in astrology. Astronomy began more or less contemporaneously with astrology and required only to be separated from it to become a true science, but alchemy was so basically mistaken that its ancestry to chemistry was indirect and, as it were, accidental. So profound was the disjunction that the publication, in 1661, of Robert Boyle's *The Scepticall Chymist,* which denied the four Aristotelian elements, may be taken as a premonitory death-knell for the venerable illusion and a first step toward practical knowledge.

II. History of alchemy

The origins of alchemy are obscure. Berthelot has a section on *Sources égyptiennes, chaldéennes, juives, gnostiques,*[16] and elsewhere there has been speculation about Indian and Chinese roots. In the Middle Ages and Renaissance, however, invention of the art was often ascribed to Hermes Trismegistus, whom we have met often in these pages and will look at directly before long. Hermes is frequently identified also as the author of basic, if rather especially mystical, texts, of which the most famous was the *Tabula Smaragdina* or *Emerald Tablet.* This was said to have

Elias Ashmole, *Theatrum chemicum Britannicum* (London: Nath. Brooke, 1652), p. 51.

An alchemical laboratory. Here the central position is given to the alchemist's balance; but furnaces are shown at bottom left and right. The central scroll reads, "Compound the Stone without contradiction (*or* repugnance)." The scroll at lower left may mean "Separate the earth from the fire by blowing upon it gently"; but if so the Latin is corrupt. The third scroll reads, "Stay near the vessel and watch the colors"—a visual method of detecting chemical changes. Sol and Luna (gold and silver) are on the alchemist's table together with what may be a mortar, and more moons appear beneath the cloth on the side of what seems to be a chest. The female and male figures in the upper corners may again represent the moon and the sun or the two sexes which must be brought to unite in a hermaphrodite.

been found, written in Phoenician characters and held in the hands of Hermes' corpse, either by Sara, wife of Abraham, or by Alexander the Great, or by Apollonius of Tyana (first century A.D.). Other accounts claim that the secrets were revealed to Adam by God and were passed down through Adam's son, Seth, to the patriarchs. The attribution of alchemical knowledge to such ancients as Pythagoras, Alexander the Great, Plato, Theophrastus, Galen, Hippocrates, Isis, Iamblichus, Mary the Prophetess, and Cleopatra suggests once more that all knowledge worth having was fathered upon persons who had lived as near as possible to the beginning of a world which ever since had deteriorated steadily. Certainly there was a Chinese alchemy—which aimed, however, merely at prolonging life—long before the Christian period and perhaps as early as the fourth century B.C.; and a hint of an elixir which conferred immortality can be found in Indian literature before 1000 B.C.[17] The sources of Western alchemy, however, appear to lie among the Alexandrian Greeks in the early Christian centuries.

At first, or in one of its forms, alchemy was a practical art associated with the work of goldsmiths. A recipe given in the *Papyrus Graecus Holmiensis,* which dates from the end of the third century, runs as follows: "Asemos [apparently a white alloy resembling silver] one *stater* or copper of Cyprus 3 *staters; 4 staters* of gold; melt them together." According to Taylor, the product would have been 19-carat or 10-carat gold, depending on which option was chosen, instead of the 24-carat gold with which the fusion was made.[18] Quite possibly, however, the goldsmiths did not recognize the product as an alloy and believed themselves to have "multiplied" the gold. The *diplosis* or doubling may, as Taylor suggests, imply a conviction that "the gold acted as a seed which, nourished by the copper and silver, grew at their expense until the whole mass became gold."[19] Certainly no reliable tests of purity yet existed,[20] but the goldsmiths may be supposed to have had a fairly accurate sense of metallic weights; if so, a literal belief in *diplosis* would have involved some self-deception. Again, early goldsmiths are known to have plated and gilded, and they appear also to have colored gold by treating it with varnishes or corrosives (which might have removed impurities).[21] In any event, the early Alexandrian treatises know nothing of the Philosopher's Stone or of an *elixir vitae.* The history of these more typical alchemical aims must be at least partly distinct.

What complicates the problem is that although the extant manuscripts nearly

Elias Ashmole, *Theatrum chemicum Britannicum* (London: Nath. Brooke, 1652), p. 44.

At the top four celebrated alchemists, Geber, Arnoldus, al-Rāzi, and Hermes Trismegistus (wearing a crown, as the first and most consummate master), lean over a balustrade to give advice to four assistants at work in the alchemist's laboratory. Geber says, "Grind, grind, grind, and grind again, and do not grow weary." Arnoldus says, "Let it drink as much as it can, up to twelve times." Al-Rāzi says, "The body is dried out as often as it is drunk up." Hermes says, "Roast this white copper (the identity of this metal is uncertain) and cook it until it becomes seed." The decorative design about the picture is conventional.

all postdate 1000 A.D. constant appeal is made to older authorities, and the substance of some works is clearly archaic. A document attributed to Zosimus seems to have been written before the destruction of the temple of Serapis, at Alexandria, in 390 A.D.[22] The early tradition must have been oral, the art being protected zealously against wide dissemination. After 400 A.D. Greek alchemists restricted themselves mostly to explanations of what older writers had meant and did not think of themselves as innovators.[23] A treatise called *The Golden Age Restored* names Abraham, Isaac, Jacob, Noah, Moses, Solomon, Ezra, and Miriam,[24] and another tract named *The Glory of the World* adds Methuselah, Adam, Hermes, Anaxagoras, and Pythagoras.[25] Additional names appear elsewhere: Cheops, Leucippus, Democritus,

DISTICON.
Has tibi necesse est scalas conscendere trinas ʃ Qui cupis æthereos, doctus adire polos,

Raimon Lull, *Liber de ascensu, et descensu intellectus* (Palma, Majorca: Michaelis Cerola and Michaelis Amoros, 1744), before p. 1. The reprint is based on a Valence, 1512, edition.

The ladder of intellect. The house of wisdom, at the top, is led to by steps labeled "Stone," "Flame," "Plant," "Brute," "Man," "Heaven," "Angel," and, at the threshold of the door, "God." The order is from lower states of being to higher. The billowing clouds are a symbol of Divinity, whose working is always partly mysterious. The circular diagram at the right, also labeled "The Ladder of Intellect," has an inner division with segments marked as "The Intelligible," "The Sensible," "The Imaginable," "The Doubtful," and "The Believable." These are categories of the knowable, the first three in the order of descending certainty, the last two a dichotomy of what must be guessed at. The segments of the outer circle, again read counter-clockwise from the top, are "The Individual," "The Species," "The Genus" (states of being in the order of ascending abstraction); "Being," "Act," "Suffering" (modes of existence); "Action" (apparently different from "Act" as a process differs from participation in it); "Nature," "Substance," "Accident" (the created universe itself, the native matter of its parts, and that matter as modified by circumstances); and, finally, "Simple," "Composite" (the contrasting states of homogeneity and compositeness). The scroll at the bottom of the disk reads "Total Intellect." The distich at the bottom, although obscure, may perhaps be translated as follows: "You must mount the steps three at a time: He who aspires to the upper regions must approach the heavens as a scholar."

Similar "ladders" appear in many contexts. In an alchemical treatise (and Lull was thought of chiefly as an alchemist), the meaning would be that the operator, if he is to succeed, must mount from lower stages of being and of knowing to higher.

and dozens or scores of others. After about 500 A.D. alchemy drops mostly out of sight, to reappear, in the twelfth century, with accretions.

The intermediaries through whom the art was resurrected were the Arabs, who in the seventh and eighth centuries made conquests in Egypt, Syria, Palestine, Persia, and elsewhere. Among these the most celebrated was Geber (Abu Musa Jabir ibn Hayyan, born probably in 721 or 722), of whose multitudinous writings about a hundred are extant.[26] By as early as 300 or 400 A.D., alchemy had become "a bewildering confusion of Egyptian magic, Greek philosophy, Gnosticism, Neo-Platonism, Babylonian astrology, Christian theology, and pagan mythology," [27] so that the doctrine which spread from Alexandria among the Muslims venerated such adepts as Egyptian gods and demi-gods (Hermes and his disciple Agathodaemon), Greek philosophers, and Jews.[28] In the meantime, so far as is known, alchemy had died in the Christian West. Its revivification began when Western scholars set about the translation of Arabic texts. The beginning of the alchemical renaissance can, indeed, be dated precisely, for the first translation in a long series, that of an Arabic *Book of the Composition of Alchemy,* was completed by Roger of Chester on February 11, 1144. Other translators, among them Adelard of Bath, Gerard of Cremona, and the famous Raymond Lull, contributed to the movement, and from this time on the art began to flourish. Its decay began in the seventeenth century, and its effectual death may be dated early in the eighteenth. The last English proponent of some note was Elias Ashmole (d. 1692), a man unusually credulous for his time but honored as the founder of the Ashmolean Museum at Oxford. He did not, however, practise.

During the five centuries of its flourishing alchemy had attracted the favorable attention of Roger Bacon, Aquinas, Albertus Magnus, and many another man of distinguished intellect and achievement right down to the time of Sir Thomas Browne (whose *Pseudodoxia epidemica* is full of hardheaded observation) and Sir Isaac Newton. Kings and emperors had been attracted: the English Henry VI and Charles II; the Scottish James IV; Marie de' Medici, Queen Consort of the French Henry IV—who had her own laboratory; the Emperor Rudolf II (1576–1612). And, of course, literature had reflected the interest. Chaucer's *Canon's Yeoman's Tale* is about deliberate trickery, and it has been suggested that Chaucer himself had been victimized. Ashmole, in his *Theatrum Chemicum Britannicum* (1651), a collection of between thirty and forty alchemical documents with which we shall have much to do, printed, along with Chaucer's *Tale,* John Gower's *Concerning the Philosopher's Stone* and John Lydgate's *Translation of the second Epistle that King Alexander sent to his Master Aristotle.*[29] Ben Jonson's play, *The Alchemist,* is well known. Jean de Meun, author of the second part of the *Roman de la rose,* was reputed to have written *Le Miroir d'alqvimie.*[30] A German dissertation has collected allusions in thirty-three English authors from Chaucer's time to the seventeenth century.[31] The purpose here, as elsewhere in the present study, will not be to interpret or collect literary allusions but to discuss the occult system itself in such a way as to make most of its parts comprehensible.

III. Alchemical processes

If at the beginning alchemy was a goldsmith's art, it soon became more ambitious and, in time, developed two distinguishable traditions. One of these was ambitiously, and often rather indiscriminately, experimental, the other philosophical or meditative. Holmyard was so impressed by the differences that he characterized the latter as a kind of poetical alchemy which had nothing to do with laboratory operations but was rather an imaginative equivalent concerned really with the purification of the soul.[32] In my opinion the separation is less complete, the distinction lying chiefly in a more highly metaphorical and imaginative style which was encouraged, among especially literate and reflective writers, both by the tradition of veiled utterance and by a tendency to draw parallels between changes imposed upon the laboratory materials and such Christian ceremonies or mysteries as baptism, marriage, resurrection, and transfiguration. Yet a demarcation can be drawn, if not always sharply, between men who toiled in smoky laboratories with small thought of their souls and others who united their operations with a spiritual discipline. The former were proto-chemists, the latter, in part, at least, mystics. Although the first sort belong to the history of science and the second to something broader, we shall look at both in turn.

At the basis of the chemical doctrine lay Aristotle's principle of the four elements (earth, water, air, and fire) and the four qualities which determined them (cold, moisture, dryness, heat). The elements were all derivative from something more fundamental still, a *prima materia* or *hyle*. In the beginning only this had existed, and if all four of the elements could be subtracted from a well-chosen substance only it would remain. The final steps in the production of gold consisted of adding to this first matter whatever was necessary to turn it into the desired metal.

A somewhat fuller statement of the theory as held at an early period is given by Berthelot.

> According to the Greek adepts, every natural body is formed of the same basic matter. To obtain a desired substance—for example, gold, the most perfect of metals, the most precious of goods—it is necessary to take analogous bodies, which differ from it only in some quality, and eliminate what characterizes them, in such a way as to reduce them to their first matter, which is the mercury of the philosophers. This can be ob-

tained from ordinary mercury by removing from it, first of all, its liquidity, that is to say a water, a fluid and mobile element which prevents it from reaching perfection. It must also be fixed: its volatility, an air or an aërial element it contains, must be extracted. Finally, some authors affirm, as Geber was to do later, that the mercury must be freed from an earth, a terrestrial element, a gross slag, which is opposed to its perfect refinement.

The first matter of all metals having been prepared in this way—I mean the mercury of the philosophers—it remains only to tint it by sulphur and arsenic, words in which were confused metallic sulphurs, various inflammable bodies of the same class (*congénères*), and quintessential materials which the philosophers professed to draw from them.[33]

The choice of mercury as the substance on which to operate may have resulted from its visual likeness to silver—the metal thought to be nearest to gold—its weight, and its curious fluidity, which suggested susceptibility to change. Having been purified, the mercury required the addition of yellowness, an evident property of sulphur; and later it came to be thought that the final product needed fixation, a "principle" inherent in salt. But since the theory did not lead to the expected results, of course the operations tended to become steadily more complicated.

We cannot trace in detail the innumerable experiments, and the modifications of doctrine which accompanied them, that characterized the development from the eighth century on among the Arabs, and from the twelfth to the seventeenth centuries by Europeans. There is subject-matter here not for a chapter but for many volumes. A hint of what toil was involved is given, however, by *The Compound of Alchymie* (1471), written by George Ripley, Canon of Bridlington in Yorkshire. Much more elaborate directions might be given, and the catalogue of terms is by no means complete.

1. *Calcination.* "The purgacyon of our *Stone,*" a process which according to Ripley takes a year or more. Although we are not clearly told how, the operator is to turn earth into water, this into air, and air into fire; he is then to reverse the process and repeat the whole twice. What results is "the hede of the Crow" (or the crow's bill, or the ashes of Hermes' tree, or "Our Tode of the Erth whych etyth hys fyll").[34]

2. *Solution* (or dissolution). The aim of this is to reduce the "hard and dry Compactyon" to become "intenuate"—thin, liquid. "Every Mettall was ons [once] Water mynerall,/ Therefore wyth Water they turne to Water all."[35]

3. *Separation,* or "dyffynycyon," which divides "The Subtill fro the groce [gross], fro the thyck the thyn." The thin is apparently again "water," the thick "Oyle." The process must be repeated "ofte tymes," "Tyll Erth remayne benethe in color bloe [blue]," and it requires the addition of water distilled seven times.[36]

Elias Ashmole, *Theatrum chemicum Britannicum* (London: Nath. Brooke, 1652), p. 12.

The alchemical initiate, in the lower left, says, "I will preserve the alchemical secrets in secrecy." The master, to the right, hands him a book as he replies, "Take God's gift under the holy seal." Above are the Holy Spirit, figured as a dove, and two angels; that on the left says, "Thou hast loved justice and hatest wickedness, therefore the Lord thy God hath anointed thee with oil" (a variant of *Psa.* 45:7), and that on the right, "Await the Lord, play the man, and He will strengthen thy heart."

4. *Conjunction* is "of dysseveryd qualytes a Copulacyon," as of the body with the purified soul, but involves a union of earth, water, air, and fire. The "Woman" (mercury) is to be impregnated with the "Man" (sulphur), after which the Woman must be stoppered up to "lygg [lie] alone" for five months.[37]

5. *Putrefaction.* Essentially this appears to be a process of causing the Woman "wyth her Chyldren all" to go "to Purgatory to purg ther fylth orygynall." There they will be "lyke lyquyd Pych [pitch] and will "swell and burbyll, setyll, and *Putrefye,*" only—later—to pass through all the colors of the rainbow and finally to turn white.[38]

6. *Congelation* is "of soft thyngs Induracyon of Colour Whyte,/ And confyxacyon of Spyrits whych fleying [fleeing] are." The effect is the reducing of the materials' consistency to that of water.[39]

7. *Fermentation,* which is not clearly explained.[40]

8. *Exaltation.* Christ said, "Yf I exalted be,/ Then shall I draw all thyngs unto me." The Wife and Man must be "contumulate" (interred, buried) and afterwards "revyvyd by the Spyryts of Lyfe"; thereafter "up to Hevyn they must Exaltyd be,/ Ther to be in Body and Sowle gloryfycate." This accomplished, they will "draw as thou shalt se/ All other Bodys to ther owne dygnyte." Presumably

the substances are at this stage vaporized by heat and then chilled back into a liquid.[41]

9. *Multiplication* results in an increase "In Color, in Odor, in Vertue, and also in Quantyte." This is done by often dissolving and congealing, or by "Iterat [repeated] Fermentacion," which requires the addition of mercury.[42]

10. *Projection,* or the transmutation of other metals. The "medicine" prepared in the way described must be "cast on" only metals which have been cleansed, or the product will be brittle. The alchemist is to multiply first by ten—that is, transmute a quantity of base metal ten times that of the "medicine"—then by one hundred, and so on up to ten thousand. This in turn will yield one hundred million, and a still further operation ten million million. If, however, "the Tyncture [that is, the proper yellow color] of thy Medcyn begyn to decrease,/ And then yt ys tyme of *Projeccyon* to cese." [43]

From this description, which is typically obscure or "veiled," some notion can be obtained of how long and expensive the operations must often have been. As Ashmole notes, the alchemists' "chiefest study was to wrap up their *Secrets* in *Fables,* and spin out their *Fancies* in *Vailes* and *shadows,* whose *Radii* seems [*sic*] to extend every way, yet so, that they all meete in a *Common Center,* and point only at One thing." [44] As has been said, the alleged motive was to prevent the learning of the secrets by men who would use them badly; but secrecy was a trait

Elias Ashmole, *Theatrum chemicum Britannicum* (London: Nath. Brooke, 1652), p. 101.

An alchemical laboratory: one assistant stokes the fire while a second is busy at another furnace. Maintenance of the proper temperatures for the various operations was crucial, but difficult before the invention of reliable thermometers in the seventeenth century. On the facing page (of Thomas Norton's *Ordinall of Alchemie*) we read, "Of manie Auctors written ye maie see,/ *Totum consistit in ignis regimine*" (everything depends on the control of the fire). The work's complexity is suggested by the seven furnaces, and its piety by the cross on the central cupola. As often, the border is conventional.

of all *occulta* and was inseparable from the very concept of esotericism, which flourishes among men who enjoy the distinction of possessing rare knowledge. As for the expense, Thomas Charnock notes in his *Breviary of Naturall Philosophy* (1557) that

Our Fire is chargeable, and will amount
Above 3. pound a weeke, who hath list to cast account . . .
Above a hundred pounds truly did I spend,
Only in fire ere 9. moneths came to an end.[45]

True, he "begun when all things were deare"; but when we recall that on the basis of a sixteen-to-one depreciation £100 would amount to perhaps $3,840 in current money, the common complaints of impoverishment and an inability to push the work to its conclusion become readily understandable. In addition Charnock must have paid the wages of assistants. According to *The Ordinall of Alchimy* (1477), by Thomas Norton of Bristol, eight servants were "convenable" but four adequate: "one halfe of them must werke/ While the other Sleepeth or goeth to

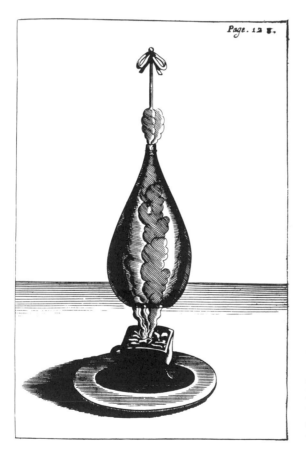

Page. 128.

Basil Valentine His Triumphant Chariot of Antimony (London: 1678), p. 128.

Another alchemical vessel, described on the opposite page (also numbered 128). The text reads as follows: "Take of *Antimony, Sulphur, Salt-nitre* [saltpeter], of each equal parts; Fulminate those under a Bell, as Oyl of *Sulphur per Campan.* is made; which way of preparing hath long since been known to the Antients. But Consider, you will have a better way, if instead of a Bell, you take an Alembeck, and apply to it a Recipient; so you will obtain more Oyl, which will indeed be of the same Colour, as that which is made of Common Sulphur, but in powers and virtues not a little more excellent, then it." A note recommends a vessel of the shape shown. *Oleum Sulphuris* (oil of sulphur) is described by Martin Ruland (*A Lexicon of Alchemy,* transl. A. E. Waite, London: 1964) as "A Vapour Extracted by Elevation from Prepared Sulphur" but is apparently identical with sulphuric acid.

Kerke." [46] On top of the cost of wood or coal and of the assistants' wages and keep was that of the furnaces—often elaborate, and usually more than one; the vessels, which were frequently broken; and the materials, some of which must have been hard of access as well as dear. Also, of course, there might be heavy expense for books or manuscripts. Yet the activity became compulsive and went on despite the lack of success, no doubt encouraged at intervals by rumors of successful projection at a distance. With the aid of illustrations in the documents, it is easy to picture a typical laboratory: fires, steam, odors, jars, alembics, cucurbits, retorts, pans, stacks of fuel, helpers working bellows, jumbled piles of miscellaneous litter on shelves and floor, smoky faces, stained aprons, and open books. The alchemists' wives must often have been driven to distraction. Again one is oppressed by a sense of waste and futility.

Because the reader may have been teased by the citations from Ripley, it may be useful to add somewhat clearer definitions of a few key terms from *The Works of Geber*, translated by Richard Russell (1678). [47] Sublimation, Geber says, "is the *Elevation* of a dry Thing by *Fire*, with adherency to its Vessel." [48] Calcination is "the *Pulverization* of a *Thing* by *Fire*, through *Privation* of the *Humidity* consolidating the *Parts*." It is done so that "Spirits" may "the better be fixed, and be the more easily dissolved into Water." [49] Coagulation is "the *Reduction* of a Thing *Liquid* to a *Solid Substance*, by *Privation* of the *Humidity*." [50] Fixation is "the convenient disposing a *Fugitive* Thing, to abide and sustain the *Fire*." [51] Ceration is "the mollification of an hard *Thing*, not fusible unto *Liquefaction*": [52] that is, the producing of a wax-like solid. Although these and similar clarifications may not much reduce the confusion of inexperienced persons, the terminology is not in fact inscrutable. Most of the words appear in good modern dictionaries, and an exhaustive alchemical *Lexicon* (1612) by Martin Rulandus has been translated into English. [53] The most stubborn opacities result from the determination of nearly all the authors, regardless of frequent promises to Tell All, really to keep the most essential secrets hidden.

Ripley's summary of the alchemist's program is only one of a very great number and should not be taken as paradigmatic. Raymond Lull's explanation, in his *Codicil*, runs as follows.

The art is divided into four parts corresponding to the four practical principles. The first part shows the way of refining what is thick by liquefaction of the component elements (*élémentation*), dissolution, and separation of the stone into four elements. The second part shows the way of lightening the heavy by distillations, calcinations, condensations, inhumations, solidifications, dissolutions, and animations which prepare the elements. The third part shows the way of vivifying by the spirit and that of nourishing the stone by imbibings, decoctions, inhumations, and sublimations of the stone. The fourth part shows the way of making the bitter sweet and the raw ripe by reductions, impregnations, inhumations, fomentations, animations, fixations, and incerations.[54]

The "stone" of the second sentence is not the Philosopher's Stone but the metallic substance with which the alchemist begins. This substance is, in turn, decomposed, refined, energized, and ripened to sweetness, and the result appears to be the Elixir, which cannot, however, always be distinguished from the Stone. It is probable that the operation began with mercury and involved the use of sulphur, for on an earlier page we read that 'Sulphur and mercury are the extremes of all the metals, and therefore all other metals are means between them." [55]

An earlier treatise, the *Mirror of Alchemy* attributed to Jean de Meun, also asserts that all metals and mineral substances are made of mercury and sulphur.[56] "Gold," the author continues, "is a perfect substance, engendered of a mercury which is lively, pure, stable, clear, and red, and of a sulphur which is clean, stable, red, incombustible, and without any fault." [57] Something, naturally, is held back: "Our final secret is very excellent and is hidden in the mineral thing from which it is to be made and composed more directly." [58] Common mercury and sulphur will not do.[59] Since heat operates in mines to produce mercury and sulphur, the means to produce them is decoction.[60] Similarly, since a mountain "is closed upon itself on all sides," the vessel into which the materials are put should be sealed "in such a way that the fire which has been put there, when it rises, will find no way to get out." The vessel should be round, small-necked, and of glass "or of some earth which represents nature." [61] The operation will produce a succession of colors: black, reddish, green, white, ashy, and golden or "red." [62] The projection made with the final product requires the heating for three days of a small part of the elixir with a thousand parts of the *corps plus voisin* (not further described) over a fire which is gradually increased from mild to intense, after which a bit of this is combined in the same way with another thousand parts of the other substance.[63] These directions advance us a little by avowing explicitly the imitation of "natural" forces thought to produce gold more slowly without human interference. Obviously the directions would be hard to follow: for instance, where are red mercury and incombustible (if that is what *non bruslant* means) sulphur to be found? Nevertheless a medieval or Renaissance reader of the treatise would not only be heartened by another testimony of the art's practicality but might be led to modify some details of his practice, as by searching for mercury associated with iron ore.

Another metal strongly recommended in a number of sources was antimony. This was especially praised in *The Triumphal Chariot of Antimony* (ca. 1500) by the shadowy Basilius Valentinus. Valentinus lists "five principal heads" of the alchemist's work, as follows: "The first is the invocation of God; the second, the contemplation of Nature; the third, true preparation; the fourth, the way of using; the fifth, the use and profit." [64] Although the difference between the fourth and fifth stages is vague, we understand easily that the work must be undertaken piously and will not succeed without God's help and also—what is not surprising—that a preliminary study of nature will reveal principles to be followed in the operations. That alchemy was not merely a physical science, and by modern standards not a science at all, appears from the necessity that the operator must "be free from all ambition, hypocrisy, and vice, as also from all cognate faults, such as arrogance, boldness, pride, luxury, worldly vanity, oppression of the poor." A wicked man can never succeed.[65] Faults in the operator's state of consciousness or even beneath the threshold of awareness will cause the substances with which he works to become recalcitrant; or else God Himself will intervene to frustrate the work, though I think the first interpretation is correct. A belief that matter itself was partly spiritual, and therefore sensitive to a mental or moral atmosphere, will appear in a number of documents which await notice.

In a later passage of *The Triumphal Chariot* we learn that minerals have been affected by astral influences.

> I find that all that is dug up from the bowels of the mountains is infused by the stars and celestial bodies, and derives its origin from a certain aqueous vapour, which, after being nourished by the stars for a long time, is reduced to a tangible shape by the elements. Furthermore, as the fire, with the aid of air, gains the ascendancy, that aqueous substance becomes dry; out of water is produced fire, and out of fire and air we obtain earth; all these elements are still found in all bodies before their separation. Water, formed into earth by fire and air, is thus the first substance of all things.[66]

The "aqueous vapour" is fed by stellar rays, dried by the elemental fire, and with the co-operation of a third element, air, is reduced to the last, earth. The "first substance" is "Water formed into earth," and according to a note by Kerchringius is identical with "the Water of Anaxagoras, the Fire of Empedocles, the First Substance of Aristotle. It is that by which trees grow, men are nourished, and metals generated." [67] "Proof" involves corroboration by the statements of three ancients who to a modern would seem to have been in dispute.

The "earth" with which the alchemist works is, for Valentinus, not mercury but antimony: not "crude, melted Antimony, which is bought in shops," but "the ore of Antimony, as it is dug up from the mine, and is first formed into glass." [68] Its preparation is by fire; oil of antimony is produced by the removal of its earth, although we had thought the antimony was itself earth, and of all other impurities.

88   EMBLEMA XXX.   *De secretu Naturæ.*

Sol indiget Lunâ , ut gallus gallinâ.

EPIGRAMMA XXX.

O *Sol , solus agis nil , si non viribus adsim,*
     Ut sine gallinæ est gallus inanis ope..
Auxiliumque tuum præsens ego Luna vicissim
     Postulo, gallinæ gallus ut expetitûr.
Quæ natura simul conjungi flagitat , ille est
     Mentis inops , vinclis qui religare velit.

Michaelis Majerus (i.e., Meier), *Secretioris naturae secretorum scrutinium chymicum* (Frankfurt: Georgius Heinricus Oerlingius, 1687), p. 88.

The sun and moon in alchemical operations. The top reads, "The sun needs the moon as the cock needs the hen." The epigram may be translated: "O Sun, thou dost nothing alone if I am not present with my strength, as a cock is helpless without a hen. I, the Moon, am present and in turn ask your help, as a cock is needed for a hen. He is lacking in wit who wishes to bind with fetters what nature forces to be joined together."

Sol—the sun, gold, and much else—and the moon—silver as well as the moon—must be joined into the hermaphrodite, an emblem of the union of male and female or the male and female principles.

The process, which is described in detail,[69] requires saltpeter, vinegar—an organic substance, hence repudiated by many authorities—salt of antimony, mercury of antimony, red oil of vitriol, and sweet oil of antimony. The operations include heating, pulverizing, distilling, "circulating" for a month in a closed vessel (the vapor being fed back through a curved neck to the bottom), subliming, rectifying, distilling in sand, and so on. The result is the "Medicine of men and of metals," a sovereign remedy for all ills.[70] This is evidently both the Stone and the Elixir. If the account is not wholly clear—none of the descriptions are that—it is none the less unusually specific.

Such summaries could be extended indefinitely; but beneath both the chemical operations we have been considering and the mystical tradition to which we shall soon turn lie certain common assumptions most conveniently accessible in the *Emerald Tablet* of Hermes, constantly referred to as exceptionally authoritative and indeed quasi-divine. The *Tablet* is brief and will be given in its entirety with interpretative notations added inside parentheses.

"1. I speak not fictitious things, but what is true and most certain.

"2. What is below is like that which is above, and what is above is like that which is below, to accomplish the miracles of one thing." (I. e., there are "corresponding planes" in various levels of creation; hence it is safe to draw analogies between macrocosm and microcosm, the mineral kingdom and the human, animal, and vegetable kingdoms, etc.)

"3. And as all things were produced by the mediation of one Being, so all things were produced from this one thing by adaptation." (Since the God who created the universe was One, created objects must have been produced from a single—that is, undifferentiated—primal matter.)

"4. Its father is the Sun, its mother the Moon; the wind carries it in its belly, its nurse is the earth." (This is an especially complex aphorism. According to Redgrove, the sun and moon probably stand here for spirit and matter.[71] This is possible, but since gold was associated with the sun and the moon with silver—the astrological symbols for sun and moon are identical with the alchemical symbols for gold and silver—the luminaries at least suggest the two most precious and dignified metals. If the moon is associated with water, as because of its "moisture" was usual, and the sun with fire, the *prima materia* is understood to have been generated by fire, born of water, brought down from the sky by wind, and nourished by earth.)

"5. It is the cause of all perfection throughout the whole world." (Naturally. Must not the source of everything good be something better still?)

"6. Its power is perfect if it be changed into earth." (The "nursing" of prime matter by the earth leaves it something different from earth, as a wet-nurse is not the same as the child she feeds. But the prime matter, if it is to be used for human purposes, must be "fixed" in a stable substance capable of being handled.)

"7. Separate the earth from the fire, the subtle from the gross, acting prudently and with judgment." (Since the volatile principle is fire—or, sometimes, air—stability is produced by its removal. Or, alternatively but less probably, the earth is impurity ("the gross") and a purified fire ("the subtle") what is wanted.

"8. Ascend with the greatest sagacity from the earth to heaven, and then again descend to the earth, and unite together the powers of things superior and things inferior. Thus you will obtain the glory of the whole world, and all obscurity will fly far away from you." (Separate the volatile part of the substance by vaporization but continue heating until the vapor reunites with the parent body, whereupon you will have obtained the Stone, which will bring you glory.)

"9. This thing is the fortitude of all fortitude, because it overcomes all subtle things, and penetrates every solid thing." (The "strong" product of the distillation and reunion will dominate less solid substances but because of its own subtlety it will "penetrate," and hence dominate, other solid things less pure and quasi-spiritual than itself.)

"10. Thus were all things created." (The alchemical operation is a paradigm of the creative process. We may note also the sexual overtones of what has preceded:

Michaelis Majerus (i.e., Meier) *Secretioris naturae secretorum scrutinium chymicum* (Frankfort: Georgius Heinricus Oerlingius, 1687), p. 106.

106   E M B L E M A   XXXVI.   *De ſecretis Naturæ.*

Lapis projectus eſt in terras, & in montibus exaltatus, & in aëre habitat, & in flumine paſcitur, id eſt, Mercurius.

E P I G R A M M A   XXXVI.

Vile recrementum fertur LAPIS atque jacere
Fortè viis, ſibi ut hinc dives inopſque parent.
Montibus in ſummis alii ſtatuére, per auras
Aëris, at paſci per fluvios alii.
Omnia vera ſuo ſunt ſenſu, poſtulo ſed te
Munera montanis quæreret tanta locis.

The *prima materia* of alchemy. The lines above the emblem read, "The stone is cast upon the earth, and is raised high in the mountains, and lives in the air, and is nourished in the streams—that is to say, mercury." The sense of the epigram is this: "The Stone is said to be worthless rubbish and to lie at random in the streets, so that rich and poor pick it up for themselves. Others place it in the high mountains, or in the air among the breezes; and still others say it is fed by the streams. All these things are true in their own way; but I urge you to seek for its great values in mountainous places." The "mercury" here is obviously the *prima materia* or *hyle* with which the alchemist begins his operations; it is everywhere accessible, not precious or rare. It is best sought in the mountains, perhaps, because it is purest there or because it should be acquired out of the public eye.

the sun as male, the moon as female, the "union" of "the powers of things superior and things inferior," the suggestion that the earth is matrix or womb, the air as the transporter of seed.)

"11. Thence proceed wonderful adaptations which are produced in this way." (From the product, the Stone or Elixir, or both, transmutations or cures will flow.)

"12. Therefore am I called Hermes Trismegistus, possessing the three parts of the philosophy of the whole world." (The "three parts" are obscure; one may be natural science, another divinity, but I am unable to identify the third. The usual explanation of Trismegistus, or "Thrice-Great," is that Hermes was the greatest philosopher, the greatest priest, and the greatest king. In any event, this paragraph assures us that the *Emerald Tablet* has unchallengeable authority.)

"13. That which I had to say concerning the operation of the Sun is completed." ("Sun" here means God, fire, gold, and perhaps other things as well.) [72]

Once the veil is penetrated the operations appear relatively simple, and simplicity was emphasized by one of the major traditions. According to this school, the adept who was in possession of the true secret began with a single substance—not with mercury or sulphur—which is never clearly identified, although the authors again and again pretend to offer adequate hints. Sometimes it seems to be ordinary earth, sometimes again water, and once, at least, sand; but in any case it was something everywhere available, which housewives cast into the streets and with which children played. Ripley's *Compound of Alchymie* speaks in this vein:

> Yet Fowles and Fyshes to us doth yt bryng,
> Every-ech Man yt hath, and ys in every place,
> In thee, in me, in every tyme and space.[73]

For members of this school the chemical manipulations were also simple. The substance was put into a vessel, which was then tightly stopped and warmed over a gentle fire until a spirit was distilled and the solid residue turned black. Further heating caused the vapor to reunite with the solid, which then turned a dazzling white; and more cooking transformed the color to "red," which marked the Stone or Elixir. As has been indicated, however, for most alchemists the processes were far more complex.

Anonymi.

Spiritus, Anima, Corpus.

Schal yow tel wyth hert mode,
Of thre Kynggys that ben fo goude,

And how thaye cam to God almyght,
The wich was ther a fweet fyght.

I figure now howr beffet *Stone*,
Fro Heven wafe fende downe to *Solomon* :

By an Angele bothe goude and ftylle,
The wych wafe than Chriftis wylle.

Elias Ashmole, *Theatrum chemicum Britannicum* (London: Nath. Brooke, 1652), p. 350.

Spirit, soul and body in alchemical operations. The cloud at the top is the usual symbol for God. From it emerges the spirit, below which are the sun and moon, here representing the soul and body. The spirit breathes into an oddly shaped bag with seven vents which open upon two human figures, apparently intended as male and female. The toad and dragons are figures for stages in the alchemical operations. On the following page the anonymous author interprets the gold, frankincense, and myrrh brought to the infant Christ by the Wise Men in terms which relate them to "howr besset *Stone*" (our best stone). The gold was the sun and "owre Bodi"; the frankincense was sulphur and "owre Soule of lyfe"; the myrrh was mercury and "oure Luneyre" or moon. The three together are "but one in mode" as the Trinity is one.

34   **EMBLEMA XII.** *De secretis Naturæ.*

Lapis, quem Saturnus, pro Jove filio devoratum, evomuit, pro monumento in Helicone mortalibus est positus.

EPIGRAMMA XII.

Nosse cupis causam, tot cur Helicona *Poëtæ*
  Dicant, quodque ejus cuique petendus apex?
Est Lapis *in summo*, Monumentum, *vertice positus,*
  Pro Jove deglutiit quem vomuitque pater.
Si ceu verba sonant rem captas, mens tibi læva est,
  Namque est Saturni Chemicus *ille* Lapis.

Michaelis Majerus (i.e., Meier), *Secretioris naturae secretorum scrutinium chymicum* (Frankfurt: Georgius Heinricus Oerlingius, 1687), p. 34.

An emblem which identifies a mythological stone with the philosopher's stone: one detail of the assiduous effort of mythographers to find hidden wisdom in ancient myths. At the top we are told that "The stone which Saturn vomited forth after devouring it instead of his son Jupiter has been placed on Helicon (a mountain in Bœotia) as a monument for human beings." The epigram reads as follows: "Do you wish to know why the poets so often say 'Helicon,' and why its summit is to be sought out by everybody? There is a Stone at the top, a monument, placed at the summit, which the Father swallowed instead of Jupiter and then spewed out. If you understand the object as the words are pronounced, your mind is stupid, for it is the alchemical stone of Saturn."

I conclude this part of the survey with observations about Paracelsus, who occupies an ambiguous position between the "chemists" and the mystics. If, on one hand, he marks, and himself perhaps made, the transition to iatrochemistry or medical chemistry—up to his time remedies had been chiefly herbal or animal—on the other hand he continues, with an argumentative insistence peculiar to him, mystical notions rooted in attitudes the very opposite of scientific.

Adam, Paracelsus thought, first invented the arts. These were engraved by his successors, in hieroglyphics, on two stone tablets, one of which was later discovered by Noah on Mt. Ararat. The knowledge passed down in this way was subsequently divided into several parts, among them astronomy, magic, the cabala, and alchemy. Abraham, an astrologer and arithmetician, carried the esoteric wisdom from Canaan into Egypt, "whereupon the Egyptians rose to so great a height and dignity that this wisdom was derived from them by other nations." The striping of the sheep by Jacob was accomplished by magic; Moses, too, was instructed (as the Bible says) in the Egyptian arts; Daniel's knowledge of them is shown by his cabalistic interpretation of "Mene, mene, Tecelphares (for "Tekel Upharsin" of the Authorized Version)." The Persian kings were called wise men, as were also the mages who visited the infant Christ. Hermes was called Trismegistus "because he was a king, a priest, a prophet, a magician, and a sophist of natural things. Such another was Zoroaster." Like the Egyptians, Homer veiled the mysteries in "enigmatical figures and abstruse histories and terms"; and Pythagoras borrowed from Moses. Hippocrates, Thales of Miletus, Anaxagoras, Democritus, and others also dabbled in the arts but did not master them because of their feeling of superiority to "barbarians." Their philosophy descended to the Latins, through whom the philosophy spread over Europe. "Many academies were founded for the propagation of their dogmas and rules, so that the young might be instructed; and this system flourishes with the Germans, and other nations, right down to the present day." [74] Although nothing of all this is new, it is important to realize that despite his very real service in opening up new vistas for medicine Paracelsus was by no means in all ways a crusading modernist.

With regard to alchemy, his most famous doctrine had to do with the three "principles" of sulphur, mercury, and salt, which he tried—up to a point—to substitute for the four traditional elements. Sulphur he thought was the source of combustibility, substance, and structure; salt was responsible for solidity and color;

112   EMBLEMA XXXVIII. *De secretis Naturæ.*

Rebis, ut Hermaphroditus, nascitur ex duobus montibus, Mercurii & Veneris.

EPIGRAMMA XXXVIII.

R Em geminam *REBIS* veteres dixêre, quod uno
   Corpore sit mas hæc fœminaque, Androgyna.
Natus enim binis in montibus *HERMAPHRODITUS*
   Dicitur, Hermeti quem tulit alma Venus.
Ancipitem sexum ne spernas, nam tibi *Regem*
   Mas idem, mulierque una eademque dabit.

Michaelis Majerus (i.e., Meier), *Secretioris naturae secretorum scrutinium chymicum* (Frankfurt: Georgius Heinricus Oerlingius, 1687), p. 112.

The alchemical Rebis as androgynous. The Rebis—a hermaphroditic compound of Sol and Luna, or of gold and silver—"is born from the two mountains of Mercury and Venus." (A sexual implication is probably intended in *mons Veneris*.) The epigram says, "The ancients said that *rebis* was a double thing because it is androgynous—male and female in a single body. For it is born in two mountains and is called 'Hermaphrodite,' which bountiful Venus brought to Hermes. Do not scorn its double sex, for the male and the female will give you the King in one and the same thing." The hermaphrodite is of course a symbol of union—what we should call "composition."

EMBLEMA IX. *De secretis Naturæ.* 25

Arborem cum fene conclude in rorida domo, & comedens de fructu ejus fiet juvenis.

EPIGRAMMA IX.

A Rbor inest hortis Sophiæ dans aurea mala,
    Hæc tibi cum nostro sint capienda sene;
Inq; domo vitrea claudantur, roréque plená,
    Et sine per multos hæc duo juncta dies:
Tum fructu (mirum!) satiabitur arboris ille,
    Vt fiat juvenis qui fuit ante senex.

D

Michaelis Majerus (i.e., Meier), *Secretioris naturae secretorum scrutinium chymicum* (Frankfurt: Georgius Heinricus Oerlingius, 1687, p. 25.

The old man and the golden apples: illustration of a typical alchemical allegory. The Latin at the top says, "Shut up the tree with the old man in a dewy house, and by eating its fruit he will be made young." The epigram beneath says, "In the gardens of Wisdom there is a tree which yields golden apples. These you are to take, together with our old man. The two are to be shut up in a glass house full of moisture for many days; then, a wonder! he will be sated with the fruit of the tree and, although formerly an old man, will become a youth." The glass house is of course a vessel; the identity of "Arbor" and "Senex" is uncertain.

mercury was the vaporous quality. Thus when a twig is burned the flame comes from sulphur, the smoke from mercury, and the ashes from salt. The admirable simplicity of the system was compromised, however, by his recognition that "There are as many sulphurs, salts and mercuries as there are objects," so that the terms became mere shorthand for the principles he thought them to embody. Also, the traditional elements were rather demoted than abolished—or perhaps dignified beyond usefulness. In one formulation the four material elements form the body, the soul is the quintessence, and the cosmic elements—earth, water, air, and fire—are "matrices" or, perhaps, four concentric spheres, of which the earth is presumably the innermost and fire the outermost. All specific objects—presumably man, animals, plants, and minerals, or perhaps only their parts—are, however, composed of sulphur, mercury, and salt. All this was confusing to many of his contemporaries and perhaps even to his disciples as well as to modern historians.[75]

From this beginning, Paracelsus proceeded to explain creation, in which the four traditional elements reappeared. "The principle . . . of all generation was Separation." The firmament or sphere of the fixed stars separated everything inside it from fire; "spirits and dreams were separated from the air"; "fish, salt, marine plants and the like were separated from the water; and wood, stone, animals, and land plants were separated from the earth."[76] If the separation proceeds far enough, it leads ultimately to *prima materia,* which is itself none of the elements.

In the account of creation Allen G. Debus, to whose understanding of Paracelus I defer, perceives Jewish influences; but borrowings came from many sources. The three principles derived from Islam, and the medicinal implications of the cosmology had a Hermetic and Neo-Platonic origin. For example, the teaching that the various human organs were governed by separate "rulers" is obviously indebted to the Hermetic *daimones* which had similar responsibilities.[77] Pythagorean or cabalistic numerology also plays a role, as it had done in the theories of Raymond Lull and Geber; and the "empiricism" sometimes hailed as a precious step toward modern scientific methods actually appears to have included a wholly uncritical acceptance of old wives' tales, which Paracelsus believed to have been tested by experience. Yet his alchemy aimed not at the production of gold but at medicine. Its ultimate effect was the opening up of a whole new range of pharmaceutical possibility, which al-

EMBLEMA XXV. *De secretis Naturæ.*   73

Draco non moritur, nisi cum fratre & forore sua interficiatur, qui sunt Sol & Luna.

EPIGRAMMA XXV.

EXiguæ est non artis opus, stravisse Draconem
 Funere, ne serpat mox redivivus humo.
Frater & ipsa soror juncti simul illius ora
 Fuste premunt, nec res fert aliena necem.
Phœbus ei frater, soror est at Cynthia, Python
Illâ, ast Orion hac cecidêre manu.

K

Michaelis Majerus (i.e., Meier), *Secretioris naturae secretorum scrutinium chymicum* (Frankfurt. Georgius Heinricus Oerlingius, 1687), p. 73.

Killing of the alchemical dragon. At the top we read, "The dragon (mercury) is not killed except with (*for* "by") his brother and sister, who are the sun and the moon (gold and silver)." The epigram may be translated as follows: "It is a work of no mean art to have prostrated the dragon in death in such a way that he may not soon be revived to creep on the earth. His brother and sister, working together, must press down his face with cudgels, nor can any other thing cause his death. His brother is Phoebus, but his sister Cynthia; Python fell by his hand, but Orion by hers."

though slow to catch on in England by the mid-seventeenth century had generated a war between Paracelsians and traditionally Galenic and Hippocratic physicians. On the continent the effects were felt from about 1550.[78] On the whole, although Paracelsus requires mention in any detailed study of alchemy, he stands well outside both the main streams. To the second, or more dominantly mystical, of these we now turn.

IV. The mystical doctrine

More even than the chemical tradition, the mystical doctrine assumed wisdom in remote antiquity and the former existence of a rich esoteric literature comprehensible only to initiates. *"Past Ages,"* wrote Ashmole, *"have like Rivers conveied down to us, (upon the floate,) the more light, and Sophisticall pieces of Learning; but what were Profound and Misterious, the weight and solidity thereof, sunke to the Bottome; Whence every one who attempts to dive, cannot easily fetch them up."* [79] Writing about 1650, he regretted the loss of precious documents by the destruction of monastic libraries: *"Indeed (such was Learnings misfortune, at that great Devastation of our English Libraries, that) where a Red letter or a Mathematicall Diagram appeared, they were sufficient to intitle the Book to be Popish or Diabolicall."* [80] The magic implied by the diagrams Ashmole thought was not illicit, like conjuring,

Gio[vanni] Battista Nazari, *Della Tramutatione metallica sogni tre* (Brescia: Pietro Maria Marchetti, 1599), p. 47.

The author is dreaming, with eyes open, about alchemy—though it would be risky to assume that the illustrator intended a likeness. The visions take the usual form of highly allegorical objects, figures, situations, and events with hidden meanings that are usually either guessed by the dreamer or explained by a personage in the dream. The open eyes may be meant to suggest the activity of reason: the dreamer responds intelligently to what he sees. The picture is repeated from point to point throughout the book.

Gio[vanni] Battista Nazari, *Della Tramuta-*
tione metallica sogni tre (Brescia: Pietro
Maria Marchetti, 1599), p. 16.

In his first dream—about false transmutation—the author sees an "aureate" figure of
an ass seated on a round stone. This, he
thinks, must be "a work of Apuleius, or
of some modern author of ours, which has
to do with his *Golden Ass.*" The ass leans
its shoulders against "a tall cornucopia full
of fruit and of useless flowers" and is playing a pipe (*sonando con certi ciffoletti**).
Around all this are "playful monkeys" who
are performing a ridiculous dance. The ass,
he decides, must signify, as among the
Egyptians, "a babbler, a liar, a sophist";
the cornucopia and its contents symbolize
a "fruitless art or invention." In short, the
device is a warning to aspiring alchemists
that they may follow wrong paths and
achieve no success.

*For the modern *zufolo.* I owe this identi
fication to my colleague Enrico De Negri.

necromancy, and witchcraft, but *"a searching into those hidden vertues which* God
has been pleas'd to bestow upon created things." [81] We have met this faith in other
chapters. One source was the difficulty of understanding the physical universe in any
other way at a time when hard scientific data were few. Before the invention of the
microscope, especially, the infrastructure of matter was invisible, so that conclusions
about it had to be inferred from concepts which had been derived from a sorting
out of mental processes and, by modern standards, were poor in physical referenda.
But there were other sanctions too, of which one of the strongest had to do with
evidence from history as that was understood.

A part of this history was Biblical. In God alone is truth, Henry Madathanas
tells us in *The Golden Age Restored,*

> and through Him alone Adam and the other patriarchs, Abraham, Isaac, and Jacob,
> were enabled to secure constant health, and a long life, and to provide for themselves
> great wealth. Through this Spirit the Seven Sages invented the Arts, and gained
> riches. With His aid Noah built the Ark, Solomon the Temple, and Moses the
> Tabernacle; through Him vessels of pure gold were borne into the Temple; through
> Him Solomon gained his excellent knowledge, and performed mighty deeds.[82]

The Glory of the World also cites the patriarchs but emphasizes their extraordinary longevity.

> By means of this most noble Medicine many men, from the death of Adam to the fourth monarchy, procured for themselves perfect health and great length of days. Hence those who had a good knowledge of the Medicine, attained to three hundred years, others to four hundred, some to five hundred, like Adam; others again to nine hundred, like Methusalem and Noah.[83]

The great age of the patriarchs was clear testimony to the existence of the Elixir. Later alchemists occasionally were rumored to have lived for five hundred, or even for seven hundred, years, and a practitioner called Artephius "claimed to have reached the age of 1025. [Roger] Bacon accepted this statement uncritically." [84] The Biblical parallels helped to make such claims credible. But "history" included much more than this. The pedigree of the arts given by Paracelsus resembles others mentioned in earlier chapters; and into many of these came the names not merely of Jews and Greeks but also of Persians, Chaldaeans, and Egyptians who not only were thought to have lived but were scarcely heard of outside the occult tradition. Zoroaster and Hermes were examples. A denial of the arts would have been a repudiation of historical evidence.

A second warrant was found in Scriptural references to stones. "Did ye never read in the Scriptures?" asked Christ. "The Stone which the builders rejected, the same is become the head of the corner." [85] Again, *Acts* 4[:11], "This is the stone which was set at nought of you builders, which is become the head of the corner," and *Romans* 9[:33], "it is written, Behold, I lay in Sion a stumblingstone and rock of offence: and whosoever believeth on him shall not be ashamed." [86] Or, once more: "Therefore thus saith the Lord God: 'Behold, I lay in Zion for a foundation a Stone, a tried Stone, a precious corner Stone, a sure foundation." [87] Every Biblical reference to a stone risked interpretation as the Philosopher's Stone. The notion caused no difficulty because it was supposed that along with the exoteric doctrine there existed also a concealed one which had been handed down orally to protect it from the foolish and wicked.

Still more impressive were parallels with central Christian truths. These are especially emphasized in *The Sophic Hydrolith*.

> Again, as our chemical compound . . . is subjected to the action of fire, and is decomposed, dissolved, and well digested, and as this process, before its consummation, exhibits various chromatic changes, so this Divine Man, and Human God, Jesus Christ, had, by the will of His heavenly Father, to pass through the furnace of affliction, that is, through many troubles, insults, and sufferings, in the course of which His outward aspect was grievously changed. . .
> And as the Sages say that the above mentioned process of chemical digestion is

generally completed within forty days, so the same number seems to have a most peculiar significance in Scripture, more particularly in connection with the life of our Lord. The Israelites remained forty years in the wilderness; Moses was forty days and nights on Mount Sinai; Elijah's flight from Ahab occupied the same length of time. Christ fasted forty days and forty nights in the wilderness; He spent forty months in preaching upon earth; He lay forty hours in the grave—appeared to His Disciples forty days after His resurrection. Within forty years from Christ's Ascension Jerusalem was destroyed by the Romans, and made level with the ground.[88]

To the modern reader some forcing will be evident here. No Scriptural warrant exists for the 40 months of preaching or the 40 hours in the grave, and the 38 years between Christ's death and the destruction of Jerusalem (if, as is probable, the crucifixion was thought to have occurred in A.D. 33) is made useable by the phrase "*Within* forty years." Neither is it fair to say that according to the sages the alchemical operation is "generally completed within forty days." Although that period is sometimes mentioned, estimates varied widely. Thomas Charnock needed 368 days. 182 to produce the Raven, 150 to cause the black mass to turn white, and 36 to modify this to yellow.[89] Miles (or William) Bloomfield makes much of the figure 40 but required forty days to make the Raven, "about" forty more to produce whiteness, and an unspecified period to achieve yellowness, which again was "fixed" for forty days.[90] Ripley's *The Mistery of Alchemists* asserts that the making of the Stone takes a year.[91] And there are many other estimates. Nevertheless the readers of *The Sophic Hydrolith* were probably not much bothered by such scruples. No doubt they had heard mention of the forty days and were gratified to have the figure brought within the ambit of other 40s associated with sacred history.

Many further parallels with Christian doctrines were adduced. *The Glory of the World* offered the alchemist comfort from "a reassuring type of the bitter passion and death of our Lord and Saviour Jesus Christ, His descent into hell, His glorious and most holy Resurrection on the third day, and His victory and triumph over sin, death, Devil, and hell."[92] The suffering of Christ is likened to the agitations of the chemicals, the solidification into the ugly Raven to the descent into Hell; the transformation to brilliant whiteness is equivalent to the Resurrection, and the action of the Stone or the Elixir is like the redemptive mission. The equating of transmutation to redemption appears also in *The Sophic Hydrolith*:

> as the Philosopher's Stone, which is the Chemical King, has virtue by means of its tincture and its developed perfection to change other imperfect and base metals into pure gold, so our heavenly King and fundamental Corner Stone, Jesus Christ, can alone purify us sinners and imperfect men with His Blessed ruby-coloured Tincture, that is to say, His Blood.[93]

Christ and the Stone are both kings, and the "redness" which alternated with yellow-ness as the color of the gold and the Stone was in the mineral realm what Christ's blood was in the spiritual. Once more, since the volatile part of a physical substance was called its "spirit," distillation might be compared to baptism: "If we men would be purified and cleansed of our original sin and the filth of Adam . . . we can obtain perfection and eternal happiness only through the regeneration of water and the Spirit, as the royal chemical substance is regenerated by water and its spirit." [94]

The Bible might also infiltrate the narrative allegories which at once served as mnemonic aids to the alchemist and lent to his processes some of the excitement of drama—often erotic. In *The Golden Age Restored,* an alleged dream is penetrated by citations from *The Song of Songs.* The writer imagines himself to be present at a procession of Solomon's sixty queens, eight hundred concubines, and countless vir-gins. Then he sees a bare-breasted woman: "Her thighs were like two half-moons, made by the Master; her navel was like a round goblet; her belly like a heap of wheat, set about with roses; her breasts like two young roes that are twins." The "Master" is, among other things, the alchemical adept, and the half-moons suggest the usual alchemical symbol for the Moon and for silver, the metal associated with it. This virgin, we are told, is "the pure and chaste virgin of whom Adam was formed and created," and her "bloody sweat and snowy tears" will strengthen the dreamer's mind and make his life peaceful. Evidently virginity suggests the *prima materia,* and the sweat and tears, which are restorative in the same way as Christ's, represent the vapor distilled from the chemical substances. Later the dreamer is told to choose a naked virgin to be his love; he does so, saying, "Her garments are old, defiled, and foul, but I will purge them, and love her with all my heart." The garments are al-most certainly the Raven, the black and unsightly mass left in the bottom of the vessel—itself suggested by the "round goblet" of the navel, mentioned earlier—after the "spirit" has been driven off. The author recurs to *The Song of Songs* after the Stone has been obtained: "My Beloved is white and ruddy, the chiefest among ten thousand. His head is as the most fine gold, his locks are bushy, and black as a raven." [95] The mythic consciousness absorbs easily such awkwardnesses as a vestige in the final product of the Raven which was to have disappeared.

Many other sanctions might be offered. From an early period, as has been ob-served in earlier chapters, numbers were thought to have mystical significations, as for Pythagoras and Plato and in the cabala. Hence readers fond of transcendent notions may have been impressed by the following passage from *The Golden Tripod.*

> I have already indicated that all things are constituted of three essences—namely, mercury, sulphur, and salt—and herein I have taught what is true. But know that the Stone is composed out of one, two, three, four, and five. Out of five—that is, the quintessence of its own substance. Out of four, by which we must understand

the four elements. Out of three, and these are the three principles of all things [the Paracelsian mercury, sulphur, and salt]. Out of two, for the mercurial substance is twofold [pure and impure, or body and spirit]. Out of one, and this is the first essence of everything which emanated from the primal fiat of creation [the *prima materia* or *hyle*].[96]

Although *The Golden Tripod* is evidently a late document—I have been unable to date it—Lull's writings were already heavily numerological.

We may look briefly at a few more allegories, paying no further attention to Scriptural proofs but focusing our attention on the role played by analogies. Some of the fictions are so transparent that the allegorical transformation must be searched for to be seen. For example, *Bloomefields Blossoms; or, The Campe of Philosophy* opens with a dream in which Time introduces the author to the Camp of Philosophy, where he meets other alchemists, true and false, among them Hermes, Aristotle, "Morien," "Senior in Turba" (a reference to a work called *Turba philosophorum*), Democritus, Albert (Albertus Magnus), Roger Bacon, "Ramund" or Raymond Lull, "The *Monke* and the *Chanon of Bridlington*" (possibly Valentinus, and George Ripley), and also Philosophy herself, who "commits" the author to "Raymund Lullie" for instruction.[97] This is to say that Bloomfield has spent considerable time studying alchemical literature and has found some authors more trustworthy than others but follows especially the doctrines of Lull. In *The Breviary of Naturall Philosophy* the meaning is less direct. Thomas Charnock appears to be saying "Pray and be charitable if you wish to succeed," but he may also intend to hint something about materials. He speaks of two poor men who ask for alms because they are going to sea for three months or more in a glass ship to abide "all tempest of the Aire," to ride dangerous roads, to have no food but water descending from a cloud, to be burned black by the moon, and finally, in another climate, to receive a spiritual body "which if it should be sould,/ Truly I say it is worth his weight in Gold." If the alchemist gives the men "one penny in their Journey to drinke," he will speed better.[98] The disguise is readily seen through. The two men are probably mercury and sulphur, the glass ship is the vessel in which they are to be heated, the tempest is agitated vapors, the dangerous roads are the chemical bubblings and alterations, the water from the cloud is condensed steam, the blackness is that of the Raven, the other climate is the quasi-spiritual one which is the ambience of the Stone or the Elixir, the reference to gold suggests transmutation, and the penny may be copper which will assist the operation if added to the mixture of mercury and sulphur.

Other allegories are more elaborate, like one quoted by Taylor from *The Visions of Zosimus,* who, if he existed, must have lived in the fourth century A.D. In a dream, again, Zosimus sees a bowl-shaped altar served by a priest in white, and sees also, as he mounts a fourth step, coming from the East, one who had in his hand a sword. And I saw another behind him, bearing a round white shining object beautiful to behold, of which the name was the meridian of the Sun [apparently cinnabar], and as I drew near to the place of punishments, he that bore the sword told me, 'Cut off his head and sacrifice his meat and his muscles by parts, to the end that his flesh may first be boiled according to method and that he may then undergo the punishment.' And so, awaking again, I said, 'Well do I understand that these things concern the liquids of the art of the metals.' [99]

The bowl-shaped altar is of course again a retort or other vessel, and the fourth step symbolizes the fourth stage of the alchemical process. The man bearing a sword comes from the East, possibly because Zosimus thought of alchemy as having had an Oriental origin, and the round white object, whether or not cinnabar, presumably also was a material which required importation from the East. At any rate, the name "meridian of the Sun" implies the Orient: as we saw in the chapter on astrology, Pico accepted a common belief that the sun had greater heat in the East than in the West and produced gems and aromatic substances only there.[100] The bowl-shaped altar is called "the place of punishment" because, as has been noted, the alchemical materials were supposed to suffer in the operations. What is more explicit in this extract than in others cited earlier is the drawing of a parallel between the mincing of an inert solid and the remorseless dismemberment of a human being or animal, as in savage warfare or revenge.

The metaphor of combat is, indeed, not uncommon. The alchemist slays or tortures his materials, or they fight with each other until one or both is killed. In *The Golden Tripod* we read the following:

> The twofold fiery male must be fed with a snowy swan, and then they must mutually slay each other and restore each other to life; and the air of the imprisoned fiery male will occupy three of the four quarters of the world, and make up three parts of the imprisoned fiery male, that the death-song of the swans may be distinctly heard; then the swan roasted will become food for the King, and the fiery King will be seized with great love towards the Queen, and will take his fill of delight in embracing her, until they both vanish and coalesce into one body.[101]

This is to say that a compounded substance must be decomposed by something else, and the two substances will then separate into purer forms; the volatile part, or vapor, will occupy most of the vial. Afterwards the "swan," the whitish material part, will be absorbed by the condensing vapor, or will absorb it—a reaction metaphorized as eating and sexual union.

Again, from the same document, we learn that gold is subdivided into its parts and made "what it was before it became gold," the "seed, the beginning, the middle, and the end—that from which *our gold* is derived." At a later point Mercury is imprisoned "under the ward of Vulcan"—is enclosed in a vessel and heated—until he is liberated by a woman. Then Saturn (lead) declares that Mercury must indeed be imprisoned until he dies and is decomposed. This sentence is confirmed by Jupiter (tin, or perhaps magnesium; or, possibly, God), and Mars gives his sword (iron) to Vulcan (the fire), so that Mercury may be slain and burned to ashes. While this is being done, the Moon (silver) begs that her husband, the Sun (gold) be liberated from the prison in which, by Mercury's craft, he has been confined; but she is not heard, for more operations must be performed.[102]

In such ways as these the esoteric doctrines are at once proclaimed and concealed. From a literary point of view, the allegories are far more attractive than less figurative texts. A few might even be staged effectively as part of a Masonic or Rosicrucian initiation. We are much less affected by the attraction Ashmole found in the "poetry" of treatises written in metrical form. The thirty-odd documents he anthologized were all metrical because he thought poetry was *"the* Ancientest, *and* Prose *but of* Latter use,"* and because the ancients did not *"wrap up their* Chiefest Mysteries, *any where else, then in the* Parabolical *&* Allusive *part of* Poetry, *as the most* Sacred, *and* Venerable *in their* Esteeme, *and the securest from* Prophane *and* Vulgar Wits"*; but he also esteemed *"the Excellent* Melody *thereof,"*[103] some taste of which has been offered in extracts printed above.

V. Mental habits: the importance of analogy

The role of analogy in the doctrines is so considerable that it may well have been germinal. A readiness to say that one thing is, or is like, another appears frequently in the claim that apparently different philosophical doctrines are identical. There is nothing unusual in Robert Fludd's demonstration that "when Aristotle wrote of the *prima materia,* Plato of the *hyle,* Hermes of the *umbra horrenda,* Pythagoras of the 'Symbolicall unity,' and Hippocrates of the deformed chaos, they were all writing in reality of the darkness or the dark abyss of Moses."[104] Aristotle's first matter is no doubt close to Plato's, and *Genesis* seems to have influenced the Hermetic *Poemander,* but differences are swept away by a desire to find the "sages" in accord.

The same predisposition may underlie a passage in Ashmole. Some descriptions of the Stone suggest that it is hard and metallic, others that it is wax-like, still others that it is liquid. Ashmole credits all the traditions: besides the Philosopher's Stone there was also a vegetable stone, a magical stone, and even an angelical stone, and these are worth glancing at. The vegetable stone was very likely responsible for *"the* Wallnut-Tree *which anciently grew in* Glastenbury Church-yard, *and never put forth* Leaves *before S.* Barnabies Day, *yet then was fully loaded with them,"* as also for a hawthorn at the same place and an oak in the New Forest of Hampshire, *"that bore greene* Leaves *at the same* Season." The magical or prospective stone will *discover any* Person *in what part of the* World *soever, although never so secretly concealed or hid . . . In a Word, it fairly presents to your view even the whole* World *. . . Nay more, It enables Man to* understand *the Language of the* Creatures, *as the* Chirping *of* Birds, Lowing *of* Beasts, *&c. To* Convey *a* Spirit *into an* Image, *which by observing the* Influence *of* Heavenly Bodies, *shall become a true* Oracle

and this not necromantically but naturally. The angelical stone, which can be tasted but not seen, felt, or weighed, causes the apparition of angels and permits conversation with them through dreams and revelations. Also, it protects against devils and preserves the body from corruption, so that Hermes, who with Moses and Solomon, but with them only, attained it, *"gave over the use of all other* Stones, *and therein only delighted."* [105] What cannot be reconciled on the manifest level must be adjusted somehow. The degree to which this tendency is active varies according to author, and by the Renaissance some are ready to pick and choose among incompatibles. Nevertheless it deserves note that the readiness to say "X is the same as Y," or if an equation cannot be made "X exists alongside Y and is the same truth in another realm or dimension," characterizes much Renaissance thought and was only gradually to be replaced by its opposite, the modern fondness for distinctions.

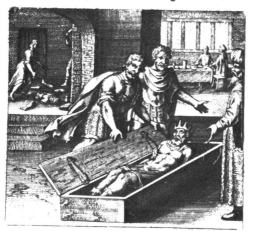

ao   **E M B L E M A XLIV.** *De secretis Naturæ.*
Dolo Typhon Oſyridem trucidat , artusque illius hinc inde diſſipat,ſed hos collegit Iſis inclyta.

E P I G R A M M A XLIV.
Syria Adonidem habet, Dionyſum Græcia, Oſirim
  Ægyptus , qui ſunt nil niſi SOL Sophiæ :
ISIS adeſt ſoror,& conjux ac mater Oſiris,
  Cujus membra Typhon diſſecat,illa ligat.
Defluit at pudibunda mari pars, ſparſa per undas,
  Sulphur enim,SULPHUR quod generavit,abeſt.
                                        Oſyridis

Michaelis Majerus (i.e., Meier), *Secretioris naturae secretorum scrutinium chymicum* (Frankfurt: Georgius Heinricus Oerlingius, 1687), p. 130.

An alchemical myth: Osiris, or the sun, as a source of sulphur. In the superscript: "Typhon (another name for Typhoeus, a giant) slew Osiris by guile and scattered his joints here and there, but the renowned Isis collected them." In the epigram: "Syria has Adonis, Greece has Dionysus, Egypt has Osiris; but these are merely the Sun of wisdom. Isis is his sister, Osiris his wife and mother; Typhon cuts his limbs into pieces, but she binds them together. The shameful part flows away to the sea and is scattered among the waves, for sulphur, the SULPHUR which it has generated, is absent." The last clause may mean "which generated him"; but in any case the meaning is obscure. The King is shown here reassembled: another emblem of the compounding of substances when the operations have reached an advanced stage.

HERMES BIRD.

Roblemis of olde likenes and fuguris,
Wych proved byn fruĉtuos of sentens;
And have auĉtorite grounded in Scripture,
By resemblaunce of notabil apperence;
Wych moralites concludyng on prudence:
Lyke as the Bibel reherseth be wryting,
How Trees sum tyme chese hemselfe a Kyng.

2. First in theyre choise they namyd the Olyve
To regne among hem, *Iudicium* doth expres;
But he hymselfe can excuse hym blyve,
He myght not forsake hys fatnes:
Nor the Fig-tree hys amorus swetnes:
Nor the Vyne hys holsum fresche terrage:
Wych gyveth comfort to all manner of age.
Ff 3

Elias Ashmole, *Theatrum chemicum Britannicum* (London: Nath. Brooke, 1652), p. 213.

Hermes Bird: what is required for success in alchemy. The dragon—often represented as two entwined dragons with a sun (gold) at one mouth and a moon (silver) at the other—is shown here as a single dragon with two necks and heads. Above it the Holy Spirit descends from the Father (hidden within the cloud); on either side are alchemists, who by their prayerful attitude show that piety is required for success in the work. Along the outer edges is indicated the necessity of Cunning or Knowledge, Experience, Practice, Prudence, and Patience (on the left); Grace, Nature, Reason, the Speculative [Faculty], and Holy Living (on the right). The anonymous "Hermes Bird," which follows, is unusual in implying that the search for the Stone is best not undertaken: "Covet not thyng that may not be." But Ashmole (p. 467) thought the rebuff applied only to "the Covetous and Ignorant Artist."

Outside the more strictly chemical texts, although it sometimes appears in them too, the passion for analogies dominated alchemical literature. Taylor saw this clearly.

> These are the primitive elements of the idea of generation: a seed, a soil, the breath of life from heaven and the gentle fostering warmth. These are the conditions that the alchemist set himself to imitate. He wants to make gold come to be, so he will grow it. He corrupts the other metals to form the soil, he can provide the gentle warmth in the dung-bed or water bath, but he requires the seed and the breath.[106]

What happened in the alembic was a model or type of natural processes outside the laboratory. Some of the more enlightened adepts thought of themselves as merely hastening what would have happened in due course anyhow. As nature strives to perfect itself in every possible way, so it is constantly engaged in purifying the base metals into gold. Thus we sometimes hear of mines being shut down in order to give more gold time to ripen. By cleansing the primary substance of its coarser parts, driving out the four elements, enclosing it in a stoppered vessel to protect it against contamination and retain heat, as a foetus is enclosed in the womb, and providing a

fostering warmth like that known to favor vegetable and animal growth, the alchemist could accomplish in a year or less what nature could do only in an age.

But the analogies go farther. To quote Taylor again: the combination of two
bodies the alchemist

> saw as *marriage,* the loss of their characteristic activity as *death,* the production of
> something new, as a *birth,* the rising up of vapors, as a *spirit leaving the corpse,* the
> formation of a volatile solid, as the making of a *spiritual body. . . .*
>
> We may, I think, regard the alchemy of this period as the practical pursuit and
> mental cultivation of the analogy between chemical changes and the life of man.[107]

These equivalences are implied by the esoteric drawings with which many alchemical
treatises are illustrated—as in a *Hermetical Museum* of 1678, which because of the
editor's bent concentrates on mystical documents. The absorption of the vapor by
the solid is pictured as a hermaphroditic body, the transformation of the Raven to
whiteness as a resurrected man rising from an open vault, the amalgamation of gold
and silver as a marriage of Sol and Luna. Everywhere we read of the union of male
and female. "The secret of our Art," says *The Book of Alze,* "is the union of man
and woman: the husband receives the tingeing spirit from his wife."[108] The male
and female principles may be named, as in *The Glory of the World:* "The water is
Eve, or the spirit; the earth Adam, or the body. And as the male is useless for purposes of generation until it be united to the female, so our earth is dead till it is
quickened by the union with water."[109] Sometimes the sexes were reversed, the
spirit, through analogy with the sun's light or with God, being regarded as the
father and the receptive solid as Mother Earth.

Other analogies pepper the documents. In the *Pater Sapientiae* the earth and
water join in a "Bed" or "Nest"; the heat produces sweating; after the substances
have "played and sweate and laboured" they will lie still, after which they should
be allowed to "coole easily, and draw their breath." Distillation and condensation are
compared to the flight of a bird: "For when the Larke ys weary above in hys stound,/
Anon he falleth right downe to the ground." Bubbling is "their voyce singing and
crying and sweating up and downe."[110] Norton's *Ordinall of Alchimy* brings in the
digestive process:

> *Digestion* in this warke hath great likenesse
> To digestion in things of Quicknes [living things]:
> And before other (as I witnesse can)
> It is most like to digestion of Man.[111]

The names given to chemicals and stages of the process were often animistic: the
Raven, the Green Lion (a corrosive acid), the Toad of the Earth, the Snowy Swan,

the Crow's Head. Other terms were metaphors having to do with human processes or diseases: Menstrual Water, Dropsy. Analogy of a different kind is apparent in Geber's warning that "if any *Man* have not his *Organs Compleat*, he cannot by himself come to the *Compleatment* of this *Work*." [112] A deficiency in the worker implies deficiency in his operations. An esoteric diagram full of circles is likened to the sky:

> Our heaven this Figure called is
> Our table also of the lower Astronomy
> Which understood thou mayst not misse
> To make our Medicen parfetly. [113]

The analogy marked here is strengthened by the association of metals with the planets and luminaries and the belief that planetary radiation formed and "imprinted" the metals found in the soil and in mines. The numerology connected with the practices of Lull, Geber, and others was related to the Pythagorean harmonics: "Joyne your Elements *Musically*," we read in Norton's *Ordinall*, for

> . . . other accords which in Musick be,
> With their proporcions causen Harmony,
> Much like proportions be in *Alkimy*,
> As for the great Numbers Actuall:
> But for the secreate Numbers Intellectuall;
> Ye must seeche them as I said before,
> Out of Raymond [Lull] and out of *Bacons* lore. [114]

In such ways as these the theory approximated the behavior of metals—and sometimes of organic substances—to relationships and processes which, like the transactions of men with one another and with sensate creatures, had something of the quality of drama.

VI. Gain and loss in the disappearance of faith

No doubt much of this was inevitable. Until a science developed which made the renunciation of observing the physical world on its own terms instead of on human ones, the avoidance of what psychologists (oddly, using an alchemical term) call "projection" was impossible. Moreover, a reverence for the past which until recently characterized most cultures encouraged an assumption that "higher" thought, no matter where it began, had to involve men or, better still, God, as it had tended to do in antiquity. The contemplation of Divinity was in former ages, to the most thoughtful philosophers, what a beautiful equation is to the modern scientist. *Life*, in the form of awareness, permeated whatever was not base. One result of the newer methods has been an unprecedented advance in real understanding of the nonhuman; and its reliability is shown by the fulfillment of predictions. But there has been loss.

The loss is the dehumanization and despiritualization of the physical universe and a consequent feeling of isolation. When metals no longer "marry," "copulate," "die," and are "resurrected," they appear alien to us. Although we can manipulate them, they remain stubbornly *other*. We dominate them, but we are separated from them by a gulf; they do not share our consciousness or our purposes. The same thing has occurred in other reflective areas. The heavenly bodies no longer pour down "sweet influence" but move in their orbits quite oblivious of our existence; devils or angels have ceased to produce apparent miracles; cabalistic phrases and symbols have no effect on the behavior of matter. The universe is cold and unfriendly, and our adjustment to it is not yet complete. If we are tempted to recapitulate, to revivify the old systems it has been the intention in these pages to examine, we should realize that in so far as the occult practices "work" they do so only subjectively and therefore depend on self-delusion. To this problem we shall return in a postscript. In the meantime, one body of Renaissance thought remains to be discussed, the Hermetic theology. Although it too is "untrue," a real nobility can be discerned in it, as in other meditative systems divorced from attempts to use the world for selfish advantage; and it carried no menace to the public like that which appalls imaginative students of astrology, magic, witchcraft, and alchemy.

NOTES: CHAPTER FOUR

1. Bruxelles: Union Académique Internationale, 1928–1931.
2. J. Bidez *et alii,* eds. (Bruxelles: Union Académique Internationale, 1924–1932).
3. Paris: Georges Steinheil, Éditeur, 1885.
4. A convenient introduction is E. J. Holmyard, *Alchemy* (Harmondsworth, Middlesex: Penguin Books Ltd, 1957). This is a general history but emphasizes Islamic materials.
5. F. Sherwood Taylor, *The Alchemists: Founders of Modern Chemistry* (New York: Henry Schuman, 1949), p. 121.
6. Berthelot, *Origines de l'alchimie,* p. 321.
7. Fritz Paneth, "Ancient and Modern Alchemy," *Science,* LXIV (October 29, 1926), 1–2 and 24.
8. H. Stanley Redgrove, *Alchemy, Ancient and Modern* (London: William Rider & Son Ltd, 2d ed., 1922), pp. 113–14 and v–x.
9. See C. Théodore Tiffereau, *L'Or et la transmutation des métaux* (Paris: H. Chacornac, Éditeur, 1889). The quotation is from p. 181.
10. Elias Ashmole, ed., *Theatrum chemicum Britannicum* (London: 1652), p. 304. I use the reprint, with an introduction by Allen G. Debus, published by the Johnson Reprint Corporation (New York and London: 1967).
11. Holmyard, *Alchemy,* p. 240.

12. Arthur Edward Waite, ed.: *The Hermetic Museum, Restored and Enlarged* (London: James Elliott and Co., 1893), I, 189–90.   13. *Ibid.*, I, 269–70.

14. *Ibid.*, I, 314 (preface to *The Great Stone of the Ancient Sages*).

15. See Taylor, *Alchemists*, pp. 179–89, for the whole story and the comment. The story is discussed also by Redgrove in *Alchemy, Ancient and Modern*, pp. 82–89, and is known to all modern students of alchemy. Helvetius' *Golden Calf* is printed in Waite, *Hermetic Museum*, II, 275–300.

16. Berthelot, *Les Origines de l'alchimie*, I, iii.

17. Taylor, *Alchemists*, pp. 68–69.   18. *Ibid.*, p. 21.   19. *Ibid.*, pp. 34–35.

20. *Ibid.*, p. 30.   21. *Ibid.*, p. 20.   22. *Ibid.*, p. 25.   23. *Ibid.*, p. 27.

24. Waite, *Hermetic Museum*, I, 66.   25. *Ibid.*, I, 188.

26. See, e. g., *The Works of Geber*, Englished by Richard Russell, 1678: A new edition with introduction by E. J. Holmyard (London & Toronto: J. M. Dent & Sons Ltd; New York, Dutton & Co. Inc., 1928), especially pp. ix–xi.

27. Holmyard, *Alchemy*, p. 25.   28. Cf. *ibid.*, p. 65.

29. See Ashmole, *Theatrum chemicum Britannicum*, pp. 227–56, 368–73, and 397–403.

30. See *Le Miroir d'alqvimie de Iean de Mehvn philosophe très-excellent, traduict de Latin en François* (Paris: Chez Charles Seveste Rüe S. Iacques, deuant les Mathurins, 1613).

31. See Lothar Nowak, *Die Alchemie und die Alchemisten in der englischen Literatur* (Breslau: Druck von Neumanns Stadtbuchdruckerei, 1934).

32. See Holmyard, *Alchemy, passim* but especially pp. 152–58.

33. Berthelot, *Origines de l'alchimie*, pp. 280–81.

34. Ashmole, *Theatrum chemicum Britannicum*, pp. 129–34.   35. *Ibid.*, pp. 135–36.

36. *Ibid.*, pp. 139–40.   37. *Ibid.*, pp. 144–47.   38. *Ibid.*, pp. 148–50.

39. *Ibid.*, pp. 161–62.   40. *Ibid.*, pp. 173–78.   41. *Ibid.*, pp. 178–79.

42. *Ibid.*, pp. 181–82.   43. *Ibid.*, pp. 184–85.   44. *Ibid.*, p. 440.

45. *Ibid.*, p. 295.   46. *Ibid.*, p. 94.

47. It should be remembered that the meaning of terms are subject to fluctuation and that Geber wrote very early (in the eighth century).

48. *The Works of Geber*, p. 74 (*Of the Sum of Perfection*, I, iv, 3).

49. *Ibid.*, pp. 101 and 103 (I, iv, 14).   50. *Ibid.*, p. 110 (I, iv, 16).

51. *Ibid.*, p. 116 (I, iv, 17).   52. *Ibid.*, p. 119 (I, iv, 18).

53. Martinus Rulandus, *Lexicon alchimiae sive dictionarium alchemisticum* (Frankfurt-am-Main: 1612). This has been translated by A. E. Waite as *Ruland, Martin the Elder: A Lexicon of Alchemy* (London: John M. Watkins; privately issued 1893; first public edition 1964). The list runs from AABAM (lead) to ZYNSER (verdigris).

54. Raymond Lulle, *Le Codicille de Raymond Lulle*, nouvellement traduit du Latin par Léonce Bouyssou (Paris: Collections La Haute Science, 1953), p. 46. Lull's dates were c. 1235–1315. The original Latin edition of the *Codicil* was published at Cologne in 1563.

55. *Ibid.*, p. 31.

56. De Meun, *Miroir d'alqvimie*, p. 6 (Chap. ii).   57. *Ibid.*, p. 7 (Chap. ii).

58. *Ibid.*, pp. 11–12 (Chap. iii).   59. *Ibid.*, p. 14 (Chap. iii).

60. *Ibid.*, pp. 19–20 (Chap. iv).   61. *Ibid.*, p. 24 (Chap. v).

62. *Ibid.*, pp. 26–29 (Chap. vi).   63. *Ibid.*, pp. 32–33 (Chap. vii).

64. Basilius Valentinus, *The Triumphal Chariot of Antimony*, with the Commentary of Theodore Kerckringius (Amsterdam, 1685), Latin version translated into English, with a biographical preface by Arthur Edward Waite (London: Vincent Stuart Ltd, 1962), p. 12.

65. *Ibid.*, pp. 13–14.   66. *Ibid.*, pp. 184–85.   67. *Ibid.*, p. 185.

68. *Ibid.*, p. 186.   69. *Ibid.*, pp. 194–97.   70. *Ibid.*, p. 197.

71. Redgrove, *Alchemy, Ancient and Modern*, p. 42.

72. I have reprinted the translation of the *Tabula smaragdina* given in Redgrove, *op. cit.*, pp. 40–41. The glosses, however, are my own.

73. Ashmole, *Theatrum chemicum Britannicum*, p. 123. Ripley goes on to call the substance "mercury," in accordance with tradition, but insists that it is "not the comyn callyd Quicksylver by name."

74. *The Hermetic and Alchemical Writings of Aureolus Philippus Theophrastus Bombast, of Hohenheim*, translated by Arthur Edward Waite (London: James Elliott and Co., 1894), I, 48–50). The excerpt I have summarized is from *The Aurora of the Philosophers*.

75. Here I have followed Allen G. Debus, *The English Paracelsians* (New York: Franklin Watts, Inc., 1965), pp. 27–28.   76. *Ibid.*, pp. 25–27.   77. *Ibid.*, pp. 30–31.

78. Cf. *ibid.*, pp. 49–126, for an extended discussion of Paracelsus' influence, especially in England. Another standard study of Paracelsus is Walter Pagel's *Paracelsus: An Introduction to Philosophical Medicine in the Era of the Renaissance* (Basel, Switzerland; S. Karger, New York: 1958).

79. Ashmole, *Theatrum chemicum Britannicum*, sig. A2.   80. *Ibid.*, sig. A2v.   81. *Ibid.*, p. 443.

82. Waite, *Hermetic Museum*, I, 66.   83. *Ibid.*, I, 188.

84. Ashmole, *Theatrum chemicum Britannicum*, pp. xix–xx (Debus' introduction to the modern reprint).

85. *Matth.* 21:42, cited from *Psalms* 118:22. Quoted in *The Sophic Hydrolith*, in Waite, *Hermetic Museum*, I, 92. Here and elsewhere I use the King James' wording.

86. *Ibid.*, I, 92–93, where only chapter references are given to *Acts* and *Romans*. A part of *Isaiah* 8:14, from which the latter passage is drawn, is quoted ("And he shall be for a sanctuary; but for a stone of stumbing and for a rock of offence to both the houses of Israel, for a gin and for a snare to the inhabitants of Jerusalem"). Other texts are also cited or referred to.

87. *Isaiah* 28:16, quoted *ibid.*, I, 77.   88. *Ibid.*, I, 101–102.

89. See Ashmole, *Theatrum chemicum Britannicum*, p. 303.

90. *Ibid.*, pp. 321–22.   91. *Ibid.*, p. 388.

92. Waite, *Hermetic Museum*, I, 168.   93. *Ibid.*, I, 103–104.

94. *Ibid.*, I, 104—again from *The Sophic Hydrolith*.

95. For the whole passage see *ibid.*, I, 57–63.   96. *Ibid.*, I, 353.

97. Ashmole, *Theatrum chemicum Britannicum*, pp. 305–11.   98. *Ibid.*, pp. 291–92.

99. Taylor, *Alchemists*, p. 65. The original Greek texts of the three visions reported by Zosimus— this is a part of the third—can be found in P. E. M. Berthelot, *Collections des anciens alchimistes grecs* (Paris: 1888), II, 107–12, 115–18; or in French translation in Vol. III—this passage on 126–27.

100. Giovanni Pico, *Disputationes adversus astrologiam divinatricem*, ed. Eugenio Garin (Firenze: Vallecchi, 1946–1952), Vol. I, 286 (III, xiii).

101. Waite, *Hermetic Museum*, I, 336.   102. *Ibid.*, I, 320–21.

103. Ashmole, *Theatrum chemicum Britannicum*, sig. B3r-B3v.

104. Debus, *The English Paracelsians*, p. 109.

105. Ashmole, *Theatrum chemicum Britannicum*, sig. B-B2.

106. Taylor, *Alchemists*, p. 10.   107. *Ibid.*, pp. 143–44.

108. Waite, *Hermetic Museum*, I, 265. I read "tingeing" for "tinging."   109. *Ibid.*, I, 238–39.

110. Ashmole, *Theatrum chemicum Britannicum*, pp. 202–204.   111. *Ibid.*, p. 61.

112. *The Works of Geber*, p. 26 (*Of the Sum of Perfection*, I, i, 1).

113. Ashmole, *Theatrum chemicum Britannicum*, facing p. 117 (Ripley, *The Compound of Alchymie*). The insert seems to be placed differently in different copies.   114. *Ibid.*, p. 60.

CHAPTER FIVE

Hermes Trismegistus

I. Background

When, about 1460, a monk named Leonardo da Pistoia brought to Florence a Greek manuscript of what subsequently became known as the *Corpus Hermeticum,* the foundation was laid for an intellectual movement which was to have a profound, if intermittent, influence in the European Renaissance. The document, which Leonardo had picked up in Macedonia, was presented to Cosimo de' Medici. Cosimo's fondness for letters was well known. He collected Latin and Greek manuscripts, had already founded libraries at St. Mark's and the abbey at Fiesole, and some twenty years earlier, as the result of conversations with the Byzantine scholar Gemistos Pletho, had become interested in philosophy. Subsequently he had read Aristotle in the Latin translation of John Argyropolos, a native of Constantinople; and his interest was drawn also to Plato, whom he ordered Ficino to translate.[1] In 1460 he was already over seventy years old and no doubt pressed by his responsibilities as merchant prince and unofficial ruler of a city state. Toward the end of 1462 or the beginning of 1463, however, he entrusted the manuscript to Marsilio Ficino, then about thirty years old and recently instructed in Greek by the same Argyropolos, with instructions to turn it into Latin. The task was completed by April of 1463, and the *Corpus,* together with a prefatory "Argument," was published in 1471. Other editions followed—sixteen before the end of the sixteenth century, not counting those in which the translation was bound with other works; and the existence of many manuscripts suggests that it had been copied frequently before it achieved print.[2] In 1494 Faber Jacobus Stapulensis (Jacques Lefèvre d'Étaples) issued another edition with a brief comment at the end. In 1505 Faber added a chapter–by–chapter analysis and attached another major Hermetic document, the *Asclepius,* which had been known throughout the Middle Ages in a Latin version thought, mistakenly, to have been made by Lucius Apuleius, author of *The Golden Ass.* Faber's commentary crept into the *Opera omnia* of Ficino published at Basel in 1576—the edition recently chosen for photographic reproduction by Sancipriano and Kristeller—where, because proper attribution is lacking, it appears to have been written by Ficino. Spanish, French, and Dutch versions appeared; in 1554 Turnebus for the first time published the Greek text from the same manuscript which Ficino had used, Codex Laurentianus 71.33; and in 1585–90 an enormous Latin discussion, by the French Hannibal Rossel, was published at Cracow in six folio volumes, which were popular enough to require a second issue.[3] As Eugenio Garin has remarked, the diffusion "si spiega solo in riferimento ad un' effettiva esigenza."[4]

What was the need? An adequate explanation would involve consideration of the total intellectual and psychological posture of the times and cannot be undertaken here. Something of the attraction of the *Corpus* for Ficino, however, can be seen from his "Argument," of which the most relevant parts run as follows.

> At the time at which Moses was born the astrologer Atlas flourished, brother of the natural philosopher Prometheus and grandfather of the greater Mercury, whose grandson was Mercury Trismegistus. Thus Augustine writes of him; but Cicero and Lactantius will have it that there were five Mercurys, and that he was the fifth, being called Theut (i. e., Thoth) by the Egyptians and Trismegistus by the Greeks. They say that he killed Argus, ruled over the Egyptians, and gave them laws and letters.

This Mercury—or Hermes, or Thoth—was venerated as a god; temples were raised to him; the open speaking of his name was prohibited; the first month was named after him; and he himself founded Hermopolis.

> They called Trismegistus thrice great because he was pre-eminent as the greatest philosopher, the greatest priest, and the greatest king. As Plato writes, it was a custom among the Egyptians to choose priests from among the philosophers, and kings from the company of priests. . . . Being thus the first among philosophers, he progressed from natural philosophy and mathematics to the contemplation of the gods and was first to discourse most learnedly concerning the majesty of God, the orders of daemons, and the transmigration of souls. He is therefore called the first inventor of theology; and Orpheus, following him, attained the next portions of the

ancient theology. Aglophemus was initiated into the rites of Orpheus, and Pythagorus succeeded him in philosophy; Philolaus, the teacher of our divine Plato, followed him. In this way, at one place a system of primitive theology, everywhere consistent with itself, was formulated by a wonderful series of six philosophers, taking its beginnings from Mercury and completed finally by Plato. Mercury, however, wrote many books having to do with the knowledge of divine things, in which, O immortal God! lie revealed mysteries as arcane as his oracles are amazing; nor, very often, does he speak so much as a philosopher as a prophet, and sings events that are to come. Here he foresaw the ruin of the antique religion, there the future judgment, the resurrection of the world, the glory of the blessed, and the punishment of sins. For this reason Aurelius Augustinus doubted whether he accomplished many things by skill in astrology or by revelation from daemons. Lactantius, however, does not hesitate to number him among the sibyls and prophets.

After specifying that among Hermes's writings two are especially divine, the *Asclepius* and the *Pimander*—Ficino's title for the entire set of fourteen *libelli* which he translated, although it is really appropriate only to the first—and describing their contents briefly, the commentator brings his introduction to a close.

> Mercury knows how to instruct . . . in divine matters. He cannot teach divine things who has not learned them; and we cannot discover by human skill what is above nature. The work is therefore to be accomplished by a divine light, so that we may look upon the sun by the sun's light. For, in truth, the light of the divine mind is never poured into a soul unless the soul turns itself completely toward the mind of God, as the moon turns toward the sun. . . . For this reason Mercury simply puts aside the fogs of sense and of fancy, bringing himself thus to an approach to mind; and presently Pimander, that is, the divine mind, flows into him, whereupon he contemplates the order of all things, whether they exist in God or flow from God. At length he explains to other men what has been revealed to him by the divine power. This, then, is his book, this is his purpose and method. Read it joyfully, O happy Cosimo, and live daily in such a way that your country may live long.

We may now look at two aspects of the "Argument," the first briefly, the other at somewhat greater length.

The historical details were not to remain undisputed. Other commentators were to assert that instead of being four generations later, Trismegistus was a contemporary of Moses, or perhaps of his grandfather Sarug; and in another place Ficino himself was to suggest tentatively that Moses, who after all was Egyptian by birth and upbringing, was perhaps identical with Hermes.[5] The differences were not, however, fundamental, all concerned scholars tending to grant the documents an origin in remote antiquity.

More interesting are the grounds suggested for an extraordinary authority. The

Renaissance mind was medieval or pre-medieval in many of its assumptions and advanced only very slowly toward the hard empirical rationality which has characterized much later thought. Thus Atlas and Prometheus are assumed actually to have existed. Euhemerism, or the theory that the pagan gods had really been exceptional men, can be found at least as early as 300 B.C. but was especially natural for any scholar who, like Ficino, combined Christian piety with a deep respect for antiquity. The alternative view, that the gods were really angels or devils—Milton is a distinguished English proponent—is here rejected. The identification of Prometheus with a natural philosopher or physicist derives from the tradition that he had given fire to men—that is, had taught its uses. Because Atlas had been thought to support the sky, he became an astrologer who affirmed the rule of terrestrial creatures and affairs by the heavens.

Still more significant is the effort to find a long pedigree for the *Hermetica*. As within the family in most times and places, authority was still largely a function of age. Before carefully tested empirical data began to weigh heavily in intellectual work, "proof" depended about equally upon logic and upon citations. Although the proportions vary widely in different arguments, support from traditional sources typically carries as much of the total burden as attempts to draw inferences from accepted premises or to adjudicate between competing premises. The attitude of King Ferdinand of Aragon in the *Crater Hermetis* of Ludovico Lazzarelli (printed 1505) suggests the expectation of readers: he interrupts the speaker frequently to ask for *aliquod* (*si quid habes*) . . . *testimonium* or again to request that *sapientum testimonia inferri*.[6] But the best *testimonia* were, at least when Ficino wrote—before the voyages of Columbus, before Copernicus had advanced his hypothesis or Bacon had recommended his *novum organum*—still the oldest. What a father had learned from a grandfather, and he in turn from a great-grandfather, had more prestige than a novelty.

The presumption underlying the retrospective orientation is conveniently stated by Ficino: *Diuina docere nequit, qui non didicit*. The wisdom of Plato must have had a source. He could not have thought it all up by himself. The source, Philolaus, must also have had a source—Pythagoras, who was thought to have acquired his knowledge in Egypt—and he another. In the end the series leads back to Hermes. And what of him? Here we pass out of the world altogether. Mercury "puts aside the fogs of sense and of fancy, bringing himself thus to an approach to mind; and presently Pimander, that is, the divine mind, flows into him, whereupon he contemplates the order of all things." The pedigree of the *Pimander* terminates in God Himself, whose word must perforce be accepted.

What emerges is *una priscae theologiae ubique sibi consona secta*, "a system of aboriginal theology everywhere harmonious with itself"; and this harmony was itself a powerful warrant of truth. The Renaissance thirst for synthesis, for syncretism, was unquenchable. Ficino was to assert the compatibility of Platonism (more accurately, Neo-Platonism) with Christianity. Pico della Mirandola was to stir together in one pot not only these two ingredients but also Hermetic doctrines and the cabala, which he thought to preserve an esoteric tradition entrusted to Moses on Mount Sinai at the same time as the written law. In the *De occulta philosophia* of Cornelius Agrippa all three co-exist easily with astrology, numerology, alchemy, and much else. As Frances Yates has recently shown, Giordano Bruno was still more boldly eclectic, with the result that he was burned as a heretic. By the beginning of the seventeenth century Robert Fludd, who was especially drawn to Rosicrucianism but wanted to abandon nothing, had become so indiscriminately receptive that Mersenne, whose mind was of a different type, was driven to say *Robertus ille Flud haereticomagus insanire mihi videtur.*[7] Much of the effort to assimilate, to adjust, to harmonize was influenced by a supposition that as men of former ages had surpassed later men in longevity and physical size (one remembers Donne's *First Anniversarie*), so also they must have been superior in native endowments.

The belief in *una prisca theologia ubique sibi consona* was to remain attractive for several centuries. A vestige of it appears in the fictive attempt of George Eliot's Mr. Casaubon, in *Middlemarch,* to work out a Key to All the Mythologies. All the Eastern religions must have been reducible to a single pattern, which no doubt would have proved to be a gentile approximation of Christian truth. The reconciling of any pagan system with Christianity at once reinforced Christian sanctions and justified respect for the great men of antiquity, who had lacked the inestimable privilege of revelation (except in so far as vague figures like Hermes had achieved some contact with Divine Mind) but had made some remarkably astute guesses. It is not surprising that Ficino saluted the discovery of Hermetic doctrines very like Christian ones by exclaiming, "O immortal God!" The greatest philosopher and priest, as well as the greatest king, of the most ancient of all known cultures was a quasi-Christian, and as such might be supposed a sage who could teach later generations forgotten wisdom.

II. The Hermetic documents

At this point we return to the Hermetic fragments, which although carefully studied by classical scholars are only now coming to be known by Renaissance specialists. It is important that our consideration of them should not be fogged by misconceptions.

First, the only Hermetic writings in question are seventeen *libelli* of what Ficino called, erroneously, *Pimander* but is now known as the *Corpus Hermeticum;*

the Latin rendering, called *Asclepius,* of a lost Greek dialogue; and certain other passages collected, about 500 A.D., by Joannes Stobaeus. The Hermes of these pages will not be an alchemist, an astrologer, a magician, or a numerologist. Except in a passage to be quoted at once, he has nothing to say about ways of operating upon the physical world or upon other human beings for one's own advantage. He is rather a philosophical mystic allied, more or less remotely, with the Rosicrucians, the Freemasons, and perhaps the disciples of Jakob Boehme or Emmanuel Swedenborg, although of the last two I know little. His object is not power but enlightenment.

The exceptional passage, which appears in the *Asclepius,* has to do with the enticement of daemons into idols and therefore with magic.

> Let us return to man and his reason, from which divine gift man is called a rational animal. For although what has been said about man is wonderful, it is less so than this. Of all the marvels this most deserves admiration, that man has been able to discover the divine nature and, indeed, to produce it. Since our ancestors erred greatly about the doctrine (*rationem*) of the gods, being unbelievers and not turning their minds to worship and the divine religion, they discovered an art by which they made gods. To this art, once discovered, they added an appropriate strength drawn from universal nature, mixing it well in. Because they could not create souls, they evoked the souls of daemons or angels and introduced them into the holy images and the divine mysteries; and from these the idols acquired the power of acting well and badly.[8]

Although the passage is cryptic it is not really puzzling, for the nature of the "appropriate strength" in nature can be guessed with some confidence. Suppose, for example, a god has been "made," that is, carved, in the form of an ibis-headed creature. Like everything else on earth, the ibis was a member of an intricate family whose members were all under the same astrological influence: minerals, plants, animals. Medals or talismans would be made of the astrologically related metals or plants, and these, perhaps inscribed with the correct astrological symbols, would be hung about or somehow connected with the image. The whole might then be incensed by the burning of a related plant and offered the flesh of a related animal as food. Innumerable examples of such families can be found in astrological literature, and some have been noted in the chapter on magic. The image, the talismans, the incense, and the food together might be expected to "draw down" a daemon from the chosen part of the sky, and this could be called upon, by persons instructed in ways of constraining it, to respond to human demands.

Considerable notice has been taken of the passage by recent scholarship. In *Giordano Bruno and the Hermetic Tradition,* Frances Yates uses it repeatedly to assimilate Hermetism (the contemplative doctrine which is our present subject) with hermeticism (esoteric systems generally). It is true that Renaissance Hermetists had wide interests, and other works which are authentically magical, astrological, or alchemical were also attributed to Hermes: one on the zodiacal signs, another on the relation of plants to astrological influences, a third on the astrological "virtues" of animals, a fourth on astrological medicine, and so on.[9] Nevertheless the grounds for the attributions are so especially shaky that no modern student of Hermes himself, from Louis Ménard in 1866 to Festugière in 1949–54, has thought the documents a part of his proper subject-matter. Further, in the Renaissance the passage often evoked strong objection. In his comment on Chapter XIII of the *Asclepius,* Faber Stapulensis begins by saying that the passage "suffers from an impurity" and concludes by asserting that persons who had undertaken such practices are "a most faulty race of men, unfriendly to God and men, and made inimical by misfortune." Augustine, he notes, "acts against this profane error of impiety, and acts, indeed, rightly, in his book *The City of God.*"[10] The relevant passage in Augustine (*Civitas Dei* VIII, 23–26, especially 24) was known also to Ficino, who cited another part of it in his "Argument," and it was frequently referred to by others. One escape was to suggest that Lucius Apuleius, who was known from *The Golden Ass* to hold scandalous opinions, had falsified his translation at this point and then destroyed the Greek original to cover his deception. In any event, the present study is concerned with the Hermes of the *Corpus,* the *Asclepius,* and the Stobaean extracts only.

Before approaching the documents we must consider their provenance and authorship. Here, fortunately, I can draw upon the studies of men far more at home than I am in classical philosophy.

As has been seen, the Renaissance opinion was that the *Hermetica* dated from remote antiquity. This view held until Isaac Casaubon, in 1614, proved decisively that the author cannot have been Hermes and that the *Hermetica* themselves were written in Christian times: "I assert that in this book is contained not the Egyptian doctrine of Hermes, but a Greek doctrine drawn in part from the books of Plato and his followers, often in their very words, and in part a Christian doctrine obtained from sacred books."[11] Apart from the word "Christian," for which Scott suggests[12] "Jewish" should perhaps be substituted, this affirmation is accepted by all competent modern scholars as correct. The basis of the judgment is also accepted: the Greek of the *Corpus* is that of a late Hellenism (*Quis priorum dixit ὑλότης, οὐσιότης, et id genus alia?*),[13] and the doctrines are those of a mystical Platonism not unrelated to that most widely known from the *Enneads* of Plotinus. In his dating of the *Corpus* at the end of the first century A.D., Casaubon is also inaccurate, erring by about a century and a half. Yet his achievement was remarkable and deserves admiration as one of many Renaissance monuments of unbiased linguistic scholarship.

If the documents postdate Christ, an explanation must be found of their attribution to a prehistoric Hermes whom Ficino and others identified with the Egyptian god Theut or Thoth. According to Festugière, Thoth was originally a local god of Middle Egypt who later became connected with Osiris as his secretary and scribe. Hence the ascription to him of the invention of writing and all sciences connected with writing. In time the priests charged Thoth with the creation of the world by his voice, which could pronounce magical formulas with the tonalities that gave them power:[14] a natural enough development at a time when names were thought to have power over objects. As the discoverer of hieroglyphs, Thoth had become the Lord of Language. An inscription at Denderah which dates from the time of Nero hails him as "Twice-Great, the Oldest One, Master of the city Hermopolis the Great, the Great God at Tentyris, the Sovereign God, Creator of Good, Heart of Ra, Tongue of Aten, Throat of the god whose name is hidden, Lord of Time, King of the Years, Scribe of the annals of the Nine."[15] From obscure beginnings, Thoth had decidedly come up in the world. The identification of him with the Greek Hermes followed as a matter of course, since Hermes was also a god of language, and was accomplished at least by the time of Herodotus.[16] Because Egypt was powerful, Thoth's fame of course spread into other lands. In the second or first century B.C. a Jew named Artapan assimilated Thoth-Hermes to Moses, who had taught the Egyptians how to navigate, to lift stones with cranes, and to manufacture arms and water-pumps and had also instructed them in writing. Behind all such identifications lies the desire of the human mind to reduce psychic conflict by modifying discrete bits of information until they no longer exist in tension.

To Thoth, accordingly, as Festugière notes, were attributed all books noted for their antiquity. Also, "according to a usage met not only in Egypt, to the god of Hermopolis was given the paternity of every writing whose prestige it was desired to raise and whose authority it was hoped to reinforce."[17] By roughly 200 A.D., we are informed by Clement of Alexandria, Hermes was accredited with forty-two books, of which thirty-six had to be memorized by his disciples. The remaining six were medical.[18] This was one aspect of the intellectual situation in Egypt at the time when the surviving *Hermetica* came into existence.

Under what circumstances were these written? A general explanation is given by the chief English specialist, Walter Scott.

> There were in Egypt under the Roman Empire men who had received some instruction in Greek philosophy, and especially in the Platonism of the period, but were not content with merely accepting and repeating the cut–and–dried dogmas of the orthodox philosophic schools, and sought to build up, on a basis of Platonic doctrine, a philosophic religion that would better satisfy their needs. . . . These men did not openly compete with the established schools of philosophy, or try to establish a new

school of their own on similar lines; but here and there one of these 'seekers after God' would quietly gather round him a small group of disciples, and endeavour to communicate to them the truth in which he had found salvation for himself. The teaching in these little groups must have been mainly oral, and not based on written texts; it must have consisted of private and intimate talks of the teacher with a single pupil at a time, or with two or three pupils at most. But now and then the teacher would set down in writing the gist of a talk in which some point of primary importance was explained; or perhaps a pupil, after such a talk with his teacher, would write down as much of it as he could remember; and when once written, the writing would be passed from hand to hand within the group, and from one group to another. Specimens of such writings have come down to us, and these are our *Hermetica*.[19]

These speculations are generally accepted as in all probability essentially correct.

The *Corpus,* the *Asclepius,* and the Stobaean extracts—surviving fragments, no doubt, of a larger body of such writings by a variety of authors—are thus the products of a late Egyptian gnosticism which, by a pious fraud, fathered its documents upon Hermes to give them prestige, much as a late Jew might publish his own composition as a Book of Daniel or of Enoch.[20] Alternatively, the writers may have intended no real deception, understanding that the trick would be seen through. In any event, the result, once the documents had existed for a time, was their acquisition of an awesome authority. The reigning philosophical doctrine in Egypt, as elsewhere, was a late Platonism. Plato, who was believed to have studied in Egypt for 13 years, had derived his doctrines from Pythagoras—perhaps at one remove, through Philolaus; and Pythagoras, in turn, was known to have studied in schools attached to Egyptian temples. What the priests taught there was unknown, for their *gnosis* was secret; but they had in their possession sacred books said to have been written by Thoth-Hermes, the scribe of the gods. A Greek-speaking Egyptian of the Empire into whose hands one of the *Hermetica* came may be supposed to have received it with respect.

The dating of the *Hermetica* is an immensely complicated problem which must be left to specialists in classical philosophy and religion. The evidence is of several kinds: linguistic (by which a date before the first century A.D. is made impossible), doctrinal, and allusive. The longest and most impressive study, that of A.-J. Festugière, ranges widely through classical antiquity and traces relationships between the *Hermetica* and a variety of philosophical and gnostic systems, with special emphasis on Platonic affiliations—particularly, though by no means solely, with the *Timaeus* —and on a "world religion," or supra-national faith, which was apparently emergent in the time of Alexander the Great and is implied by Cicero's *De natura deorum*. Another influence is a late Stoicism which instead of being competitive with Platonism had absorbed much of it.[21] Allusions to the *Hermetica,* sufficiently rich to fill nearly five hundred pages of Scott's fourth volume, range from Athenagoras, who wrote about A.D. 177, through Fulgentius (about A.D. 500) and beyond. Outside these three general categories of evidence, other stray hints can be picked up. Scott thought he had discovered in the year A.D. 270 a situation "prophesied" retrospectively in *Asclepius* 25–26;[22] but A. S. Ferguson, who after Scott's death edited the latter's fourth volume, found what he believed to be an adequate historical parallel in A.D. 115.[23] The whole problem of dating is made intricate by the necessity that the seventeen *libelli* of the *Corpus,* distinct sections of the *Asclepius,* and the Stobaean extracts be investigated separately. On the whole, we must rest satisfied with the guess that the *Hermetica* were composed between the latter half of the second century A.D. and the end of the third.

To what extent are the Hermetic philosophy and theology Egyptian? The most charitable possible conclusion was offered by Ralph Cudworth in 1678, long after Casaubon's exposure of the forgeries. Although Cudworth allows that "there have been some pious frauds practised upon these Trismegistick writings" and that passages or even whole books have been "counterfeited by pretended Christians," nevertheless "it does not at all follow . . . that therefore all of them must needs be such." Even if they are, they prove what Cudworth is especially eager to assert, "that the Egyptian Pagans asserted one supreme Deity, *viz.* because every cheat and imposture must needs have some basis or foundation of truth to stand upon." There must

> have been something truly Egyptian in such counterfeit Egyptian writings, (and therefore this at least of one supreme Deity) or else they could never have obtained credit at first, or afterwards have maintained the same. The rather, because these Trismegistick books were dispersed in those ancient times, before the Egyptian paganism and their succession of priests were yet extinct.

The fact that the books were written in Greek is not conclusive because "at least from the Ptolemaick kings downward, Greek was become very familiar to all the learned Egyptians, and in a manner vulgarly spoken." The presence of Greek doctrines is not surprising because "Pythagorism, Platonism and the Greek learning in general was in great part derived from the Egyptians."[24] Modern opinion is less generous. Scott, for instance, believes that the only authentically Egyptian element is a "greater intensity of religious fervour" than was common among Greeks.[25] We may, I think, assume with confidence that the Renaissance enthusiasts—and G. R. S. Mead, a Theosophist who asserted similar views in 1906—erred in believing that the documents have preserved accurately, and in detail, Egyptian religious doctrines which mount to high antiquity.

III. General characterization of the doctrine

The documents themselves, at which we may now look directly, are accessible in four volumes edited by A. D. Nock and translated by A.-J. Festugière (author of *La Révélation d'Hermès Trismégiste,* also in four volumes) and are dated at Paris in 1945–54. French and Greek—or, for the *Asclepius,* Latin—are on facing pages. The English-speaking reader who does not know Greek, Latin, or French can go to the four volumes of *Hermetica* published by Walter Scott at Oxford in 1924–36; but he should be warned that Scott, although an excellent Greek scholar, emends the text boldly and rearranges both sentences and whole sections, especially in the *Asclepius,* in ways that he thinks will produce greater coherence. The Nock-Festugière edition will be used by careful scholars. It will be remembered that the first fourteen books of the *Corpus Hermeticum* (hereafter referred to as *CH*) were available in print after 1471 in Ficino's Latin translation. The remaining three *libelli* were printed in the *editio princeps* of the Greek text, by Turnebus, in 1554 at Paris.[26] The *Asclepius,* which Lactantius (died ca. 340 A.D.) knew in Greek as the Λόγος Τέλειος, or *Perfect Discourse,* and Augustine in Latin, never quite disappeared and from the twelfth century was often cited. Finally, the Stobaean extracts were partly edited by Trincavelli at Venice in 1535–36 and again by Gesner in 1543, 1549, and 1559 but were not completely published until 1575, by Canter.[27] Other less important fragments, the so-called *Fragments divers* and *Fragments de Cyrille,* had little or no currency in the Renaissance and in any event add nothing to our understanding of the system.

Hermetism was basically a Greek contemplative mysticism developed on Egyptian soil. Its sources were mainly in popular Greek philosophical thought—Platonism, Aristotelianism, and Stoicism; but details appear to have been borrowed from Judaism, Persian religion, and, more doubtfully, from Christianity. Striking resemblances to Christian gnosticism have been found, but these may have resulted rather from similar backgrounds and a similar psychological function than from direct contact.[28] The only unmistakable references to Christianity appear in the *Asclepius* at the point (24–26) where the subversion of Egyptian religion by foreign invaders is prophesied. *Libellus* IV of the *Corpus,* entitled the Κρατήρ or Basin, suggests Christian baptism (βάπτισον σεαυτήν, "Dip yourself!"), and the irrelevant title of *CH* XIII, "Secret Discourse on the Mountain," may remind us of the Sermon on the Mount, but the hints are probably delusive. Jewish influences appear especially in *CH* I and III, which contain accounts of the creation evidently affected by the Septuagint; and the use, here and there, of ὁ κύριος, "the Lord," for the supreme god is contrary to usual Greek practice. Anti-Stoicism is apparent in the denial of the extra-cosmic void offered in *CH* II.[29] Clear Mithraic influence is shown, I think, in *CH* I, 25–26, in which the soul is said to be purged of a different sin as it passes through each of the seven celestial spheres on its way to the eighth, or Ogdoad, where it becomes a Power and sings hymns to the Father. Misleadingly, the entire *gnosis* is sometimes presented as peculiarly and exclusively Egyptian, as when, in *CH* XVI, 1–2, we are told that the doctrines will lose clarity and weight if translated into the loose and extravagant Greek tongue. Ways exist of knowing whether a document in one language has been translated out of another. For example, in the *Asclepius* a Greek origin is indicated by the occasional use of a genitive after a comparative or a singular verb after a neuter plural subject. From the time of Casaubon on, no respectable dissent has been offered to the judgment that the *Hermetica* were originally written in Greek.

A consequence of multiple authorship and divergent influences is that the documents are not everywhere mutually consistent. Most notably, a predominant optimistic strain is contradicted by a recurrent pessimistic one. *CH* XII, 12 asserts that if man uses his gifts properly he will differ in no way from the immortals and will ultimately be guided to the choirs of the gods and the blessed. *CH* VI, 3–4 says that in man nothing of good exists but the name and that the cosmos is "one mass of evil." The usual warnings against imparting esoteric doctrine to the public are compromised by a missionary spirit in *CH* I and VII. The warm praise of the generative act in *Asclepius* 21 runs counter to a pervasive tendency to condemn all sensory pleasure as bad. The encomium of man in the *Asclepius* (*magnum miraculum est homo,* etc., *Ascl.* 6) is balanced by seven pessimistic propositions out of forty-eight listed in *Stobaeus XI:* nothing corporeal is true, nothing on earth is good, man is evil, everything on earth is unknowable, everything earthly deserves reproach, earth is without reason, man is changeable and bad. Three separate accounts of the creation (in *CH* I and III and in *Stobaeus* XXXIII, the Κόρη Κόσμου or "Eye-Pupil of the Universe") are quite incompatible. And there are other inconsistencies. Not all the contradictions are necessarily irreducible. For example, men may become good in some absolute sense only after death and yet attain beatitude, as Christianity teaches; and no great surprise need be aroused that the keeper of an esoteric doctrine should once or twice be tempted to preach it in the marketplace. Yet it would be effort wasted to pretend that all the authors possessed identical beliefs. The defense of an attempt to achieve an overall view is that from this distance of time and mental habits the inconsistencies are less striking than the constants. The purpose of these pages is not to make a meticulous study of details but to suggest general purport in such a way as to illuminate a Renaissance influence.

One of the first characteristics to strike a modern reader is the poverty of empirical content. To be sure, much stress is laid on the orderliness of cosmic processes as evidence of a divine rule. God created man in order that man might see Him in His works; and we are frequently exhorted to marvel at the regular movements of the heavenly bodies in their orbits. We are not, however, to watch the movements intently. *Asclepius* 12–13 warns lovers of pure philosophy against arithmetic and geometry (together with music, which taught the "harmony" of proportionate distances), precisely the studies necessary to an astronomical science. Elsewhere appeals to sensory phenomena are virtually non-existent. A disciple's objection in *Stobaeus* IV, 1–2, based on the observed behavior of ants, birds, and quadrupeds, is disposed of quickly. The notion that hypotheses about the natural world should be carefully checked against sensory evidence appears scarcely to have been imagined, and an effort to quantify data with the aid of carefully constructed and operated instruments was still further beyond the intellectual horizon. Here, indeed, may be found one of the clear differences between the philosophical *Hermetica* and the quasi-scientific, magical, or theurgical documents we shall not consider. In the purely mental universe of the *Hermetica,* a desire to operate on the world does not arise. The tendency to scorn physical work as proper to slaves offers a partial explanation, but a further influence is also at work. The milieu of the *Hermetica* was not that of temple, court, or city but a retired hermitage—or many hermitages—within which a master and his few disciples meditated, prayed, and perhaps grew a few vegetables but did not make war, hunt, or trade and hardly even performed sacrifices. Not only is there no aim of effective participation in worldly affairs; both the affairs and, in a sense, the world itself are rejected. "Possessions" are a frequent object of attack, and in *Asclepius* 11 are said to include the body. According to *CH* VII, 2 the body is a dark jail, a living death, a tomb, a robber who lives in your house, a jealous and hating companion. The philosopher accepts in theory the rather vague duty of "tending" the earth but in fact aspires to live wholly in a universe of thought.

What substitutes for the interpretation of empirical evidence is Νοῦς, or Mind: intellect working, it might be supposed, more or less in a vacuum. Actually, of course, each master began with a body of doctrine learned from his teacher, who had learned from another, so that, to a degree at least, tradition carried the authority now borne by evidence. Nevertheless the prestige of mind is striking. The supreme god himself is sometimes Νοῦς. Men who have mind hate their senses (*CH* I, 22), whereas those who do not are wicked and will be pricked on to the commission of greater sins so that their punishments may be heavier (*CH* I, 23). Knowledge, we are told, differs from sensation in being independent of external objects (*CH* X, 5). Alternatively, knowledge, which is incorporeal, is attained through mind, and mind uses the body—presumably the senses (*CH* X, 10). God Himself is knowable only through mind: *mente sola intellegibilis, summus qui dicitur deus* (*Ascl.* 16). We may infer His existence from the beauty of the created world but can understand Him only through contemplation, which is most effective when the senses are suspended and the mind emerges from the body into the realm of pure thought. We see such suspension vividly in *CH* I, in which the narrator has a vision of the world's creation while his senses are inactive like those of a man in deep sleep. Philosophy consists in a simple desire to know God through steady contemplation (*frequens obtutus*) and holy piety (*Ascl.* 12). A rare qualification appears in *CH* IX, 1, in which we are told that sensation should not be separated from thought (νόησις) in men, although in animals it is related wholly to nature. The power of soul (ψυχή) praised memorably in *CH* XI, 19–20, is really a power of what we should call mind: order your soul to transport itself to India, and it is there; send it to the ocean, and it seems not to have to travel to be where you wish it. What power you have, and what speed! The consistent implication that thought has little to do with objects is borne out by *Stobaeus* XVII, 6, where we are told that thoughtfulness or mental activity (ὁ περινοητικὸς λόγος) works over conjectures thrown up by the reason. No mention is made of observation as providing the materials. The philosopher glances now and then at the stars but mainly sits quietly and cogitates. The ascetic tendency so strongly marked in the documents—abandon the body, win the fight, and begin the ascension (*Stob.* IIB, 8)—derives in large part from a conviction that although the orderliness and beauty of the world are admirable matter itself deserves contempt.

Yet reflection contrives to operate without substantive data. The method is too complex to be described fully but can be illustrated and partly analyzed.

> What is called the sensible world is the receptacle of everything sensible which has semblance or quality or body; and none of this can have life without God. All things therefore are God, and come from Him and through His will; and the whole is good, fitting, and provident; inimitable, and sensible and knowable only to Him; and without Him nothing has been, is, or will be. (*Ascl.* 34)

We may begin by looking at these fairly typical sentences.

What is asserted up to the first semicolon is self-evident. Once the synthesizing impulse so characteristic of the documents has caused the postulation of a sensible world which contains the totality of sensible (i. e., sensory) objects, it follows necessarily that whatever is sensible is a part of the sensible world. The next clause, "none of this can have life without God," connects what has just been said with the result of an earlier movement of the same impulse. After God has been posited as the source of everything good, life, as a good, must be recognized to derive from Him. "All things therefore are God" because God, like the world, is construed as a totality of which all things are parts; and by a metonymy it may be said that whatever is a part of God "is" God. What follows uses honorific adjectives—"good," "fitting," "provident," "inimitable"—of the whole in consequence of the relation established with God, to whom every commendatory adjective is appropriate. This praise appears to follow from the preceding affirmations but in fact is a corollary of a prior honorific quality inhering in the concept "God." The whole, we are told, is "knowable only to Him" because everything other than God is assumed to be inferior to Him not only in the degree of its inclusiveness but in every conceivable way, and therefore also in knowledge. The final phrase, "without Him nothing has been, is, or will be" declares that the state of affairs shown to be logically necessary must always have been and will continue to be logically necessary, hence incapable of suffering change. The reflective process is thus basically deductive. Inferences are drawn from propositions antecedently thought to be true, or connections are found among them. Since the propositions are all generalities, the plane is that of high abstraction, and sensory evidence which runs counter to the argument is not easily accessible.

A further insight into rational patterns is provided by a glance at a brief exchange in *Asclepius* 2.

—Every human soul, Asclepius, is immortal, but they are not all immortal in the same way. They differ according to manner or time.

—Then, Trismegistus, all souls do not have the same quality?

—How quickly you turn away from the true consequences of reason (*de uera rationis continentia*), Asclepius! Have I not said that everything is one and that the one is everything, inasmuch as everything was in the Creator before He created all things?

The retort would appear to indicate that Asclepius' former opinion was right; all souls are indeed one. But the meaning seems instead to be that souls which differ in quality are yet united in the whole, which is God. The tendency evident here to find an identity behind every difference even when the focus is apparently on difference is another pervasive trait in the documents. Unity is a very high value. The mind is reassured, satisfied, by the discovery that seeming distinctions are reconciled in a higher similarity and that ultimately All Is One. (Precisely this generalization has more than once been said to be made by all Oriental philosophy and to distinguish it from Western.) The lower abstractions are subsumed in successively higher ones, so that in the end the philosopher can concentrate his mind upon God and exercise the piety which is hardly more than emotional acquiescence to the non-sensory vision in which he is absorbed. An example of the lower level of abstraction is the assertion that the separate *genera* or kind of beings have their own forms, so that each is unitary (*Ascl.* 4), and an example of the higher level is the statement that the whole (πλήρωμα) made up of all beings is one and in the One, since everything is unity (*CH* XVI, 3).

Other intellectual values appear, some of them disconcerting to modern readers. One of these is impassivity. Suffering, in the sense of undergoing or being subjected to any activity other than a self-initiated one, is bad. God is completely impassive and cannot be moved to any emotion (*Ascl.* 31, *CH* VI, 1). Stability, or physical immobility, is another good. God moves only "within the immensity of

His stability" (*Ascl.* 31); and the fact implies His superiority to the world He has created, which is good (except in the "pessimistic" passages) but moves. *Stabilitas enim utpote defixa quod sustinere, quae agitabilia sunt, possit, beneficio firmitatis merito obtinet principatum* (*Ascl.* 31): stability, because it is firm and can support things capable of movement, has priority by reason of its steadfastness. The world, *CH* X, 10 tells us, is bad in that it moves, although good in being immortal; and man is doubly bad because he is both mobile and mortal (*CH* X, 12). One is tempted to relate such preferences to the monarchical system of government, in which the sovereign aspires to complete independence from external pressures and absolute autonomy in willing. Fixity—not, as for moderns, development, progress— is a good. The philosopher's removal from town to a retreat in which he is sur-rounded only by a few respectful disciples implies his yearning for physical and moral stasis.

Such values, however, are prior to the reasoning process, about which more can be said. Some of the peculiarities are obvious: for example, a fondness for what might be called sets of Chinese boxes. This is in that, that in the other, the other in a third. According to *CH* XI, 2, God makes the world, the world makes time, time makes becoming; eternity is within God, the world moves in eternity, time is in the world, becoming occurs within time. Similarly, in *CH* X, 13, the mind is said to be in the discursive reason, the reason in the soul, the soul in the breath, and the breath, by means of veins, arteries, and blood, moves the body. The series can be run in the opposite direction. At death the breath retires into the blood, the soul into the breath, and the intellect receives a body of fire and ranges through space, leaving the soul to judgment (*CH* X, 6). Evidently the thought of contain-ment gave a satisfaction analogous to that we obtain nowadays from the discovery of causal connection. Again a social parallel may be discerned. In the relatively "primitive" cultures of antiquity, when a keen sense of individuality had not yet emerged, the typical human being must have been deeply aware that he existed within a family, the family within a clan, the clan within a larger community, and the community within a nation or race (the Greeks differed from "barbarians"). The larger unit thus regularly subsumed the smaller, and involvement often substituted for causality. The "becoming" of matter required something more inclusive, time, as its *locus;* time required the world, the world eternity, eternity God. In this way each member of the series except the last derives from and is dependent on the next higher one.

Other intellectual habits appear. In order not to prolong this part of the dis-cussion unduly I will offer only one additional illustration. In *CH* XIV, 2 we are informed that what comes into being does so through something else. Section 3 proceeds as follows.

This [other thing] must be more powerful and one and single, and really wise about all things, because it has no elder. It is first (ἄρχει) in number, in greatness, and in difference from created things, and in the continuity (συνεχείᾳ) of its creativeness. Therefore, although created things are visible, it is invisible. For this reason it creates in order that it may be seen. Accordingly it creates eternally and is indeed visible.

The passage may detain us briefly.

The pre-eminence imputed by the first sentence to what is older (πρεσβύτερος) is consistent with the social dignity of primogeniture. The first-born son is nearer than younger children to the authority-figure, the father, and in time will succeed him. The father, who is older still, has higher dignity and greater power. The assumption that wisdom accompanies age (and experience) is natural—our recent American envy of youth is abnormal—and persists in such vestigially traditional cultures as the Japanese. The admiration of Renaissance scholars for ancient literature, philosophy, and even morality and government implies a similar respect for priority. The First Cause, therefore, is "wise about all things." Like a father, it has watched the development of what it has generated; but the ground of the assertion is an instinctive association of wisdom, like power, with age and priority. Moving on, we observe that the First Cause is prior in other ways: in number, since One is the first number and the source of all others; in magnitude, since what produces other things is assumed to surpass them in size (we would not say, in our period, that an atom is "greater than" what is produced by its fission); and in difference from what it creates, as a painter differs from his picture or a carpenter from his table. The statement that the First Cause must continue eternally to create may derive from any one of a number of presuppositions, or from several in combination. An awe inhering in the Hermetic concept of God forbade the limitation of His activities. Observation of the natural world suggested that creative potentiality expressed itself not once but many times; and the combination of this perception with the recognition of God's immortality led necessarily to the notion of eternal creativity. What has been defined—indeed, partly imagined—as a creative force inevitably exercises the energy of which it is an embodiment. The affirmation that the First Cause is invisible, whereas created objects are visible, suggests a desire to clarify intellectual distinctions by positing qualitative differences; and the ultimate degree of difference is contrariety. Finally, the assertion that God creates in order that He might be seen is a consequence of the belief that He does create with knowledge that the world is visible. The world must, therefore, have been created in order that it might be visible. The effect of divine activity cannot be separated from purpose.

Much else might detain our attention. The conception of space offered by *CH* XI, 18 is curious: the τόπος, or place, of a body is the area which contains it, nothing more, so that "Place is corporeal—a motionless body—and what it contains cannot have motion." The inference is not that motion is impossible but that "All things are in God" (*ibid.*), evidently very much as a thought is in the mind. What corresponded to the modern idea of space in antiquity was the Stoic or Epicurean doctrine of the void, and this is explicitly denied (*CH* II, 10–12; *Ascl.* 34). Another characteristic tenet is that the good—and, supereminently, God—is incommunicable. When Tat achieves regeneration in *CH* XIII, the experience is mystical. Also, it must be borne steadily in mind that there is little (in most documents, no) thought of converting the public. The doctrine is esoteric, and the pious are repeatedly said to be few. According to *Ascl.* 22, they can be counted: *pauci, ita ut numerari etiam possint*. The attempts at open preaching made in *CH* I and VII are uncharacteristic. We have, however, lingered long enough on preliminaries. What has already been said will have indicated the method and something of the tone and will make unnecessary further insistence on the philosophical and theological, as opposed to a thaumaturgical or theurgical, tenor of the whole.

IV. Detailed analysis

Greater rational interest inheres in the ideas and attitudes the Hermetic authors started with and the mental processes by means of which they built up their substantive doctrines than in the doctrines, which modern readers are unlikely to find persuasive. Nevertheless the doctrines must be summarized in order to provide a means by which Hermetic influence on the Renaissance can be recognized. Many of the assumptions and mental habits persisted until, in "advanced" thought, they were challenged, and eventually overcome, by empirical procedures; but such a remark as Milton's about "those *Daemons* that are found/ In fire, air, flood, or under ground" (*Il Penseroso*, 93–94) may—or may not—imply a direct acquaintance with Hermetic sources. We shall consider, in turn, the Hermetic cosmology, theology, and anthropology.

The origin of the universe is described in *CH* I (and also in *CH* III and *Stob.* XXIII, the Κόρη Κόσμου; but these had less repute than the *Poimandres* from which the entire *Corpus* was frequently named). The unidentified narrator, presumably Hermes, while thinking about "beings" (ὄντων), found that his senses were suspended like those of a man in deep sleep. There appeared to him a huge figure who called him by name (not given) and said, "What do you want to hear and see, and learn to know by thought?" Asked who he was, the figure replied, "I am Poimandres, the Mind (Νοῦς) of absolute sovereignty." (This is not a claim that Poimandres is the highest god of all.) The writer said that he would like to be instructed about beings and to know God.

Poimandres changed his appearance, and suddenly a vision produced itself: a limitless expanse of light, joyous and serene. Soon an obscurity followed, tending downward in the form of spirals, like a serpent; and this, in turn, became a sort of "wet nature" (ὑγρὰν τινα φύσιν) which heaved and gave forth a vapor like smoke, at the same time uttering a groan. Then came an unarticulated cry like a voice from fire itself, and, emerging from the light, a holy word covered Nature while fire leaped out of the dampness toward the higher region and air followed it, leaving the earth and water in such a way as to appear suspended from fire, the fire and earth meanwhile remaining mingled, shaking under the breath of the Word.

Poimandres's explanation follows. The light, he says, is himself, Mind, "your God," who existed before the dampness and appeared out of the darkness. The Word which issued from Mind is the Son of God (a passage which Renaissance commentators were quick to reconcile with Christianity); and the two are not divided, for their union is Life.

"Fix your spirit on the light," said Poimandres; and he looked directly at Hermes for a time. By thought, rather than sight, Hermes perceived a light which consisted in an immense number of "powers" (δυνάμεσιν) and became a limitless world, except that the fire now appeared to be constrained by force into a fixed position. Poimandres said, "You have seen in mind (or thought) the archetypal form (εἶδος) or first principle which preceded the beginnings of things and is boundless." The elements of nature have proceeded from God's will, which saw and imitated the beautiful archetype of the world, making the cosmos orderly and fit to produce souls. God the Mind, being both male and female and existing as life and light, by a word gave birth to a second God, the Demiurge, which then, being a god of breath (πνεύματος) and fire, made seven governors (the planets) that circled about the perceptible world; and their rule was called Destiny or Εἱμαρμένη (for which the Latin translation is *Fortuna*).

At once the Word left the downward-tending elements to mount to the pure upper area, and there it united itself to the Demiurge-Mind, with which its substance was identical, and so left the inferior elements to be simple matter not endowed with rationality. Together with the Word, the Demiurge-Mind next set the spheres to turning; and this movement, as Mind wished, produced irrational animals, making them of the lower elements (earth and water), and caused the air to produce birds and the water fish. Earth and water now being separated by the desire of Mind, the earth produced quadrupeds and reptiles.

Next Mind, the Father of all beings, engendered a Man like himself, and loved him, and gave him all that had been produced; for the man was beautiful, reproducing his Father's image, since God was amorous of His own image. When man saw creation he wanted to produce something himself; and the Father gave him permission. The governors also loved him and gave him power, each of his own kind. Man then broke through the frame of the sphere (Scott thought this was the sphere of the moon), and his likeness showed God's beautiful form to lower nature. Nature saw the reflection of this form in the water and its shadow on the earth and smiled with love; and man loved the reflection and wanted to dwell with it. At once his will was accomplished, and he inhabited irrational form (ἄλογον μορφὴν), being totally mingled with nature. This is why man alone of all beings has a double nature and is mortal in his body but immortal in his human part. He also was male and female; and so were the governors, so that Nature, being unable to wait, immediately produced seven men, also bisexual, who corresponded to the natures of the seven governors. The female element in them was earth, the male element water. Man himself, being life and light, underwent a change, life becoming soul and light mind. And thus things remained until the end of the first age (μέχρι περιόδου τέλους).

That period being over, God broke the bond which united all things, and male and female were separated in both man and animals. At once God said, "Increase and multiply (Αὐξάνεσθε ἐν αὐξήσει καὶ πληθύνεσθε ἐν πλήθει), and let beings with intellect recognize themselves as immortal; and let them know that the cause of death is love (τὸν αἴτιον τοῦ θανάτου ἔρωτα), and let them know all beings." Thus Providence, with the help of Destiny, established the generations, each person who knew himself arriving at his chosen good, and each who loved the body tarrying in obscurity and suffering what belongs to death. And Hermes understood that the body originates in darkness (or obscurity) and lives in a sensible form that finally dies, whereas the one who knows himself realizes that he issues from the Father of All.

There was a puzzle in this recognition, and Hermes inquired whether all men do not have mind (so that they will know themselves, etc.). By no means, came the answer; mind belongs to those who are good, merciful, and pious, love the Father, and thank Him in blessings and hymns. Such men hate their senses, and Poimandres will prevent their bodies from doing them harm. But those without intelligence (ἀνοήτοις), the vicious, the impious, will be exposed to the vengeful daemon, who will prick them on to more evil that they may receive a greater punishment.

Hermes next wished to be instructed about the "way up." First of all, Poimandres replied, the body is delivered to change (death), and the usual self is given over to the daemon. The senses return to their sources and are reabsorbed, except that irascibility and concupiscence go off to irrational nature. Thus man throws himself upward toward the spheres and is purged of a different vice as he passes through each. Finally, possessing only his own power, he enters the eighth or Ogdoad and enters the hymning choir, hearing also the songs of Powers which dwell higher still. Mounting thus toward the Father, he himself at length can become a Power and enter into God.

Having said so much, Poimandres himself mingled with the Powers under the eye of Hermes, and Hermes began to preach to men about what he had learned.

I have dwelt at perhaps excessive length on *CH* I because a Renaissance man who read any part of the newly discovered *Corpus* must have read that, and because the prestige of *Libellus* I resulted in the giving of its title to the whole *opus*. Also, many of the Christian parallels which helped produce the concept of the *una prisca theologia ubique sibi consona* will have been evident. If the *libellus* is not limited to cosmology and therefore exceeds the present topic, it none the less has the advantage of presenting directly or indirectly several themes to be noticed later.

We must now shift our attention to the structure of the completed universe (κόσμος in the Greek texts, *mundus* in the *Asclepius*).

The universe, we gather from indirections, is spherical in shape. God—the High God, *summus deus*—is outside it, in "a place without stars and lacking corporeality" (*est enim ultra caelum locus sine stellis ab omnibus rebus corpulentis alienus, Ascl.* 27). Beneath Him is a "body which surrounds the whole world" (περιεκτικὸν τῶν ἁπάντων εἶναι σῶμα, Stob. VI, 3), apparently something like the shell of the Ptolemaic universe. Inside this are the Thirty-Six Decans (*ibid.*), whose talismanic representations, in human form, were known to the Renaissance; each presided over ten degrees of the cosmic sphere. Alternatively, the decans are stationed within the sphere of the fixed stars (*XXXVI, quorum uocabulum est Horoscopi, id est eodem loco semper defixorum siderum, Ascl.* 19). The duty of the decans is to support the exterior envelope, restrain the envelope's speed, and hasten the movements of the planets (*Stob.* VI, 3–4). They thus "preside" over everything and maintain cosmic order. They also influence men's affairs collectively and individually and cause large social events such as changes of kings, famines, pestilences, floods, and earthquakes (*Stob.* VI, 8). In doing this they are aided by servants whom they themselves engender. These have the shapes of stars and act as soldiers, producing, it seems, only malevolent actions (*Stob.* VI, 12).

Next in order—if separate from the sphere of the decans—comes the sphere of the fixed stars. From the stars, and especially from the zodiacal signs, astrological influences rain down on the earth. Inside the stars are the spheres of the sun, the five planets, and the moon. The sun is sometimes made out to be very important, as it is in astrology. According to *CH* XVI, it sends down substance (οὐσίαν) and draws up matter; its light illuminates both the upper sky and the lower earth; like a chariot driver, it assures the world's stability, using as reins life, the soul, breath, immortality, and generation (*CH* XVI, 5–7). As an agent of God, it also makes things, assigning eternal duration to the immortals and vivifying by its light what is below; and it causes changes and metamorphoses (*ibid.,* 8). Around it are many choirs of daemons, who perform the gods' commands, again especially in punishing men (*ibid.,* 10). When a form fails, the sun reabsorbs it (*ibid.,* 12); and if the reasonable part of the soul receives light from the sun, the daemons are powerless against it (*ibid.*, 15–16). Yet it should be remembered that the sun lacks real autonomy. It "receives from God the good which is its creative activity," so that "God is the Father of everything, the sun the creator, and the world the instrument of creation" (*ibid.*, 17–18).

This brings us down to the sphere of the moon; and so far, aside from the decans and perhaps the daemons' functions, little will be unfamiliar. The essentials of the physical cosmology go back far beyond Hermetism, as do the daemons, which we have seen to be vestigial from the *numina* men in a low stage of intellectual development sense everywhere; and the decans are "hermetic" only if the word is given the extended meaning which has been renounced in the present discussion.

The earth of course sits at the center. According to a description in *Stob.* XXV, 11–13, it is surrounded by four general divisions of space and sixty subdivisions. The division nearest the earth has four subdivisions and extends no higher than the highest mountains. The next division has eight; in these the birds fly and the air moves. The third division has sixteen subdivisions and is filled with a subtle air; the fourth and last has thirty-two subdivisions and contains an air which is absolutely unmixed and transparent. The highest subdivision borders on the high heavens (the sphere of the moon? that of the fixed stars?), which are igneous. The subdivisions evidently relate to the sixty orders of souls which are described in the Κόρη Κόσμου (*Stob.* XXIII, 14–16) as having been created out of sixty layers of the primordial matter produced by God, with holy incantations, from breath and fire, each of the layers being inferior to the preceding one.

These are the essentials of the physical structure of the universe, plus hints of divine forces without which it was impossible for the Hermetists to compose their vision. The elements are the usual four—earth, water, air, and fire—plus, here and there, mention of a fifth, aether, and of breath (πνεῦμα), which perhaps may be identified with air.

And how was the universe governed? What were its laws? The questions provide a transition to Hermetic theology.

At the top of the hierarchy is God, called usually θεός but sometimes ὁ κύριος, the Lord, or, in the *Asclepius, deus* or *summus deus*. His ascendancy is unquestioned, and it was to Him that virtually all worship was to be directed. The polytheism of the documents is consistently contradicted by a tendency to offer intense piety only toward the apex of the cumbersome system of divinities which is so frequently and exhaustively explained. Immediately beneath the High God comes the Creator God who is His Word or Son—but only according to *CH* I, the *Poimandres*. Elsewhere the "luminous Word issued from Mind who is the Son of God" (ὁ δὲ ἐκ Νοὸς φωτεινὸς λόγος υἱὸς θεοῦ, *CH* I, 6) is missing; but in many places we are told that the cosmos or world is the Second or Visible God, and in the *Poimandres* we hear also of the Demiurge Mind as a second god. God Himself is the good (τὸ ἀναθὸν, *CH* II, 15) and is distinct from mind, which emanates from Him (*CH* II, 14), as does also truth (*CH* II, 12). He is everything that exists (οὐδέν ἐστιν οὗτος ὅ δ' οὐκ ἐστι), the visible and the invisible, what the mind contemplates and what the eyes see (*CH* V, 10). He is the bodiless and also the Omniform, hence has no name or all names (*CH* V, 10; *Ascl.* 20). The Second God or cosmos is inferior in being beautiful but not good and in being subject to becoming. Nevertheless it was difficult for the Hermetists to avoid imputing mind to the Second God also. The world, we are told, is a head (κεφαλή). The cosmos is round; the roundness suggests a human head, and the head suggests intelligence, so that what is nearer the circumference of the universe consists more of soul than of body (*CH* X, 11). If the Second God is eternally creative, he is so by participation in the High God. God's function, we learn, is creating, and He cannot stop creating (*CH* XI, 13); but He performs His work by willing (*CH* X, 2), and what He wills the universe or Second God creates. In the main, the Second God is simply the visible universe, which by its beauty and orderliness implies the existence of a creator. The Creator must be single, since if there were two creators, or several, they would be jealous of each other and would try to usurp each other's functions (*CH* XI, 9). That a single God should create life, the soul, immortality, and change is no more wonderful than that a man should see, speak, hear, smell, touch, walk, think, and breathe (*CH* XI, 12). Again, if the same painter can paint sky, gods, earth, sea, men, and objects which lack reason and soul, is it not possible to God to make everything (*CH* XIV, 8)? God is like a sower who sows barley here, wheat there, something else in another place (*CH* XIV, 9–10). The universe is constantly in movement and eternally creates, reabsorbs, recombines. We regard it properly with awe and gratitude but should refer our profoundest veneration to the unseen Principle that lies behind it and, like an earthly monarch, issues orders carried out by subordinates who themselves possess great dignity.

   This is the place at which a comment can most appropriately be made about a statement of which much has been made by persons who have written—for example —about Hermetic influences on Thomas and Henry Vaughan. *Asclepius* 20 says that God is filled with the fecundity of both sexes (*utraque sexus fecunditate plenissimus*) and, being constantly pregnant in will, gives birth constantly to whatever He wishes to procreate. The doctrine, however, is not emphasized in the *Hermetica,* and it is immediately followed (*Ascl.* 21) by the assertion that all animate and inanimate beings are also bisexual. The Christian God too might be said to be bisexual in this sense, since He created without a female partner; and Adam, we remember, was divided into a man and a woman. *Asclepius* 21 goes on to praise human generation, in the course of which "the females acquire the males' strength and the males grow weary in feminine torpor" (*et uirtutem feminae marum adipiscuntur et mares femineo torpore lassescunt*). Andryogny, if thus technically a characteristic of God, has a reflection in human beings and bears no weight in most of the documents.

Below the First and Second Gods the hierarchy is complex and not wholly consistent. According to *Ascl.* 19, the οὐσιάρχης or Dominant Being of the heavens is Jupiter. Elsewhere the sun is given primacy (e. g., *CH* XVI, 4–5); but the description of the decans in *Stob.* VI, especially, seems hardly to allow their subordination to anything below the First and Second Gods. Except for astrological influences and the daemons, to which I shall recur in a moment, below this level there is confusion. Egyptian gods—Isis, Horus, and the great Hermes or Thoth—appear in the Κόρη Κόσμου (*Stob.* XXIII), which is concerned with the making of the universe and its creatures. So also do the Greek Kronos, Zeus, Ares, and Aphrodite, plus, on a lower plane, a rich miscellany of personified abstractions like Nature, Invention, Terror, Silence, Sleep, Memory, Justice, Necessity, Fortune, Hope, Peace, Contest, Anger, Quarrel, Love, Adrasteia or Nemesis, and even the Elements. Of the abstractions, Necessity, Fortune, and Destiny are most strongly emphasized in the *Hermetica* as a whole. *Fortuna* appears in *Ascl.* 19, along with the air, through which all things are made, as an οὐσιάρχης of the seven planets. In *Ascl.* 39 Ἑιμαρμένη, Fortune or Destiny, is said to be either the cause of all things (*effectrix rerum*) or the Supreme God or the Second God made by the Supreme God or the order of all heavenly and earthly things fixed by divine laws. Destiny is prior to Necessity and gives birth to the beginnings of things; Necessity drives them to the ends which follow from the beginnings; and Order maintains the connection of what Destiny and Necessity have disposed. But there are accident and chance mixed with whatever is earthly (*Ascl.* 40). A tendency to see divinity everywhere has generated a hospitality to all the Egyptian, Greek, and Roman gods whose names were current at the time the documents were written. The effort to arrange them all in a hierarchically subordinated series did not succeed; but it went almost without saying that everything must be linked in a continuous chain (*necessitas omnium quae geruntur, semper sibi catenatis nexibus uincta, Ascl.* 39). No other basis for order than hierarchy was conceivable.

We return to the heavenly bodies and the daemons, which often seem to be related as force and agent. We are told in *CH* XVI, 10 that the daemons act immediately as the sun's agents, but ultimately as God's, in punishing men's impiety by means of storms, earthquakes, famines, wars, and other afflictions. They cause trouble generally for cities and nations (*CH* XVI, 14) but also for individuals. They mold our souls, being seated in our muscles, marrow, blood vessels, brains, and even our entrails; for when we are born we are put under the charge of the daemons who preside over that astrological moment. They replace each other constantly, each working in its own way. Our reason, however, is not under their power and remains free to know God (*ibid.*, 14–15). The individual is what he is, as regards the "form" which is constituted by the combination of his corporeal and incorporeal elements, in consequence of the time of his birth (*Ascl.* 35). Identical forms cannot be engendered at different times and places because the forms change as often as an hour has minutes within the revolving circle of the god who is called the Omniform (*ibid.*). The daemons are also subject to the commands of the stars, whose groups or squares (πλινθίδας) they serve in equal numbers (*CH* XVI, 13). Festugière's brief summary, "Dieu administre le monde par l'intermédiaire du soleil et des démons (serviteurs des astres)" (I, 228) is thus accurate. As God's ministers, the daemons deserve a certain reverence; and we have seen (*Ascl.* 37) that they can be constrained to dwell in idols and serve men. *CH* XVII defends the worship of such idols on the ground that as the incorporeal can be reflected in the corporeal, so the intelligible world can be reflected in the sensible world: "Hence do obeisance to the statues, O King, since they contain the forms (ἰδέας) of the intelligible world." An Agathos Daimon, or Good Daemon—apparently always the same one—is mentioned in several places (for example, *CH* XII, 1), and *CH* XVI, 13 says that some daemons consist of mingled good and evil. Nevertheless the tendency is to offer the daemons a respect not strongly toned with cordiality. In *CH* IX, 3 they are regarded as wholly bad: the purposes (νοήματα) aroused by them in men have to do with adulteries, murders, the abuse of parents, sacrileges, impieties, suicides, "and everything else which is the work of daemons" (καὶ ἄλλα πάντα ὅσα δαιμόνων ἔργα). Evidently their forces were exerted upon men's bodies, which as material substances were thought contemptible. Since they could not affect mind, the hope was that if the mind was raised above physicality malevolent pressures originating in the stars and mediated by the daemons could be evaded.

One more comment may be added because it suggests the predisposition which underlay the whole theory of daemons. Again and again we are told that the whole world is alive. "If therefore the world is always a living animal—was, and is, and will be—nothing in the world is mortal. Since every single part, such as it is, is always living and is in a world which is always one and always a living animal, there is no place in the world for death" (*Ascl.* 29). When, in our own day, C. S. Lewis's fictive character Ransom first traveled through space, the word "space," the reader is told, was "a blasphemous libel for this empyrean ocean of radiance in which they swam. He could not call it 'dead'; he felt life pouring into him from it every minute." [30] The Hermetic universe was similarly vitalistic, permeated with life. So is the universe of the low savage, the *Naturmensch;* but long before the second and third centuries of our era the primitive belief had been rationalized.

Man's theological duties are contemplation of the High God and the piety which is its inevitable accompaniment. Although theoretically man should tend the earth, having been created partly for that purpose, the impression is given that the philosopher can safely delegate this responsibility to others. The man who has achieved *gnosis*—the good man—expounds his esoteric doctrine to one, two, or three disciples at a time, often concluding the sessions with prayer or praise, but he is not seen watering a garden or leading the vine to wed her elm. Neither need he devote much energy to the general service of mankind. *Stobaeus* IIB begins, "I compose this treatise, O child, especially for love of man and piety toward God"; but when Tat asks "How can we live well?" the immediate reply is "Be pious, O child; he who is most pious will philosophize." Philosophizing, Hermes adds, consists of understanding existent beings, their orders, and by whom and why they exist. The acquisition of understanding will result in the giving of thanks, and this in piety (*Stob.* IIB, 1–2). The theological duties of men—of which, however, only a few are capable by reason of their contempt of sensory pleasures—are thus comprised in the activities of knowing and adoring. The process of coming to know appears to consist chiefly of looking, thinking, and waiting for revelation. Nowhere is a disciple enjoined to read a section of Plato's *Timaeus* or an *Ennead* of Plotinus for the next day's assignment. As yet, research was undertaken rather by a compiler like Cicero or Pliny than by the master who already knew.

As piety is the highest theological virtue, impiety is the worst of all crimes. The gods, we are told, take account of no sin which may be committed through error, Destiny, or ignorance, but impiety falls under their judgment (*CH* XVI, 11). How little social orientation the theology had is suggested by a question and answer in *Asclepius* 29: "What persons deserve the greatest punishment?" "Those who lose their lives violently because they are condemned by human laws and seem to have returned their souls to nature not as something owed but as a punishment for their deserts." The gods make no assumption that their moral discriminations are superior to those of men. Yet in *Stobaeus* VII we learn that justice is administered by a great daemon who sits at the center of the universe to watch men and punish their crimes, and in *Asclepius* 28 we are told that mortals will be the more subject to punishment in proportion as their transgressions have remained hidden, divine omniscience fitting the penalty to the quality of the trespasses.

Eschatology might be treated as an aspect of theology but can also be discussed in connection with a doctrine of man, to which we now turn. Since the total theory is complex and not entirely self-consistent, we must again confine ourselves to an effort to perceive general outlines.

Stobaeus XXVI, 1, "Of Incarnation and Reincarnation," describes the sources whence human souls come. These are the sixty regions mentioned earlier. Royal souls come from the highest region, those of lowest rank from the lowest regions, and others from in between. (Again there is no perception of human injustice. Every man deserves the station he occupies.) An easy inference suggests that the souls are made from the sixty layers of the finer and purer (λεπτότερα καὶ τε καθαρωτέρα) matter which boiled to the surface of the mixture of breath and fire stirred by God in *Stobaeus* XXIII, 14–16. A Keeper of Souls (ψυχοταμίας) has charge of unembodied souls, and an Escort of Souls (ψυχοπομπός) assigns them their places (*Stob.* XXVI, 3). The bodies which are to receive the souls are varied appropriately, the receptacles of lively souls being made lively, those of lazy souls being made lazy, and so on (*ibid.*, 4). Birds are appropriately furnished with wings, quadrupeds with horns, teeth, claws, and hooves; reptiles are given soft bodies so that they may glide, and because an excess of water makes them feeble they are given rows of teeth or spined armor (*ibid.*, 5). Souls endowed with judgment are embodied in human forms (*ibid.*, 6). Specific classes of souls are ruled by special gods. The king of the souls of the dead is Osiris; the king of medicine is the first Asclepius, son of Hephaestus; the king of counsel (βουλῆς) is Hermes himself; the king of philosophy is Har-neb-eschenis (*ibid.*, 9). Souls which come from the region of fire work with fire and nourishment; those which come from moist zones become sailors (*ibid.*, 11). Bodily qualities result from the mixture of the elements. For example, an excess of air causes the body to be light, bouncy, unstable (*ibid.*, 15). The souls of men contain much fire, little air, and equal amounts of water and earth, the excess of heat becoming intelligence (*ibid.*, 20). This scheme is developed at some length. Health, we are told, depends on the preservation of the elements in their original proportions (*ibid.*, 25).

Accordingly, from one point of view man is a single kind of creature among many, all of whom are endowed with souls. As in primitive cultures—totemism is a common institutional manifestation—nature is believed to be unitary. Pessimistic conclusions can be, and sometimes are, drawn from this premise. *CH* VIII seems to deny personal immortality on the grounds that at death the human body is resolved into its elements, which are then recombined: "thus a privation of perception occurs, but not a destruction of the bodies" (καὶ ὄντω στέρησις γίνεται τῆς αἰσθήσεος, ὀυκ ἀπώλεια τῶν σώματων, *CH* VIII, 4). Since this sentence is followed, however, by the phrase "The third living creature is man" (*CH* VIII, 5), the intention may not be to deny human consciousness after death. In any event, the view of man projected by the *Hermetica* as a body is so optimistic as to permit suspicion that the Renaissance exaltation of man (as in Hamlet's "What a piece of work is a man!") may have been given impetus by the currency of the documents which Ficino translated. The pessimism of *CH* II (only God is good, and it is an impiety to call even other gods good, *CH* II, 14) and of *CH* VI (man is wholly bad, and what appears good in him is only less bad, *CH* VI, 3) is balanced, and overbalanced, by a doctrine so positive as not merely to encourage but even to exhilarate.

The *locus classicus* of this view in the *Hermetica* is *Asclepius* 6:

Wherefore, O Asclepius, man is a great wonder—an animal worthy of adoration and honor. He passes into the nature of a god as if he were himself a god; he knows the race of daemons, inasmuch as he is aware that he has the same origin with them; he despises the purely human element in himself, trusting in the divinity of the other part. O how much more happily is man's nature composed! He is joined with the gods by his shared divinity; he despises within himself the part that makes him earthly; he binds to himself by a knot of love (*caritatis*) all the other things to which he knows he has been made necessary by heavenly disposing; he looks up at the sky. Thus he is placed happily in a middle position so that he might love what is below him and be loved by those who are above. He takes care of (*colit*) the earth; by the speed (of his thought) he is mingled with the elements; by the sharpness of his mind he probes the depths of the sea. Everything is permitted to him; he does not find the heaven too high, for he measures it as if from nearby with the shrewdness of his mind. No mist in the air confuses his straining intelligence; the compactness of the earth does not impede his work; the profound depth of the water does not dull his view. He is everything at once, and everywhere.

By virtue of his middle position man has a double nature. In part he resembles God, in part he is material. After the Creator God had made the cosmos and saw it to be good, He formed man to contemplate it and gave him a body that he might minister to it (*ibid.*, 7–8). Hence man's dual composition of reason and matter. He is able to wonder at God and the heavenly beings, to adore and obey them; but individual men who are weighed down by the lower elements are assigned a caretaker's duty (*curandis elementis hisque inferioribus, ibid., 9*).

In virtue of this special position man is a third god, having a dignity immediately below that of the Lord of Eternity and of the world (*ibid.*, 10). As a composite being, he can rise by mind and spirit to a kind of divinity or be pulled down by his earthly part to animality. His good is piety and contempt of what satisfies his material part. He is, in fact, "man" in an honorific sense only if he scorns sense and possessions. At best, he can lose his mortality and become wholly godlike; and this can occur even before death. *CH* XIII describes Tat's regeneration ($\pi\alpha\lambda\iota\gamma\gamma\epsilon\nu\epsilon\sigma\acute{\iota}\alpha$), as a result of which he attains knowledge of joy ($\gamma\nu\hat{\omega}\sigma\iota\varsigma\ \chi\alpha\rho\hat{\alpha}\varsigma$, *CH* XIII, 8), becomes steadfast ($\acute{\alpha}\kappa\lambda\iota\nu\acute{\eta}\varsigma$), and perceives things not with his eyes but with the intellectual energy he obtains from the Powers (*CH* XIII, 11). Trismegistus, we are told by the same document (*ibid.*, 3), has progressed so far that although he appears outwardly the same in fact he no longer has color, the sense of touch—i. e., tangibility—or extension in space ($\mu\acute{\epsilon}\tau\rho\sigma\nu$).

CH XII contains the same positive doctrine. Mind ($\nu\sigma\hat{\nu}\varsigma$) is drawn from God's substance, not by being cut off from Him but by emanation from Him, and in men is itself God, so that some men are gods or very near to deity in their humanity ($\sigma\hat{\nu}\tau\sigma\varsigma\ \delta\grave{\epsilon}\ \acute{\sigma}\ \nu\sigma\hat{\nu}\varsigma\ \acute{\epsilon}\nu\ \mu\grave{\epsilon}\nu\ \acute{\alpha}\nu\theta\rho\acute{\omega}\pi\sigma\iota\varsigma\ \theta\epsilon\acute{\sigma}\varsigma\ \acute{\epsilon}\sigma\tau\iota\cdot\ \delta\iota\grave{\sigma}\ \kappa\alpha\grave{\iota}\ \tau\iota\nu\epsilon\varsigma\ \tau\hat{\omega}\nu\ \acute{\alpha}\nu\theta\rho\acute{\omega}\pi\omega\nu\ \theta\epsilon\sigma\acute{\iota}\ \epsilon\acute{\iota}\sigma\iota,$

CH XII, 1). After death men can become actual gods. The ancestor of Hermes's disciple Asclepius even now aids suffering men by his divine power as god of medicine, and Hermes's own ancestor, the greater Hermes, dwells in his native city giving help to everyone who calls upon him (*Ascl.* 37). Everything in the universe is alive, and everything has a soul (ψυχή, *anima*); but in animals the souls consist of irascibility and concupiscence, and in beings without consciousness they are external to the bodies they move and remain a part of the divine body (*Stob.* III, 8–9). To man alone is given the capacity to become divine; and pious men, in consequence, are in a sense even better than the gods (*per uoluntatem dei hominem constitutum esse meliorem et diis, Ascl.* 22). One sign of this superiority is man's ability to make gods: and there follows the famous passage about idols (*Ascl.* 23–24).

Among men, it may be added, Egyptians are particularly favored. (This claim is one of the few clear signs that the *Hermetica,* although written in Greek, had an Egyptian origin.) In *Stobaeus* XXIV, 11, Horus asks his mother Isis, "By what cause, Mother, do men who live outside our most holy place lack our quickness of apprehension?" The reply might have been included in the section on cosmology but fits here also because it bears on the satisfaction Egyptian Hermetists might feel in their human situation.

The earth, we are informed, lies on its back in the center of the universe facing the heaven in order that it may make adjustments in itself suitable to those in the sky. It has as many parts as a man's body has members. Its head is in the south, its right shoulder in the east, its feet under the Great Bear, its middle parts in the middle. This is proved by the fact that southerners have well-developed heads and handsome hair, easterners are prone to attack and are archers (i. e., are right-handed), westerners usually fight with their left hands, northerners have well-turned legs, and the Italians and Hellenes, who adjoin them, have good thighs and buttocks, for which reason their men are homosexual. The most holy land of our ancestors, however (says Isis), lies in the middle of the earth; and since the heart is the region of the soul, Egyptians, without being inferior in other respects, are exceptionally intelligent and wise. The climate is also advantageous, being constantly serene. Consequently the Egyptians are in all respects superior and, like a good satrap, share their victories with the conquered. (For the whole passage see *Stob.* XXIV, 11–15). The sharing presumably extends to the Hermetic philosophy; but we must not forget the constant exhortations to secrecy and the insistence (for example, in *CH* X, 24) that not all men possess mind. This is one reason why even in Egypt those who have *gnosis* are sometimes laughed at, hated, and despised (*CH* IX, 4) and in the future will be virtually exterminated (*Ascl.* 24–25). The threat offered to the intellect by man's material part is constant.

Is God responsible for the threat? No—evil of every kind is like rust on metal or dirt on the skin and results from duration in time. Evil and ugliness cannot be laid to God's account; on the contrary, He has provided for change in order that created nature might constantly be purified (*CH* XIV, 7). In addition, man possesses a limited free will. In becoming attached to a human body, the soul becomes irascible and concupiscent; but these qualities can be managed in such a way that irascibility becomes courage and concupiscence becomes temperance. These two qualities, in turn, by their union produce justice (*Stob.* XVII, 1–3). Despite the pressure of astrological influences on the body and the presence of daemons in all his organs, the reasonable part of the human soul can become the receptacle of God (*CH* XVI, 13–15). Ἑιμαρμένη or Destiny governs all human actions, so that the rational man (ὁ ἐλλόγιμος) who has not committed adultery or murder will suffer as if he were guilty of it; but he can prevent the suffering from being an evil by withdrawing his soul from pleasure, which is the source of spiritual disease (*CH* XII, 5–7, 3).

The purification just mentioned proceeds, so far as men are concerned, by means of death, the recombination of the corporeal elements into other bodies, and the transmigration or deification of the soul. Transmigration (metamorphosis, metempsychosis) is conceived differently in different documents. *CH* X tells us that every soul, once it is parted from total soul (μιᾶς ψυχῆς), enters upon a series of changes, some souls moving upwards, others downwards. Creeping souls pass into aquatic animals, aquatic souls into terrestrial animals, terrestrial souls into birds, aerial souls into men, and human souls into daemons, to end finally in the choir of gods, either that of the planets or that of the stars. This is the upward path. If, however, the human soul is vicious, it runs the same course in the opposite direction. The vice which presses the soul downward is ignorance; the virtue which lifts it is *gnosis* (*CH* X, 7–9). A later passage of the same fragment runs directly counter to this doctrine: the impious soul hunts for another body to enter, but the body must be human, for the divine order prohibits the human soul from being embodied in an irrational animal (*CH* X, 19). Such a contradiction within a single *libellus* indicates vividly the composite nature of the documents as we have them.

A final, or at least very advanced, stage of illumination is described in *CH* XIII, which contains the account of Tat's palingenesis or regeneration. Hermes, who acts as his sponsor, as it were—not his teacher, for rebirth cannot be taught—has already, as was remarked earlier, entered into an immortal body and been born into mind, so that he is less material than he appears (*CH* XIII, 3). The agent of rebirth is the Son of God, the One Man (ὁ τοῦ θεοῦ παῖς, ἄνθρωπος εἷς, *CH* XIII, 4; Festugière translates "un homme comme les autres"), but the effective cause is apparently the will of God (τοῦ θελήματος τοῦ θεοῦ, *CH* XIII, 2). Tat's rebirth is shown in process; and it is preceded merely by a question, "Am I, then, incapable of it, Father?" and the reply, "Hush now, child, and observe a reverent silence, so that God's pity may not be kept from us" (*CH* XIII, 7, 8). There is no theurgy, no sacramental action performed to constrain or invite the experience.[31]

What follows, in a confusingly numbered series (*CH* XIII, 8–9) which is incomplete but can be worked out as far as it goes, is an invasion of powers. (1) Knowledge descends and drives out ignorance. (2) Joy drives out sadness. (3) Continence replaces incontinence. (4) Endurance or Patience (καρτερίαν) expels concupiscence. (5) Justice replaces injustice. (6) Communion or Fellowship (κοινωνίαν—Festugière translates "la bonté qui partage") drives out cupidity. (7) Truth drives out cheating or fraud (ἀπάτη). This schedule gives us clearly enough seven of the twelve punishments of matter (*CH* XIII, 7); and the five which remain—Envy, Deceit (δόλος), Anger, Rashness, and Baseness or Malice (κακία—Festugière, *méchanceté*) have already been enumerated in Paragraph 7. The remaining three good powers, Good (τὸ ἀγαθόν), Life, and Light, complete the catalogue in Paragraph 9, but without being contrasted to specific Punishments.

The reason for the breakdown of the numbered series may be guessed from what follows in Paragraph 10. Hermes explains that the coming of the Decade has resulted in intellectual birth (νοερὰ γένεσις) and has driven away the Dodecade. Although now made steadfast by God and capable of perceiving not by his eyes but by the intellectual energy he has received from the Powers, Tat inquires naturally enough how it happens that twelve Punishments can be expelled by only ten Powers (*ibid.*, 11). The reply, given in Paragraph 12, associates the Twelve with the zodiacal signs, which, however, form pairs: for example, Rashness is inseparable from Anger, and one may suppose that Fraud and Deceit are also associated. A deeper explanation, which follows immediately, is that the Decade is a magical number: Unity contains the Decade, and the Decade contains Unity. Possibly the obscuring of the last five Punishments and the grouping of the last three Powers results from a difficulty in working out the details of the system.

CH I, the *Poimandres,* contains a different list and suggests a further reason why the enumeration in *CH* XIII ended with the seventh vice. In Paragraph 25 the man whose physical envelope has been dissolved rises through the seven spheres toward the Ogdoad, or eighth, where (*ibid.*, 26) he will sing hymns to the Father; and as he passes through each he leaves behind some of his bad human characteristics. In the first zone he abandons his power of growth and decrease, in the second his Deceit, in the third his covetous Fraud, in the fourth his Aspiration to Rule, in the fifth his Wicked Daring and Bold Rashness, in the sixth his Evil Resources of Wealth (τὰς ἀφορμὰς τὰς κακὰς τοῦ πλουτοῦ), and in the seventh his Plotting Falsehood (ἐνεδρεῦον ψεῦδος). The coincidences of this schedule with that in *CH* XIII are of the slightest; Fraud, Rashness, and Deceit appear in both lists, but in different places. The seven degrees of enlightenment in Mithraism, which appear to be related to the seven spheres, offer an obvious parallel, and the breakdown of the attempt to oppose Powers to Punishments—or Virtues to Vices—may reflect an inability to adjust the notion of the Decade and Dodecade together to the number of spheres through which the illuminated soul ascends to blessedness.

Such is the experience of regeneration, which comprises both what we should call illumination and what we should call salvation. Once rebirth has occurred, the use of the senses is suspended in favor of sheer intellection. It would be correct, I think, to say that intuitive knowledge, or immediate understanding without reflection on observed phenomena, has replaced discursive thought. And the higher state, once attained, is permanent. Will his new body, asks Tat, made up as it is of Powers, suffer dissolution? "Hush!" comes the answer. "Do not speak the impossible." Tat has become a god and a son of the One ($\theta\epsilon\grave{o}s \ \pi\acute{\epsilon}\phi\upsilon\kappa\alpha s \ \kappa\alpha\grave{i} \ \tau o\hat{\upsilon} \ \acute{\epsilon}\nu\grave{o}s \ \pi\alpha\hat{i}s$, *CH* XIII, 14). But it may be observed once more that readiness for the new birth is achieved not by theurgy and not by good works but by a piety which consists of an intense concentration of the mind on God and by a suspension of sensory observation which makes the initiate accessible to something not entirely different from Christian grace. When the rebirth has been completed, however, and a hymn of praise sung, Tat does not issue into the world to preach a gospel. On the contrary: he is to tell no one about his miraculous powers or the manner in which he has received them, lest both he and Hermes be numbered among the divulgers (*CH* XIII, 22).

V. Hermetic influence on the Continent

The impact of this body of doctrine upon the continental Renaissance deserves notice. Unlike references to astrology, witchcraft, magic, and alchemy, allusions to philosophical or theological Hermetism may slide across the reader's mind without attracting much attention. The system itself is not widely known, and what has little meaning is quickly forgotten. What follows includes only explicit references to Hermetism, and of them only a few are given. A fuller discussion might easily become a volume, though perhaps a volume of interest only to specialists.

That the Hermetic texts were frequently republished has already been said. Once the condemnation of the *Asclepius* by St. Augustine, which had made good Christians somewhat wary of it, was canceled out by the rediscovery of the *Corpus,* the tendency in some quarters was to regard the *Hermetica* as nearly, or occasionally quite, equal in authority to Holy Writ. The vogue reached its height in the fifty years on either side of 1500,[32] but continued strong well into the late sixteenth century and regained prominence from time to time until the 1650s, after which it subsided. At Siena the cathedral pavement bore an image of Hermes with the inscription "Hermes Mercurius Trismegistus Contemporaneus Moysi." At Florence sermons and official orations delivered from balconies called attention to him. "Priests, professors at universities, politicians, and charlatans," says Eugenio Garin, "invoked his authority at every step. That Leonardo jotted down his name does not appear strange." [33] Antonio Agli, Bishop of Fiesole and later of Volterra (d. 1477), cites the *Asclepius* in *De immortalitate animae*.[34] Such deference might, of course, evoke resistance. Johannes Pannonius charged Ficino with the revival of pagan theology, and Ficino's first biographer, Giovanni Corsi, thought that he had passed through a pagan period.[35] Nevertheless the influence was powerful.

> By the time of the *Protesto* of Pier Filippo Pandolfini, on July 13, 1475, we find that Hermes has substituted his own holy testimonies for the accustomed ones of Aristotle and St. Thomas; and the elder Dati refers to Trismegistus in his wandering official discourses. Hermetism took on the tone of a new religion, or at least a new way of interpreting Christianity and its universal operation in human history.[36]

The supposed pedigree of the documents, their association with the Egypt known by Moses, and parallels with Christianity—of the *Poimandres* with *Genesis*, of the Logos as Second God with the Son, and the like—were elements favoring an enthusiastic reception.

Among the early propagandizers was Giovanni Pico della Mirandola, whose association with Ficino was close. Many references to Hermes appear in the famous 900 propositions which he offered to defend against all comers at Rome in 1486. His *Oratio de hominis dignitate,* in its second sentence, quotes the *Magnum, O Asclepi, miraculum* passage and proceeds to argue, in basically Hermetic terms, that man is a mixed creature, formed by God to love and wonder at the universe, and capable both of sinking into animality and of rising to divinity. Whether Pico's devotion to Hermes survived his revulsion against astrology is uncertain, but the early support of a man who was learned, attractive, and of noble birth contributed to the system's prestige.

Ludovico Lazzarelli, roughly a contemporary, was even more radically Hermetic. He saluted Hermes in his *Vade Mecum* as "father of theologians, magicians, and alchemists" [37] and asserted elsewhere that, contrary to Ficino's opinion, "Hermes flourished not after the time of Moses . . . but rather long before Moses's age, as can be gathered clearly from the books of Diodorus." [38] In his *Calix Christi et crater Hermetis* (Paris, 1505) the deference shown to Hermes is extreme. Did not Hermes search all knowledge and leave documents to posterity, so that wisdom passed from him to the Hebrews through Moses, who is said in *Acts* to have been the best instructed of all Egyptians? Lazzarelli is not ashamed to be known as both a Hermetist and a Christian.[39] Of the ninety-two notes added by the modern editor to the *Calix,* thirty-one offer Hermetic sources and parallels; and Lazzarelli was also probably the author of the *Epistola Enoch,* to which we shall recur shortly.

Influences continue to appear. Champier Symphorien, a disciple of the French Faber Stapulensis, in 1507 published at Lyons a long, four-part work called *Commentaria in definitiones Asclepii* (i. e., *CH* XVI). In the first and last parts he argues that all Greek philosophy derives from Hermes.[40] Cornelius Agrippa cites Hermes scores of times in the *De occulta philosophia* (first dated edition 1533) and in an oration delivered at Pavia (*Oratio habita Papiae*[41]) took as his subject Hermes's "dialogues on wisdom and on the divine power."[42] Like Lazzarelli in the *Epistola Enoch,* he identifies Hermes with a grandson of Abraham, thus pushing the theology's antiquity back several generations beyond Moses's grandfather.[43] He cannot find enough innovations to impute to Hermes, whom he accredits with the discovery of writing, the giving of names to objects, the inventing of gymnasia, the originating of theology, the first cultivation of olive trees, and much else.[44] Although many of his citations are of the *Hermetica,* already the recovery of the *Corpus* had led to the resuscitation of other documents associated with Hermes, so that the distinguishing of the theological and philosophical Hermes from the alchemical, astrological, and magical one becomes increasingly difficult.[45] Still another vigorous Hermetist was Giorgio Veneto (or Zorzi), whose *De harmonia mundi,* published at Venice in 1525, is almost illimitably syncretic but grants a special pre-eminence to Hermes.[46] Veneto's efforts to reconcile Hermetic tenets with Biblical doctrines are sometimes especially quaint, as when he explains the Hermetic saying that mind comes from water as hinting at the Second Person of the Trinity, who "smacks of" or "tastes like" (*sapit*) water.[47]

A number of other names must be lumped together in a paragraph. Copernicus quoted Hermes on the sun as the visible God.[48] Agrippa d'Aubigné (1552–1630) and Marguerite of Navarre praised Hermes in poems.[49] Giordano Bruno, until recently thought a martyr to empirical science, has been proved by Frances Yates to have been primarily a magician who worked along what he thought were Hermetic lines.[50] Tommaso Campanella, as Miss Yates has also abundantly proved, was drenched in Hermetic ideas. Pontus de Tyard, Bishop of Châlons, quotes the holy Egyptian school;[51] and Athanasius Kircher praised Hermes in his *Oedipus Aegyptiacus* in 1652, long after Casaubon's demonstration that the documents were forged.[52] The most dramatic single appearance of Hermes on the public scene, however, came through one Giovanni Mercurio da Correggio, of whom the fullest single account is given by Lazzarelli in the *Epistola Enoch* previously mentioned.[53]

Giovanni's apparition is curious enough to merit a chapter to itself. On Palm Sunday, 1484, he appeared in Rome, clad very oddly in symbolic garments and attended by men similarly accoutered. On the banks of the Marana River he put on winged shoes (to indicate his identity with Hermes) and placed on his head a crown of thorns topped by a crescent moon on which was written an inscription beginning,

"This is my son Pimander, whom I have chosen" and ending "Thus speaks the Lord God and the Father of every talisman of the whole world, Jesus of Nazareth." After much more business, involving among other things the waving of a seven-jointed reed, the mounting of a rented white ass draped with symbolic objects, and a long speech which mingled Hermetic quotations with excerpts from the Bible, he distributed sheets containing what he had said and asserting in addition that he, Giovanni Mercurio of Correggio, was also "the angel of wisdom, Pimander, in the highest and greatest manifestation of the spirit of Jesus Christ." He then proceeded to the Vatican, stopping on the way to assert that he had descended from heaven with eternal majesty and power to judge the quick and the dead. At the Vatican, impressed or intimidated guards made way for him through curious crowds, so that he was able to lay his mystical garments and many of his symbolic trappings on the altar of St. Peter. Of the spectators, Lazzarelli says, some thought he was crazy, some guessed that he went through the rigamarole because of a vow, "but some truly, and more truly, acclaimed him as a prophet." [54] Lazzarelli appears himself to have been impressed and perhaps converted by Giovanni.

We see Giovanni also at other times and places: at Florence in 1486, where because of a suspicion of heresy he was put in the stocks; [55] breaking into a consistory of cardinals held at an uncertain date; and in Lyons, this time "with his wife and children, all . . . wearing a chain of iron about the neck." The king of France had Giovanni interrogated by his physicians and was informed that indeed he "knew more than other mortals." [56] He was not only dear to the French king but was protected by Lorenzo de' Medici and seems, indeed, to have created enough excitement possibly to have influenced the Church's discouragement of Hermetism after about 1490. But and this is the point Giovanni was not a grammarian or learned in oratory.[57] This is to say that he did not know Latin and could not have had access either to Ficino's translation of the *Corpus,* which appeared only thirteen years before the earliest of these events, or—unless he saw it in manuscript—to Benci's still unpublished Italian translation. Evidently the Hermetic influence was not limited to the scholarly world but filtered down among the populace, and that with surprising rapidity.

That a predisposition existed in all classes of society to take seriously what would seem to most of us to be a ludicrously pretentious symbolism suggests vividly an intellectual temper within which Hermetism could sink roots. The new gospel, apparently so easily assimilable to the old, had for a culture still given to syncretism and superstition and not yet ready to desert pure speculation for empirical science an attraction which, in spite of inevitable fluctuations, was to endure for another century and a half.

VI. Hermetic influence in England

We proceed finally to a consideration of Hermetic influence in England, looking, however, at a very few authors, and at them largely with the purpose of inviting reflection on a very important distinction between awareness and indebtedness. It is essential, in such studies, not to exaggerate, not to find in a new idea—particularly if it is esoteric, surprising, and so freshly discovered or re-emphasized that as yet little use has been made of it—a key to virtually every unsolved problem and a means to the re-interpretation of what is already accurately understood. I include this section partly in order to focus at last upon England but mostly because of uneasiness about possible responses to the present book. In my opinion no real service is done to scholarship by faddism, which swings wildly from one new interest to another, always overestimating the value of new insights in the total body of authentic knowledge. Although in the foregoing chapters I have documented the existence in the Renaissance of several occult systems, it has been no part of my intention to suggest that educated and intelligent men generally were engrossed by them and thought or wrote of little else. I begin with remarks about John Colet and Sir Thomas More, hoping to imply indirectly that commonplace ideas may in-cautiously be attributed to specific sources and that hints can be extrapolated much farther than the evidence justifies.

Colet (?1467–1510) had studied in Italy about the time of the elder Pico's death and refers to Pico's *Heptaplus* in *Letters to Radulphus on Genesis I.*[58] When he says that Moses mentioned fertility and vegetation before the stars in order to show that the stars did not determine the earth's fertility, it might be assumed that he has been prejudiced against astrology by a reading of Pico's *Adversus astrologiam*. Again, his remark that the inhabitants of the fire and air which are beneath the stars are called by profane authors *demones igneos et aerios*[59] might imply his acquaintance with the entire Hermetic doctrine of daemons. From this point the hope for discovery might generate a belief that Colet had not only read the entire Hermetic *Corpus,* as well as everything written by Pico, but was deeply influenced by it. Once made, the conviction would be confirmed by the finding of a possible reference to the *Poimandres*.[60]

It is nevertheless extremely doubtful that Colet was in any meaningful sense of the word a Hermetist. The severity of his temperament and an animus against "unclean" literature protected him against an urge either to prove Christian truth by pagan parallels or to find in pre-Christian writings esoteric extensions of Christian doctrines. And there are other reasons for disbelief. Opposition to astrology need not imply an acquaintance with Pico's attack. Cicero and Juvenal, among others, had opposed astrology much earlier. An allusion to Pico's *Heptaplus* does not assure

Colet's knowledge of Pico's other writings, or, if it did, his agreement with every-thing said in them. As for the aerial and fiery daemons, belief in them was by no means peculiar to Hermetists. The daemons derived, probably, from an association of the four elements with an aboriginal tendency, several times commented on, to project consciousness upon what is inert. Anyhow, the mention of "profane authors" (*quos si quosdam prophanos sequar, debeo appellare demones igneos et aerios*) sounds deprecatory. Colet himself may have thought of the spirits, in the orthodox way, as angelic. What remains is the single allusion to the *Poimandres,* which alone will not bear much of a superstructure. From the *Letters to Radulphus* only—chosen here as an illustrative document—one ought, I think, to infer no more than that Colet had read *CH* I.

The case that can be made out for Hermetism in More is no better. More pub-lished a condensed version of the life of Pico written by Pico's nephew Gian-Francesco, and according to Cresacre More attempted to pattern his own life on Pico's.[61] Under the circumstances, and in view too of the natural religion described in his *Utopia,* the ascription to More of some knowledge of the *Hermetica* seems plausible. Yet in the *Life* of Pico the 900 conclusions offered for debate at Rome are said to have been offered in pride and to have been "partly fetched out of the secret mysteries of the Hebrews, Chaldees and Arabians, and many things drawn out of the old obscure philosophy of Pythagoras, Trismegistus, and Orpheus, and many other things strange and to all folk (except right few special excellent men) before that day not unknown only but also unheard of." [62] The mention of "special excellent men" hardly suffices to draw the sting of "old obscure," "strange," and "not unknown only but also unheard of." The excellence of the special men, moreover, lies in their learning, not in the strange things they know about but are not said to approve. In the *Utopia,* the native religion includes worship of sun, moon, and planets and even of virtuous or famous men of antiquity. Among the greater and more prudent part of the citizenry, however, worship centers upon a single god whose name is unknown but who is eternal, immense, inexplicable because He is beyond the grasp of human intellect (*quod supra mentis humanae captum sit*), and diffused throughout the universe not by size but by goodness (*virtute*).[63] This better system, if not, perhaps, incompatible with Hermetism, does not clearly depend upon it. Also, small praise is imputed to it by the readiness of the Utopians not to extend but to abandon it when Christianity is explained to them by Hythloday and his companions. To be sure, Christianity was "near to that sect strongest among them-selves"; but the reporter Hythloday believed also to be very influential (*hoc quoque fuisse non paulum momenti crediderim*) the fact that among primitive Christians, as among the truest (*germanissimos*) Christians still, provisions were held in com-mon.[64] Further, the name given to the unknowable God in the Utopian language was Mythra,[65] a choice which suggests Persian rather than Egyptian influence. Although a defense of More's Hermetism might be contrived by the astute manipulation of such details, a sounder conclusion would be that the Utopian religion, which we should remember has not been revealed by a divine Νοῦς and seems to have had no prophets, is "natural" in a way that Hermetism is not. Far more persuasive of Hermetic influence than quantities of such flimsy evidence is a single explicit acknowledgment, like that of George Puttenham that Trismegistus is "the holiest of Priestes and Prophetes."[66] Here no doubt can arise: Puttenham found admirable whatever parts of the *Hermetica* he knew.

In such a man as Richard Hooker, who wrote toward the end of the century, acquaintance with the *Hermetica* is indisputable but vigorous propagation of the Egyptian wisdom is not attempted. Although *The Laws of Ecclesiastical Polity* (Books I–IV printed 1593; V, 1597; VI and VIII, 1648; VII, 1662; but Hooker himself died in 1600) repeatedly cite the Hermetic fragments, the quotations usually appear in footnotes and never carry a heavy burden of proof. For example, the sentence, "Christ's own apostle was accounted mad: the best men evermore by the sentence of the world have been judged to be out of their right minds" is glossed by a passage from *CH* XV which in English means, "Those who have knowledge do not please the many, or the many them, but seem to rave and deserve laughter."[67] Similarly, the claim that the soul of man has "the ability of reaching higher than unto sensible things" is supported by a passage from *CH* X, 25 which begins, "Man raises himself to the sky and measures it";[68] and "while we are in the world, subject we are unto sundry imperfections" is footnoted with a rather botched excerpt from *CH* VI, 3–4, beginning "Only the name of good exists among men, Asclepius, but the deed itself nowhere."[69] Occasionally, as in I, v, 3, Trismegistus is elevated into the text: "The wise and learned among the very heathens themselves have all acknowledged some First Cause, whereupon originally the being of all things dependeth. Neither have they otherwise spoken of that cause than as an Agent . . . Thus much acknowledged by Mercurius Trismegistus, τὸν πάντα κόσμον ἐποίησεν ὁ δημιουργός οὐ χερσὶν ἀλλὰ λόγῳ" (The demiurge made the whole world not by hands but by the word).[70]

The same thing happens at a few other places. For example, after a citation of Plato's tendency "to excite men unto love of wisdom, by shewing how much wise men are thereby exalted above men," Trismegistus is quoted on the virtues of a righteous soul: " 'Such spirits' (saith he) 'are never cloyed with praising and speaking well of all men, with doing good unto every one by word and deed, because they study to frame themselves to *the pattern* of the Father of spirits.' "[71] At a later point Hooker recurs to the Platonic notion that " 'the most part of good have some evil, and of evil men some good in them.' So true our experience doth finde those Aphorisms of *Mercurius Trismegistus*"; and the passage which I have called botched (because Hooker's text differed from our more reliable one) is repeated.[72] Finally, a phrase from the end of the *Asclepius, puram et sine animalibus coenam,* is cited in a note to the explanation that "When men fasted it was not always after one and the same sort," abstinence being sometimes complete and sometimes selective.[73] For the rest, in the eight books I have been able to find only one other possible allusion to the *Hermetica,* the subject being this time the worship by pagans, as *dii inferi,* of fallen angels who dispersed themselves in air, earth, and water.[74] But such worship was less encouraged by theological Hermetism than—for example—by the state practices in Greece and Rome, so that little should be made of the passage.

On the basis of this evidence, may it be said that Hooker was influenced by theological Hermetism? "Yes" in the sense that he had certainly read the *Corpus Hermeticum* and the *Asclepius* with some attention, "No" if we mean by "Hermetism" an acceptance of the doctrines as quasi-inspired and mainly true. Hooker used Hermetic excerpts, where he found doing so convenient, very much as a modern scholar might cite parallel passages from different literatures to show that an idea or attitude was widespread. Nowhere does he impute cognitive priority or a decisive intellectual or spiritual weight to the citations. No doubt he was gratified when he found in the *Hermetica* a hint of properly Christian beliefs; and for the whole body of writings he may have felt a qualified respect like that a modern may feel for Plato's moral dialogues. It was good to have them; the reasoning in them was interesting and sometimes cogent; their spirit was occasionally noble; and in their period and pagan milieu they were rather remarkable. They were not, however, sanctioned by the true God, and their authority is not equivalent to that even of the minor Scriptures. The most that can be granted is a possible expectation that the *Hermetica* would have for some of Hooker's readers an import somewhat greater than a learned audience would now recognize in them. But this admission, if made, would imply the existence of a diffuse, if limited, Hermetism in the immediate intellectual climate.

By the 1590s Puritanism was vigorous in England, and because its effect even on non-Puritans was strong the syncretic impulse in theology was weakened. A Protestantism which acknowledges no guide except the Bible in matters of faith and morals is necessarily suspicious of ideas coming from other sources. Roman Catholicism, in contrast, had always valued an oral tradition which varied according to place, and its organizational structure, like that of the Imperial administrative machinery on which it had been modeled, although capable of severity tended usually to tolerate cultural differences. Once the Reformation had begun in earnest, the kind of Hermetism we have observed in Italy became difficult everywhere, and in England it was virtually impossible. Only abnormally eccentric Englishmen like Robert Fludd and Thomas Vaughan can be expected to have developed an enthusiasm for the Egyptian mysteries as great as that we have observed in the young Pico and in Lazzarelli.

Of course interpretation is often difficult, for the influence might be disguised.

A Platonizing poet like Spenser might perhaps draw in Hermetism along with much else from Ficino and his school, or a curious and ranging mind like that of Sir Kenelm Digby—a Catholic—might dip into the *Hermetica* and react vigorously to them before moving on to some other interest. The problem of Spenser, however, is much too complicated to engage us here, since in poetic, and especially in allegorical, transformation Hermetic ideas may be scarcely recognizable. At the request of a friend, Digby himself wrote a letter (published in 1643), called "Observations on the 22. Stanza in the 9th Canto of the 2d Book of Spencers Faery Queen," [75] in which he undertook to prove that from a single stanza Spenser could be shown to be "throughly verst in the Mathematicall Sciences, in Philosophy, and in Divinity." [76] The demonstration, which is irrelevant to a discussion of theological Hermetism, turns mostly on geometrical symbolism; and another set of "Observations" by Digby, this time on Sir Thomas Browne's *Religio Medici,* refers to Trismegistus and to "the *Hermeticall Philosophers"* without showing an intimate acquaintaince with either.[77] An antiquarian polymath like Robert Burton or a man who, like Browne, besides being almost universally well-read was divided between tough-mindedness and mysticism, will repay attention better than marginal figures like Digby and Spenser.

Burton's *Anatomy of Melancholy* (1621, 1624, 1628, 1632, 1638, and 1651, with steady augmentation; later editions in 1660 and 1676) mentions Hermes or Trismegistus by name no fewer than thirteen times; and in addition there are occasional references to Ficino, Pico, Paracelsus, Campanella, and other persons associated in some way with Hermetism. Sometimes an allusion is indirect, as when Burton remarks that "the Kings of *Egypt* were Priests of old, chosen and from thence,— *Idem rex hominum Phoebique sacerdos:* but those heroical times are past." [78] Burton appears to accept, provisionally at least, the alleged pedigree of Hermetic wisdom. Ficino, among others, "seems to second" the opinion that spirits are as numerous as the stars, taking the view most likely from Plato, who on the authority of Socrates "made nine kinds of them," Socrates, in turn, having drawn "from *Pythagoras,* & he from *Trismegistus,* he from *Zoroaster."* [79] An earlier passage carries the same implication.[80] Many of the spirits, however, are devils, and some of those, we learn from Tertullian, delight in sacrifices, "as *Trismegistus* confesseth in his *Asclepius,* and he himself could make them come to their images by magic spells." [81]

The cited pasages are typical. Hermes is used like other authors and is granted no special pre-eminence, is not brought in triumphantly to resolve disputes or to discredit authors whose knowledge had no divine source. Like Averroës (an Arab) and Orpheus (a still more shadowy theologian than himself), Hermes gave a positive answer to the question, "Does the world have a soul (*An terra sit animata*)?" [82] Along with Musaeus, Orpheus again, Pindar, Pherecydes Syrius, Epictetus, the Chaldaeans, and the British druids, he affirmed that the soul is immortal.[83] The affirmation is cited a second time with some alteration in the list of authorities and with a hinted reservation: "that *Scyrian Pherecydes, Pythagoras* his Master (i. e., Pythagoras's Master), broached in the East amongst the Heathens first the immortality of the Soul, as *Trismegistus* did in *Egypt,* with a many of feigned Gods." [84] Being a heathen, Trismegistus is not consistently trustworthy. He may deserve a certain limited admiration: "The Philosophers, *Socrates, Plato, Plotinus, Pythagoras, Trismegistus, Seneca, Epictetus,* those *Magi, Druids, &c.* went as far as they could by the light of Nature." [85] Special illumination is explicitly denied, and Hermes is one philosopher among many. So elsewhere. Cardan, in *De Subtilitate,* we are told, "brings many proofs out of *Ars Notoria,* and *Solomon's* decayed works, old *Hermes, Artesius, Costaben Luca, Picatrix, &c."* that cures can be made by the aid of daemons and charms. Burton himself, however, is strongly against magic: "Why should we rather seek to them than to Christ himself, since that he so kindly invites us unto him, *Come unto me all ye that are heavy laden, & I will ease you?"* [86]

None of the remaining allusions [87] alters the implications of these passages. In much the same way as Hooker, Burton is acquainted with the *Hermetica,* finds them interesting, and cites them occasionally, but he is not awed by them or by their reputed antiquity. He treats them, in fact, like other ancient and modern texts which in isolation prove little or nothing but through coincidence with one another can become impressive. Even so they need not always be accepted, for what seems to approach the *semper et ubique* must be rejected if it conflicts with Christian truth.

The attitude of Sir Thomas Browne is more complex. On one side, every undergraduate student of literature knows Browne's fondness for an *O altitudo.* "Where I cannot satisfy my reason, I love to humour my fancy"; and again, "Where there is an obscurity too deep for our Reason, 'tis good to sit down with a description, periphrasis, or adumbration; for by acquainting our Reason how unable it is to display the visible and obvious effects of Nature, it becomes more humble and submissive unto the subtleties of Faith; and thus I teach my haggard and unreclaimed Reason to stoop unto the lure of Faith." [88] The theme is picked up repeatedly. "I have often admired the mystical way of Pythagoras and the secret Magick of numbers. . . . The severe Schools shall never laugh me out of the Philosophy of Hermes, that this visible World is but a Picture of the invisible." [89] Again: "Now, besides these particular and divided Spirits, there may be (for ought I know) an universal and common Spirit to the whole World. It was the opinion of Plato, and it is yet of the Hermetical Philosophers." [90] And once more: "Therefore for Spirits, I am so far from denying their existence, that I could easily believe, that not onely whole Countries, but particular persons, have their Tutelary and Guardian Angels. It is not a new opinion of the Church of Rome, but an old one of Pythagoras and Plato" [91] —and, he might have added, of Hermes. Finally, in speaking of an "obscurity" in the early chapters of *Genesis,* he says, "those allegorical interpretations are also probable, and perhaps the mystical method of Moses bred up in the Hieroglyphical Schools of the Egyptians."[92] So far it might appear that in Browne we have an authentic convert to the Egyptian theology.

The conclusion would be premature, for outside the *Religio Medici* the leaning toward what is incomprehensible is muted or absent. The author of the *Religio* is also the author of *Pseudodoxia epidemica,* or *Vulgar Errors,* and from this a quite different image arises. It is that of an indefatigable philosopher whose chambers are crammed with specimens on which he has been experimenting: a kingfisher hanging by its bill, an egg suspended in water, tadpoles in various stages of development, bits of a noisome whale recently cast up on a beach, birds whose throats had been dissected in the search for an epiglottis; organs, medicaments, acids, metallic substances, a litter which must have irritated even an indulgent wife and limited the indoors playing area of the couple's twelve children. This skeptical scientist is quite as much Browne as the contemplator of infinity, and in the five volumes of the *Works* he looms as large. To the end of his days Browne appears to have treasured the "Hermetic" definition of God (not present in the *Hermetica* but traced back by modern scholars to a twelfth-century *Liber XXIV. philosophorum*[93]), "God is a circle whose center is everywhere and whose circumference is nowhere." He is never tired of alluding to this sentence: in *Christian Morals,*[94] in *The Garden of Cyrus,*[95] in *Religio medici,*[96] in *Pseudodoxia epidemica,*[97] and perhaps elsewhere. Unless belief in a God who is at once immanent and transcendent is thought wholly incompatible with empirical science, such a vestigial respect for "Hermes" need not surprise us. Yet on the whole Browne is rather strikingly anti-Hermetic. No more than in Burton will we find in him a disciple whose soul dilates and whose eyes shoot forth sparkles at the slightest memory of the Egyptian theologian.

The reason is that despite the interest in abstruse notions and fantastic calculations which led Browne (for instance) to muse about "the mystical way of Pythagoras, and the secret Magick of numbers,"[98] to write a whole book on the quincunx, to speculate that Adam might easily have espoused a ninth-generation descendant without marrying within the seventh degree of consanguinity, and to compute the possible population of the earth at a time halfway between the Creation and the Flood at 1,347,368,420 people,[99] his temperament included a strong skepticism. In few writers besides Bacon, in the English Renaissance, is a more direct and damaging attack made on the common assumption that ancient wisdom was superior to modern.

"The mortallest enemy unto Knowledge," he declared sweepingly in *Pseudodoxia epidemica,* "and that which hath done the greatest execution upon truth, hath been a peremptory adhesion unto Authority, and more especially, the establishing of our belief upon the dictates of Antiquity." This is bad because "Men hereby impose a Thraldom on their Times, which the ingenuity of no Age should endure, or indeed, the presumption of any did ever yet enjoyn." The past was once the present: "that is, as our own [times] are at this instant, and we our selves unto those to come, as they unto us at present." It is no more than "the humour of many heads, to extol the days of their Forefathers, and declaim against the wickedness of times present." The testimonies of antiquity are not always reliable. Many affirmations are qualified by *aiunt, ferunt, fortasse* ("they say," "they report," "perhaps"). Some writers are found "taking upon trust most they have delivered, whose Volumes are meer Collections"—for example, Pliny, Aelian, Athenaeus. We must remember the "fabulous condition" of former ages, when men were credulous. Many things found in old texts are "but ordinary, and come short of our own Conceptions," or are so obvious that "no reasonable hearer but would assent without them." Finally, "While we so devoutly adhere unto Antiquity in some things, we do not consider we have deserted them in several others," as, for instance, in knowledge of the eighth sphere's movements, of the torrid zone (which the ancients thought uninhabitable), and of the antipodes (which they declared not to exist).[100] If Browne had a congenital impulse to pant reverently whenever he held an ancient text between his fingers, he succeeded in bringing it under control.

Trismegistus is not excepted from these strictures. "That the Sun, Moon, and Stars are living creatures, endued with soul and life, seems an innocent Error, and an harmless digression from truth; yet hereby [the Devil] confirmed their Idolatry, and made it more plausibly embraced."[101] The Hermetic belief in an animate universe is thus emphatically denied. The Egyptians, Browne remarks elsewhere, were "great admirers of Dogs in Earth and Heaven" and worshiped Anubis or Mercurius, "the Scribe of Saturn, and Counseller of Osyrus, the great inventor of their religious rites, and Promoter of good unto Egypt," who was "translated" into Sirius, the dogstar.[102] The tone here is that of a collector of curious information, not that of a propagandist; of a scholar, not of a convert. "To begin or continue our works like Trismegistus of old, *Verum, certè verum, atque verissimum est,* would sound arrogantly unto present Ears in this strict enquiring Age, wherein, for the most part, *Probably,* and *Perhaps,* will hardly serve to mollify the Spirit of captious Contradictors."[103] Although the reference here is to the pseudo-Hermetic *Tabula smaragdina,* the skepticism is typical of the later Browne.

Of course it would be wrong to imply that a withholding of assent necessarily is equivalent to scorn. "Egypt itself is now become the land of obliviousness and doteth. Her ancient civility is gone, and her glory hath vanished as a phantasma. . . . She poreth not upon the heavens, astronomy is dead unto her, and knowledge maketh other cycles."[104] Evidently at one time Egypt was comparatively, if not absolutely, civil, glorious, and wise in knowledge of the stars, and a contrast of her present with her past evokes a mild nostalgia. Nevertheless Browne is no more a Hermetist than Hooker. He too knew something of the *Hermetica,* although, surprisingly, for him the author of the *Corpus* and the *Asclepius* is also the alchemist and astrologer,[105] and he found the documents interesting. He shows no disposition, however, to think the alleged antiquity of the documents a testimony of their credibility, and Hermes is not for him a theologian favored by God only slightly less than the authors of Scripture and also enjoying a quasi-infallibility.

So much I have felt it advisable to say about Colet, More, Hooker, Burton, and Browne in the hope of discouraging the more enthusiastic and undiscriminating kinds of influence-hunting. For the rest, it will be possible only to lump together in a long

Athanasius Kircher, *Oedipus aegyptiacus,* Vol. I (Rome: Vitalis Mascardi, 1652), frontispiece.

Egypt as the source of all wisdom: Oedipus solving the riddle of the Sphinx. The first three books of this volume treat Egyptian geography, politics, and "Theogony or Architecture of the Gods." (No mention is made of Hermes Trismegistus.) Later books have to do with the Hebrews, Indians, Chinese, Japanese, Tartars, Mongols, and New World people, among all of whom "manifest traces of Egyptian superstition are revealed to the reader" (Synopsis Tomi Primi). In short, Kircher was an Egyptian disseminationist. In the plate reproduced above, the open book claims authoritative support from Latin, Greek; Hebrew, Chaldaic, Syriac, Arabic, Samaritan, Armenian, Egyptian, Coptic, Persian, Ethiopian, Italian, German, Spanish, Gallic, and Lusitanian sources. The scroll about the two angels reads, "By reason and experience." The medallions beneath the book are labeled "Egyptian wisdom," "Phoenician theology," "Chaldaic astrology," "The Jewish cabala," "Persian magic," "Pythagorean mathematics," "Greek theosophy," "Mythology," "Arabian alchemy," and "Latin theology." A heroic figure in the foreground, armed with helmet and spear (Oedipus, or a figurative representation of Kircher himself?) stretches out a hand toward the Sphinx, whose secrets he is about to reveal.

paragraph other indications—a few of many that might be collected—that the *Hermetica* had some English vogue.

William Gilbert's *De magnete* (1600) includes two rather lyrical chapters, in one of which an anti-Aristotelian bias expressed itself as approval of Hermes. Aristotle would have us believe that in the whole universe only the earth is "imperfect, dead, inanimate, and subject to decay," whereas "Hermes, Zoroaster, Orpheus, recognize a universal soul. As for us, we deem the whole world animate." [106] Henry Reynolds, in *Mythomystes* (?1632), affirms that Zoroaster was "the first Author of that Religious Philosophy, or Philosophical Religion, that was after followed & amplified by Mercurius Trismegistus, Orpheus, Aglaophemus, Pythagoras, Eudoxus, Socrates, Plato, &c." [107] Milton refers three times to Hermes: in *Il Penseroso* (lines 87–88, where Hermes is evidently an astrologer); in *Ad Joannem Rousum* (line 77, where the question is of *placidam . . . requiem, sedesque beatas* to be granted partly by Hermes); and in *De idea Platonica* (lines 33–34, where *Ter magnus Hermes* appears as "knowing in secrets," *arcani sciens*). According to J. H. Hanford, "Hermes was included in Milton's ed[ition] of Justin," i. e., in the edition of Justin Martyr's *Opera* published at Cologne in 1636. [108] Milton was willing also to consider whether "any knowledge comes to us about those beings which are called Lares, Genii, and Daemons"; [109] and in *De doctrina christiana* he granted the probability that "there are certain angels appointed to preside over nations, kingdoms, and particular districts." [110] But such angels, although strongly suggestive of the decans said in *Stobaeus* VI, 8 to influence men's affairs collectively and of the daemons asserted in *CH* XVI, 14 to cause trouble for cities and nations, are probably derived mainly from Christian tradition. Henry More mentioned Hermes favorably in a poem:

> Plato's school
> . . . well agrees with learned Pythagore,
> Egyptian Trismegist, and th'antique roll
> Of Chaldee wisdome, all which time hath tore
> But Plato and deep Plotin do restore. [111]

Indeed, according to Carol L. Marks, the Cambridge Platonists generally "accepted Ficino's view of an unbroken tradition of early wisdom, passing from Moses to Hermes and percolating through Zoroaster, Pythagoras, Plato, Orpheus, and yet more obscure philosophers." [112] Some of the writings by members of this school were accessible, we are told by Rufus M. Jones, in New England, "and may have been read by an occasional liberal, though there is little evidence that they colored the stream of thought. Plato's complete *opera,* with some of the works of Porphyry, Iamblichus, and Hermes Trismegistus, were early put into the Harvard Library." [113] Ralph Cudworth's opinion of the *Hermetica* has already been described: although the documents were untrustworthy in detail, they must have preserved some of the authentic Egyptian teachings of a relatively high antiquity.

The list of writers might be extended indefinitely. A small scholarly industry (not, in my opinion, always adequately informed) has grown up about the alleged Hermetism of Henry and Thomas Vaughan, and careful study would be needed to discover whether apparently Hermetic ideas in Thomas Traherne owe anything, or much, to the Trismegistic fragments. Nevertheless, I think it safe to risk a tentative generalization that outside the small group of Cambridge Platonists, whose doctrines included ideas drawn from Plotinus, Iamblichus, Proclus, and other ancients brought into notice by the fifteenth-century Florentine school, theological Hermetism was never a powerful intellectual force in England. Moreover, the degree of direct Hermetic influence within Cambridge Platonism may have been less than would be implied by an easy association of Trismegistus with the Neo-Platonics. Certainly there was awareness of the newly recovered *Corpus* in England, and frequent references were made to its supposed pedigree. In the present state of our knowledge, however, the Hermetic influence on thought would seem to have been small.

Small as it was, protest arose against it in the form of a vigorous attack on Cambridge Platonism, which in Samuel Parker's *Free and Impartial Censure of the Platonick Philosophie* (1666) was declared to be "ungrounded and Fanatick Fancy."[114] Parker himself preferred "the Mechanical Hypotheses before any other" but was so far skeptical that he doubted the possibility of attaining more than "true and exact Histories of Nature for use and practice; and . . . the handsomest and most probable *Hypotheses* for delight and Ornament."[115] So positivistic a temperament inevitably was rubbed the wrong way by Hermetism. The Platonic mysteries are allegedly derived "from *Pythagoras,* who in his Travels into Aegypt and the East had either immediately received them from the Jewes themselves, or from the Aegyptian Priests, and the Chaldean Wise men."[116] But it is no credit to have borrowed from the Egyptians, whose "Theological Learning was lamentably frivolous, obscure, fabulous, uncouth, magical, and superstitious," as can be seen from the remains of "supposititious Authors, such as *Zoroaster* and *Hermes Trismegistus"*: remains identifiable in the writings of Psellus and even of Pico, admirable as he was, as "grand and pompous Futilities."[117] We learn from the "lost labour and fruitless industry of *Kirchers Oedipus Aegyptiacus"* that the Egyptian hieroglyphics were "childish fooleries." The Egyptian priests, indeed, were like credulous monks in the darkest ages of Popery.[118] Parker believed that no one who asked the Platonists for rational evidence would ever become a disciple.[119] As for himself, he wanted no traffic with "the giddy and fanciful Conjectures of a very *warm Brain."*[120]

The rejection emerged from, and was appropriate to, a new intellectual temper sharply different from that of the syncretizing Renaissance; and the mood was destined to prevail. Hermetic theology is now likely to appear "true" only to persons who combine an abnormal responsiveness to moral elevation with the lack of a

SYNT. III. DE ORIG. IDOLOLAT. ÆGYPT.   189   CAP. IV.

Athanasius Kircher, *Oedipus aegyptiacus,* Vol. I (Rome: Vitalis Mascardi, 1652), p. 189.

"Description of Isis, Great Mother of the Gods, according to Apuleius." This is another product of the syncretic passion so pronounced in Kircher. The left-hand column lists "Other names of Isis," of which most will be familiar. Rhea or Earth was the mother of Romulus and Remus. Pessinuntia (as often, *c* for *t* before *i*) is the Cybele worshiped at Pessinus, a town in Galatia. Rhamnusia is the Themis worshiped at Rhamnus, in northern Attica. Bellona is a goddess of war. Polymorphus daemon is, rather vaguely, a shape-shifter. In the right-hand column a key is given to the symbols which accompany the figure. A represents divinity, the world, the heavenly orbs. BB symbolizes the winding path of the moon and the power to confer fertility. CC is a high headdress built over a cone, symbol of the moon's influence on vegetation. D, a stalk, shows that Isis discovered grain. E, a cotton dress of many colors, represents the moon's various faces. F again symbolizes the discovery of grain. G—the lower part of the hat or a separate headband—symbolizes dominion over all vegetation. H, the lower part of the robe, suggests the moon's rays. I, the *sistrum* or Egyptian rattle, represents Averruncus, a genius or local god of the Nile who averts calamities. K represents the moon's waxing and waning. L is the moon's power to moisten. M is its power to conquer and to prophesy. N is its rule over water and sea. O indicates the earth and stands for Isis as the discoverer of medicine. P is the fruitfulness produced by irrigation. Q represents the moon as mistress of the stars. R shows that she is the nourisher of everything. S, M suggest that she is goddess of earth and sea.

The Greek phrases at the middle top and at bottom mean "Isis the all-receiving and multiform daemon, myriad-named nature, matter" and "Supreme mother of the gods, she the many-named."

disciplined historical and philosophical sense. Nonetheless I urge again that theological Hermetism was in all probability the least harmful of the occult systems examined in these pages. Because its emphasis was meditative, Hermetism absorbed little or no wealth, made no false predictions about daily activities, provoked no persecutions, and did not encourage malice. If conversion to its doctrines sometimes produced a delusion of superior wisdom, and perhaps, less often, an arrogance not uncommon among members of a band of *illuminati,* it is unlikely to have caused much overt suffering. On the contrary: like contemplative Buddhism, it had a certain nobility, and its pietism may have enriched a few lives which otherwise would have been emotionally poor. In the context within which we have seen it, it may be judged charitably.

NOTES: CHAPTER FIVE

1. Eugenio Garin, *La Cultura filosofica del rinascimento italiano* (Firenze: G. C. Sansoni Editore, 1961), pp. 105–106.
2. Cf. P. O. Kristeller, *Supplementum in Ficinianum* (Firenze: L. S. Olschki, 1937), I, cxxix–cxxxi.
3. For the early publishing history see, e. g., Garin, *Cultura filosofica,* p. 152; also Walter Scott and A. S. Ferguson, *Hermetica: The Ancient Greek and Latin Writings Which Contain Religious or Philosophic Teachings Ascribed to Hermes Trismegistus,* 4 vols. (Oxford: At the Clarendon Press, 1924–1936), I, 31ff.
4. Garin, *Cultura filosofica,* p. 152.
5. See Frances A. Yates, *Giordano Bruno and the Hermetic Tradition* (London: Routledge and Kegan Paul, 1964), p. 26. The reference is to Ficino's *Theologia Platonica,* VIII, i (*Opera omnia,* Basel, 1576, I, 400).
6. Eugenio Garin, ed.: *Testi umanistici su l'Ermetismo* (Roma: Fratelli Bocca, 1955), pp. 61 and 59. Along with many other important texts, the entire *Crater Hermetis* is reprinted here.
7. *Ibid.,* p. 16, n6.
8. *Corpus Hermeticum,* texte établi par A. D. Nock et traduit par A.-J. Festugière, 4 vols. (Paris: Société d'Édition "Les Belles Lettres," 1945–1954), II, 347 (*Ascl.* xiii, 37).
9. For a general discussion of non-philosophical and non-theological works attributed to Hermes, see A.-J. Festugière, *La Révélation d'Hermès Trismégiste,* 4 vols. (Paris: Librairie Lecoffre, 1949–1954), I, Chaps. v–viii.
10. Marsilio Ficino, *Opera omnia:* Riproduzione in fototipia a cura di M. SANCIPRIANO, con presentazione di P. O. Kristeller, 2 vols. (Torino: Bottega d'Erasmo, 1959), II, 870. This is a reproduction of the *Opera omnia* published at Basel in 1576.
11. *Isaaci Casauboni . . . exercitationes XVI. Ad Cardinalis Baronii prolegomena in annales . . .* Londini, MDCXIIII, *Exercit.* I, 10, p. 70ff.
12. Scott, *Hermetica,* I, 41, n2.   13. *Ibid.,* I, 42.

14. Festugière, *Révélation*, I, 67–68.   15. *Ibid.*, I, 69.

16. Scott, *Hermetica*, I, 4, n4: "Herodotus 2.67 calls the city of Thoth Ἑρμέω πόλις; and in 2.138 he mentions a temple of 'Hermes' (meaning Thoth) in Bubastis."

17. Festugière, *Révélation*, I, 74. This statement is confirmed by the opening sentence of Iamblichus' *On the Egyptian Mysteries*, which says that "our ancestors too dedicated the discoveries of their wisdom by calling all their own writings by the name of Hermes" (ᾧ δὴ καὶ οἱ ἡμέτεροι πρόγονοι τὰ αὐτῶν τῆς σοφίας εὑρήματα ἀνετίθεσαν, Ἑρμοῦ πάντα τὰ οἰκεῖα συγγράμματα ἐπονομάζοντες).

18. Festugière, *Révélation*, I, 75.

19. Scott, *Hermetica*, I, 1–2.

20. For the suggestion see *ibid.*, I, 3.

21. See especially *ibid.*, I, 9.   22. *Ibid.*, I, 8 and 61–76.   23. *Ibid.*, IV, x–xvi.

24. Ralph Cudworth, *The True Intellectual System of the Universe* (London: J. Walthoe, etc., 1743), I, 319–26.

25. Scott, *Hermetica*, I, 11.

26. Book XV, which was put together by Turnebus from three Stobaean extracts—see Scott, *Hermetica*, I, 19—is quite properly restored to its proper place; but Turnebus' numbering of XVI–XVIII has been retained.

27. See Lynn Thorndike, *History of Magic and Experimental Science*, 8 vols. (New York: Columbia University Press, 1923–1958), V, 449.

28. Cf. Nock, *Corpus Hermeticum*, I, vii.

29. Scott, *Hermetica*, II, 77.

30. C. S. Lewis, *Out of the Silent Planet* (New York: Macmillan and Co., 1943), p. 29.

31. Cf. Scott, *Hermetica*, II, 374.

32. Cf. Garin, *Cultura filosofica*, p. 397; but he says the second half of the fifteenth century.

33. *Ibid.*   34. *Ibid.*, pp. 112–13.

35. P. O. Kristeller, *Studies in Renaissance Thought and Letters* (Roma: Edizioni di Storia e Letteratura, 1956), p. 52.

36. Garin, *Cultura filosofica*, p. 138.

37. Garin, *Testi umanistici*, p. 75.   38. *Ibid.*, p. 71, n8.   39. *Ibid.*, pp. 55–56.

40. Cf. Kristeller, *Studies in Renaissance Thought*, p. 241.

41. See Garin, *Testi umanistici*, pp. 119–28.   42. *Ibid.*, p. 122.

43. *Ibid.*, pp. 122–23.   44. *Ibid.*, p. 123.

45. E. g., Lazzarelli says that Hermes wrote 26,525 books, "in which he reveals wonderful secrets, the most occult mysteries, and astonishing oracles"—*ibid.*

46. Cf. Garin, *Testi umanistici*, pp. 91–92: Hermes, Veneto says, worked 28 years to acquire "mind" (*mentem*) and be filled with the divine light.

47. *Ibid.*, p. 99.

48. Yates, *Giordano Bruno*, p. 238.

49. Garin, *Testi umanistici*, p. 14.

50. In *Giordano Bruno*.   51. *Ibid.*, p. 174.   52. *Ibid.*, pp. 417–18.

53. Reprinted in Garin, *Testi umanistici*, pp. 34–44.   54. *Ibid.*, p. 41.

55. See Eugenio Garin, *Giovanni Pico della Mirandola* (Comitato per le Celebrazione Centenarie, 1963), pp. 39–40.

56. Thorndike, *History of Magic*, IV, 438. The citations are to J. Trithemius, *Annales hirsaugienses* (St. Gallen: 1690).

57. Garin, *Testi umanistici*, p. 37.

58. John Colet, *Opuscula quaedam theologica: Letters to Radulphus on Genesis I, Together with Other Treatises*, edited and translated by J. H. Lupton (London: George Bell and Sons, 1876), p. 170.   59. *Ibid.*, pp. 176 and 178.   60. *Ibid.*, p. 179; cf. note on p. 22.

61. For the latter statement see Thomas More, *The English Works*, edited W. E. Campbell (London: Eyre and Spottiswoode (Publishers) Limited, 1931), "Introduction" by A. W. Reed, I, 18.   62. *Ibid.*, I, 351.

63. St. Thomas More, *Utopia (1516)* (Leeds, England: The Scolar Press Limited, 1966), sig. liii *r*.

64. *Ibid.*, sig. liii *v*.   65. *Ibid.*, sig. liii *r*.

66. *Art of English Poesie*, I, viii.

67. Richard Hooker, *Of the Laws of Ecclesiastical Polity*, 2 vols. (Everyman's Library: Dutton, New York), I, 105 (Preface, par. 1). This edition is quite reliable and has the advantage of a much clearer Greek type than in the early printings.   68. *Ibid.*, I, 167 (I, vi, 3).

69. *Ibid.*, I, 203 (I, xi, 3).   70. *Ibid.*, I, 151 (I, ii, 3).

71. *Ibid.*, I, 166 (I, v, 3). The citation is from *CH* X, 21.

72. Book VII of the *Polity* is omitted from the Everyman Edition, which includes only Books I–V. See John Keble, ed., *The Works of that Learned and Judicious Divine, Mr. Richard Hooker* (Oxford: Clarendon Press, 1874), III, 315.

73. Everyman Edition, II, 378 (V, lxxii, 6).   74. *Ibid.*, I, 164 (I, iv, 3).

75. London: Printed for Daniel Frere Bookseller, at the Red-Bull in Little Britain, 1643. Reprinted in Edward W. Tayler, ed., *Literary Criticism of Seventeenth-Century England* (New York: Alfred A. Knopf, 1967), pp. 203–13.   76. *Ibid.*, p. 4; Tayler, p. 204.

77. For a discussion of the commentary on the *Religio* see Frank Livingstone Huntley, *Sir Thomas Browne: A Biographical and Critical Study* (Ann Arbor: The University of Michigan Press, 1962), pp. 140–42.

78. Robert Burton, *The Anatomy of Melancholy*, ed. A. R. Shilleto, 3 vols. (London: George Bell and Sons, 1903–1904), I, 367 (I, ii, iii, 15).

79. *Ibid.*, I, 215 (II, ii, i, 2).   80. *Ibid.*, I, 202–205 (I, ii, i, 2).

81. *Ibid.*, I, 218 (II, ii, i, 2).   82. *Ibid.*, II, 60 (II, ii, iii).

83. *Ibid.*, I, 185–86 (I, i, ii, 9).   84. *Ibid.*, III, 379 (III, iv, i, 2).

85. *Ibid.*, III, 387 (III, iv, i, 2).   86. *Ibid.*, II, 6 (II, i, i) and 16 (II, i, iii).

87. See I, 84 ("Democritus to the Reader"); I, 206 (II, i, i, 2); and I, 457 (I, iii, i, 3).

88. Sir Thomas Browne, *The Works of*, ed. Geoffrey Keynes, 6 vols. (London: Faber & Gwyer Limited, New York: William Edwin Rudge, 1928–1931), I, 14–15 (*Religio Medici*, I, 10).

89. *Ibid.*, I, 17 (*Religio medici*, I, 12).   90. *Ibid.*, I, 40 (*Religio medici*, I, 32).

91. *Ibid.*, I, 41 (*Religio medici*, I, 33).   92. *Ibid.*, I, 43–44 (*Religio medici*, I, 34).

93. Published by Clemens Baeumker in *Studien und Charakteristiken zur Geschichte der Philosophie insbesondere des Mittelalters* (Münster, 1928).

94. Browne, *op. cit.*, I, 134 (*Christian Morals*, III, 2).

95. *Ibid.*, IV, 121 (*The Garden of Cyrus*, Chap. v).

96. *Ibid.*, I, 14, margin (*Religio medici*, I, 10).

97. *Ibid.*, III, 269 (*Pseudodoxia epidemica*, VII, 3).

98. *Ibid.*, I, 17 (*Religio medici*, I, 12).

99. See *ibid.*, III, 198 (*Pseudodoxia epidemica*, VI, 6).

100. *Ibid.*, II, 42–50 (*Pseudodoxia epidemica*, I, vi).

101. *Ibid.*, II, 82 (*Pseudodoxia epidemica*, I, xi).

102. *Ibid.*, III, 74 (*Pseudodoxia epidemica*, IV, 13).

103. *Ibid.*, I, 122 (*Christian Morals*, II, 3).

104. *Ibid.*, V, 462–63 ("Fragment on Mummies," which is not, however, certainly by Browne).

105. *Ibid.*, II, 221 (*Pseudodoxia epidemica*, III, xii).

106. Quoted by Paul H. Kocher, *Science and Religion in Elizabethan England* (Huntington Library: San Marino, California, 1953), p. 181.

107. See the reprint in Tayler (Note 75, above), p. 248.

108. See J. H. Hanford, *John Milton: Poet and Humanist* (Cleveland: The Press of Western Reserve University, 1966), p. 106, n161, and p. 86.

109. See *The Works of John Milton,* Vol. XII (New York: Columbia University Press, 1936), 264 (seventh *Prolusion*).

110. *Ibid.,* XV, 102. I have again quoted from the translation on the opposite page.

111. *Philosophical Poems of Henry More,* ed. Geoffrey Bullough (Manchester: University Press, 1931), p. 12. But I have taken the reference from C. A. Patrides, *The Cambridge Platonists* (London: Edward Arnold (Publishers) Ltd, 1969), p. 6.

112. Carol L. Marks, *"Thomas Traherne and Cambridge Platonism,"* PMLA, LXXXI (Dec., 1966), 523.

113. Rufus M. Jones, *Mysticism and Democracy in the English Commonwealth* (Cambridge: Harvard University Press, 1932), p. 120.

114. Sam. Parker, *A Free and Impartial Censure of the Platonick Philosophie* (Oxford: Printed by W. Hall for Richard Davis, 1666), p. 2.

115. *Ibid.,* p. 46.   116. *Ibid.,* p. 93.   117. *Ibid.,* pp. 95–96.

118. *Ibid.,* p. 97.   119. *Ibid.,* p. 87.   120. *Ibid.,* p. 107.

Postscript

No reader who has pushed through the preceding chapters will have found everything in them new. Every literary person knows, or thinks he knows, at least a little about astrology, witchcraft, magic, and alchemy, or about one or more of them, if not, perhaps, about Hermes Trismegistus.

The Renaissance specialist of course knows more. He may be able to interpret the technical passages in Jonson's *The Alchemist,* talk learnedly, if briefly, about the witchcraft in Marlowe's *Dr. Faustus,* make helpful comments about the magic in Greene's *Friar Bacon and Friar Bungay,* and answer simple questions—or perhaps some not simple—about astrological allusions. Sometimes his knowledge has been drawn from the footnotes to edited texts or from published discussions of the works or their authors; but it may be more solidly grounded. Such titles as D. C. Allen's *The Star-Crossed Renaissance,* Lynn Thorndike's *History of Magic and Experimental Science,* and R. H. Robbins's *Encyclopedia of Witchcraft and Demonology* are readily accessible to every scholar, and presumably the books have been read, or at least skimmed through, by a good many. Some knowledge of Ficino and Pico—perhaps a good deal—can be expected, and also recognition, and perhaps some knowledge about, such names as Agrippa, Cardan, Bruno, Campanella, and Erastus. Nevertheless the typical English-speaking *literary* scholar, of whom alone I have been thinking, is unlikely (I suppose) to realize vividly, along his bones as it were, the extent and intensity of the Renaissance interest in *occulta*. For example, because he has not read widely in the discussions of daemons (and why should he be expected to have done so?) he may believe that Ariel and Caliban, in *The Tempest,* like the Earth-Spirit in Shelley's *Prometheus Unbound,* are poetic inventions which no contemporary reader or spectator could have imagined to be anything else. Again, he may take it for granted that Prospero's magic, for Shakespeare and the more knowing persons in his audience, was an immediately transparent metaphor for aesthetic creativity and that except for some especially raw yokel the fairies in *A Midsummer Night's Dream* were fanciful borrowings from an exploded folklore.

If I underestimate the literary specialist's knowledge, as I may well do, I apologize. No one can guess accurately the contents of his professional associates' brains. I suspect, however, that the characterization I have offered is reasonably fair. As for the specialist in Renaissance history or thought, I shall speculate merely (and in saying this I intend no reproach) that apart from scholars who have been drawn especially into *occulta* few have crawled, or cantered, over more than one or two of the five areas upon which the preceding chapters have focused. Like the present, the past is illimitably complex, and no man can be expected to know all its corners. Yet it is possible, by reading around one's area of specialization as well as within it, to obtain a fuller and sharper sense of milieu; and the result may be altered understanding. In the remaining pages I propose to suggest, with all possible brevity, two of many insights which have accrued to me and may also have accrued to some of my readers.

The first has to do generally with Renaissance scholarship and more specifically with Latin scholarship. Like other undergraduates, I was told many years ago that the Humanism which distinguished the Renaissance was marked by a diversion of attention from the scholastic philosophy and from theology to the *belles lettres* of antiquity and especially to the Greek masterpieces, now available to educated men in the recovered Greek language. As a graduate student I was informed (and I accepted the anecdote as illustrative) that Cardinal Bembo, although a prelate, refused to read the Vulgate Bible because he feared it might corrupt his own Ciceronian style. Perhaps because my orientation was primarily literary, as time went on my impression that classical scholarship was mainly belletristic was strengthened. Works like *The Senecan Amble,* by George Williamson, and a number of studies by M. W. Croll suggested, more by implication than by statement, that Latin stylistics was an overriding preoccupation.

Nothing of this was totally wrong except the inference I drew from it. I continue to esteem the scholars and to admire the scholarship. Moreover, we may remember that when "English" was created as a discipline, the price was the carving out of an area recognizable by its preoccupation with *belles lettres* as opposed to history, philosophy, theology, and other specialized studies, so that when professors of English moved outside the vernacular it was natural that their attention should continue to be given primarily to *litterae humaniores*. Now that the discipline is firmly established the need to stay within restricted bounds has decreased, and once outside it one finds one's horizons remarkably altered. To judge only from the documents with which we have been concerned here, the Latin scholarship of the Renaissance had to do less with imaginative conceptions than with ideas thought to be objectively true; and with pure Latinity and rhetorical elegance it had no commerce at all, or a commerce obscured by a far deeper interest in something else. I do not recall that in any of the documents the turn of an ancient's sentence or the beauty of his Latin or Greek is saluted. This view too, of course, is partial; but it can act as a corrective of the other.

This leads to my second comment, which is that I have emerged from the reading with my opinion of our modern culture, and particularly of the physical sciences, enormously raised, and this despite the fact that I long ago ceased to have a romantic admiration of the past. I have suggested that in the Renaissance the ancients appear to have been respected less as skilled writers than as wise men. The respect is justified if we recall their limited opportunities or consider only their handling of subjects like ethics, in which misinformation is unlikely to play a vital role; not otherwise. The deference to antiquity of the writers discussed here is hardly qualified except, perhaps, when authorities conflict, and even then an attempt is often made to save both opinions. To such a degree is this true that I continue, notwithstanding innumerable earlier surprises, to be astonished by a sentence like this in Agrippa: "We find in Scripture that the Pythoness made Samuel return in this way (i. e., from the dead); and so, in Lucan, the Thessalian sorceress raised a dead body" (*sic Thessala vates apud Lucanum cadaver erexit*, III, xli). The acceptance of Scripture as revealed truth is one thing, the presumption that a first-century Latin poet of moderate distinction is equally reliable quite another. (The passage appears, incidentally, in a context which discusses the topic *Quid de homine post mortem opiniones variae* by means of sixteen pages of citations mainly from pagan writers and only five pages of citations from Christians.) The excerpt is characteristic not of Agrippa only—who in his *Oratio habita Papiae* piously submits everything he has said about Hermes to the judgment of Holy Church—but of nearly all the writers on occult science; and a modern may well find it staggering.

Taken alone, the passage might seem to imply a remarkable failure to realize that the truth of poetry is rather metaphorical than factual; and innumerable comments in the works I have described support that inference. Statements not only by Lucan, whose subject was actual history, but also by Ovid, Homer, Virgil, and other poets are often read quite literally and credited as factually reliable. The matter, however, is more complicated. When a pious Christian mind revolted against the literal sense, "truth" was often—I am tempted to say regularly—salvaged by an assumption that it had been "veiled" by fictions in order that an esoteric doctrine might be hidden from unfit readers. How this practice worked can be seen in the *Iconologia* of Cesare Ripa, the *Mythologiae* of Natalis Comes, and the *Mythomystes* of Henry Reynolds. I shall take a single illustration from the last.

Pico, says Reynolds in speaking of *"Magia naturalis,* or naturall wisdome," defined it as *"exacta & absoluta cognitio omnium rerum naturalium*—the exact and absolute knowledge of all naturall things (which the Auncients were Masters of)." Among these Masters *"Praestitit Homerus,* Homer excelled" because he knew *omnes . . . scientias* but dissimulated them, as under the guise of Ulysses' travels. So too Orpheus and Zoroaster. The latter was "one of the greatest (as first) of Naturall Magicians, or Masters of the absolute knowledge of all Nature," as is seen in his doctrine of the *Scala a Tartaro ad primum ignem,* or ladder from Tartarus to the realm of the first fire (the upper heavens). In this Reynolds found the *"Seriem naturarum universi a non gradu materiae, ad eum qui est super omnem gradum graduate protensum*—the series or concatenation of the universall Natures, from a no degree (as he speakes) of matter, to him that is above or beyond all degree graduately extended."[1]

What is noteworthy here is the ascription of "exact and absolute knowledge of all naturall things" to the earliest writers, and especially to shadowy pagans like Homer, Orpheus, and Zoroaster. The sources of the prestige are never dilated upon sufficiently to satisfy my curiosity, at least, about them. It would be interesting to know how important was the role played by the Christian belief that mankind, as the result of accumulated sins, had degenerated steadily ever since the commission of Original Sin, and more interesting still to obtain a full and generalized reply to the question, "How did the remotest ancients come to know so much?"

The nearest approach to an answer in the documents we have noticed is given by Ficino in the argument to his *Pimander,* a passage which may be repeated here although a considerable excerpt from it was cited earlier.

> He cannot teach divine things who has not learned them; and we cannot discover by human skill what is above nature. The work is therefore to be accomplished by divine light, so that we may look upon the sun itself by the sun's light. For, in truth, the light of the divine mind is never poured into a soul unless the soul turns itself completely toward the mind of God, as the moon turns toward the sun. The soul does not turn toward mind except when it becomes mind itself. Indeed, mind does not exist until it has laid aside the deceptions of the senses and the mists of fancy. For this reason Mercury (i. e., Hermes Trismegistus) simply puts aside the fogs of sense

and of fancy, bringing himself thus to an approach to mind; and presently Pimander, that is, the divine mind, flows into him, whereupon he contemplates the order of all things, whether they exist in God or flow from God. At length he explains to other men what has been revealed to him by the divine power.

The trustworthiness of the *Pimander,* or *Corpus Hermeticum,* derives from the fact that Hermes turned toward God, renounced sensory perception and imagination, and laid his intelligence open to divine ideas, which thereupon performed the work of illumination. In this way the problem of how a Gentile might be inspired by the Christian God was neatly shortcircuited.

Here was one means, if not the only available one, of believing that Homer, Orpheus, Zoroaster, and the rest of the "Masters" owed their understanding to a similar process. We need not, I think, separate divine knowledge from the knowledge of "all naturall things," for the distinction between matter and spirit was indistinct. Hermes himself tells us in detail how the physical cosmos was structured and governed. As for lesser personages—Lucan, for example, with a reference to whom we began—it is at least conceivable that the authority they also enjoyed resulted from a combination of their fame (certified by the preservation of their works and perhaps also by respectful allusions in the writings of others) with their comparative nearness in time to even greater authorities from whom they might be supposed to have borrowed, or within the circle of whose radiance they stood. The explanation is far from complete or satisfactory and perhaps not accurately stated; but we cannot, I think, avoid concluding that reliability tended to be connected with temporal priority in a way quite uncharacteristic of post-Renaissance thought.

Ficino's comment about "the deceptions of the senses" requires separate notice. From a very early period men had been aware that even ocular evidence—regularly thought to be the most trustworthy of all that obtained through the senses—was deceptive. The clearest instance was perhaps that of a stick thrust partly into water so that it looked bent but could be felt to be straight, but other examples are not far to seek: mirages, sleight-of-hand, the reversal of sides in mirror images. In addition, perception is distorted by mental states and imperfect organs. One man's report of a complex event seldom coincides with that of another. The recognition that the senses could delude co-operated with a disposition to regard spirit as both more dignified and ultimately more real than matter, or the behavior of matter as determined by a non-corporeal power either residing within it or affecting it from outside. In any event, a conviction arose, or perhaps existed from the beginning and was never successfully challenged, that true wisdom must be sought by sheer intellection, without recourse to empirical evidence except, mainly, *a posteriori,* and then usually as a source of exemplification (as in Plato). By definition, almost, "higher" things were non-corporeal or corporeal in such a way as not to permit handling—for instance, the "bodies" of earthy, watery, aerial, and fiery daemons or the "attractive virtue" of a magnet. Thus theology and the higher reaches of philosophy were insulated from close contact with physical reality and had to proceed on the basis mainly of logic (in which the Renaissance was highly skilled) and whatever authoritative pronouncements were available.

What of other intellectual disciplines—astrology, magic, and alchemy, to mention only those on which the preceding pages have centered? Here, surely, we may expect to find an intimate, perceptive grappling with precisely those aspects of the phenomenal world which philosophers and theologians were debarred from considering anxiously.

Not at all. In the controversy about astronomy sketched in Chapter One, the only defense that makes an honest approach to empirical methodology is Bonatti's *Astrosophia* (1687), which dates from long after the emergence of Copernican astronomy, the publication of Bacon's *Novum organum,* and, in England, the founding of the Royal Society. The remaining treatises appeal usually to authorities and, when they bring in "experience," do so in terms of the careful records supposedly kept by the Babylonians or of reports, often made at third- or fourth-hand, of predictions verified by events, many of them blatantly *post factum* and some depending on a birth-date selected to yield the necessary data. How, indeed, could things have been otherwise, when no zodiacal sign was actually in the position it was supposed to occupy in the horoscope, and when observation with an astrolabe would often have shown that the positions of the planets marked in the tables or Ephemerides were wrong? (It will be remembered that no two sets of tables coincided.) So much for the apologetic writings. When the astrologers wrote for each other, their concern was usually the superiority of one authority to another or the reconciling of conflicting claims, not the establishing of a specific influence—for the sake of illustration, let us say the effect on musical aptitude of a retrograde planet under defined conditions. But, in fact, the "science" was so constituted that no single influence could have been isolated. The light, heat, and "virtues" of a single luminary were thought to depend upon the angle of its rays, its relation to zodiacal signs, and its positions among other wandering stars, all these, in turn, being affected by the division of the celestial sphere into houses according to one or another of a number of competing systems. The exact configuration might not recur for thousands of years, if ever. Accordingly controlled and repeated experimentation was impossible. The real ground for belief was faith, again in authorities—and so it remains to this day. The difference from the situation in the more abstruse departments of knowledge arose from the more obvious discrepancies of assertions that dealt with specificities, not in substituting a different basis for certainty.

In natural magic, which involved not only astrological forces but also concrete physical objects susceptible of manipulation, the intellectual habits differed only marginally, as appears from the perseverance of a conviction that the toad "hath yet a precious jewel in his head" or that salamanders are not harmed by fire. To take up only one of the illustrations, did no curious investigator, in a period of 1,500 to 2,000 or 2,500 years, actually put a salamander into a fire? If so, either his report was not believed or he contrived somehow to persuade himself that his results were atypical. Innumerable ways can be found of discrediting sensory evidence. The animal, perhaps, was not after all a salamander, or was a salamander of the wrong kind— not what the ancients had written about. The fire was not "pure," but included some noxious energy besides heat. The animal, again, had suffered some mortal injury before being put to the test, or was diseased.

In the other form of magic, witchcraft, psychological states had such importance that failure could easily be attributed to a fault in the operator's attitude. His attention had wandered, or his faith was insufficient, or the Devil had perceived that he had made a mental reservation about the compact. Or, again, he had failed in the performance of the ceremony by omitting or mispronouncing some all-important word or phrase; one of his materials was of the wrong kind or imperfect; or perhaps the operation was impeded by powerful counter-magic. Sometimes, inevitably, the magic succeeded. A chickenyard was cursed and a hen died; a human object learned he had been hexed and fell ill; a charm put into the victim's food was really poisonous. Failures, however, no more automatically led to rejection of the theory than continued dry weather causes the Zuñi Indians to cease their rain-dances. A child who leaves a gift in the crotch of a tree for an imaginary playmate goes right on with his fantasy despite his discovery on the next morning that the gift is still there. As for alchemy, the curious report of Helvetius is insufficient to unsettle a conviction that in many hundreds of years not a single experimenter of hundreds or thousands ever succeeded in attaining his goal.

What progress required was skepticism of the authorities, exact instruments for making observations, controlled conditions, and, not least important, a refusal to let wishes interfere with perception. At length, very slowly and painfully and against strong instinctive resistance, an inductive revolution began and at length gradually produced real knowledge, which has now so accumulated that our understanding of the physical universe, if of nothing else, is historically unprecedented. (Of course I do not assume that hunches, guesswork, and sudden intuitions have no role in true science. The point is that they result from contemplation of verified data and are themselves subject to experimental corroboration.) Outside the exact sciences much of our wisdom (if I may give it that courtesy title) remains primitive. In certain areas, perhaps, we have regressed; and no one would pretend for a moment that our industrial culture is faultless or our political institutions and practices ideal. A value of historical perspective, however, to which I hope the present work has in some degree contributed, is that it deepens our perception of immediate predicaments. No matter what troubles may arise in the future, the tremendous cost of the occult sciences in human disappointment, wasted effort and resources, and direct suffering like that caused by witchcraft and the persecutions it inspired ought never again to be invited. The current reaction against science as a cold, impersonal, and oppressive force which is destroying humanity can better be directed toward ways of using the results of scientific discoveries for the enhancement of life—and perhaps, although this is more difficult, toward the application of scientific methods to new areas— than toward the resuscitation and popularization of thought-ways which discourage and harm more often than gratify and which, in any event, deceive rather than illuminate. The humanizing of research methods, as opposed to uses, is, however, undesirable and dangerous, for the price of exact and reliable knowledge is precisely the suspension, in purely intellectual work, of the emotional involvement which well through the European Renaissance perplexed and distorted not only abstract thought but also the objective perception of happenings.

NOTES: POSTSCRIPT

1. Henry Reynolds, *Mythomystes,* in Edward T. Tayler, ed., *Literary Criticism of Seventeenth-Century England* (New York: Alfred A. Knopf, 1967), pp. 247–48.

Bibliographical Note

An attempt to give exhaustive bibliographies of the topics discussed in the five chapters of the text is prohibited both by the richness of the materials and by a desire not to swell further what is already a large and expensive book. Each of the topics is enormously complex, and a full bibliography of all, if it were possible, would run to a shelf of volumes. The discussion I have offered must be understood as synoptic: I have tried to arrive at a general comprehension of each system but have stopped reading at the point where a steady diminishing of returns suggested that further study would provide merely additional illustrations of conclusions already more fully documented in my notes than space would allow in the chapters. A reader whose interest has been aroused—for example, in alchemy—can begin with the notes, where he will find enough titles to get him off to a running start. As he proceeds he will find additional titles accumulating on his note-cards, and before long he will discover that unless he is willing to devote a lifetime to research and undertake extensive travel in search of rare titles he must limit his purpose radically.

Since the location of books is important, it may be useful for me to say that I began the present study with books accessible at the University of California Library in Berkeley (many of them in the Rare Book Collection) and continued it in London, where I read sometimes at the British Museum but much oftener at the Warburg Institute of the University of London. Finally, after a decision had been reached that illustrations should be provided, I spent part of a short holiday at the Henry E. Huntington Library in San

Marino, California. Excellent as these collections were, a number of important texts were missing from them, and I sometimes had to be satisfied with a translation when I would much have preferred reading the original.

For the rest, I add comments about books which the course of my exposition did not allow me to notice adequately and books to which I have not had access. No esssential service would be provided by simply alphabetizing titles accessible in the notes.

Kurt Seligmann's *The Mirror of Magic* (New York: Pantheon Books, 1948) and Grillot de Givry's *Le Musée des sorciers, mages et alchimistes* (Paris: Librairie de France, 1929) are two of the relatively few books which range over a considerable part of my subject-matter. Both are lavishly illustrated, the latter also containing a number of beautiful color plates. Except visually, Seligmann's is by far the better. A popular study which is less superficial than may at first be thought is *Spirits, Stars, and Spells* (New York: Canaveral Press, 1966), by L. Sprague de Camp and Catherine C. de Camp. The nonacademic reader, at least, may find it both informative and entertaining. Far more important than any of these to the scholar is Lynn Thorndike's *A History of Magic and Experimental Science* (New York: Columbia University Press, 1923-1958). A disadvantage is that any topic of particular interest may have to be run through the eight volumes with the help of indexes.

More to suggest the limitations of the discussion of astrology in Chapter I than to pretend exhaustiveness I add the titles of a few texts not cited there. Symon de Phares, like the English John Dee a rather silly man, when in trouble with the courts because of his occult practices wrote, about 1497 or 1498, a work called *Recueil des plus célèbres astrologues et quelques hommes doctes* (ed. from the Bibliothèque Nationale ms. by Ernest Wickersheimer, Paris: Librairie ancienne Honoré Champion, Éditeur, 1929). Its interest lies in a desperate attempt to justify astrology by citing as practitioners "des sains patriarches, prophetes, papes, cardinaults, arcesvesques, evesques, empereurs, roys, ducz, contes et de plusieurs autres nobles hommes, sages, graves personnes et grans docteurs, philosophes et clers" (p. xi). The list begins with Adam and contains some 1800 to 1900 names. In 1533 Nicolaus Prucknerus published at Basel a book called *In Iulii Fermici Materni Iunioris Siculi V[iri] C[onsularis] ad Mavortium Lollianum astronomicum libri VIII . . . ab innumeris mendis vindicati.* Only the editing belongs to the Renaissance; but the Warburg copy of the volumes contains also the *Centum aphorismorum liber* attributed to Hermes Trismegistus—an important work which connects Hermes with astrology, as his *Tabula smaragdina* connects him with alchemy—and Otho Brunfelsius's *De diffinitionibus et terminis astrologiae libellus.* Benedictus Pererius, a Jesuit theologian of note, published *De magia, de observatione somniorum, et de divinatione astrologica* (Romae: Fran. Zanettus et Barthol. Tosius, 1562). The *Zodiacus vitae* of Marcellus Palingenius or Pietro Angelo Manzolli (Lugduni: Apud J. Tornaesium, 1581; but first published in 1534), of which an English version called *The Zodiake of Life* has been edited by Rosemond Tuve (New York: Scholars' Facsimiles & Reprints, 1947), was a popular work which besides being astrological in its general plan is heavily so in Book XI, "Aquarius." Even Claudius Salmasius, the French Goliath who was overthrown by the English David, Milton, in a controversy about the execution of Charles I, wrote *De annis climactericis et antiqua astrologia diatribae* (Lugdunum Batavor—i.e., Leyden: Ex Officina Elzeviriorum, 1648), a massive work which although not totally anti-astrological attacks the whole notion of seven-year "climacteric" periods because they were "unknown to the ancient mathematicians" (or astrologers) and are untrustworthy, anyhow, because of differences made by the zodiacal signs and the houses (sig. g7*v*–g8*r*). These, however, are only samples; the resources, as I have said, are intimidatingly vast. I add, finally, a title to which I was led by an interest in the beginning of a Renaissance "Blütezeit" in astrology resulting from an invasion of Western Europe by Byzantine scholars: Deno John Geanakoplos, *Greek Scholars in Venice: Studies in the Dissemination of Greek Learning from Byzantium to Western Europe* (Cambridge: Harvard University Press, 1962). The connections of this with astrology are marginal.

The literature of witchcraft (Chapter II) is also huge. Besides the more trustworthy histories mentioned in the text I cite, as a treatment to be used with extreme caution, Montague Summers's *The History of Witchcraft and Demonology* (London: Kegan Paul, Trench, Trubner & Co. Ltd, 1926). Yet although Summers's smug assumption that all his authorities are credible is astonishing and his enthusiastic approval of the "law divine" that a witch must not be suffered to live is appalling, his knowledge of the subject was considerable; and English readers are indebted to him for numerous translations of hard-to-find Latin works. In this section I was more plagued than elsewhere by an inability to find books. I mention the following: Pierre Le Loyer, *IIII Livres des spectres* (1586, republished 1605; transl. into English by Z. Jones, 1605); Battista Condronchi, *De morbis veneficis ac veneficiis, libri quattuor* (Venice: 1595); Franz Agricola, *Von Zaubern, Zauberinnen und Hexen* (1596); William Perkins, *Discourse on the Damned Art of Witchcraft* (Cambridge: 1608); John Cotta, *The Triall of Witchcraft* (London: 1616); Thomas Cooper, *The Mystery of Witch-craft* (London: 1617); James Mason, *The Anatomie of Sorcery* (London: 1617); Alexander Roberts, *A Treatise of Witch-craft* (London: 1618); Edward Fairfax (the translator of the *Orlando Furioso*), *A Discourse on Witch-craft* (c. 1622; ed. Wm. Grainge, Harrogate, 1882); Richard Bernard, *A Guide to Grand Jurymen* (London: 1627); Thomas Beard, *The Theatre of God's Judgements* (3d ed., London: 1631); Thomas Ady, *A Candle in the Dark* (1656), republished as *A Perfect Discovery of Witches* (1661); and John Webster, *The Displaying of Supposed Witchcraft* (London: 1677). As will be seen, most of these are in English, and further search might have turned most of them up. Possibly I unconsciously tended to work harder on Latin titles because of an assumption that those would indicate more accurately a European climate of opinion. Because I have not seen them, the bibliographical notations are incomplete, and I do not vouch for the accuracy of all the dates. A treatise of some importance which I used but did not discuss is Thomas Erastus's *Deux Dialogues touchant le pouvoir des sorcieres: et de la punition qu'elles meritent* (originally written in Latin but accessible to me, along with Jean Wier's *De prestigiis daemonum,* in a reprint called Jean Wier, *Histoires, disputes, et discours des illusions et impostures des diables,* 2 vols., Paris: A. Delahaye et Lecrosnier, Éditeurs, 1885). Among modern discussions I have not seen are

Wallace Notestein, *A History of Witchcraft in England from 1558 to 1718* (Washington: 1911) and R. Trevor Davies, *Four Centuries of Witch Beliefs* (London: 1947).

The course of the discussion in Chapter III, on natural or white magic, did not permit notice of many highly relevant works. The subject was not, I thought, sufficiently well known to allow the kind of leaping about possible without serious disorientation only on relatively familiar ground. As was said in the text, treatises written against witchcraft occasionally also discussed magic. Book I of Martin Delrio's *Disquisitiones magicae* (Mainz: 1603) is entitled *De magia generatim, & de naturali, artificiali, & praestigiatrice.* Leonardo Vairo's *De fascino libri tres* (Paris: Apud Nicolaum Chesneau, 1583) is rather about magic than witchcraft in Book I. Anti-astrological books, too, sometimes treat other superstitions as well. Book VII of Gian-Francesco Pico's *De rerum praenotione* (written 1503, published 1506; accessible in *Opera omnia,* Basiliae, 1572–73) has ten chapters *adversus magiam* (II, 627–674). A number of other titles may be added: Hieronymus Torella, *Opus praeclarum de insignibus astrologicis* (Valentiae: Alphonsus de Orta, 1496); Symphorien Champier, *Dialogus . . . in magicarum artium destructionem* (Lugduni: Apud Guillermum Balsarin, ?1500); Antonius Lodovicus (Antonio Luíz, or Luis, of Lisbon), *De occultis proprietatibus libri quinque* (Lisbon: Lud. Rodriguez, 1540); the work of Benedictus Pererius mentioned earlier, *De magia, de observatione somniorum et de divinatione astrologica* (Romae: Fran. Zanettus et Barthol. Tosius, 1562); Petrus Pomponatus (Pietro Pomponazzi), *De naturalium effectuum causis sive de incantationibus* (Basiliae: Henricus Petri, 1556); Francesco Patrizzi, *Magia philosophica* (Hamburgi: 1593), which emphasizes Zoroaster, the Chaldaic oracles, and Hermes Trismegistus; Le Sieur De L'Isle (Charles Sorel), *Des Talismans, ou figures faites sous certaines constellations* (Paris: Anthoine de Sommaville, 1636), an attack on the *Curiosités inouïes* (1629) of Jacques Gaffarel; Meric Casaubon, ed., *A True and Faithful Relation of What Happened for Many Years between Dr. John Dee and Some Spirits* (London: 1659—the spirits were hoped, at least, not to be devils); and also, perhaps, Thomas Vaughan's *Anthropo sophia theomagica* and *Anima magica abscondita* (1650). But Vaughan offers a whole nest of special problems which I have not wanted to stir up. These titles are a few of many; diligent search in Thorndike and elsewhere will turn up others. Two general discussions deserve special mention: Charles G. Nauert, Jr., *Agrippa and the Crisis of Renaissance Thought* (Urbana: University of Illinois Press, 1965) and D. P. Walker, *Spiritual and Demonic Magic from Ficino to Campanella* (London: The Warburg Institute, 1958). Frances Yates's *Giordano Bruno and the Hermetic Tradition* (London: Routledge and Kegan Paul, 1964), although in my opinion occasionally overstated, is indispensable. I have not seen a work by Thomas A. Spalding called *Elizabethan Demonology* (1880) and do not know whether it relates more properly to witchcraft or to magic. Some light, finally, is thrown on the classical backgrounds of daemonic magic by J.-A. Hild's *Étude sur les démons dans la littérature et la religion des Grecs* (Paris: Librairie de L. Hachette, 1881).

As was said in the text, the literature of alchemy is virtually unlimited. Among modern studies a special interest attaches to C. G. Jung's extensive treatments. The basic discussion is in *Psychology and Alchemy,* 2d ed., transl. R. F. C. Hull (New York: Bollingen Foundation, Inc., 1953—Vol. 12 of the *Works*). A "Prefatory Note to the English Edition" (p. v) explains that Jung's attention was drawn to alchemy by a remarkable similarity between alchemical symbols and the dreams of twentieth-century Europeans and Americans. Another volume by the same author is *Mysterium Coniunctionis: An Inquiry into the Separation and Synthesis of Psychic Opposites in Alchemy,* also transl. R. F. C. Hull (Bollingen Series XX, New York: Pantheon Books, 1963). This is Vol. 14 of the *Works.* Vol. 13 of the same series is entitled *Alchemical Studies.* Jung was an excellent Latinist and, working partly from mss. in his own collection, obtained a surprisingly detailed knowedge of the subject but believed, I think wrongly, that actual efforts to obtain the Stone or the Elixir were rare. In the main, the tradition appeared to him not only secret but symbolic. Mircea Éliade's *Forgerons et alchimistes* (Paris: Flammarion, Éditeur, 1956), of which the second half is on alchemy, also focuses on symbolism. For the rest, discussions tend to be divided between history of science, on one hand, and the mystical tradition, on the other. A number of useful titles have been listed in Chapter IV. A concise sample of the former is Allen G. Debus's "The Chemical Dream of the Renaissance" (The Churchill College Overseas Fellowship Lecture, No. 3: Cambridge, W. Heffner & Sons Ltd, 1968), a good sample of the latter A. E. Waite's *The Secret Tradition in Alchemy* (London: K. Paul, Trench, Trubner & Co. Ltd, 1926). An attempt to draw connections between alchemy and freemasonry apparently is made in a book I have not seen, Oswald Wirth's *Le Symbolisme hermétique dans ses rapports avec l'alchimie et la francmaçonnerie* (Paris: Laval, 1962–63). Still another book to which I have not had access is M. A. Atwood's *Hermetic Philosophy and Alchemy: A Suggestive Inquiry* (originally published in 1850; reprinted New York: The Julian Press, 1960). According to F. Sherwood Taylor it is "a remarkable work, which every student of alchemy should read, if he can obtain it." There is also a modern alchemical dictionary, Gino Testi's *Dizionario di alchimia e di chemicà antiquaria* (Rome: 1950). This may supersede Martin Ruland's *Lexicon,* which, alas, like Du Cange's *Glossarium mediae et infimae latinitatis,* now and then is helpful but usually lacks precisely the term for which one is searching. A German introduction to the whole subject is Karl Frick's *Einführung in die alchemiegeschichtliche Literatur* (Wiesbaden: 1961). I can only remark again, despairingly, that the resources are nearly inexhaustible. Bibliographical reference works are cited in Chapter IV.

With regard to Hermes Trismegistus, the student's most troublesome problem is resisting the lure of by-ways: into Orphism, Neo-Platonism generally, the Rosicrucian movement, Freemasonry, Swedenborgianism, Gnosticism, Egyptian history and religion, the Cambridge Platonists, and much else—in short, *occulta* of every conceivable kind. Since I at first intended to write only on Hermes, the present volume is a testimony to my own inability to avoid all the distractions. Nevertheless here, if anywhere in these shadowy regions, no real conquest is possible without division. On the other side, particular interests —for example, the "Hermeticism" of Thomas Vaughan—tend to be attacked by persons whose general knowledge of esotericism is inadequate, so that what is ordinary may appear to them to imply only one source of a possible fifty. We therefore find ourselves in a dilemma: a total comprehension of esotericism is impossible, but without it we are sure to go astray in studying specifics. I possess no magic key to this difficulty but wish none the less to call attention to its existence. To illustrate by means of Robert Fludd, upon whom one seems inevitably to wash ashore at some point no matter what occult system one has undertaken to investigate, a wise preliminary assumption would be, in my opinion, that his mind was in the highest degree eclectic but the structuring of the ideas he absorbed from a multitude of sources original. In this situation my own choice has been to eliminate from consideration in Chapter V everything but the Hermetic philosophy and theology accessible in the *Corpus Hermeticum,* the *Asclepius,* and the Stobaean fragments.

The dissemination of the Hermetic texts, once fourteen books of the *Corpus* had been Latinized by Ficino, is discussed briefly in Vol. I, 31ff., of Walter Scott's *Hermetica* (Oxford: The Clarendon Press, 1924-1936). A list of modern editions and studies is given *ibid.,* p. 43ff.; of these, I recommend especially those of Louis Ménard and R. Reitzenstein. The best edition of the *Hermetica,* by far, is that of A. D. Nock and A.-J. Festugière used in my discussion, and the most reliable and far-ranging study is Festugière's *La Révélation d'Hermès Trismégiste,* 4 vols. (Paris: Librairie Lecoffre, 1949-1954). The treatment by G. R. S. Mead (London: John M. Watkins, 1949; but first published in 1906) is that of a modern theosophist and is quite unreliable. In the other volumes enough is available to detain the serious student for several months. Of the early commentaries, the *Pymander Mercurii Trismegisti* of Hannibal Rosseli, in six huge volumes (Cracow: Ex Officina Typographica Lazari, 1585-1590) is the most detailed, but the others are by no means negligible. Keeping one's bearings while reading all this is no mean task, but doing so is barely possible. The spread of Hermetic ideas in Italy is discussed briefly in the text, where references to the chief sources are given. Their influence in France has been studied by D. P. Walker in "The *Prisca Theologia* in France" (*Journal of the Warburg and Courtauld Institutes,* Vol. XVII, 1954, 204-59). A specific extension appears in Gilbert Gadoffre's "Ronsard et la pensée ficinienne" (*Archives de philosophie,* Vol. XXVI, 1963, 45-58). At some point Hermeticism begins to become indistinguishable from Neo-Platonism generally; an introductory consideration of the latter in England can be found in Sears Jayne's "Ficino and English Platonism" (*Comparative Literature,* Vol. IV, 1952, 214-38). Neo-Platonism, in turn, had earlier absorbed influences from Gnosticism, discussed by Jean Doresse in *The Secret Books of the Egyptian Gnostics* (London: Hollis & Carter, 1960). A vigorous reaction against the *prisca theologia* appeared in Johann Heinrich Ursinus's *De Zoroastre Bactriano, Hermete Trismegisto, Sanchoniathone Phoenicio, eorumque scriptis, & aliis, contra Mosaicae scripturae antiquitatem* (Norimbergae: Typis & Sumptibus Michaelis Endteri, 1661). I have seen this only as the second half of a compound volume owned by my colleague George Starr; pp. 72-180 are given over to Hermes. A contrary reception was that of Athanasius Kircher, whose *Oedipus aegyptiacus* (Rome: Vitalis Mascardi, 1652) traces all wisdom, Oriental as well as Occidental, to Egyptian sources. A reader who wishes to know more about the Egyptian craze will be enlightened by Erik Iverson's eminently sensible *The Myth of Egypt and its Hieroglyphs in European Tradition* (Copenhagen: GED GAD Publishers, 1961). Don Cameron Allen's *Mysteriously Meant* (Baltimore: The Johns Hopkins Press, 1970) ranges over pagan symbolism and Renaissance interpretations widely and with learning.

There is, I say once more, no easy road through this intricate tangle, a titillating view of whose complexities it has been a chief purpose of this note to suggest. Since I have come to believe that the traditional understanding of Renaissance thought is, if not wrong, no more than half right, I welcome future researchers into the areas in which I have wandered, picking up an unconsidered trifle here and there. At the same time I urge them, with as much passion as is appropriate to these pages, to keep their heads clear, if they can, while involved with the blossoms and brambles. In these regions, confusion and even enthusiasm offer as grave a threat as superficiality. I add finally that without competence in Latin the student will find himself regularly checkmated just as he seems to be on the point of making some crashing discovery or, worse still, will imagine he has discovered a novelty in what is really a commonplace.

 # Index

The indexing of a work rich in mental concepts is difficult, and some guidance may be helpful.

First, as to form. The effort—although it will not prove fully successful—has been made to guess under what words the reader would be most likely to look. For example, a recurrence of the word "aspects" may provoke a reader already thinking about astrology but forgetful of what he has been told earlier to search for a definition, so the index lists not "astrological aspects" but "aspects, astrological." Similarly, "congelation" may be searched for directly, without detour through an analytic process which would lead him to "alchemical processes" or, more indirectly still, to "processes, alchemical." (Nevertheless he would find the term if he went to the pages given under the former heading.) Conversely, "planetary associations" is given in that form because the entry is more likely to attract a reader looking for information about planets than one looking for information about associations. But there are many double entries, and *"see"* and *"see also"* appear frequently. For the rest, it will suffice to add that excessive groupings under subject headings have been avoided. "Sabbats" appears separately, not under "witchcraft" or "witches"; "pentagram" is not merged with a dozen other items under "magic." Not much purpose would be served by duplicating the groupings of the "Contents."

The entries are necessarily limited, and, inevitably, not all readers will find the author's choices ideal. By no means all the proper names are included. Listing them all would not only have swelled the number of pages uneconomically but would also have caused annoyance at finding a name frequently listed merely among those of a dozen or twenty "authorities." Titles are also omitted except when the author is unknown (for example, *The Golden Tripod* or even, although it is incorrectly attributed to Hermes Trismegistus, *The Emerald Tablet*). They must be searched for under the names of the authors.

The chief problem has had to do with possible varieties of interest. Although the book's structure is conceptual, some readers are sure to be interested also, or mainly, in details. Hence a selection of such terms as "apes' blood," "cinquefoil," "elephants," and "ragwort" has been included. Yet the degree to which the author's hope is attained both of helping readers to find again what has interested them and, by skimming, to be led to fresh discoveries will vary from reader to reader.